THE HUNDRED
THOUSAND FOOLS
OF GOD

THE HUNDRED THOUSAND FOOLS OF GOD

Musical Travels in Central Asia
(and Queens, New York)

THEODORE LEVIN

INDIANA UNIVERSITY PRESS
Bloomington and Indianapolis

This book is a publication of

Indiana University Press
601 North Morton Street
Bloomington, IN 47404-3797 USA

http://www.indiana.edu/~iupress

Telephone orders 800-842-6796
Fax orders 812-855-7931
Orders by e-mail iuporder@indiana.edu

©1996 by Theodore Levin
Originally published in 1996 by Indiana University Press.
First reprinted in paperback in 1999.

The paper used in this publication meets the minimum requirements of American
National Standard for Information Sciences—Permanence of Paper for Printed Library
Materials, ANSI Z39.48-1984.

Manufactured in the United States of America

Library of Congress Cataloging-in-Publication Data

Levin, Theodore Craig.
   The hundred thousand fools of God : musical travels in Central
Asia (and Queens, New York) / Theodore Levin.
      p.   cm.
   Includes bibliographical (p.   ) and discographical (p.   )
references and index.
   ISBN 0-253-33206-0 (alk. paper)
   1. Music—Asia, Central—History and criticism. 2. Jews,
Bukharan—New York (State)—Queens (New York) —Music—History and
criticism. 3. Ethnomusicology. 4. Music and society—Asia,
Central. 5. Music and society—New York (State)—Queens (New York)
I. Title
ML3758.A783L48 1996
780'.958—dc20   96-7607
                                                                          MN

ISBN 0-253-21310-X (paperback)

2 3 4 5 6 04 03 02 01 00 99

For K. D. and N. L.

A god can do it. But how, tell me, shall
a man follow him through the narrow lyre?
His mind is cleavage. At the crossing of two
heartways stands no temple for Apollo.

Song, as you teach it, is not desire,
not suing for something yet in the end attained;
song is existence. Easy for the god.
But when do we *exist?* And when does he

spend the earth and stars upon our being?
Youth, this is not it, your loving, even
if then your voice thrusts your mouth open, —learn

to forget your sudden song. That will run out.
Real singing is a different breath.
A breath for nothing. A wafting in the god. A wind.

From *Sonnets to Orpheus* by Rainer Maria Rilke
(translated by M. D. Herter Norton)

CONTENTS

MAPS

PREFACE

I first visited Central Asia in 1974 and have been traveling there ever since. Most of my travels have been concentrated in two periods: 1977–1978, when I studied Uzbek music at the Tashkent State Conservatory, and 1990–1994, when I joined forces with my Uzbek friend and fellow musical explorer Otanazar Matyakubov (At-a-na-ZAR Mat-ya-KU-bov), whom I shall henceforth call by his initials, OM, for reasons soon to be explained, to survey musical life in Transoxania.

OM preferred the old geographic term to the Soviet neologisms Uzbekistan and Tajikistan because, as he saw it, "Transoxania" stressed the region's underlying geographical and social coherence rather than its more recent ethnic and political divisiveness—divisiveness that OM attributed to the machinations of Soviet politics. It was only in the 1920s that the Soviet Central Asian republics, the predecessors of today's nominally independent states, had been carved willy-nilly from the remains of Russian Turkestan and the feudal city-states of Bukhara and Khiva—a vast territory of steppe, desert, mountain ridges, and riverine oases that had once been united under the rule of Timur and Chingis Khan. And it was Soviet political and cultural strategists who had forged the present-day Central Asian "nationalities"—Uzbek, Tajik, Turkmen, etc.—from Transoxania's myriad clans, tribes, and family lineages, none of which had given much heed to the concept of "nation."[1]

Traveling around Transoxania and drawing on a wide network of musical friends and contacts, OM and I hoped to assemble a living musical-ethnographic map that chronicled the way musical life reflects the often fluid boundaries and identities that both divide and unite the various social groups that live there. My own sense of this musical life, based on what I had gleaned during earlier visits to the region, was that it was far more complex, alive, and intimately linked to the innermost lives of people than one might have guessed from watching the glitzy professional folk troupes that became the official cultural ambassadors of the Central Asian republics during the Soviet years and represented nearly all that was known in the West about Central Asian music. I wanted to explore the musical landscape that lay beyond the folk troupes, where musicians performed

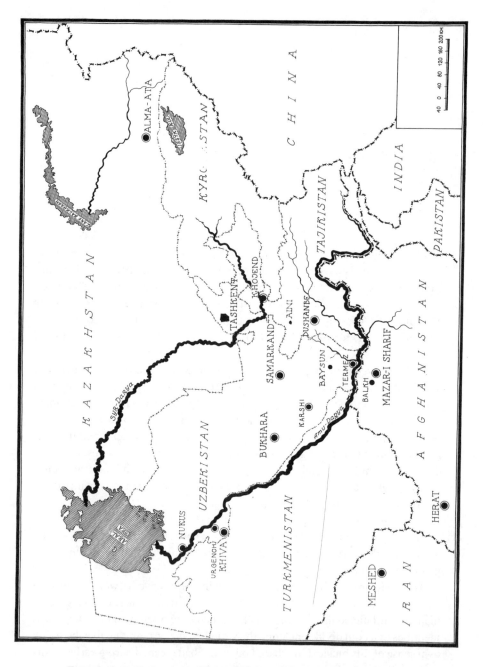

Transoxania (or Transoxiana), "Beyond the Oxus." The name is adopted from Arabic *mâ warâ al-nahr,* "that which is beyond the river." The region includes the territory that arcs eastward from the Aral Sea between the Amu Darya (the River Oxus of antiquity) and the Syr Darya, comprising most of the present-day republics of Uzbekistan and Tajikistan and portions of Kyrgyzstan and Kazakhstan; in antiquity, Soghdia and Khorezm.

not for a paycheck but out of a sense of service to community and to God. OM had said that he knew such people and that we could meet them.

The map that we set out to create would be one stitched together by the music and autobiographical stories we gathered from musicians in the villages, cities, and towns we visited. Echoing Central Asia's strong tradition of regional and clan loyalties, local musicologists and folklorists had tended to focus their fieldwork on a single region of Uzbekistan or Tajikistan—usually the region of their own familial roots—and surveys of different regions' music were rare.[2] By contrast, our goal was to view the cultural realm of Transoxania comprehensively, as a whole.

At the same time that we hoped to gain a better sense of the way musical styles articulate with social groups in Transoxania, we also were eager to use our musical window into traditional practices, beliefs, and social relationships and their transformations into mainstream Soviet culture to learn more about the history of Soviet colonization. Much of this history is little known beyond the region's borders. In the Soviet Union, historians and ethnographers working on Central Asia published under extraordinary ideological constraints, while foreign researchers have suffered from severely limited access both to Central Asia itself and to reliable information about it.[3] But as the Soviet Union broke apart and Moscow's grip on Central Asia loosened, indigenous traditions of spiritual and expressive culture that survived Soviet rule in the privacy of family life reemerged into public view. Newly assertive nationalisms in the former Soviet republics have bolstered the role of "national" languages and cultures with the intent of rooting out vestiges of Russian colonialism, as the century-and-a-quarter of tsarist and Soviet rule in Central Asia is now freely called by local politicians and intellectuals.

Yet no amount of enthusiasm for the recovery of a vanished pre-Soviet reality has been able to stop the inertia of seventy years of Soviet rule. The innovations of Soviet culture policy continue to cast a long shadow over the cultural landscape of Central Asia, and many of these innovations have become so much a part of the landscape that one can hardly imagine Central Asian life without them. The "traditional" practices, beliefs, and social relationships that OM and I set out to explore in fact comprise a patchwork of traditions of various provenance: Soviet traditions intermingled with Soviet transformations of pre-Soviet traditions and with reemergent pre-Soviet traditions, reconstructed and reinterpreted to serve the farrago of nationalist, socialist, capitalist, ethnic, and religious interests that have shaped, and are shaping, post-Soviet society and culture.

My musical travels with OM were not confined to Transoxania. Since the late 1970s, when Leonid Brezhnev opened the hermetic borders of the Soviet Union to Jewish emigration, tens of thousands of Bukharan Jews (as they have been called for centuries by European and Russian Jews and now call themselves), that is, Jews who came—or were forced to come—from Persia to the great Silk

PREFACE

Route cities of Central Asia beginning more than a millennium ago, have left Bukhara, Samarkand, and Tashkent to settle in Israel or the United States. Jewish musicians played a leading role in the ecumenical social world that Bukharan Jews had shared for centuries with Central Asian Muslims, and as many of those musicians emigrated, OM and I followed them to the brick apartment blocks and tidy row houses of Queens, New York, and looked on as they began to recreate their musical lives within the social milieu of a reimagined Transoxania. How would Central Asian music fare in the middle of New York City? In a mirror image of my own travels, OM made several trips from Uzbekistan to New York, while I, the local host, continued to frequent the Bukharan émigré community on my own.

OM and I never discussed our professional relationship in terms of a formal research collaboration, but the principles of a partnership emerged from a blending of common interests and individual needs. We agreed to share freely all information that we gathered, both separately and together, during the course of conversations and recording sessions and, on the basis of this collective information, to collaborate on certain projects at the same time that each of us pursued individual projects. Together we have produced two compact discs and organized several concert tours for Central Asian musicians in the West.[4] On his own, OM has completed two book-length manuscripts, neither of them published as of this writing, and is at work on a third.[5] The present book represents the centerpiece of my own work.

Traveler-writers invariably reveal not only what has drawn them to their chosen part of the world but also the reasons for their choice of a particular route or destination. Sometimes the choices are whimsical, arising from fancy or fantasy; in other cases, they may arise from a scholarly agenda, from military or diplomatic necessity, or from a spiritual commitment. In my own case, once the larger geographical boundaries were in place, the particular areas of focus turned out to be somewhat a matter of chance. That I have reported on Bukhara but not Samarkand, on Khorezm but not the Ferghana Valley, is not because Samarkand or the Ferghana Valley lack musical interest. Rather, I focused on Bukhara and Khorezm because they were the places where OM—for historical reasons of his own—had the best contacts and where I could most easily submerge myself in local musical life. Since OM's network was based primarily in cities rather than in the countryside, we agreed to round out our survey of Transoxania by visiting several rural regions that were musical *terra incognita* to both of us. These regions, we happily discovered, supported some of Transoxania's richest and most distinctive musical traditions.

If travelogues typically speak from a precisely bounded ethnographic present that reflects the chronology of a single, continuous journey, then the ethnographic present of my own work shifts backward and forward in time, highlighting events, conversations, and impressions from many trips to both Central Asia and Queens separated by months or even years. Chapter 1 ("Tashkent") explores the musical life of Central Asia's largest city, where the influence of Russian and European models on indigenous forms of art—as well as the reaction to these influences—has been a major theme during the whole of the twentieth century. Chapters 2 ("Bukhara") and 4 ("Khorezm") document the symbiotic relationships that permeate urban and suburban cultural life in two of Transoxania's most famous oases—symbioses between Muslims and Jews in Bukhara and between herders and city dwellers in Khorezm. Chapters 3 ("The South: Surxandarya and Qashqadarya"), 5 ("The Upper Zaravshan and Yagnâb"), and 6 ("Shahristan") illustrate the sometimes seamless, sometimes jarring meetings of older and newer traditions, of local practices and imported politics, in rural Transoxania. Finally, chapter 7 ("Queens") examines the fate of a musician shaped by Soviet cultural conventions who struggles to survive as an émigré in a new social order from which he looks back nostalgically on his former life.

Since both the original Transoxania and the reimagined Transoxania that I describe within the book's elastic ethnographic present constitute societies undergoing rapid social change, I have taken care to note the dates of visits and conversations that have particular bearing on the facts being reported. In other instances, however, cultural continuities made it sensible to merge conversations and events from different trips in the interest of narrative coherence: for example, certain conversations with musicians in Bukhara that are presented as having taken place during one and the same visit in fact occurred during visits spread out over three years.

One more wrinkle on the ethnographic present: much of the ethnographic information in the text comes from recorded conversations in which friends and acquaintances reconstructed for me with extraordinary verisimilitude a portrait of their own past—a kind of informal oral history. (A number of those cherished raconteurs have since died, pushing our conversations firmly into the realm of history.) Thus not only is *The Hundred Thousand Fools of God* a description of one person's travels at a certain historical moment; it also appeals to a freer sense of travel, not only through the present but backward in time, through memory and reminiscence.

I make no claims to completeness. If anything, the ground I have covered suggests the extraordinarily rich cultural terrain that awaits other musical travelers who might consider visiting Transoxania—or Queens. Perhaps this guide will show them the way to the starting point.

ACKNOWLEDGMENTS

Most of all, I wish to thank Otanazar Matyakubov and his family, and in particular, Svetlana Matyakubova, for welcoming me into their household, and into their lives during my five years of work on *The Hundred Thousand Fools of God*. Without their knowledge, guidance, and support, this book would have been, literally, inconceivable. As ought to be evident from the text itself, I was the constant beneficiary of Otanazar Matyakubov's intellectual largess during the months we spent together, and our spirited dialogue remains one of the greatest satisfactions of my Transoxanian travels.

This book would also have been inconceivable without the offerings given to me so freely by the musicians about whom I have written. They shared generously their knowledge and their music, as well as, usually, their guest room. That I experienced Central Asian music within the context of traditional Central Asian hospitality made it so much the richer. I am also grateful to the many nonmusician hosts who cared for us during our travels.

I am indebted to Alexander Djumaev for his research assistance in Tashkent and for reading an early draft of the book with the impeccable attention to detail that characterizes his own rigorous scholarship. Leonid and Irina Antonov also assisted me in Tashkent by drawing the maps reproduced herein, adapted from a variety of Russian and Soviet sources. Nancy Toth, a student at Dartmouth College, drew the map of Queens.

Other readers of a first draft, to whom I am grateful for comments, corrections, and in some cases, hard-nosed copy editing, include Katheryn Doran, Jean During, Dale Eickelman, Walter Feldman, Timothy Hill, Molly and Joseph Levin, Svetlana Nikitina, and Mark Slobin. To Mark Slobin, and also to Harold Powers, I offer special thanks for pointing me toward Central Asia in the first place—now almost two decades ago. I also acknowledge my gratitude to Walter Feldman and Jean During for their generosity in sharing with me over the years their profound knowledge of Central Asia and its musics. Unable always to identify their specific contributions—for what I have learned from them has become so much a part of my own thinking—I am left with a general sense of indebtedness to two first-rate intellects and intrepid musical explorers.

ACKNOWLEDGMENTS

To Janet Rabinowitch, my editor at Indiana University Press, I express thanks for her initial enthusiasm about an incomplete manuscript and, throughout the process of revision, for her sure sense of what to add, cut, and leave alone.

My research and writing has been aided by grants from the National Endowment for the Humanities, the Social Science Research Council, and the International Research and Exchanges Board (IREX), and I am grateful to the anonymous referees who took a chance by supporting this work in its early stages. A faculty fellowship from Dartmouth College enabled me to devote full attention to writing and editing as the project neared completion. Dartmouth also generously subsidized the costs of preparing photographs, music examples, and recordings for publication.

I also acknowledge the assistance of Smithsonian/Folkways Recordings and OCORA/Radio France, who granted permission to include recordings on the accompanying compact disc that I have previously released on those labels: Mahdi Ibadov, "Shahd," and Tohfaxân Pinkhasova, "Taralilalalai," from *Bukhara: Musical Crossroads of Asia,* Smithsonian/Folkways 40050, and Turgun Alimatov, "Segâh," and Munâjât Yulchieva, "Bayât-i Shirâz Talqinchasi," from *Asie Centrale: Traditions classiques,* OCORA/Radio France C560035–36. Blue Flame Recordings granted a license for use of its recording of Yulduz Usmanova, "Shoch va Gado," from *Alma Alma,* Blue Flame 398 40572. The poem that appears at the beginning of the book is from *Sonnets to Orpheus* by Rainer Maria Rilke. Copyright 1942 by W. W. Norton & Company, Inc., renewed copyright 1970 by M. D. Herter Norton. Reprinted by permission of W. W. Norton & Company, Inc. Thanks also to Molly Levin for preparing the index, and to Boris Dubrinin and Alexander Krol for making possible a new recording of the excerpt from A. F. Kozlovsky's "Lola," performed by the Moscow Radio-Television Symphony Orchestra under the direction of Alexander Mikhailov.

KEY TO SELECTIONS ON COMPACT DISC

The sequence of selections on the accompanying compact disc does not follow the order in which they are discussed in the text. Rather, the sequence aims to make the compact disc musically coherent on its own. Urban music—some of it reflecting a fusion of European and Central Asian influences—is gathered in the first part of the disc, while rural and ritualistic music and chant appear toward the end. Readers who wish to program a compact disc player to play the selections in the order in which they are discussed in the text should use the following sequence of track numbers: 2, 7, 5, 4, 12, 3, 1, 9, 10, 8, 15, 17, 14, 13, 16, 11, 18, 19, 20, 21, 22, 23, 6.

KEY TO SELECTIONS ON COMPACT DISC

GUIDE TO PRONUNCIATION AND TRANSLITERATION

Transoxania's turbulent legacy of ethnic intermingling could hardly be better expressed than in the blending of languages, one of the region's most salient features. Uzbek, a Turkic language, and Tajik, an eastern dialect of Persian, share a large number of words, many of them adopted from Arabic. These days, conversations in Uzbek or Tajik typically abound in Russian loanwords, while native Russian speakers routinely use words of Persian, Turkic, or Arabic origin. Meanwhile, English creeps into the vocabulary of younger speakers of all the region's languages.

Uzbek, Tajik, Russian, and Arabic may all be transliterated into the Latin alphabet according to international conventions that use a variety of specialized phonetic symbols. In this work, however, I have avoided using most such symbols in favor of spellings that make intuitive sense to readers of English. My goal has been to simplify for the nonspecialist the task of reading and pronouncing non-English words with reasonable phonetic accuracy. For sounds that cannot be intuitively or unambiguously transliterated into English orthography, I use the following conventions:

Sound	Letter(s)	Example
"ch" as in Scottish "loch"	x	*baxshi* (epic reciter, healer) [for Uzbek/Tajik words]
	kh	*kolkhoz* (collective farm) [for Russian words or Uzbek/ Tajik words with conventional English spelling, e.g., *khan* (ruler)

GUIDE TO PRONUNCIATION AND TRANSLITERATION

Sound	Letter(s)	Example
"gh" similar to "ch" in "loch," but voiced to sound like "logh"	gh	*ghijak* (spike fiddle)
"c" as in "cot" (a hard c, formed in the back of the throat)	q	Qahhâr (personal name)
"a" as in "father"	â	*âsh* (food, celebratory meal)
"a" as in cat	a	*bacha* (boy dancer)
"j" as in "joke"	j	*jân* (soul)
"g" as in "loge"	zh	*zhirau* (Karakalpak: bard)
"aii" as in "Hawaii" (a weak glottal stop)	'	Nawâ'i (name of poet)

In all cases, I have preserved transliterations that have become standardized in English, even when they do not conform to the phonetic equivalences shown above; for example, Tashkent, not Tâshkent; Bukhara, not Buxârâ. Transliterations of Uzbek and Tajik song texts reflect local dialects where these diverge from the standard literary forms.

THE HUNDRED
THOUSAND FOOLS
OF GOD

TASHKENT

Yol azâbi, gur azâbi
(The suffering of the road is like the suffering of the grave).

—Uzbek aphorism

MOSCOW TO TASHKENT

Could there be a less auspicious point of departure for the mysterious East than the dreary Intourist lounge at Moscow's Domodedovo Airport? That dingy suite of rooms, created to segregate foreign travelers from the indigenous throngs who use the even more decrepit facilities in the main part of the airport, is a monument to the banality of travel. Since 1981, it has marked the beginning of my journeys from Moscow to Tashkent, the capital of Uzbekistan and the gateway to Transoxania.

Before that, I took the train. The train traverses the two thousand-odd miles between Moscow and Tashkent at an average speed of thirty-five miles an hour. It can be a pleasant trip, if you have two-and-a-half days to kill and don't mind the invasive conviviality endemic to long journeys on Russian trains. But I stopped taking the train after one trip during which a pair of drunk Georgians—Caucasian Georgians—threatened to kill me.

The Georgians, traveling in a neighboring compartment, had brought along an ample supply of vodka and, in the spirit of traditional Georgian hospitality, insisted on sharing their drink with fellow passengers in our car. Well into one communal drinking session, the Georgians began to argue about an incident that had occurred the day before. On that day, while stopped at a small depot in the desolate flatness of the Kazakh steppe, our train had been boarded by policemen. The policemen had consulted briefly with a conductor and then made straight for the compartment that I shared with a frail physicist returning to

Tashkent after heart surgery. When we met upon boarding the train in Moscow, the physicist had immediately wanted to know why I spoke Russian so poorly. "Are you drunk?" he had asked. When I told him that I was an American, he had grinned and said, "Oh, in that case, you speak Russian very well."

The policemen informed us politely that they were required to search our compartment. Someone on the train had reported a sum of cash missing, and the physicist had come under suspicion when the conductor noticed him locking and unlocking the door of our compartment from the outside with a homemade key. Normally such latchkeys were carried only by conductors. The policemen performed a cursory search of our luggage, found nothing suspicious, and retreated after an unenthusiastic inspection of several other compartments. One of the Georgians had then asked me whether the policemen had scrutinized my books during their search. I had said no. This answer became the subject of the Georgians' dispute. "Yesterday, he said yes, they did look at his books," one Georgian shouted to his friend. "He's just contradicted himself."

"That's not a contradiction," retorted the second Georgian. The argument rapidly escalated, and in no time at all, the Georgians had grabbed weapons—the jagged neck of a liquor bottle and a pocketknife—and were carving each other up.

The physicist thrust himself between the two Georgians in an attempt to stop their fighting. The Georgian with the pocketknife, lunging to stab his friend with the liquor bottle, missed his target and instead slit open the physicist's thigh. The physicist crumpled to the floor, howling in pain. Just then, a conductor arrived and, with help from several burly passengers, managed to yank the snarling men apart. The Georgians were installed in separate compartments while their wounds were bandaged with makeshift tourniquets and dressings. As one Georgian's bloodied nose was being swabbed with vodka, the man grimaced at me and, in a gush of Georgian logic, explained that since I had defiled his honor and caused him to fight with his friend, I would have to die, preferably, as far as he was concerned, before we reached Tashkent. I took the threat seriously and spent the rest of the voyage locked inside my coupé. So much for taking the train.

During the dozen years of plane trips between Moscow and Tashkent that followed that last train journey, five leaders have ruled the Kremlin, the Soviet Union has ceased to exist, the ruble has shrunk in value from $1.60 to less than a tenth of a penny, and McDonald's opened its largest restaurant in the world in Moscow's Pushkin Square. But at Domodedovo, the Moscow airport that services internal routes to the southeast and east, the Intourist lounge remains proudly, strangely, unchanged. There are still the 1950s' vintage tan upholstered chairs lined up back-to-back down the center of the room, the dim fluorescent lights, the large wall map entitled "Air routes of the Soviet Union." The buffet still features the same foul-smelling hot dogs, pickled tomatoes, and slices of bread with thick chunks of fatty sausage. Tea is still made with water poured from a large samovar that in my experience has never been more than lukewarm.

Only the unfortunate travelers who find their way to this remote outpost have changed. When I first came to the Intourist lounge, it was filled with Arab, African, and Vietnamese students on their way to study engineering *cum* Marxism-Leninism at an assortment of provincial Soviet institutes and universities. Soviet sports teams in blue warmup suits and tourist groups returning from highly sought-after vacations in Bulgaria were occasionally processed through the Intourist facility as a special privilege.

But which foreigners were flying on the evening of March 19, 1993? Korean and Pakistani businessmen, a skinny German with a shaved head dressed in the uniform of some religious cult, and a flock of American tourists with name tags pinned to their lapels. One of them clutched a booklet with "Dream Vacations" written across the front in liquescent purple lettering.

There is something disconcerting about flying to Tashkent. You leave Moscow at one o'clock in the morning, and the flight is scarcely three-and-a-half hours long. But somewhere beneath, in the middle of the night, Europe changes to Asia. Where is the boundary? It is marked by the Volga and the Urals, geographers tell us with certitude; a clean, north-south dividing line. Yet down on the ground, as you cross the Volga, the boundary seems no less arbitrary than when it flits through your mind as an idea in the middle of the night while you hurtle through the air six miles above Kazakhstan.

In the memories of my first train trip to Tashkent, in 1977, the towns along the railroad track that links Europe and Asia all dissolve into a single composite Soviet town. On the outskirts, supply depots and factories are planted in muddy yards piled high with industrial flotsam and surrounded by concrete slab fences. Then shabby concrete apartment blocks come into view, laid out along a grid of perpendicular avenues. Flatbed trucks and yellow buses ply the avenues, belching trails of dark exhaust. On the station platform, a heterogeneous crowd of faces reveals countless personal histories of West meeting East. Even as the train approaches Tashkent, passing through cities with names such as Kzyl-Orda, Chiili, Yanykurgan, and Turkestan, the amalgam of facial types tips only slightly more in the direction of Asia.

On that journey, the most revealing clue that the train had crossed into Asia came on the morning of the third and final day, when I awoke to find that the cloying Russian pop music played endlessly through speakers in the corridor of the train car had been replaced by Oriental-sounding Uzbek pop music. Perhaps the boundary between Europe and Asia is just a matter of imagination anyway, determined, in this case, by the whim of the *provodnik,* the woman who punches tickets, prepares tea, and decides which tape cassettes to play through the train's speaker system.

Descending into Tashkent by air, you seem no surer that you are arriving in the East. Flying low on the approach to the airport, the plane passes over neatly cultivated patches of field bordered by low-slung farm buildings, then over

3

neighborhoods of tin-roofed houses with small, walled yards, and finally, over a sprawling landscape of oblong apartment blocks, industrial buildings, and broad, straight boulevards that seem to have been dropped harum-scarum across a swath of oasis in the middle of the steppe. If this is the East, then it is an aggressively Europeanized and modern-looking version of the East. You have to search hard to find vestiges of an older, more traditional East in the evanescent aerial portrait that passes by the plane window in the few minutes before landing; but those vestiges are there, as surely as they are there in the lives of the people moving about down below through the haze of Tashkent's sulphuric air.

AN UZBEK FELLOW TRAVELER

I was not traveling alone on the night flight from Moscow to Tashkent. I arrived with Otanazar Matyakubov, the man I have called OM, who had accompanied me from New York. It seems simplest that I should refer to OM by his initials, since by doing so, I avoid becoming mired in the present-day polymorphism of Uzbek names, among which the name of my friend offers a particularly vexing set of alternatives. Beginning in tsarist times, when Russian rule spread to Central Asia, Uzbek names were Russified by adding to patrilineal first names the suffixes "ov" and "ev" to create surnames. Matyakub (a contraction of Muhammad Yakub), the given name of Otanazar's father, became Matyakubov, analogous to the Russian Ivanov or Petrov. Now many Uzbeks are dropping the Russian suffixes. Otanazar has begun using the surname Matyakub in some circles but still calls himself Matyakubov in others. In Uzbek company, however, no one pays much attention to surnames. The tradition is to use first names, followed by one of a variety of terms that convey respect. For example, no one but a close family relation or intimate friend would pronounce "Otanazar" without adding *aka,* literally "Otanazar-older brother." Russians, though, do not use the Uzbek *aka,* but for politeness or formality construct a Russian-style patronymic, e.g., Otanazar Rahimovich: "Otanazar the son of Rahim" (in this case, the son of Matyakub Rahimov; Otanazar's surname should have been Rahimov, like his father's, but the office that registered his birth certificate made a mistake and listed him as Matyakubov).

During our five years of intensive work together, OM's life and my own became intertwined in a complex calculus of mutual assistance, which, to our good fortune, has continued to draw nourishment from its roots in an abiding friendship. Born in 1946, OM is five years older than I. He is of medium height with a hefty build that tends toward paunchiness, short-cropped black hair, and an olive complexion. Thick black glasses set over an ample nose and a large, square face give him a commanding presence. This presence is reinforced by a loud and almost exaggeratedly slow speaking voice that becomes even louder and slower when he is addressing a foreigner. Foreigners sometimes take OM's loud and slow speech for imperiousness, especially when it is couched in the prolix Soviet oratorical style of which he is a master. His speech never struck me that way because OM is so devoid of pretense, arrogance, or guile.

We met in 1977, the year that I first came to Tashkent to study Uzbek music at the Tashkent Conservatory. OM was the senior graduate student in the Conservatory's Department of Eastern Music, a much respected young scholar who would soon receive the *kandidat* degree, which is the functional equivalent of a Ph.D. in the Soviet and post-Soviet academic hierarchy. We had a cordial but not close relationship. In 1977, an American student, even (or, perhaps, particularly) one whose interest was Uzbek music, was assumed to be working for an intelligence service. An instructor in the Conservatory's Political Department had issued a warning that American spies could effect all sorts of disguises, even that of a musicologist, and that one had to be careful not to be fooled. OM was a leader in the Komsomol (Communist Youth) organization and for the most part kept a healthy distance from me. Once, near the end of my ten months at the Conservatory, he invited me home for Sunday dinner. Years later, he told me that he had first asked permission of a KGB official and had been instructed which route to use to take me to his house.

After I returned to the United States in 1978, OM and I lost touch. Fed up with musicology, I had finished my dissertation on the old Bukharan court music repertory called *Shash maqâm* and dropped out of academic life. Searching for a way to live, work, and study music in the Soviet Union, I fell in with a New Age impresario from California who, in the euphoria of the early glasnost years, had developed a business taking American celebrities to the USSR to fulfill what could only be called glasnost fantasies: a rock concert in Kazakhstan, a journey to an off-limits ancestral village in the Ukraine, an expedition to record the sounds of freshwater seals under the ice of Lake Baikal—nothing was too far-fetched.

It was one such adventure that brought me together again with OM. An American pop musician wanted to take his band on a concert tour through Central Asia. He was an Orthodox Jew and wouldn't perform or travel on the Sabbath. Grounded in Tashkent over a long Sabbath weekend, I dropped by the Conservatory on an impulse and found OM teaching a class in the Eastern Music Department. I handed him a wad of tickets for the next evening's show and suggested, a bit nervously, that it might be an interesting experience for his students. To my surprise, OM came to the concert himself with a group of fellow teachers and a few of his pupils.

We saw one another again the following summer, and it was then that I had proposed working together. OM had displayed no wariness about the political implications of our collaboration, and it was only later that I understood his considerable courage in undertaking a project with such a strong focus on

5

Bukharan Jews, even in those heady early years of glasnost. In Uzbekistan's strongly nationalistic society, many of OM's Uzbek colleagues at the Conservatory and at Tashkent's Xamza Institute of Art Studies regarded (and still regard) his research on Bukharan Jews as a form of cultural treason.

OM lives in what by Tashkent standards is a spacious apartment. It is a fifth floor walk-up in a 1960s' vintage pale concrete block that fronts the corner of Zhukovsky and Xamza streets, about a ten-minute walk from the Conservatory. The living room contains a dining table, a sofa, a spinet piano, and, along the back wall, two shiny wooden commodes separated by a large television set, the only one of four in the apartment that works. A too-bright red shag carpet with fluorescent green and yellow guls covers most of the floor, and a factory-woven *ersatz* Oriental rug hangs on the wall behind the piano. In the kitchen-dining area, the only wall decoration is a small prayer rug with a crude portrait of the Uzbek writer Aibek woven into the central mirab. Carpets with portraits are a Soviet invention, perhaps a literal implementation of Stalin's decree that art should be "nationalist in form and socialist in content." OM likes Aibek's writing, and he is fond of the rug, both as weaving and as socialist kitsch.

OM is married to Svetlana Matyakubova, a fellow musicologist who teaches European music history and theory at the Tashkent Conservatory. Her mother was Russian; her father, for convenience, had registered himself as an Uzbek, since he lived and worked in Uzbekistan. In fact, her father claimed descent from an Arab lineage and spoke Uzbek and Tajik with equal fluency. Svetlana also speaks Uzbek and Tajik fluently but is more comfortable in Russian. When she was born, her parents couldn't agree about whether to give her a Muslim or a Christian name. Her mother prevailed, but her father's relatives never accepted "Svetlana" and called her instead Sa'âdat, "luck." Now, depending on whom she is talking to, she switches back and forth between the two names. In recent years, she has become a devout Christian.

OM is Uzbek on both his mother's and father's side. He acknowledges being a Muslim, but what he has in mind is that as an Uzbek, he is Muslim by default. I have never known him to pray, inside or outside a mosque. He grew up in Khiva, in the northwest of Uzbekistan, where few Russians live, but he mastered Russian as a teenager and, as a consequence of having gone to school in Bukhara, also speaks fluent Tajik. The four Matyakubov daughters have been raised bilingually in Uzbek and Russian. Depending on which extended family members or guests are present, the language of the household switches seamlessly back and forth between the two. Uzbek, Russian, and, to a lesser extent, Tajik are interwoven throughout the day as the family fields telephone calls and visitors come and go.

Visitors determine not only the language that is spoken in the household but also its internal geography and the comportment of the various family members. Female visitors and close friends or extended family members of either sex are invited to sit at the table in the kitchen-dining area, drink tea, and chat. But OM does most of his entertaining in the living room. Particularly if his guests are Uzbek, the entryway from the kitchen-dining area to the living room becomes a dividing line between the male world and the female world. The female Matyakubovs enter the living room only to bring and remove food and drink; they make minimal conversation with male guests.

Arzu, the oldest Matyakubov daughter, has been in the United States for over five years. She came originally for four months to live with me and my wife, take care of our young daughter, learn English, and allow me to practice Uzbek. My Uzbek barely improved, but Arzu's English became fluent. She stayed on and now attends an American college. Yaira, the second eldest daughter, also attends school in the United States. She has played the violin since early childhood and, after winning a scholarship for summer study at the Interlochen Arts Academy, was invited to join Interlochen's year-round program. Raihân, the third daughter, attends a prestigious private high school in Tashkent. She is an outstanding writer and has a brisk, take-charge manner that has brought her success in her after-school job as the family food shopper. She nimbly bargains with fruit and vegetable sellers in the bazaar and knows at which hours and with which documents and what kinds of containers she needs to appear at the various government food depots to procure cooking oil, sugar, flour, and the few other staples that are not purchased at the bazaar. The youngest daughter, Anâr, is in primary school. OM says that in the future it will be important for Anâr to feel comfortable as an Uzbek, but notwithstanding his conscious effort to converse with her in Uzbek, Anâr is drawn toward Russian.

PLAN OF THE CITY

Tashkent's population of over two million contains countless thousands of families like the Matyakubovs that are not only biethnic but, in their daily lives, actively bicultural. When the Russians first came to Tashkent, the city's geography starkly reflected the division between native Central Asians and their colonial rulers. Uzbeks and other Asians lived on one side of the Anhor River, while Russians built their town on the other side. Despite the blurring of ethnic boundaries and the appearance of mixed marriages during the Soviet era, social divisions between Uzbeks and Russians, and more broadly between Asians and Europeans, run deep, and Tashkent's cultural geography still reflects these divisions.

These days, Tashkent is really four cities in one. There is what remains of the old Muslim Tashkent and Russian Tashkent; there is Soviet Tashkent; and there is the new Uzbek Tashkent. Muslim Tashkent, which local residents call the Old City, is a warren of crooked streets, walled-off houses set in courtyards covered by grape arbors, and small neighborhood shops and bazaars. Since the earth-

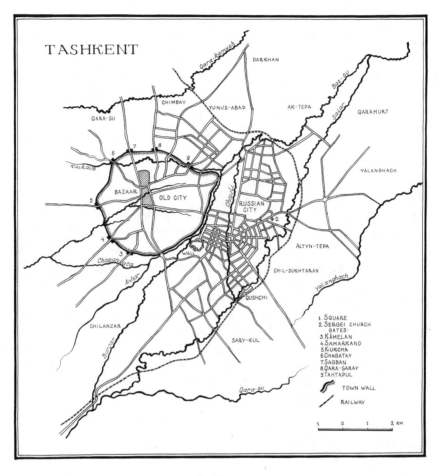

Tashkent

quake of 1966, the Old City has gradually receded behind bulldozers and wreckers' balls in favor of the oblong apartment blocks and asphalt boulevards that are such visible landmarks from the air.

On the opposite side of the Anhor—at present, more a muddy canal than a river—is the town built by Russian colonizers in the decades following General Chernaev's capture of Tashkent from the Khokand Khanate in 1865. Unlike the old city, Russian Tashkent was planned with colonialist precision. At the center was a square of park, and from the square, broad avenues radiated in four directions. Spread out among these avenues were smaller networks of streets along which the Russians and other Europeans built thick-walled one-story bungalows and villas set in walled gardens.

Planned though it may have been, Russian Tashkent was a colonial city conceived on a far more modest scale than, say, British Calcutta or Lucknow.

8

Eugene Schuyler, an American scholar and diplomat who visited Central Asia in 1873, reported that the Russian town consisted of 600 houses and a population of 3,000, "exclusive of the garrison of about 6,000."[1] No Russian architectural monuments in Tashkent stand to rival Calcutta's railroad station or Victoria Memorial. In fact, precious little of prerevolutionary Tashkent survived the earthquakes of 1866 and 1966 or the vast postearthquake urban renewal program that is still in progress.

Creeping out like a fungus into both Russian Tashkent and the Old City is Soviet Tashkent. During seventy years of rule, the Soviet Union did its utmost to reinforce the physical continuity of Soviet Eurasia with a cultural rapprochement between East and West. But Soviet-style rapprochement meant East meeting West on Western terms. Until the postearthquake rebuilding began, the architecture of Soviet Tashkent paid little respect to local sensibilities in the way, for example, that Lutyens adapted Mogul motifs in designing buildings for British New Delhi.[2]

Finally, on the periphery of Soviet Tashkent is the new Uzbek Tashkent. It is here that Uzbeks have reimagined their own traditional way of life in newly built neighborhoods of unattached houses, each with its own walled courtyard. In these neighborhoods, the Uzbek *nouveaux riches* try to outdo one another in the grandeur of their houses, particularly in the design of the *mehmânxâna,* literally "guest room," where male guests (or women, if they are foreigners) are entertained. And yet, in these mansions, where you are seated in the plushest of carpeted chambers with delicately carved and painted wooden molding, plisse-covered walls, and silk curtains, where you eat off the finest china and drink French brandy out of crystal goblets, you can ask to be shown to the toilet and be led outside to the garden, where the odor from the outhouse leads to a door in a far corner of the walled yard. A cold water spigot in the garden provides water for washing your hands. According to one architect acquaintance of mine, the revival of traditional living in the new Uzbek Tashkent is, from an architectural point of view, tipped more toward reimagination than tradition. Many of the architect's clients got their ideas about design by studying the mansions in the immensely popular Mexican soap opera "The Rich Also Cry," which has had a long run on Uzbek television. Brick facades and circular staircases are particularly in vogue, he told me.

While a new residential Uzbek Tashkent rises at the periphery of the city, Soviet Tashkent, which occupies the center, is undergoing de-Russification. In the few years since Uzbekistan became an independent republic, both the physical appearance and the spirit of the city center have changed. The changes are more in details than in large landscapes, but they are telling for a visitor who has been absent for a year. Russian colonialism is officially on the retreat. While many Russians remain in Tashkent, Russian language has disappeared from nearly all public signs, once bilingual in Russian and Uzbek or written in

Russian alone. On the metro, the recorded announcement that plays at each station stop is in Uzbek only. In the main shopping district, commercial shops offer imported liquor, tape recorders, cosmetics, and lingerie. In one such shop, a shiny Qur'an is propped up casually amid a display of lipsticks, instant coffee, and hair sprays. There is a new class of people in these commercial shops that I have never seen here before: fashionably dressed and manicured, more self-confident, more at ease with Western goods. The bookdealers who sell from tables set up on the street are offering Western fare translated into Russian, which, despite the elevation of Uzbek to the status of "state" language in Uzbekistan, is still the *lingua franca* of the former republics. One table that went up daily outside my apartment block featured novels by Danielle Steele and Stephen King, Dale Carnegie's *How to Win Friends and Influence People,* a variety of computer manuals, and a mysticism, magic, and psychology section that indiscriminately lumped together everything from manuals on witchcraft to translations of Freud to L. Ron Hubbard's *Dianetics.*

THE CONSERVATORY

When I came to Tashkent in 1977, I became the fifth American to study there as part of the academic exchange program that had been set up by the U.S. and Soviet governments during the "cultural thaw" of the Khrushchev years. My predecessors had studied Central Asian history, languages, and literature. I was the first to study music and to be attached to the Tashkent State Conservatory rather than to the university.

My only experience of Uzbek music had taken place the previous year during a brief visit with Mark Slobin, an ethnomusicologist who had conducted fieldwork in Afghanistan and made several visits to Tashkent, where he had picked up recordings of the repertory that would become the subject of my dissertation, the Bukharan *Shash maqâm* (Persian: "six *maqâms*").[3] The *Shash maqâm* was a large compendium of instrumental and vocal pieces that embody classical Central Asian aesthetic ideals in music and poetry. Linked to the classical *maqâm* music of other Islamic lands by a common heritage of music theory and musical terminology, the *Shash maqâm* nonetheless displayed features of melodic style and formal structure that set it apart from this heritage. Central Asian musicians and scholars reveled in what they regarded as the mystery of the *Shash maqâm*'s origins. Which masters had created it? When, and for whom? Did the melodic modes of the *Shash maqâm* reveal deep consanguinities with Turkish, Arabic, and Persian classical music that were no longer apparent on the musical surface? Were there even older connections with the *maqâm* system of the Uighurs, the Turkic Muslim people who have inhabited the oasis cities of Chinese Xinjiang since ancient times?

10

The *Shash maqâm* was without doubt a repertory of major importance in the atlas of Asian art musics and, at the time I came to Tashkent to learn about it, one that was practically unknown in the West, even to cognoscenti of Oriental musical traditions. However, even with my enthusiasm for the unknown, I found it difficult to reconcile the *Shash maqâm's* high cultural status with what I heard on the recordings that I borrowed from Mark Slobin: lugubrious music, performed by a bloated, cacophonous-sounding ensemble of instruments and vocalists from the Tashkent radio station that sounded as if it were being played and sung out of tune and at half speed. But my graduate advisor at Princeton University, Professor Harold Powers, had offered encouragement. "Look," he had said, pointing to yellowing photos of bearded Uzbek musicians reproduced in a volume of musical transcriptions he had picked up on his travels. "These are serious-looking men, and they must play serious music. You'll survive. Maybe you'll even grow to like Uzbek music."

At the Conservatory, I was assigned to the dormitory that housed students from out of town. I shared a tiny room with a young Uzbek violinist named Sardar. The Conservatory curriculum featured both Central Asian and European music, and while I had come to Tashkent to study *Shash maqâm,* Sardar was studying the European classical repertory. That semester, he was working on the Bach violin concerto in E major. He practiced in the room night and day while I read and typed notes on a portable Olivetti typewriter set on a wobbly table that always tilted to one side when I struck the "o" and "p" in the upper right corner of the keyboard.

I had left for Uzbekistan imagining that I was going to undertake musical fieldwork. Indeed, imagination played a large role in my enthusiasm about studying Uzbek music, for I had no training in anthropology and had never discussed with anyone how I would actually do fieldwork. Strangely, that didn't bother me. I had believed Harold Powers when he told me not to worry, that once I was there, I'd figure out how to do it.

Whatever the degree of my ignorance, I knew when I first met Professor Karomatov, who supervised the Department of Eastern Music at the Conservatory, that his plan for how I would spend my time in Tashkent didn't sound like fieldwork. In fact, it quickly became clear that Karomatov and I viewed my presence there quite differently.

I imagined myself an emerging ethnomusicologist, come to coax music and musical ideas from Uzbek "informants" and, on the basis of these, to fabricate an original thesis about how and why the Uzbeks made music. Karomatov, on the other hand, regarded me in the same way that he regarded students from developing African and Asian countries sent to Tashkent to receive a Soviet-style education: his task was to ensure that I understood Uzbek music and its history *his* way, that is, according to the officially canonized Soviet version.

Karomatov's aim was clearly to keep me on a short tether. I was to enroll in classes at the Conservatory, learn to play an Uzbek instrument, the *dutar* (a two-stringed lute), from an instructor at the Conservatory, read scholarly articles, and study musical transcriptions in the Conservatory library. My vision of the fieldworker traveling to villages to query and tape-record musicians was unimaginable in Karomatov's scenario. Perhaps this clash of expectations was the initial cause of a strong and abiding malaise about my life and work in Tashkent that set in soon after my arrival and gradually and steadily intensified.

Professor Karomatov, or Faizulla Muzafarovich, as we called him in the formal Russian style of the Conservatory, was of medium height and small frame with high cheekbones, a dark complexion, and thinning hair combed straight back. He habitually stabbed clenched knuckles into the top of whatever surface happened to be at hand to emphasize a point in his clipped, staccato speech. His smile revealed a mouth full of gold teeth. The smile never struck me as friendly, but rather as a ploy to put one at ease while the vulpine Karomatov mused on the predicament of his prey and calculated the best angle of attack.

Karomatov was the doyen of Asian music studies in Uzbekistan. The story of his career exemplifies in many ways the cultural transformation of Central Asia under Soviet rule. Born in Bukhara in 1925 into an educated and musical family with long roots in that city, he grew up with the sounds of Uzbek and Tajik music. He also studied the violin and attended a Russian-language school, as was customary for the children of Uzbek and Tajik families with intellectual, social, or political ambitions. Under the nationalities policies inspired by Lenin and implemented by the first People's Commissar for Nationality Affairs, a Georgian by the name of Joseph Stalin, non-Russian peoples in the USSR were to pursue cultural advancement both by outright adoption of European cultural models and by adapting these models to their own artistic forms.

Karomatov came to Tashkent in 1938 to further his study of violin at the Glière Musical School. Later he matriculated to the Conservatory, where he played violin in the orchestra and studied music history and theory. He finished the Conservatory in 1950 and went to Moscow to become a graduate student of Viktor Beliaev, Russia's foremost scholar of Central Asian music, under whom he wrote a dissertation on Uzbek-Soviet folk songs. Returning to Tashkent, he worked at the Xamza Institute of Art Studies and organized expeditions to record and collect Uzbek music. In the late 1960s and early 1970s, Karomatov emerged from the quiet world of folk-song collecting to spearhead efforts to organize a department of Eastern music at the Conservatory. Central Asians ought to be able to study the musical achievements of their own culture, he argued. Like OM, Karomatov was trilingual (Uzbek, Russian, and Tajik) and bicultural. He could trade stories with Uzbek and Tajik musicians like one of their own (although I never heard him perform any kind of Central Asian music), or he could talk music theory with scholars from the other side of the world.

Karomatov's dual talent was not in itself remarkable. That, after all, is the ethnomusicologist's stock in trade. But the idea of becoming an academic specialist in the music of one's own backyard was something new to me. In America, the conventional initiation for ethnomusicologists has consisted of submerging oneself in a language and culture different from one's own. Conducting fieldwork close to home—at least until recently—has had little cachet. Karomatov's work, however, was modeled not on American ethnomusicology but on nineteenth-century German folklore studies, a model adopted in Russia and subsequently in the Soviet Union, with all its Romantic and nationalist overtones intact. According to this model, there could be no higher aim than studying the oral literary and musical traditions of one's own *Volk,* and this is indeed what the vast majority of Uzbek folklorists and musicologists did.

In Uzbekistan, at least, native scholars' devotion to the study of their own expressive culture has led to a growing certainty that they are the only ones in a position truly to understand it. The contributions of the Russian musical ethnographers of the 1920s and 1930s—Beliaev, Uspensky, Romanovskaya—are viewed respectfully but a bit skeptically by Karamatov and the students he trained. In the same way, my presence at the Conservatory seemed to evoke contradictory feelings among the Uzbeks: on the one hand, pride that an American had come to study *their* music; on the other hand, bemused skepticism that I would ever understand anything about it.

The Tashkent Conservatory grew out of the Turkestan People's Conservatory, which was established in Tashkent in 1918, a year after the Bolshevik Revolution. It occupies a rambling, three-story yellow stucco building on Pushkin Street, in the former Russian town. In the immediate postrevolutionary years, the People's Conservatory brought together diverse elements of Tashkent's European and Asian communities: members of the former tsarist military orchestras, Czechs who had been taken captive in World War I and interned in Tashkent, Jewish and Russian opera singers and instrumentalists, and cadres of local Uzbek students passionate to assimilate Western musical skills in the spirit of Soviet internationalism. At the same time, a school for Uzbek music was opened in the Old City. Viktor Alexandrovich Uspensky, a graduate of the Saint Petersburg Conservatory who had grown up in Central Asia, served as a military officer, then returned to Tashkent to help develop the People's Conservatory, believed that Russian musicians ought to learn Uzbek music, just as Uzbek musicians ought to learn European music.

Amid the idealism of the 1920s, the notion that cultural fusion between Europe and Asia could be a two-way process—of East meeting West but also of West meeting East—was a living idea that had not yet acquired the Eurocentric overtones of Soviet ethnic politics in the 1930s. According to such politics, the cultures of non-Russians living on Soviet territory could progress—in the Socialist sense—only by assimilation or adoption of Russian or, more broadly, European models. In music, for example, the eventual development of monophonic Central Asian music into European-style harmonic music was seen as an historical inevitability. Joined to this Eurocentrism was another shibboleth of Soviet composers that perhaps arose as much from musical tradition as from politics but that in any event attained the status of a cultural dogma by the early 1930s: the use of folk song as a central resource for art music composition. (There was, of course, ample historical precedent for this brand of musical Realism in the Russian composers of the 1860s, exemplified by Musorgsky.)

With increasing intensity, programs aimed at reorganizing musical life to reflect the ideologically ordained convergence of Uzbekistan and Europe began to penetrate music performance, composition, pedagogy, and scholarship. Russian performers, composers, and music historians came, or were sent, to Tashkent to teach native cadres the tools, styles, and techniques of Western music, beginning with reading and writing staff notation and ending with composition and orchestration. At the same time, they taught their students how to transcribe and arrange Central Asian folk music, how to compose it, and how to use the folk idiom as a source of melodic material for both classical and popular works, such as *agitprop* marches and musical dramas.

A RUSSIAN COMPOSER FINDS THE EAST

Some of the composers who taught conservatory students how to build musical bridges between Western musical forms and Eastern musical content were also building such bridges in their own compositions. The most talented of these composers was Alexei Fedorovich Kozlovsky. I never met Kozlovsky— he died early in 1977, half a year before I arrived in Tashkent—but I became a close friend of his widow, Galina Longinovna Kozlovskaya, who lived until 1991. At age eighty-four, a year before her death, Galina Longinovna completed a monograph-length work which she called "The Days and Years of a Wonderful Life: Reminiscences about the Composer Alexei Kozlovsky."[4] As she explained in a preface, the reminiscences were less a formal biography than an effort to explain "the poetry of life itself which sculpts and creates an artist and directs the development of his spiritual life."

When I met her, Galina Longinovna was seventy-two and suffering from an assortment of physical infirmities so debilitating that when I left Tashkent at the end of 1978, I doubted I would ever see her again. But she defied the pessimistic prognoses of all who knew her and lived for another thirteen years, during which, save for rare visits to a medical clinic, she never left the cloistered, overgrown garden and tiny bungalow that she and Alexei Fedorovich Kozlovsky had shared for two decades. She had no use for the Tashkent that had replaced the quasi-mythical city of her memories, and within the insular world of the garden and the memorabilia-laden room in which she worked, slept, dined, and received visitors, she led an extraordinary life of the imagination.

Galina Longinovna Kozlovskaya. Photo by Dmitri Mikhailov.

Galina Longinovna had never had children, but after Alexei Fedorovich died, she wasn't left completely alone. She lived with a crane, named Guppy, who had fallen into the Kozlovskys' large garden after half a wing had been shot off by a hunter, or so the story went. Galina Longinovna had become passionately attached to the bird, and it had become completely domesticated. It preferred the house to the garden and would often stand transfixed in front of the television set (whether or not it was turned on). Sometimes Guppy would dance, flapping his stump of a wing and hopping up and down lightly on his long, spindly legs. He danced only for men, never for women, Galina Longinovna assured visitors.

In the early years of our friendship, before she became blind and almost completely bedridden, Galina Longinovna had run what amounted to a salon for an admiring coterie of Tashkent's young artists, musicians, and literati. Attending her salon was a heady experience, for the salon had a history that stretched back to long before most of those in attendance were born and, in its early years, had included a distinguished group of cultural luminaries. Particularly during the war years, when Tashkent became a center for evacuees from Moscow and

Leningrad, the Kozlovskys had extended a welcome to their displaced artistic brethren. Anna Akhmatova and Alexei Tolstoy were frequent guests. The composer Maximilian Steinberg and his wife, Nadezhda, the daughter of Rimsky-Korsakov, often joined the Kozlovskys for evenings of impromptu musical performance. Another evacuee, one of Galina Longinovna's closest childhood friends, was Zhenya (Evgeniia Vladimirovna) Pasternak, the artist who became the first wife of Boris Pasternak.

The salon invariably unfolded in the same way. Late in the evening, after a few shot glasses of vodka and a filling Russian supper prepared by one of the succession of volunteer housekeepers who looked after Galina Longinovna and cleaned up after her bird, Galina Longinovna came into her own. Coiffed, gowned, and made up in the slightly garish style of a prerevolutionary *grande dame,* she seemed miraculously to abandon the frangible body that caused her such physical suffering and become once again the pert young woman I knew from photographs and from the startlingly detailed reminiscences that she shared during these late-night sessions.

Galina Longinovna Gerus was born in 1906, in Krasnodar. "It was an accident that I was born in Krasnodar," she recounted. "My father was imprisoned there for his part in the 1905 Revolution, and my mother had gone to Krasnodar to be near him. When the Second Duma came to power, Papa was chosen as a deputy while he was still in prison. The people from Kuban who had elected him carried him on their shoulders from the prison right to the train station and sent him off to Petersburg.

"Papa—his name was Longin Fedorovich Gerus—served in the Duma, but he wasn't a very tactful person. Once he went to the Preobrazhensky Regiment and supposedly started to make some sort of call for armed rebellion. I don't think he really did exactly that, but he used some sort of revolutionary words that weren't allowed. He was accused of plotting to overthrow the government and had to flee to Finland. He didn't even have time to say goodbye to my mother. A little later, he learned that he'd been sentenced in absentia to twenty-five years of penal servitude in Siberia. Despite his sentence, he slipped back into Russia to say goodbye to Mama, traveling across the lakes and rivers of the north to the Don, and down the Don to Rostov. He spent a week in Rostov then crossed over the southern border of Russia and traveled through Bessarabia to Austria and finally to America.

"My mother and I went to America later. We sailed from Antwerp to New York, and from there we went to Chicago to meet Papa. We stayed in Chicago four years, then Papa decided to move to Utah to start an agricultural commune. He gathered some Russian immigrants—not intellectuals but workers and former peasants—and they bought an enormous piece of land in a place called Park Valley near the Great Salt Lake. There were no houses on the land, and we lived in tents.

"Each day I walked seven kilometers to a country school, and that way, I met some of the local farmers. One of them gave me a baby pig as a present. I called her Peggy, and we became the closest of friends. Other boys and girls had ponies or horses, but I had Peggy. Our land wasn't irrigated, and for three years there wasn't enough rainfall to make anything grow. Most of what we ate came from cans. The food was monotonous, and the workers began to ask why I should have a pet pig when it was really just a pig and they had a craving for pork. One day, when I was at school, they slaughtered Peggy. When I came home, there were pork chops on the dinner table. I've never been able to forget about Peggy, and about those terrible workers. It was at that moment that I first felt very deeply the biological hatred of plebeians for intellectuals. It was a very clear, particular feeling that they expressed to my parents. My parents were one, and they were another. And it all ended with that commune self-destructing. Everyone left, except my parents, and my father had to earn a living with his tractor, plowing other farmers' fields.

"After the February Revolution of 1917, when I was twelve, the Provisional Government sent Papa a ticket for passage back to Russia. We were living in Salt Lake City when the Revolution came. Papa was being congratulated in all the newspapers; he was giving interviews, writing, and speaking. We took a train to San Francisco and from there a steamship to Japan and then to Vladivostok. Papa went to Petrograd, while Mama and I returned to Rostov to live with my grandmother. It took a month on the train to get there."

Despite her father's revolutionary activities and party ties, Galina Longinovna maintained a lifelong antipathy toward Soviet politics and what she regarded as the philistinism of socialist culture, the tastelessness of the new Soviet man in matters of art, music, and literature. "I love the aristocracy and the peasants," she once told me proudly, in the ever-so-slighty accented American English that she remembered from her childhood but had barely spoken in seventy years. Alexei Fedorovich Kozlovsky, she assured me, had shared her feelings.

Kozlovsky was born in 1905 into a musically talented family of the minor nobility. One great-grandfather, a Polish count, had been an accomplished cellist. For his role in the failed First Polish Uprising of 1830, the count was sentenced to penal servitude in Siberia, but he managed to flee to Paris, where he befriended his émigré countryman Chopin. Later, under the name Bartolocci, he concertized widely in Europe. Kozlovsky's mother took piano lessons from her older sister, a graduate of the Warsaw Conservatory, who, it was said, had studied with a student of Beethoven's. Growing up in Kiev, Alexei Fedorovich and his two brothers played the piano from early childhood and, as schoolboys, became active participants in the musical life of the city.

At age twelve, Alexei Fedorovich entered the Kiev Conservatory and became a piano and composition student of Boleslav Leopoldovich Yavorsky, known in musical circles for his theory of modal rhythm.[5] Yavorsky moved to

Moscow in 1919, and sixteen-year-old Alexei Fedorovich Kozlovsky followed two years later. After initial studies at the First Moscow Musical Technicum, a specialized secondary school that Yavorsky founded under the wing of the Conservatory, Kozlovsky enrolled in the Conservatory itself, where he studied composition with Miaskovsky, orchestration with Sergei Vasilenko, and conducting with Alexander Khesin.

In Moscow, Kozlovsky was swept into the musical and theatrical life of the early postrevolutionary years. After graduating from the Conservatory in 1931, he served for a time as an assistant conductor for the opera productions of the renowned Stanislavsky Theater. Later he busily composed music for avant-garde theater productions. One by one, however, Kozlovsky's musician friends were arrested or disappeared as the Stalinist terror bore down on Moscow's artistic elite. And as Galina Longinovna recounts in her reminiscences, "The day came [in 1936] when they took Alexei Fedorovich to Lubyanka. Notwithstanding the investigator's efforts to frighten, blackmail, and provoke him, he came up clean. He didn't sign a single paper, didn't slander a single person, despite the threats made against him. A so-called troika [panel of three judges] sentenced him to three years of exile in Tashkent without the future right to reside in the six most important cities of the Soviet Union. They charged him with having a noble background and thus with being hostile to the existing regime. He was told to gather his belongings and leave Moscow immediately, but in a sudden rush of unexpected goodwill, the investigator extended the period of departure several days to allow him to be present at a concert in the Hall of Columns where they were performing his *a cappella* choruses." Regarding Kozlovksy's trial and exile, the composer's brief biography in *The New Grove Encyclopedia of Music and Musicians* is more laconic: "In 1936, he moved to Tashkent."[6]

When Alexei Fedorovich arrived in Tashkent, he had to report immediately to the Office of State Security, where his passport was taken away and replaced with a gray sheet of paper. For the next three years, he was required to present himself to the authorities every ten days to have the gray paper stamped as proof that he hadn't tried to flee the city.

When the Kozlovskys arrived in Tashkent (Galina Longinovna had accompanied her husband on his administrative exile), they knew nothing about the city and had no friends there. But Alexei Fedorovich was not a total stranger to the cultures of the East. As a fifteen-year-old, he had read Madame Blavatsky's *Secret Doctrine,* the bible of Theosophy, and become fascinated with Indian spirituality. Yet for all of Alexei Fedorovich's interest in India, the East had remained always on the far side of a barrier of intentional mystery. The move to Tashkent, even as political exile, offered the composer a way to break down that barrier and experience the East firsthand.

Soon after their arrival, the Kozlovskys rented a room in an Uzbek quarter of the city. Their house faced another house across a large garden, and there, as

Galina Longinovna wrote, "in the intimacy of the garden, traditional [Uzbek] life showed itself more clearly than it ever did again; the whole of family life unfolded before our eyes, almost as in the theater." That theater of family life provided Alexei Fedorovich Kozlovsky with his first sources of Uzbek folk music. Galina Longinovna's memoirs describe a typical domestic scene: "No sooner would the mother of the family go out to visit friends than the two daughters would begin to wash down and sweep the yard. But it wasn't work for them; rather, it was some kind of spontaneous dance which they did to their own quiet singing. Their suppleness and innate need for movement was amazing . . . and they weren't exceptional. Girls that age all danced. Almost everyone, adults and children, sang or played on various instruments. As the sun set over the garden, which reeked of the irreproducible odor of moist Central Asian earth, girls of different ages began to come by. One brought a drum and set it over coals to heat up. From the back wall of the covered porch, another retrieved a *dutar,* and the girls took turns singing, dancing, and smiling about something that was their own, something happy. Then, after getting to know Alexei Fedorovich and seeing how much he loved listening to them, they taught him their songs and tunes on the *dutar.* These girls were his first teachers in the practical study of Uzbek music. But for a long time they couldn't figure out what he did for a living, and only after he showed them a few simple magic tricks and completely overwhelmed them by swallowing a knife did they exclaim gleefully, 'Ah, you work in the circus!' After that, everything fell into place."

Kozlovsky, in turn, was enchanted by the musicality that he experienced in his new Uzbek surroundings. He wandered in Tashkent's old city, manuscript notebook in hand, transcribing the singing of teahouse musicians, the chants of wandering dervishes, the cries of peddlars, the music that accompanied itinerant tightrope acts or goat fights at the hippodrome, the tunes and songs that went along with every sort of folk festivity. Little by little, the music from his notebook found its way into his compositions.

Kozlovsky's first symphonic composition in Uzbekistan, called *Lola* (Persian/Turkic: "tulip"), was inspired by a spring tulip festival that took place in Isfara, then a village and now a small city, in northern Tajikistan. Galina Longinovna describes the festival: "In the spring, when tulips bloom on the mountains that surround the Ferghana Valley, men with horse carts would go up to the mountains at sunset to the accompaniment of songs sung by local villagers. They'd spend the night in the mountains, and at dawn they'd gather tulips and fill their carts with them. In those days, the inhabitants of Isfara would scout the outlying area beyond the village and find the oldest, strongest tree. They'd cut it down and, singing and dancing all the while, carry it, with the oldest male in the village seated on it, to the outskirts of the village in order to meet the returning tulipers (as the tulip gatherers were called). After a merry meeting, all present decorated themselves with as many flowers as possible, then began to decorate the tree with enormous bunches of tulips. The tree, ablaze in the scarlet of the tulips, was carried with the old man astride it to the main square of the village. The dancing and singing went on for three days. On the third night, after a clap from the old man, everyone silently sat on the earth. The holiday had come to an end."[7]

Kozlovsky's *Lola* is a symphonic tone poem in three movements that paints three different scenes from the tulip festival. While Kozlovsky is not immune from the Orientalist clichés of his famous nineteenth-century Russian predecessors—for example, the high, tremulous drones in the opening of both *Lola'*s first and second movements could have stepped right off the pages of Borodin's "In Central Asia"—*Lola* largely transcends those clichés. Kozlovsky shies away from the banner techniques of such Russian Orientalist favorites as Rimsky's *Sheherazade,* Borodin's *Polovtsian Dances,* and the *Lezginka* from Glinka's *Ruslan and Ludmila:* fetching modal harmonizations, quirky rhythms, and furiously paced dance numbers with exotic scales. In their place he offers a kind of true-to-life musical impressionism based on his own direct and protracted experience of the music he portrays. Rather than citing Uzbek melodies and rhythms with the aim of reproducing the musical surface of his sources, Kozlovsky draws on orchestral timbre and coloration to convey a more abstract sense of the atmosphere of a place and the feeling of the events that occurred there. One movement from *Lola,* "Night in a Ferghana Garden," is presented on the accompanying compact disc (track 2).

Alexei Fedorovich was not the only Russian in Uzbekistan who submerged himself deeply in local culture as a source of artistic inspiration. The set designer for his opera *Ulugbek,* a dramatization of the life of the great fifteenth-century Samarkand astronomer (and grandson of Timur), was a Russian artist, Alexander Vasilevich Nikolaev, who converted to Islam and took the name Ustâ Mumin (Master Mumin). Ustâ Mumin had been a student of Malevich and Filonov and, unlike Kozlovsky, came to Central Asia of his own volition as the result of what Galina Longinovna described as a "deep personal drama." Ustâ Mumin and a group of like-minded artists inhabited a large house and farmed a plot of land in Samarkand, which in Russian artistic circles was half-jokingly called the Paul Gauguin Collective Farm, referring to Gauguin's exploits in Tahiti. Ustâ Mumin went native in the deepest possible way. He became completely fluent in Uzbek and fully adopted the life of a rural Uzbek *dehqân,* or agricultural worker.

Working together on *Ulugbek,* Alexei Fedorovich, Ustâ Mumin, and Galina Longinovna, who wrote the libretto, faced the challenge of creating a work that was not simply a Russian opera on an Oriental theme intended for a Russian audience, like Glinka's *Ruslan and Ludmila* and Rimsky's *Legend of the Invisible City of Kitezh,* but an opera that reached out to both Russians and Uzbeks in the spirit of Uzbekistan's cultural politics of the

20

1940s. Galina Longinovna offers a splendid description of the early reception history of *Ulugbek:*

"The production was ready and everyone was just waiting for the premiere. But then something terrible and unexpected happened. The opera was shown to the First Secretary of the Communist party of Uzbekistan, Comrade Usman Yusupov. He announced to everyone that he wasn't going to give permission for the opera to be shown unless the authors changed the character of Ulugbek. 'How can you show a gentle scholar when there's a war going on and he should be shown to the people as a warrior and a defender of the Motherland?' It was like a thunderbolt. Yusupov was demanding historical falsification in the interests of upholding official dogma.

"We were shaken by outrage in our souls, and we couldn't look at the faces of the opera troupe without horror and sadness. They couldn't ask us in words to submit to the demands of the petty tyrant [Yusupov], but their eyes spoke of their despair. Was all of their work and inspiration going to be for nothing? In order to save our common creation, we grit our teeth and changed the finale of the opera [in which, on the order of conservative mullahs, Ulugbek is murdered for his heretical beliefs; in the bowdlerized version, Ulugbek vanquished the legions of the mullahs and lived on]. It contradicted historical truth. The artistic and historical conception of the tragedy was destroyed. But the petty tyrant allowed the production to go on.

"On the very first evening of the show, two kinds of responses became clearly defined. The opera, which had been translated into Uzbek, had an enormous success with the Russian part of the public but clearly didn't get through to the majority of Uzbek listeners. For them, everything was new, unfamiliar, and alien. And this was natural and to be expected. I'm explaining this in such detail because *Ulugbek* was a turning point in the history and development of operatic music in Uzbekistan. Before Kozlovsky, all the [Uzbek] composers who worked in this genre were very timid and cautious about working up Uzbek musical material. They were afraid of scaring away Uzbeks, afraid that 'Uzbeks wouldn't get it.' They didn't develop what was most inherent in the form of opera and didn't understand the laws of musical dramaturgy. All of their work was dominated by a simple kind of musical citation, which led to forms known in Uzbekistan as 'musical drama.' The [Uzbek] people gradually got accustomed to this sort of art and began to like it.

"Before *Ulugbek,* Uzbek listeners weren't familiar with large-scale polyphonic works. They were accustomed to unison singing and couldn't grasp the free and independent vocal lines in duets, trios, quartets, and so forth. [In *Ulugbek*] they first heard leitmotivs, leitrhythms, and the development of musical references that arise from them. The opera was saturated with folk melodies, motives, and rhythms, but they were all realized in the dynamics and forms of operatic dramaturgy. To all of this was added one more circumstance.

21

The majority of Uzbek listeners complained that they didn't understand the words of the translation [from Russian into Uzbek]. Only a small number of educated people understood the classical literary language in which the poet Mirtemir wrote his translation. What they knew was the everyday language of the streets and the modest vocabulary used in newspapers. So the official opinion formed that *Ulugbek* was an opera by a Russian composer on an Oriental theme, not an Uzbek opera. But then a historical paradox occurred. When, after sixteen years, *Ulugbek* was revived in the original Russian version, something amazing happened. Uzbek listeners proclaimed, 'This is *ours, our real Uzbek opera.*' That's what time did. People got accustomed to it. A lot of opera music was broadcast on the radio, and people's tastes adapted to musical forms with which they had once been unfamiliar. Everything was cleared up and fell into place."

The change in perception and reception that transformed *Ulugbek* from an Uzbek-language "Russian opera" to a Russian-language "Uzbek opera" is particularly ironic in light of the fact that so-called Uzbek national opera was at root a Soviet invention. What Uzbek audiences came to view as their music had indeed never before existed in Central Asia. But for Soviet cultural strategists, "national opera" (as opposed to Russian or European opera, i.e., "opera" *simpliciter*) provided yet one more means of concretizing the cultural and ultimately the political fealty of Uzbekistan and other non-Slavic Soviet colonies to Mother Russia.

THE LAST OF THE JADIDS

If Kozlovsky was a European composer who immersed himself in Central Asian music to enrich his Western musical roots, then Mutavaqqil Burxanov is his mirror image: an Uzbek who studied European musical forms and techniques to provide an expressive vessel for his Central Asian musical heritage. Burxanov, born in 1916, is a living legacy of the Jadids, the Central Asian Muslim reformists who in the interregnum years between the dissolution of the Bukharan Emirate and the consolidation of Soviet rule, tried, and in the end failed, to fuse Central Asian social and religious tradition with European Enlightenment thinking.

Burxanov is a tall, gaunt man who exudes an emotional intensity that belies his age and frail physical condition. He calls himself a dervish. He never married and lives alone in a small, spartan apartment that mirrors both his predilection for austerity and his lack of financial means to live any other way. "When I die, the Burxanov line will die with me," the composer said with resignation when we met one day at OM's.

Burxanov's music is not technically complex, but it achieves remarkably strong effects from the spare harmonization of folk songs that became his stylistic signature. Burxanov has written collections of harmonized folk songs gathered from many different peoples of Central Asia and has a fine sense of the subtle distinctions that mark these various folk musics. But he has never had a recording of his music released.

Some years ago, Burxanov wrote his autobiography in a manuscript that he called, after the Persian scholastic tradition, "Burxanname" (Book of Burxan). He kept the manuscript to himself, however, even after OM showed great interest in writing his own biographical sketch of Burxanov. Burxanov finally revealed the manuscript to OM and me early in 1993 in the course of several conversations about his life and career, to which he agreed with great reluctance. "Why would anyone want to know about me?" he asked OM incredulously. Once we began to talk, however, Burxanov's diffidence dissipated; in fact, he seemed relieved, as he recounted orally the contents of his "Burxanname," that his life might not go unremembered.

"I grew up in Bukhara, where my father was a mathematics teacher in the *madrasah* (theological college). My mother was from the *xâja* lineage and was supposedly descended from one of the early rulers of Bukhara, Ismail the Samanid (d. 907). But there was tuberculosis in her family and to try to break the vicious cycle of the tuberculosis, her family gave her to a lower lineage for marriage; not a low lineage, but the middle lineage of my father, the mathematics teacher. That caused a scandal among the *xâja*s.

"I had one brother, who was born in 1905, and three uncles on my father's side. They were Jadids. One uncle, Mukammil Burxâni, was the Minister of Justice in Bukhara under the last emir. After the fall of the emir, he was the first ambassador of the Bukharan Republic to Russia. He was educated in Istanbul, at the university. When he went to Istanbul, he took his younger brother, Muammir, because the emir wanted to take Muammir, who was very handsome, into his service. Mukammil studied mathematics but was also interested in music.

"In 1919, the emir clamped down on the Jadids, who were trying to establish a democratic socialist republic in Bukhara, and my father, Muzainiddin, was implicated in some sort of provocation.[8] A man came to the *madrasah* where my father taught and told him that he was going to be sentenced to have his children killed in front of his eyes, and then be killed himself. When he heard this, my father went into shock. He rushed home and told my mother to hide the children. My mother had a relative who was a mufti [a legal advisor consulted in the application of religious law], and he went to the emir's father and explained that according to the Qur'an, it was illegal to punish someone who was physically or psychologically ill. The emir ultimately changed the sentence to house arrest. But my father never recovered from his shock, and died a month later.

"My uncle Mukammil saw my interest in music, and when I was eight years old, he ordered a little *tanbur* for me. I studied with Ata Ghias, one of the most famous musicians in Bukhara. When I was twelve, I entered the Institute of Music and Dance in Samarkand, which had become the capital of the new Soviet republic of Uzbekistan. It was both a place for scholars and a pedagogical institute that prepared students for the Conservatory. At the same time that we studied Oriental music, they played us records of the music of Beethoven, Bach, Rimsky-Korsakov, and Tchaikovsky."

I asked Burxanov, "What did you think of this music?"

"Of course, it was strange for me. I had been raised on monophonic music. But I wanted to learn more about the great music of Europe and Russia, and so I went to Moscow. I became a student at a preparatory school for the Conservatory, and the next year, I started the Conservatory itself.

"In 1934, just before I went to Moscow, my brother was arrested as an 'enemy of the people' and sentenced to five years in Siberia. I remember that one day, after I had been in Moscow for several years, I was told to go to the office of one of the secretaries of the Conservatory. The secretary said that an old man had come to see me and was waiting on the street. I went outside and found him. He asked, 'Are you Burxanov?' He said that he had known my brother in a camp in Siberia and that my brother had been a great help to him. He took out a wrinkled paper envelope and gave it to me. It was from my brother. There was a letter in Russian, but wrapped up inside this letter was a small piece of paper on which there was writing in the Arabic alphabet. My brother wrote to me, 'Muhal-*aka,* please believe that I am not an enemy of the people. I am suffering so much here. I beg you to take this letter [the one in Russian], put it in an envelope, address it to Comrade Stalin, and go to a mailbox near the Kremlin and mail it to him.' Even the people in the camps had faith in Stalin then. I did as my brother asked. I went to a mailbox near the Kremlin, waited until no one was looking, and dropped the letter in. Until I received that letter, I, too, had believed that my brother was an enemy of the people. That was the first time that my idea changed. My brother was released from the camp in Siberia a year early, in 1937, and returned to Tashkent. But the reason he was returned was so that he could be shot, together with my three uncles. They were shot because they had been Jadids. I only learned recently about the circumstances of my brother's death.

"The Jadids trusted Lenin. They wanted to unite with the Communist party. I also liked Lenin. He ate potatoes. I wrote an 'Ode to the Party,' but I never joined the party. I remember people who came back to Bukhara from Germany. They knew German, they were very cultured, and they cried when Lenin died. They were so sincere. It was a mistake. They didn't know they'd be systematically exterminated. The problem was, the Jadids were more progressive than the Communists. Religion was very strong in Bukhara at the time of the Bukharan Revolution. [Abdurauf] Fitrat [one of the most prominent of the Jadids, who served as Minister of Culture in the short-lived Bukharan Republic], who was married to my older sister, insisted that religion had to be permitted in Bukhara.

Then Lenin said, 'Well, we can't take you in [to the Soviet Union] unless you can get rid of religion.' Fitrat replied, 'That's impossible. What will the people say?'."[9] Lenin prevailed, of course, and later Fitrat was accused of being a bourgeois nationalist and pan-Turkist, and put before a firing squad.

"I stayed in Moscow until 1941. At first, I studied at the 'workers' depart-ment,' or *Rabfak* [for *rabochii fakul'tet*]. The *Rabfak* was an accelerated program to prepare the children of workers for higher education. The *Rabfak* had connections to an opera studio that opened in Moscow to train cadres from Uzbekistan for the opera theater. There were opera studios for other republics as well. I enrolled in the Uzbek opera studio, and in 1939 I entered the Moscow Conservatory itself as a student in the composition department."

In many ways, Burxanov's harmonized folk songs, his symphonic pieces, and the opera *Nawâ'i* that he completed in 1991, based on the life of Mir 'Ali Shir Nawâ'i, the fifteenth-century Timurid poet, epitomize the kind of concert music that Soviet cultural strategists hoped would take root in Central Asia. Burxanov, in a sense, was an Uzbek clone of the nineteenth-century Russian composers—in particular, Glinka, Rimsky-Korsakov, Tchaikovsky—who served as models for Soviet composers charged with the creation of "national" music inspired by indigenous folk songs. The difference was that the nineteenth-century Russian impulse for folk-song-inspired concert music arose much more from a blending of romantic populism with the aesthetics of realism than from ideological doctrine imposed from above, as became the case in the Soviet Union beginning in the early 1930s. And, of course, Burxanov's Central Asian folk-song sources were considerably more distant even than Russian folk genres from the European harmonic style that formed the common language of Soviet "national" musics. Nonetheless, at age seventy-six, Burxanov still conveyed a sincere belief in the idea that Uzbek folk songs can be—and ought to be—merged with European concert music, and that such musical merging is the rightful task of Uzbek composers.

"The Russian composers with whom I studied—Glière, Vasilenko, Sposobin—they all convinced us to love our folk music. 'You can study harmony and counterpoint, but don't forget your own folk music,' they told us. There was a singer here who was sent to Italy to study, and when he came back, people listened to him, and someone said, 'You went away a nightingale and came back a sparrow.' When you take up someone else's style and lose your own identity, you end up repelling people. When you use what's your own, you attract them—even people who aren't from your nation. Take Tchaikovsky's piano concerto. Even peasants on a Samarkand collective farm will admire parts of it."

I had looked at scores of Burxanov's music, but I wanted to hear it performed. Music notation could explain Burxanov's conception of East-West cultural convergence on the level of musical form and structure, but how did performers interpret that convergence in actual sound? To what extent did notation-reading singers convey the distinctive timbres and pulsing dynamics that mark the vocal style of Uzbek folk song? Since Burxanov's music had never been released on a commercial recording, I went to the radio station in Tashkent, where the director of the Uzbek National Chorus, Juraqul Shukurov, kindly agreed to arrange a private concert of some of Burxanov's folk-song settings. One of these settings, "Yarlarim," which Burxanov composed in 1952, is included on the accompanying CD (track 7). The text is as follows:

> Where now is a soulmate like you?
> Having seen your flower-like face in the garden
> I will hold your love as long as I live
> Wherever I find myself, I want to be with you.

> Endi sendek jânajânân qaydadur
> Korib gul yuzingni bâghda bandadur
> Saqlay ishqing tâki jânim tandadur
> Ozim har jâydaman konglim sendadur.

Burxanov's setting is sprightly but spare. Male and female choirs alternately declaim the melody in a thinly harmonized unison layered over a textless ostinato of male voices that imitates the rhythmic cycle (*usul*) of the frame drum (*dâyra*). The effect is one of directness and lack of pretense, and while the surging dynamics seem a little contrived, they provide an admirable simulacrum of Uzbek folk song as performed by village singers in a traditional style.

Juraqul was a demanding conductor, and his chorus was well-rehearsed and well-disciplined. Although I was satisfied with the first recorded take of "Yarlarim," Juraqul repeated the piece six times until he achieved a performance that he thought sounded right. "We don't have the right to spoil the way the people sing it," he said. "We're a hundred percent responsible for preserving what the people have. For example, I ignore rests and join phrases together, developing the musical apogee [*awj*] through ornamentation [*nâla*]. In this style of singing, the ornaments pull upward while the notes themselves move like a falling wave through the rests. You have to base a performance on the pulse of a piece, and that pulse determines the shape of the falling wave. If you don't feel the pulse, you'll distort the piece."

"If Burxanov had wanted you to join phrases together and ignore rests, couldn't he have conveyed that through notation?" I asked.

"He could have conveyed it, but the chorus that existed at the time he wrote the piece was made up of Europeans. They couldn't sing in the folk style. The conductor was Russian, and the singers distorted the pronunciation of the texts. You can perform Burxanov's music in an academic, European style, but since this is our *national* chorus, we should preserve the national features of the music. Burxanov came to hear our performance and was very happy with it. You can show almost everything in notation, but oral tradition also plays a role. It's the same with Tchaikovsky. We're interpreters. These sorts of issues come up at every step of our work."

Burxanov's opera, *Nawâ'i,* was to be performed in Tashkent during one of my visits, and OM and I attended a preview performance for a large group of Burxanov's friends and acquaintances. Tashkent's opera house dates from 1947. It was designed by Alexei Shchusev, the architect who created the Lenin Mausoleum, and the similarity between the two buildings is unmistakable. The opera house is in a style that might be called Uzbek Stalinist: an imposing classical facade with columns and plinths leads to spacious marbled lobbies and a grandiose proscenium hall whose walls are inscribed with floral and arabesque patterns in an Oriental motif. Aphorisms from a pantheon of both Central Asian and European artistic luminaries are carved in bas-reliefs set into the exterior side walls. Unfortunately, for all of its grandeur, the hall's acoustics never seem to have been taken into account. From the fourth row, singers at the front of the stage are barely audible.

The opera theater has a yearly season that features European and Russian classics and, on rare occasions, a contemporary Uzbek opera like Burxanov's. Attendance has been declining steadily over the years; these days, what audience there is consists mostly of organized groups of tourists, students, and workers who receive their tickets for free.

OM's gloss on *Nawâ'i* was that Burxanov had used the great poet and his futile search for love and justice in the fifteenth century as a form of allegory that represented his own life. But the asceticism with which Burxanov infused his main character seemed finally to diminish the opera's musical coherence. Burxanov had warned us that *Nawâ'i* contained only one aria. "What is important to me is to show Nawâ'i the man, not the way he could use his voice. Characters show themselves better through recitative than through aria," Burxanov said.

Unfortunately, the production did not help Burxanov make his case. The staging was maladroit, the performers' movements seemed contrived and mechanical, and the orchestra played out of tune. The opera itself lacks dramatic tension. Men and women only once appear in the same scene, only once, fleetingly, touch hands. The characters don't seem to engage one another, either physically or musically.

After the preview, the director of the opera theater invited the audience to remain for a discussion with the composer and principal artistic personnel. Burxanov seemed less than pleased with the production. The orchestra conductor apologized for his ensemble's performance. He explained that in the past year the orchestra had lost many of its best players—Jews who had emigrated to Israel or the United States, as I later learned. After an extended discussion that featured often tactless critique of the work, an official from the Ministry of Culture rose and offered what sounded like a rehearsed valedictory speech. His conclusion: opera has a bright future in Uzbekistan.

27

Some time after the performance of *Nawâ'i,* I dropped by the Ministry of Culture to speak with a Deputy Minister about why his government was devoting scarce financial resources to supporting artistic institutions, like opera, that were holdovers from the era of Russian colonialism. The Deputy Minister replied, "Because we want to become part of the rest of the world; we want our artists to have the same chance that artists from other countries have to compete in international competitions, and we want them to know of the accomplishments of world culture."

I think this minister was speaking sincerely. However, another reason for maintaining the status quo must be bureaucratic inertia. Hundreds of thousands of people were trained to run and maintain the archipelago of Soviet cultural institutions. As OM put it, "To fundamentally change those institutions, you'd literally have to change the blood of the people running them, and that's not about to happen." The musical merging of Central Asia and Europe by fiat—the commissioning of operas and symphonies on Uzbek themes, the training of composers to write those works and of musicians to play them—will grind on. But the generation that embraced this artistic experiment with a passion and commitment that far exceeded the demands of political expediency is passing from the scene. These musicians are not likely to be replaced.

Burxanov sticks stubbornly to his position as a cultural centrist, a kind of neo-Jadid, in the debates about Eastern and Western influences: "Composers should know their own musical and cultural roots thoroughly. They should know languages like Arabic and Persian so that they're not learning everything through Russian. At the same time, they ought to know the great achievements of European and Russian music in all of their subtleties. Some people now say that we don't need symphonies, operas, or choirs here. I don't agree. We need composers, but we need fewer of them—just the good ones."

What is a "good" composer in Uzbekistan these days? Ulugbek Musaev, Chairman of the Union of Composers of Uzbekistan, had strong ideas about the direction of the nation's postcolonial musical life. In a conversation I had with Musaev in the summer of 1994, the Chairman, an energetic, chain-smoking man in his mid-forties, was respectful of Burxanov, the Union's musical elder statesman, but made it clear that he considered Burxanov's brand of neoromantic folklorism to be a kind of cultural fossil that revealed a particular stage of Uzbekistan's evolution but provided an unsuitable model for its future development.

"We love our traditions too much," Musaev complained to me, rising to fetch a pack of Marlboro cigarettes from his office safe (otherwise empty, as far as I could tell). "People are still writing in the style of Borodin and Tchaikovsky. It's almost the twenty-first century, and people are still writing that stuff. I can't stand to listen to it. We're still doing everything *à la russe.* We had the premiere of a new opera—*Omar Khayyam*—about two weeks ago.

It was written by Mustaffah Bafâev. He's about forty-eight, forty-nine years old, and he knows folklore well. I listened to the opera carefully a few times. It's again more Tchaikovsky, freshened up a little. There's a bit of dissonance here and there, but it's the same old operatic forms. I said to him, 'Why don't you write a twentieth-century opera? You have to write music that's part of our own time, not the last century.' But no, he doesn't want to do that. 'We have our Uzbek folk music, our history, our legends, our fables,' he said. I've seen how such a composer works. He takes a book of Uzbek folk songs and puts the folk songs side by side with his libretto. He wants to write an aria, so he looks for a poetic text whose rhythm is the same as the part of the libretto that he's trying to harmonize. Then he takes the folk melody from that text and harmonizes it. There's no creative process, no creativity.

"We're living in a complicated time. People aren't well educated now. When we were part of the Soviet Union, I used to be able to call Moscow and say, 'I need to go to Italy.' And they'd send me. I'd listen to music, bring back records. Now we're independent, but we can't go anywhere. There's no money. At a time when we need more than ever to be integrated into the rest of the musical world, we have no information. It's like someone turned out the lights after independence. Our concerts are nothing but folklore and dancing. I'm against the idea that you have to be a prisoner of folklore. The interest in folklore is exaggerated now. It's a political action. You can't throw everything you have into folklore. We all have the stamp of communism in our heads, and it's hard to escape from it.

"This last year, [President] Karimov went to France and they took him to the opera theater. So when Mitterrand came here, they invited him to our opera theater. But first they had to reconstruct it. We had an order: fix up the opera theater. People have to understand that you can't just order an evening of culture to be put on for a visiting president. People have to understand that it's something that has to exist at a certain level all the time. A composer earns ten dollars for writing a cello concerto. How can you live on that? He might have spent a year writing that piece. For writing an opera now, you can't even buy a suit of clothes. As head of the Composers Union, I receive fifteen dollars a month. I've rented out half the Union's building to a Pakistani firm that's in the textile business. They help us with hard currency. Maybe in five or ten years we will have moved through all of this. But it's going to be dangerous if it continues. We should be a cultured nation that can communicate with anyone. East and West should develop together. One can't develop without the other. The East has had an enormous influence on the West—its poetry and so on. But it doesn't make any sense just to play folklore. A tradition is only interesting when it develops in relation to the rest of the world's humanity. So it's become clear that what the Russians gave us was not all bad. There was a lot of good in it."

NEOFEUDALISM WITH A HUMAN FACE

OM was eager for me to meet his friend Xudâbergan (XudâberGAN), a fellow Khorezmian, who was staying for several weeks in Tashkent. OM didn't know exactly why Xudâbergan had come to Tashkent, but he supposed that the reason might have been connected to a crackdown in Khorezm on what is loosely called "the mafia."

In Transoxania, as elsewhere in the former Soviet Union, the word *mafia* is used casually and widely to describe people whose wealth comes from sources other than a regular salary. These people run the gamut from extortionists, racketeers, and murderers-for-hire to money launderers and the secular version of simonists, who sell state benefices and property for personal gain, to legitimate businessmen who have enjoyed financial success. OM emphasized that Xudâbergan was an example of a positive hero among mafiosi: a man who used his connections to help others and, in particular, to help artists and musicians. He was, in short, a sort of philanthropist and patron of the arts trying to fill a philanthropic void in a society making the difficult passage from state monopolism of arts patronage to the blend of personal, private-sector, and government support characteristic of capitalist societies. Xudâbergan ran his commercial and philanthropic empire while holding an official position as coach for the amateur boxing team in a cotton oil factory in Urgench, the capital of the Khorezm region. (Later he became president of an officially registered firm that managed his various enterprises.)

Xudâbergan showed up one night with one of the beneficiaries of his generosity, a young and obviously well-fed Khorezmian musician named Rahmat. Xudâbergan was an unprepossessing patron of the arts. He was of medium height and average weight with receding short black hair and a flattened nose. His gold upper front teeth matched the expensive-looking gold watch and watchband that girdled his left wrist, not quite covering a faintly tatooed blue "x." He was dressed in a dark blue warm-up suit, the jacket unzipped over a shiny black silk shirt.

We ate dinner and made small talk. After dinner, Xudâbergan and Rahmat excused themselves and left OM's apartment, promising to return in about half an hour. OM whispered to me, "They're going to smoke opium." Opium, or *taryak,* is widely used among Uzbek men. A ball of opium paste is sometimes stuck to the side of a tea bowl, where it slowly dissolves into the hot tea as it is drunk. Inhaling or ingesting a small amount produces a feeling of langorous well-being that puts users in the right mood for an intimate evening of conversation or music.

When Xudâbergan and Rahmat returned, they suggested that we go to my apartment—a small place that OM's brother-in-law had bought as an investment property and temporarily made available to me—to continue our conversation. We settled onto wooden stools set around the gas stove in the tiny kitchen, and Xudâbergan, relaxing from the effect of the opium, began to tell his story. He had been born in Urgench, in 1955, one of ten children. His father had been a worker and, despite little money and crowded conditions, made a habit of picking up homeless people and offering them food and shelter. Once he had taken home a Russian man who was begging in a restaurant, and the man had lived with them for four months. Xudâbergan had tried to emulate his father's generosity. "I passed a homeless person once on the street. I was in a hurry and I didn't stop for him right away. But my conscience bothered me, and I returned and picked him up. I took him home, and later he robbed us. But it didn't matter that he stole. What was important was that I didn't pass by this person. I honored my father.

"I had a talent for sports and became a boxer. I had a lot of self-confidence, and I was cocky and tough. In 1977, I beat up four guys. They spent a long time in the hospital, and I was sent to jail for eight years. Until 1977, I'd barely read a single book. But when I was in prison, I began to write poetry. After I got out, I dreamed about that life, about the sweetness that I felt in writing poetry. I can't compare it to anything. Now, books give me greater pleasure than anything else. I love Babur and Nawâ'i. They've helped me, because they also suffered, and in their works, I found parallels to my own life.

"In 1985, I left prison. My friends had grown up, and they helped me. I worked in the construction business. I made lots of contacts, and I was successful. My success was based on *dasturxân* [literally, "tablecloth"]—on friendship and hospitality. All my life, I've placed a high value on good friends.

"I'm a believer, but I don't go to the mosque. You know what kind of life we had here. You could be sent to jail for going to the mosque. The most important thing is to believe in your heart, to live through the principle of *himmat*—generosity unsullied by self-interest; to help others without feeling proud about it. I serve the good—that's my goal. I look at other people who have perfected themselves to a greater extent than I have, and these people are like a compass for me. You can strive toward that perfection."

I asked, "How do you help others?"

"I set up my relatives very well. I got work for them. I helped them build houses. I gave them building materials and I sent craftsmen to do the work. But it spoiled them. They started arguing among themselves, and they became lazy and hypocritical. I realized that I wasn't doing them a favor but a disservice. So I took away their work. People get spoiled from a good life. I'm not interested in material things. For me the most important is for someone to have a soul."

"What about artists?"

"I've helped musicians like Rahmat [the singer from Khorezm who came that evening with Xudâbergan] build their houses. I sent bricks and cement and

31

wood, and master builders and craftsmen. I've paid for musicians to perform at the weddings of relatives and friends."

Rahmat, the young leader of a folk music ensemble called Lazgi who lives in an ostentatious new house, nodded in agreement. "God gave me my house," he said, referring to Xudâbergan's philanthropy. "I earn 9,000 rubles a month [about $12] from the Philharmonia [a government organization that serves as an official manager for music ensembles]. I get up to 100,000 rubles for a wedding. My conscience won't let me take more than that. But by the time I take care of my eight musicians and dancer and then pay for transportation and sound equipment, I'm left with only 15,000 rubles [$20]. During the wedding season, we play sixty to seventy weddings. But only about fifteen of them are on the basis of a fixed agreement. For the rest, we just show up, not knowing what we're going to earn, because the people who have invited us are friends or relatives and it's impolite to discuss money with them."

The discussion wore on until the early hours of the morning. Xudâbergan wanted OM to tell him about dervishes, and in particular about the life of Jalâlâddin Rumi, the founder of the Mevlevi Sufi order. OM obliged with a long description of Rumi's life and of his poetic masterpiece, the *Mathnavi*. OM is one of Xudâbergan's compasses, someone who offers him spiritual and intellectual direction. They seemed an unlikely pair, the erudite musicologist and the boxer with the pug nose, but Xudâbergan appeared entranced by OM's explanations of the Sufi *tariqa*—the mystical path—and of the poetry and music that it has inspired.

The next day, OM was expansive about Xudâbergan and about how he exemplified many of the qualities of traditional Central Asian Islamic life, even if he didn't articulate the connections himself. "For example," said OM, "his love [*ishq*] of music and poetry. There's an aphorism: Ishqi yoq eshek, dardi yoq qisek [A person without love is like a donkey; a person without passion is like brimstone]. *Ishq* and *dard*—love and passion, these are the ideals of life here. And then look at his level of activity. He's always on the move. That love of travel is also a quality that's been important in traditional life. There's another aphorism: Keçgen—darya, oturgan—boyra [A person who moves is like a river, a person who sits is like a straw mat]. The idea is that you stay fresh by traveling, that you atrophy if you stay still." I wasn't convinced about Xudâbergan. It wasn't clear to me whether he was always on the move because of a traditional Islamic love of travel or to stay one step ahead of the authorities who were trying to bust the Uzbek mafia.

"Xudâbergan is an example of a good man, a man who serves the good in life," OM continued. "Look at the importance that he places on friends and friendship. That's also something of the greatest importance in local tradition. Friends are higher than anything. Friendship is in the highest category. Not Soviet-style 'friendship among peoples,' but just friendship. The worst thing is not to be able to trust people; to be lied to."

I asked, "When Xudâbergan builds houses for his friends and relatives, isn't he taking the building materials illegally from the state?"

"He doesn't steal from the state; he just has very close relations with it that are not obvious. What you and I couldn't buy for two million rubles, he can get a ton of for two kopecks."

Later, OM talked about Xudâbergan and his philanthropy as an example of a newly forming paradigm of social organization in Uzbekistan that OM called neofeudalism. If the nobility of a traditional feudal society derives its wealth by extracting profit from the ownership of land, then the nobility of Uzbekistan's neofeudal society comes by *its* wealth mainly by "money laundering" (the term is translated literally into Russian and Uzbek). The laundered money comes in some cases from old party coffers and in other cases from the diverse illegal schemes that comprise the infamous "parallel economy" of the former republics. But unlike capitalist societies, in which the source of personal wealth, especially when it appears mysteriously and is conspicuously displayed, can be a matter of intense public scrutiny, Uzbeks are publicly nonchalant about their neofeudal *nouveaux riches*. The present attitude is a stark contrast to the old order in which the conspicuous display of personal wealth could lead easily to a criminal investigation. Since salaries—almost all under the control of state enterprises—were universally low, it was assumed that anyone with substantial assets had acquired them dishonestly. In the majority of such cases, the assumption of theft and corruption was correct. In any event, people who had money tended to keep it well hidden.

The sort of private patronage exemplified by Xudâbergan—providing material support to a favored musician or employing skilled craftsmen in the construction of elegant homes—is not, of course, new to Central Asia. OM had stressed in his encomium to Xudâbergan that patronage has deep roots in old feudal centers of mercantile wealth such as Bukhara, Samarkand, and Khiva; that it was the substitution of monolithic bureaucratic patronage proffered by the state for the idiosyncratic artistic tastes of the feudal nobility that had led to such odious standardization of music, architecture, and decorative arts during the seventy years of Communist rule. At the same time, it seemed clear from listening to OM and Xudâbergan that state patronage had never completely replaced the traditional patronage of individuals, even at the height of Communist power.

OM pointed out that during his lifetime there had always been individuals like Xudâbergan who had helped artists; that, in fact, the entire unofficial cultural network and economic system that supported the central events in Uzbek social life—the *toy* (wedding), *âsh* (literally, "food"—an early morning quasi-religious gathering of men given separately by the fathers of both bride and groom before every Uzbek marriage), and *ziyâfat, gap, gurung,* or *majlis,* as intimate evening gatherings of friends for conversation, food, and music are variously called—had existed all along in the shadow of the official cultural life played out in concert halls and theaters, at public ceremonies and on radio and television.

THE SINGING MULLAH

One of my guides to the world of *toy, âsh,* and *gap* was a mullah, poet, and musician from Khojend, in northern Tajikistan, named Ma'ruf Xâja Bahâdor. Ma'ruf Xâja and OM were old friends, and OM had introduced us once when OM and I stopped briefly in Khojend en route from Tashkent to Samarkand and Bukhara. OM had not visited Ma'ruf Xâja's house for some years—they usually saw one another in Tashkent—and he had forgotten how to find it. But everyone in Khojend seemed to know Ma'ruf Xâja and was prepared to direct us to his house. We had to ask for directions repeatedly, and as we came nearer to our destination, the people we approached for directions not only told us how to find Ma'ruf Xâja but also invited us to have tea with them before we saw Ma'ruf Xâja himself. They clearly felt a communal pride that Ma'ruf Xâja was their neighbor and thus a communal responsibility in serving as hosts to a visitor from abroad.

Among Uzbeks and Tajiks, an invitation to have tea (*chai*) always implies that more than tea will be offered. Tea is only one element of *dasturxân,* which, although it literally means "tablecloth," serves as the general term for hospitality proffered at the table. An invitation for *dasturxân* specifies only tea out of a tradition of modesty. The simplest *dasturxân* always includes bread, fresh or dried fruits, nuts, and hard candies, but a *dasturxân* is rarely that simple. Usually these obligatory snacks are accompanied by salads and followed by soup and finally *palav* (pilaf). According to convention, once a guest has stepped across the threshold of a house, he has committed himself to accepting *dasturxân.* At the same time, he has surrendered control over the complexity of the *dasturxân* and the length of the séance, for these are entirely at the discretion of the host. Pleading for a small *dasturxân* on the grounds of having just eaten has no effect whatsoever.

When OM and I traveled away from our home base in Tashkent, we could have easily filled the whole of each day with nothing but *dasturxân,* and thus we were perpetually having to decline invitations for "tea." This task was itself a matter of great delicacy. The polite way to decline an invitation is to smile, nod slightly, put hand over heart, and answer simply *"raxmat":* (thank you). However, that is also precisely the way to accept an invitation (a third option is to answer *"Xudâ xâxlasa"*—"God willing," understood as "I'm not ruling it out, but I can't do it right now"). The logic behind this seemingly ambiguous etiquette seems to be that in order to show that an invitation is appreciated, even if it is declined, a "no, thank you" ought to be indiscernible from a "yes, thank you." "Thank you" is thus disambiguated in the following way: in order to signal "no, thank you," one smiles, nods, and repeats "thank you" several times without making any movement that suggests surrender to the host. According to custom, however, the prospective host will continue to extend his invitation three times, changing the wording of the invitation with each repetition. Only after the third decline does the host desist.

Ma'ruf Xâja had received us graciously when we finally reached his house but told us with refreshing frankness that it was not a good time for a long chat. He had commitments that required his presence as a mullah and proposed that we meet in Tashkent another time. He had many friends there and would welcome a chance to visit them as well as us. And so it was that Ma'ruf Xâja, age seventy-three, hitchhiked the hundred-odd miles from Khojend to Tashkent and showed up on my doorstep one April day, a little over a year after our original encounter in Khojend. He brushed off my protests that he should have taken the bus. "For me, hitchhiking is easy," he said with a grin. "Everyone knows me." Ma'ruf Xâja thought that he would stay about a week, but all he carried with him for his stay was his *tanbur.* He was wearing a dark, baggy suit over a blue warm-up uniform, his shaved head covered by a *doppi,* the traditional Uzbek and Tajik skullcap, that had worn a groove around his scalp. Ma'ruf Xâja looked directly at you when he spoke and his deeply lined face broke frequently into a smile, which made the lines look even deeper. Despite his white goatee, he seemed younger than his age, which is rare for men—and even rarer for women—in Central Asia. That impression stemmed largely from an extraordinary quality of alertness in his body that was crystallized in the directness of his gaze during conversation.

As a younger man, Ma'ruf Xâja had lived in Tashkent for twenty years, and he still had a wide circle of friends there. On this trip, soon after arriving at my apartment, he had gone to the place where he was most likely to run into his old friends: the Friday Mosque in the Old City. There he met an acquaintance, a shopkeeper, who invited him to a *gap*—literally, a talk, a conversation—that evening. The *gap* is an old institution in Transoxania. It goes by many names— *ziyâfat, tokme, dawra, majlis, gurung.* The ambience of the *gap* may vary from intimate and subdued to the far side of bacchanalian, depending on the inclination of the participants. Even in times of strict Islamic rule, some *gaps* featured wine and *bachas* (dancing boys). Others featured mullahs who nourished discussions about religious or spiritual topics. During the Communist era, *gaps* did not disappear, but they became secularized. Even in trusted company, religious themes were avoided, and mullahs were not invited. The *gap* became simply an evening out and invariably featured copious amounts of alcohol. According to OM, nearly all men in Tashkent's Old City go regularly to at least one *gap,* and it is not uncommon to go to more than one. While the *gap* is considered primarily a male institution, women also have their *gaps,* these days often served by an *aya mullah*—a female mullah.

In early evening, Ma'ruf Xâja, OM, and I were driven to a quiet neighbor-hood of one-story bungalows on the very outskirts of Tashkent, just beyond the circumferential highway. The host of that evening's *gap,* a man named Tursunbai, worked as a watchman at a nearby automobile repair station. He welcomed us into a simple and tasteful *mehmânxâna* illuminated by a dim chandelier. At one end were the traditional glass cabinets for storing teapots and bowls and bedding for guests. The ceiling of the room was supported by eleven crossbeams. OM explained that it was traditional to have an uneven number of crossbeams as a symbol of the fact that Allah is one and has no double. Twelve men, each wearing a *doppi,* sat on long quilted pads placed around a large table that was completely covered with food: nuts, raisins, dried apricots, fresh fruit and vegetables, pastries, bread, and bottled sodas.

When we entered the room, everyone stood, and OM, Ma'ruf Xâja, and I walked around the table, shaking hands with each man and exchanging salaams. We sat and said a collective "amen." Tea was poured, and the conversation continued. Ma'ruf Xâja seemed to know everyone, but he introduced neither OM nor me. No one asked who we were or what our business was, yet in our anonymity we were made to feel welcome and relaxed. A mullah with a wispy gray beard sat at one end of the table leading a discussion about *sharia*—religious law—and what it had to say about women and the veil. The men asked terse questions, to which the mullah responded with long soliloquys. It turned out that he had studied the Qur'an at home, with his father, and taught *tajwid*—Qur'anic cantillation—at the *madrasah* in Tashkent. The mullah who had previously served this *gap* had moved to a different city, and the present mullah, or *dâmla* (literary: *dâmulla*), as the men called him, using the reverential name for a teacher, had been attending for less than two months on a trial basis. If the group felt that the chemistry was right, the mullah would be invited to become a permanent attendee.

When the group went outside to say evening prayers, one man—Qochqâr was his name—stayed behind with us. Qochqâr told us that he was a lawyer and had been invited to join the *gap* eleven years ago. "It was 1982. I was working in the Supreme Soviet. Jumabây-*aka* worked there, and we became friends. He invited me. He said, 'We have a group and it's good company.'" Qochqâr thought that the *gap* had been going for quite a few years before he joined. The *gap* had thirteen members. There had been fifteen, but two had died. All were around the same age—late fifties, early sixties. They met twice a month on Friday evenings, rotating among the houses of the members. Some members were professional men with higher educations; others were merchants or worked in service businesses. The president of the *gap,* as he was called, had risen from the bottom to a position of responsibility in the railroad.

The conversation was not elevated or intellectual; rather, it dealt with practical aspects of religious law and custom, with how to live as a Muslim.

The mullah explained the position of the *sharia* on a variety of issues and illustrated each issue with an example. His tone was earnest but not imperious or shrill. He never told the men, "You must do such-and-such."

As the evening wore on, *shashlik* (shish kebab) was brought in, and after everyone had finished eating, Ma'ruf Xâja was asked to perform a song. He sang several, accompanying himself on the *tanbur.* The men listened respectfully and silently. As Ma'ruf Xâja was packing up his *tanbur,* one man casually turned to OM and asked him to introduce himself and his guest. Until that moment, no one had asked either one of us a question.

OM spoke briefly and modestly about himself and at greater length about me. In the conversation that followed, the men learned that OM had visited the United States three times, and these visits became an object of curiosity. Gradually the religious focus of the early part of the evening shifted to more worldly topics. OM offered a rambling discourse on U.S. supermarkets, automatic teller machines, laser scanners, and welfare, all of which produced expressions of wonder and disbelief on the faces of the assembled.

Later OM analyzed Ma'ruf Xâja's performance at the *gap.* "He's like a musician from a museum. Once there were a lot of musicians like Ma'ruf Xâja, but now there are almost none left. His music is meant for direct contact with people in small groups like the *gap.* He's a master psychologist who can judge his audience and adjust his music to fit their mood and their needs. He'll sense what poet's lyrics they want to hear. He'll know whether it's time for them to pray, and in that case, he'll make his song a little shorter. You could see how attentively the men listened to the two texts of Mashrab and the text of Ulfat [a twentieth-century poet from Khorezm]. Ma'ruf Xâja is a good poet himself, and it's typical of musicians of his generation that they are never just musicians. They always do something else: they're musician-poets, or musician-philosophers, or musician-comedians. Moreover, Ma'ruf Xâja, you might say, is a musician-*abdâl* [pronounced *abDAL*]—a 'fool of God.' You can see that for him being a musician is more than simply an occupation—a means of earning a living—and music serves a higher aim than that of simply entertaining. For a fool of God, music first and foremost conveys a moral and spiritual power, and performing music is a calling that carries a moral responsibility."

Abdâl is an Arabic word that in Sufi thought refers to a hierarchical class of mystical saints—usually forty in number—who, along with other hierarchical classes of saints, surround the *qutb* (axis, pole), or highest spiritual authority present on earth at any given time.[10] In Transoxania, *abdâl* may connote not only a "friend of God" or a "fool of God," that is, one who has given himself to the life of the spirit and is under the special protection of God, but also a dervish or an ascetic—a person not entirely "of this world." Somewhere in a conversation with OM—the precise memory of when and where has been lost—the expression had come up as a way of describing a particular musician who, in both his musical activities and his personal life, seemed to embody the high ethical standards, humility, and altruistic spirit that characterized the figure of the *abdâl*—the fool of God. The term had stuck in our conversations and become a kind of shorthand for referring to musicians who lived exemplary lives of devotion not only to their art but also to the notion of musicianship as a form of service in which the musician, like the *abdâl,* assumes the moral weight of guiding humankind toward the just and the good.

The analogy wasn't a precise one. In Sufi tradition, the *abdâl* are hidden or veiled from public view, while in present-day Transoxania, the *abdâl*-dervish is understood to be a person who gravitates toward the margins of normative social life. Those whom OM and I had cast as *abdâl*-musicians certainly included such shadowy, dervishlike figures, Mutavaqqil Burxanov being a prime example. But there were others, like Ma'ruf Xâja, who led very public and highly esteemed musical lives. What bound all of these fools of God together, however, was their unwavering devotion to a life of service through music, to the notion of music as a moral calling, to the idea of a connection between the way they lived their lives and the moral quality of their art. Such a connection didn't necessarily imply abstemiousness, for some of the fools of God lived well, though never luxuriously. Yet fame and wealth (in the local understanding) were borne with a modest dignity, as if to make clear that they were not ends in themselves but only the casual by-products of a life of public service. And if canonical Sufi tradition set the number of contemporaneous *abdâl* at forty, then OM and I, in our musical reimagination of the fools of God, opened up membership to all who qualified. We knew at best several dozen in Transoxania whose life spans overlapped, or had overlapped, with ours. But there might have been a hundred, a thousand, or even a hundred thousand who had come before. Others would surely follow.

After the *gap,* Ma'ruf Xâja stayed in my apartment for several days. Between sorties to visit friends, he shared his music and poetry and talked about his life and about the transformation of Central Asia that was taking place as whole populations were swept up in animosities and feuds nourished by, as he saw it, artificial nationalist and regionalist loyalties. I began to feel not only that Ma'ruf Xâja was a musician from a museum, as OM had described him, but also that he represented an entire worldview that had gradually disappeared in the decades of Soviet rule in Central Asia. Ma'ruf Xâja's vision of Central Asia was of a land where Muslims belonging to different clans and speaking different languages would nonetheless feel the bonds of their common religious heritage. He told a little story to illustrate his point: "Once, someone asked the Prophet, 'What nation are we from?' The Prophet answered, 'We're from the nation of Ibrahim.' So you see, it's not language that makes a nation. There's no such thing as an Uzbek or Tajik nation. Khojend is about forty percent Uzbek and a little more than that Tajik. Some districts on the outskirts are completely Uzbek. Tajiks live in the center. But everyone is bilingual. An Uzbek wedding is no different than a Tajik wedding. But now our politics are that people say, 'I'm Uzbek,' 'I'm Tajik,' or 'I'm from Khojend,' 'I'm from Samarkand,' 'I'm from Kulyab.' Look where that kind of thinking is leading us. Everyone is afraid of everyone else."

Returning to the subject of music, Ma'ruf Xâja spoke about how he had begun his musical life. "I was thirteen years old when I first took a *tanbur* in my hands. It was 1933, and I had ordered a *tanbur* from an old man. It was after I heard a famous musician named Sadir Khan, who had sung at the funeral of one of our neighbors. You know, a famous person performs, and a young person hears him and wants to be like him. I was like that. The young man doesn't know what sort of voice he has or what his potential is. But people listen to him, and he starts to sing. Unfortunately, Sadir Khan died, at the age of eighty-two, shortly after I heard him perform. But his records were in the hands of his students, and I listened to those records. Then the people who had been around Sadir Khan began saying that I was his successor, that my style was similar to his.

"I worked in a silk factory and studied in the factory's school. They had a school where you'd study for four hours and then work four hours. I was fourteen when I started. The factory had an amateur music group that I participated in. After a while, someone came to hear us and said to me, 'You have a good voice.' In 1937, they invited me to the radio. They said, 'We'll pay you; go ahead, perform.' I performed folk music. They allowed folk music, but they didn't allow religious music. There couldn't be any mention of God or the Prophet. So we performed folk music.

"I quit my work in the silk factory when I was eighteen because I was earning enough to get by at the radio and I had also started to play in the theater. When I was twenty-one, I got married. My wife's father managed a bread store. By that time, the war had started, and you'd do anything for a piece of bread. He said, 'Son, you're working with such bad people, people without a conscience.' That used to be a typical view of musicians. You could sing, but it was considered undignified to carry an instrument. 'Stop that work,' he said, 'and come and work as a salesman in the bread store.' I told him, 'There's a war going on; I'm supporting myself, and I have an exemption. If I leave the radio and theater, they'll take me into the army.' I stood him off once, twice, three times, and finally I told him, 'Take your daughter back.'

"My second wife had tuberculosis. Her first three children all caught it in infancy and had to go to a children's tuberculosis hospital. They got it from her milk. Then the doctors told me that I'd better take care of myself or I'd also get the disease. I moved to Dushanbe and she stayed in Leninabad [as Khojend was called during most of the Soviet era]. I told her to move in with her father, and she asked for a divorce. I gave her the house and everything in it and left. She never married again. She's still alive, living in that house, but she goes to a tuberculosis hospital every year for treatment. She can barely walk. After the divorce, I married a third wife. She died not long ago. In all, I have eleven children—three sons and eight daughters."

Before our week with Ma'ruf Xâja, OM had spoken expansively of him as a modern-day incarnation of a Central Asian Renaissance man: a poet, singer, and instrumentalist who builds his own musical instruments, a mullah who could recite the Qur'an from memory, a scholar steeped in the tradition of *ilm-i musiqi* (musical science) that had crystallized in the central Islamic lands as early as the tenth century in the scholastic treatises of Al-Fârâbi and, slightly later, Ibn-Sinâ (who wrote in Arabic and benefited from the cultural patronage of Abbasid Baghdad but was of Turkic descent, as Uzbek historians are fond of pointing out). *Ilm-i musiqi* is broadly analogous to the discipline of music theory associated with European art music, and the musical elite of cities like Bukhara and Samarkand would in the past certainly have been familiar with its canon. It turned out, however, that Ma'ruf Xâja knew nothing of *ilm-i musiqi* and couldn't recall ever having read a book about music or music theory. His knowledge of music was thoroughly practical and empirical, not theoretical or speculative. Ma'ruf Xâja himself was well aware of this and seemed more comfortable placing himself in a less elevated tradition of Islamic learning than the one where OM had suggested he belonged. When I mentioned this to OM, he looked disappointed. "If Ma'ruf Xâja doesn't know about *ilm-i musiqi,* then no musician in Central Asia does," he groused.

OM was right. The living intellectual tradition of *ilm-i musiqi* that arcs backward in Central Asia through the treatises of Darwish Ali Changi (late sixteenth–early seventeenth century), Kawkabi Bukhari (late fifteenth–early sixteenth century), Qutb al-Din al-Shirazi (late thirteenth–early fourteenth century), Safi ad-Din (mid-thirteenth century) to Ibn Sina (late tenth–early eleventh century) and al-Farabi (mid-tenth century) has come to an end in Transoxania. It survives now as an object of historical inquiry, like an ancient language, in the curricula and research plans of academic institutions where scholars study the musical past.[11] It is not that musicians have stopped thinking about music. On the contrary, Ma'ruf Xâja, like many of the musicians I know, is an endless font of ideas that concern the relationship of music and poetry, music and religion, music and ethnicity. But these ideas stem from a different kind of thinking than the scientific rationalism that permeates *ilm-i musiqi*. It is thinking that is more mythological than logical, more concerned with the power of music to convey affect (*Affekt*) and meaning than with the elaboration of rational systems and schemata.

Confirming OM's misjudgment of Ma'ruf Xâja's musical knowledge, I had at first been more than a little disappointed. The idea of a medieval tradition of music theory surviving hermetically down to the present among an elite school of Central Asian musicians had been an alluring one. But my disappointment was mitigated by the realization that what did survive in the musical worldview of Ma'ruf Xâja and his fellow fools of God comprised vestiges of a music theory, albeit informal, that were arguably much older. For Ma'ruf Xâja's beliefs about music's power, and in particular about the power of a judicious alliance of word and sound to affect listeners in a moral way, mirrors the concept of *Affekt* that was a cornerstone of ancient aesthetic theories of Western music—theories that found their way into the Middle East and Central Asia through the Arabic notion of *ta'thîr*.[12] Is it possible that this oral tradition of musical *Affekt*—the tradition that animated the fools of God—was indeed a popular vestige of medieval Islam's assimilation of ancient learning through the translation of Greek texts into Arabic? Was it, in fact, an aspect of "musical science" that had survived in living practice long after the scholarly theoretical tradition that described it had vanished?

In light of Ma'ruf Xâja's strong views about music as a moral occupation, it seemed not surprising that he should have been at once musician and mullah, the guardian of religious morality. I asked Ma'ruf Xâja whether he felt any of the tension between music and religion that had led some orthodox Islamic clergy to condemn music because of its potential to stimulate immoral behavior. "If it were in the Qur'an that music isn't allowed, there wouldn't be a question," he said. "But there isn't any such statement in the Qur'an. I learned both to read the Qur'an and to play the *tanbur* from my father."

"Your father had a Qur'an?"

"Yes, an Arabic Qur'an. It was illegal to have a Qur'an then. If they found a Qur'an in your house, they'd put you in jail. When I was little, I studied Arabic at a secret class in a woman's house."

"How did you study with your father?"

"When he had some free time, he'd say, 'Sit down. God created you, you should know about God. Go ahead, read this.' At first, we just learned lines by memory. Only later did I begin to understand their meaning."

"When did people start to call you a mullah?"

"According to Muslim custom, you can't consider yourself a mullah until you're forty. God cultivated Muhammad until he was forty, then he told him he was a prophet.

"There are different kinds of mullahs. I didn't graduate from a *madrasah* or a conservatory. I'm not a professor. But the Prophet said, 'learn, learn, learn,' and I've sat with a lot of teachers and learned what I needed from them. I'm invited to weddings and to memorial services to read the Qur'an. I serve as an assistant to the *qâri* (reciter of the Qur'an) at the Maslahaddin mosque. He's a young man who studied for five years in Tashkent and for five or six years in Algeria or Tunisia."

"Does it offend the *qâri* that you play music?"

"No, he knows who I am. No one says anything about it. What's important is how you show your character to others. My father told me, 'People listen to you and see you with their two eyes, so behave like you ought to behave.'"

"Have you ever drunk when you've been playing music?"

"Yes, when I lived in Dushanbe. The Council of Ministers, the Communist party—they called me to sing. I was famous then. They'd sit and drink, and if I didn't drink, they wouldn't call me a second time. But I'd just drink a little."

"Did you feel it was a sin?"

"Yes, it's a sin. If you drink a little, it's all right. But if you drink a little more, then it starts to be a sin. The Prophet said that the mother of sins is drunkenness."

"Are you uncomfortable when you're invited to a wedding and people drink?"

"It used to make no difference. I'd sit and do my work. One musician from Namangan came to Leninabad and said, 'If people drink vodka, I'll get up and leave.' He was beaten. People said, 'What business is it of yours? Just sing your songs, take your money, and that's it.' That was a lesson for me. What business is it of mine? I have to endure people's company and not spoil their good time, even if I don't want to drink."

"Are you sorry that your sons didn't follow you into music?"

"On the one hand, it pains me, but on the other hand, it's a good thing. If they had followed my direction, imagine what it would be like for them now, at this moment. All the weddings have European music. They still call me for the morning, for the *âsh,* but they don't invite me to evening weddings, and even if they invited me, I wouldn't go. There's all sorts of drunkenness, and the musicians have to play Western music so that twenty or thirty young men and women who lack any conscience can get up and dance. It's like kasha. It would be the worst thing that could happen to me if I were to get mixed up in that; it would be shameful for me. Am I going to go in there with my beard? I'm seventy-three years old. A singer has to sing songs that correspond to his age. What would it be like if I went out and performed songs like 'I love your beautiful eyes'? People would laugh. You have to be young to sing those songs. So what should I sing? I should sing songs that help show young people the right path. If I show them the wrong path, then both their sins and my sins before God will be like a weight around my neck. I have to be responsible for what comes out of my mouth—it can go to people's heads. I'm responsible to myself, and to my listeners before God."

OM had a friend, a professor of engineering and member of the Academy of Sciences, whose son was about to be married, and OM's friend had invited him to an *âsh* on the Friday following Ma'ruf Xâja's arrival in Tashkent. OM suggested to Ma'ruf Xâja and me that we come along and that Ma'ruf Xâja bring his *tanbur.* I protested that it seemed a violation of etiquette to appear at a private family ceremony to which one had not been personally invited. OM laughed. "On the contrary," he said. "The host would be angry with me if he found out that I hadn't invited you. Everyone who wants to come is welcome at a wedding. I've been to weddings where there are five thousand people."

The Friday *âsh* was to be put on not by OM's friend but by his counterpart, the father of the bride-to-be. The following morning, OM's friend would give his own *âsh* for largely the same group of male guests. When OM, Ma'ruf Xâja and I arrived at 6:00 A.M, the *âsh* was already well under way. The street in front of the host's house had been blocked off and about 150 men sat at long tables on the street and in the courtyard of the house. A stream of boys and men were carrying platters of *palav,* stacks of *nân* (puffy bread), and clusters of teapots from the house across the street and placing them on the tables.

In front of the host's house, a *tanbur* and a *dutar* player sat in folding chairs on a carpet-covered platform. The *tanbur* player was Fattaxan Mamadaliev, a well-known musician from Andijan, in the Ferghana Valley, who had moved to Tashkent. Fattaxan worked several days a week at the radio station, taught at the Conservatory, and did a good deal of freelance work—mostly *âsh*s like the one we had just joined. Fattaxan was accompanied on the *dutâr* by his *hamnafas (ham:* "also"; *nafas:* "breath"), or "musical alter ego." The *hamnafas* is more than a mere accompanist. He is a trusted friend or sometimes a loyal student, and the musical relationship between the *hamnafas* and the musician with whom he performs can often assume the character of a friendly competition, with each musician provoking the other.

Fattaxan played slow, serious music, delicately plucking his *tanbur* with precise strokes of the *nahun*—the metal pick that he wore on the index finger of his right hand—while drawing out each note with slides, slurs, and ornaments executed by the left hand. Unfortunately, the subtlety of his *tanbur* playing and singing was lost in the immensely loud and grotesquely distorted sound that attacked the captive audience from loudspeakers placed on poles on the street. What seemed even more unfortunate was that no one appeared to mind, including the musicians. Fattaxan-*aka* sat, Buddhalike, absorbed in his *tanbur* and seemingly oblivious to the deafening but distant likeness of his voice that emanated from the speakers.

The *âsh* is a religious occasion, an extension of morning prayers, as Ma'ruf Xâja had explained, that constitutes an offering to God and to family ancestors. In this offering, the fathers of the bride and groom pray for the continuation of their family lineage through their children's union. The music at an *âsh* conveys the serious nature of the event: spiritual poetry set to slowly paced, drawn-out melodies.

When Fattaxan and his *hamnafas* took a break, they invited Ma'ruf Xâja to fill in. He enthusiastically unzipped his *tanbur* case, tuned up his instrument, and launched into a classical song. Later he beamed to OM and me about his brief performance. The host had paid him 1,500 rubles (a little more than a dollar), which Ma'ruf Xâja viewed as confirmation that his talent had been appreciated.

Because the *âsh* is a religious event, Russians and other Europeans who presumably are not Muslims are rarely invited. I noticed two Russians among the guests at this *âsh*. But whether an Uzbek or Tajik is a practicing Muslim—in any of the ways that "practicing Muslim" might be defined—matters not at all when it comes to inclusion at ceremonial events like an *âsh, maraka* (memorial), or *sunnat* (circumcision). Simply being an indigenous Central Asian gets you in the door. Bukharan Jews are frequently invited to Muslim ceremonial events.

It is not considered polite to stay until the bitter end of an *âsh*, but OM and I did stay with a small group of men who were sitting close to the musicians and listening intently to the music. Gradually the guests at other tables departed, passing through a receiving line to shake hands with the host and male members of his family as they left. One table of men continued to linger, and someone at the table motioned for me to join them. A man was pouring what looked like clear water from a teapot. I imagined for a moment that this water pouring was a ritual that I did not know about—perhaps a symbolic rendering of the analogy between the purity of water and the purity of the marital bond. But when I was handed a tea bowl, I realized that the water was vodka. "I thought that people don't drink at an *âsh*," I said with surprise. One of the men threw his head back and laughed. "The *âsh* ended at 7:00 A.M. Now we're just schmoozing."

A second *âsh*, given by the father of the groom, took place the following morning at the same early hour. It was held in a café done up with contemporary Oriental motifs—blue fluorescent arabesques set in the ceiling and mirabs carved in the walls with imitation harem lamps in the center. Most of the café's business is wedding-related, I was told. Few customers walk in off the street, but mornings, especially on weekends, the café is busy serving up *palav* for an *âsh*, and Saturday evenings are booked far ahead for the festive part of a wedding called *bazm*.

The groom's family was from Khorezm, and both the music and the food had a Khorezmian accent. Each table was set with plates of *dinya*, the delicious green melon that is Khorezm's specialty. A young musician with slicked-back black hair and dressed like Liberace played the *tar* (plucked stringed instrument) and sang, while another musician, also in Liberace clothes, accompanied him on an accordion. Their music seemed even more breathtakingly loud than that performed the previous morning, which perhaps had to do with the cellarlike acoustics created by the café's stucco walls. OM's friend, the father of the groom, came around to our table to shake hands and said that he was looking forward to seeing us that evening at the *bazm*, where the actual marriage ceremony would take place.

The *bazm* was held in a marbled banquet hall in the basement of the new public library building. The hall was a large, circular room divided into a center ring, where a band had set up an electric keyboard, speakers, and microphones at the edge of what would serve as the dance floor, and an outer ring, separated from the center by a balustrade and filled with long tables laden with food and drink. Flashing colored lights were strung around the perimeter of the center ring, and at the back of the hall the names of the bride and groom were formed on a glittering floor-to-ceiling marquee from hundreds of small twinkling light bulbs.

Brides used to be taken from their houses to the *bazm* with processions of *karnai*s (long ceremonial trumpets) and *surnai*s (loud oboes). The *karnai* and *surnai* still make an appearance at most Uzbek weddings, but now the wedding procession is usually made by taxi or private car and the *karnai* and *surnai* players come directly to the banquet hall and wait for the bride and groom to arrive. Once guests had made their way to the tables and begun to munch on appetizers and to open bottles of champagne, cognac, and vodka, the actual wedding began. The band played the traditional welcoming song, "Toy Mubarak" (Welcome to the Wedding), and family members from both the bride's and the groom's side marched together with linked arms through the center of the ring to their own tables. The bride and groom made their appearance to the sound of the *surnai*s and *karnai*s and walked forward, each with a witness, to a table set up in the center. There a woman representing ZAGS, the Law of the Act of Civil Registration, took a microphone and offered a long-winded explanation of the procedure of civil registration, after which she congratulated the couple. The bride and groom signed the ZAGS registration book, and at that moment they became husband and wife. They were both students at the medical institute, and the marriage had apparently been their idea, not their parents'. OM said that arranged marriages are still common in the countryside but that in the cities, more and more young people are making their own choices about whom to marry.

Once the official part of the wedding had been completed, the band turned on its amplifiers and cut loose with a program of schmaltzy, Russian-Uzbek techno-ethnic folk-pop music. The dance floor in the center was immediately filled with couples doing a mixture of *ersatz* Uzbek dance, which emphasizes liquescent arm and hand movements, and the hybridized contemporary dancing, found all over the former Soviet Union, whose body language is based on hopping up and down while shaking the hips. The music was earsplittingly loud. A synthesizer was joined by an electrified *tar* and a *dâyra* (frame drum), and the instrumentalists accompanied several different vocalists, each of whom had to be amplified in equal measure to the instruments.

FROZEN MUSIC

The electrified Uzbek folk-pop genre claimed a large audience that happily submitted itself to frequent nightlong feats of aural endurance at *bazm*s like the one I had attended. Moreover, audiences didn't lack for choice of ensembles: the market for wedding musicians was a free market. Dozens of bands competed for employment, and potential employers were free to cut their own deals. Wedding music culture, one might say, was a culture shaped essentially from below, by popular taste, thus leaving itself vulnerable at any moment to evolutionary pressures stemming from changes in that taste.

Uzbek classical music, however, was different. Although groups of men still listened to solo or duo performances of classical music at a morning *âsh* or an evening *gap,* the *Shash maqâm,* the centerpiece of the classical repertory that I had come originally to Tashkent to study under the tutelage of Professor Karomatov, was a musical tradition propped up from above by the policies of Uzbekistan's culture *apparat.* Patronage was, to be sure, not new to the *Shash maqâm.* Like other art music traditions in the core Islamic world, the *Shash maqâm* had always been the domain of professional musicians whose support came largely from wealthy merchants and the nobility. With its sophisticated poetics, complex melodic modulations, and glacially paced tempos, the *Shash maqâm* was an aristocratic music intended for cultivated audiences whose knowledge of music and poetry made for a kind of spontaneous dialogue between performers and listeners. But that knowledge had gradually receded, and the art of the *Shash maqâm* had begun to stagnate.

Though I couldn't put my finger on it, something had seemed not right about the performances of *Shash maqâm* I heard when I first came to Tashkent. Put simply, they lacked life. As taught and performed at the Tashkent Conservatory, the *Shash maqâm* could have been compared to a dying person being kept clinically alive on a respirator. The respirator was controlled by the Ministry of Culture. It was the Ministry that had approved the resuscitation of the moribund *Shash maqâm* in the late 1950s and had stage-managed its ideological repositioning as a leading exemplar of Uzbekistan's "national" music (this after a near-death experience in the early 1950s in which the Ministry had decreed that the *Shash maqâm* had been too close to the feudal culture of the emirs, too distant from "the people," too infused with undercurrents of Sufism, and thus had to be suppressed).

For both Soviet and post-Soviet Uzbekistan, the *Shash maqâm* comprised an important cultural property that provided evidence of an Uzbek literary and musical great tradition. Soviet cultural politics had fostered the creation of such great traditions for each official Soviet nationality, often aided by a reimagination of cultural history that produced notable distortions in the way that both cultural boundaries and cultural commonalities were perceived and reified. For example, in cities such as Bukhara and Samarkand (presently in Uzbekistan) and, as Maruf Xâja had pointed out, in Khojend (Tajikistan), musicians thoroughly bilingual in Uzbek and Tajik have traditionally performed lyrical songs whose texts are drawn from poetry in both languages. Singers switch almost unconsciously from one language to the other, and it is not uncommon to find Uzbek and Tajik couplets mixed together in the same song.[13] But during the Soviet era, in order to bolster Soviet-created national identities ("Uzbek," "Tajik," etc.), the bilingual art song repertory of Bukhara, Samarkand, and other cities was commonly divided into two separate entities: "Uzbek classical music" and "Tajik classical music," each with poetic texts exclusively in the "national" language of the appropriate republic. Commercial recordings, radio and television performances, musical pedagogy, and publications of musical notation all reflected this essentially political nomenclature. The *Shash maqâm,* for example, was split in two: a Tajik *Shash maqâm* was published in Dushanbe, Tajikistan, with Tajik texts, and an Uzbek *Shash maqâm* was published in Tashkent, with Uzbek texts. The Tajik publication made no mention of the Uzbek *Shash maqâm,* and the Uzbek publication made no mention of the Tajik *Shash maqâm.*

By the early 1980s, the absurdity of this artificial division had become too obvious to support, and the separate Tajik and Uzbek *maqâm*s were reterritorialized into what became known in Uzbekistan as the Uzbek-Tajik *Shash maqâm* and in Tajikistan as the Tajik-Uzbek *Shash maqâm.* The Uzbek-Tajik, or Tajik-Uzbek, *Shash maqâm* has survived until the present, but in the current highly nationalistic atmosphere of Uzbekistan, the *Shash maqâm* seems to be undergoing yet another reterritorialization from above aimed once again at promoting Uzbekization: singers at the radio station in Bukhara, a thoroughly bilingual city (Uzbek and Tajik), have apparently been told to use only Uzbek texts in their broadcasts of *Shash maqâm* music.

In the Conservatory's Department of Eastern Music, the *Shash maqâm* was taught from a six-volume set of musical transcriptions compiled by Professor Karomatov and a fellow musicologist, Is'haq Rajabov. Students memorized the various songs and instrumental tunes in the *Shash maqâm* by reading the transcriptions. The transcriptions were in standard staff notation and provided a single melodic line that gave the core pitches of each song and tune. Details of interpretation—dynamics, melodic ornamentation, tempo—were conveyed by teachers during private lessons with such unerring exactitude that they may as well have been inscribed in granite.

The *Shash maqâm* is not the only Islamic court music repertory to have been transcribed in Western staff notation. Iranian *dastgâh,* Arabo-Andalusian *nuba,* Ottoman *makam*—all have their volumes of transcriptions compiled by scholars whose aim has been to fix a certain version of these traditional repertories as an authoritative canon for contemporary performance. But in none of these repertories do performers so rigidly adhere to the canonical transcriptions as in the *Shash maqâm.* I was startled by the extent to which the *Shash maqâm* had been frozen, not only on paper but also in performance.

The man who froze the *Shash maqâm* was a musician and self-styled musicologist, Yunus Rajabi (1897–1976). For a musicologist, Rajabi is unusually famous in Uzbekistan.[14] Born in Tashkent, Rajabi sang and played the *dutar* from an early age. His talent attracted the attention of some of Tashkent's older musicians, and he was quickly drawn into the musical community of the city. As a listener, Rajabi was also familiar with Russian and European popular music. Thanks to the regimental brass band of the occupying Russian garrison in Chimkent, not far from Tashkent, where he had worked in a slaughterhouse before the Revolution, Rajabi came to know the standard repertory of Russian marches and dance music.

Rajabi entered the Turkestan People's Conservatory in 1919 and studied in the division of folk music, where he learned not only to perform, but also to transcribe folk music in staff notation, compose it, and arrange it for ensembles. He wrote a number of the *agitprop* marches and folk songs, as well as musical dramas, that were the vogue of the immediate postrevolutionary period. In 1923, Rajabi was dispatched to Samarkand to teach music in a high school and organize music for the Samarkand Theater of Musical Drama. In 1927, when the fledgling Uzbek radio called for the organization of a national folk music ensemble, Rajabi was a logical choice to serve as director. His conservatory training, combined with his traditional background, placed him in an ideal position to form just the sort of bridge that was needed between prerevolutionary and postrevolutionary musical culture.

Rajabi did for Uzbek music in the first part of the twentieth century what scribes and bards living at the dawn of literacy had done for oral literature like the Genesis story and the Homeric epics: he listened, and he wrote down what he heard. And as was presumed to have been the case with his ancient Near Eastern and Greek predecessors, he didn't listen to just one source. Rajabi had a wide circle of musical contacts. He listened to many versions of a single song and took the one that he considered "most authentic." When he didn't find a version he liked, he took bits and pieces of different musicians' versions and used them to synthesize his own.

Assembling his chosen versions of the *Shash maqâm*'s many songs and instrumental melodies, he created a redaction of the entire repertory. In light of the ongoing skirmishes between Uzbek and Tajik cultural ideologues for control of the *Shash maqâm,* it is ironic that Rajabi's primary informant and many of his secondary informants were Bukharan Jews.[15]

It is the Rajabi version that is taught in the Conservatory, and Conservatory graduates in turn teach it to younger students in music high schools. The radio and television ensemble—largely composed of Conservatory graduates—performs the Rajabi version and has recorded it on a twenty-volume set of long-playing records. The Rajabi version has also been enshrined in a biannual *Shash maqâm* Competition at the Conservatory—a kind of provincial imitation of Moscow's famed Tchaikovsky Competition. Somber performers dressed in suits or formal gowns take the stage and compete before a panel of judges to see who can offer the most excruciatingly exact rendition of a song or melody from the Rajabi canonization.[16]

Most recently, Uzbekistan's strongly nationalistic post-Soviet leadership (essentially the same lineup as that which served the republic's erstwhile Soviet masters) has adapted the cultural strategies of Soviet nationalities policies to serve its own ideological aims. The foremost of these aims is arguably the abiding struggle to consolidate national consciousness in a society in which social groups and group identity traditionally revolved around clans, tribes, religious affiliation, and territories ruled by local nobility. National consciousness can have no future without a past, and thus post-Soviet Uzbek cultural strategists have found themselves in essentially the same bind as their Soviet predecessors: obliged to forge a singularly Uzbek great tradition from a cultural history that more objective accounts show to have been interlaced with the influences of myriad social groups.

The manipulation of the *Shash maqâm* for ideological ends has not been motivated only by the "national question," as it was known in the former Soviet Union. Another kind of manipulation stems from the same founding postulate of Leninism that influenced Uzbek composers like Mutavaqqil Burxanov: the notion that the adoption of European art forms held the key to cultural advancement for the indigenous peoples of what became Soviet Asia. One of these European art forms was what one might call music for large ensembles. A veneration of ensembles and music composed or arranged for ensembles has been one of the enduring vestiges of the cultural politics of rapprochement and fusion (with Europe) in non-Russian parts of the Soviet Union. In Uzbekistan, the creation of ensembles modeled on European orchestras and choirs began in the 1920s with workers' choirs that performed a mixture of arranged folk songs and newly composed revolutionary songs. After that came the infamous folk orchestras, which featured traditional Uzbek instruments altered to facilitate a merging with European music. Rajabi adopted ensemble performance as a key element in his renovation of the *Shash maqâm*. The *Shash maqâm* ensembles represented in some sense a merging of a workers' choir and a folk orchestra: between a half-dozen and a dozen singers, both male and female, sang in a unison monophony that alternated with solo episodes, all backed up by a consort consisting usually of at least eight instruments (*tanbur, dutar, ghijak, nay, qâshnay, chang, Kashgar rabâb, dâyra*), and often included doublings. The result was that the limpid, filigree texture of the melody lines that is such an essential feature of the *Shash maqâm* became lost in the ensembles' bloated heterophony of voices and instruments.

Notwithstanding the post-Soviet Uzbek leadership's nativist tendencies to try to expunge the most conspicuous vestiges of Soviet and Russian colonialism from Uzbekistan's cultural landscape, the *Shash maqâm* ensemble, like the Uzbek National Chorus, has remained an *idée fixe* of both musicians and the cultural *apparat*. The *maqâm* ensemble that Yunus Rajabi founded in 1958 still rehearses five mornings a week at the Tashkent Radio Komitet building, and one morning in the fall of 1994, I attended their rehearsal.

With my prejudices against the heavyhanded, ideologically motivated en-semblization of *Shash maqâm* performance, I had expected Abduhashim-*aka* to be an odious, robotic music director. I couldn't have been more mistaken. As I watched Abduhashim rehearse his group, it became clear that he was a talented musician who conveyed a real passion for his work. He knew the Rajabi redaction of the *Shash maqâm* from memory, and neither he nor the musicians looked at musical notation at any time during the rehearsal (Abduhashim and the singers occasionally glanced at looseleaf notebooks of song texts). When questions arose about how to perform a particular passage, Abduhashim sang the passage, and both singers and instrumentalists repeated it. "I teach from the voice," he said. "If the musicians worked from notation, it would be as if they were playing the piano."

"I love our national music," Abduhashim told me during a break in the rehearsal. "My whole life has been devoted to it, and I'm doing what I do from my soul. Our national music is alive. It's not like a house, not like a mausoleum. It has to live. You have to add something. After you, someone else will add something different. You have to hear the music and add your own soul; you have to find a place to add things so that it will be interesting. I'm trying to continue and develop the work of Yunus-*aka* [Rajabi]. I've been the artistic director of the ensemble for eight years, and in those eight years, we've made more than fifty changes in the way Yunus-*aka* performed the *Shash maqâm*."

"Fifty changes in eight years?" I repeated Abduhashim's statement back to him to make sure I had understood correctly.

"Yes, fifty changes," Abduhashim repeated proudly, "mostly in ornamenta-tion." For all of Abduhashim's talk about music being alive and about the importance of adding one's own soul, musical liveliness and soulfulness did not for him seem linked either to radical innovation or to a fundamental rethinking of the Rajabi canon and the Rajabi-ordained performance style. Rather, Abdu-hashim seemed like a devoted caretaker of the Rajabi shrine. His efforts were aimed at recovering, or where evidence failed, deducing, the great man's true musical intentions where they had been distorted by a lack of performers with the technical means to realize them.

I could understand and respond to Abduhashim's passion for music, and I could appreciate his efforts to help his performers play and sing musically. Yet the results of his passion and his musical energy seemed in the end no less lackluster than I had found them eighteen years earlier, when, considering a doctoral dissertation on the *Shash maqâm,* I had listened to the old Melodiya recordings of the radio station ensemble and almost dropped the idea of going to Central Asia because the music had seemed so dull. But reader-listeners may judge for themselves. I have included on the accompanying compact disc (track

5) an excerpt from the performance of the *maqâm* ensemble, recorded with Abduhashim's permission during the rehearsal I attended. The excerpt is from the beginning of the *saraxbâr* section of *maqâm-i segâh*. (The sudden fluctuations of dynamic level are not the result of a technical defect in the recording but represent Abduhashim's efforts to extract musicality from his performers.)

OM's analysis of the *maqâm* ensemble phenomenon was larded with a gloom that had come to characterize his outlook on officialized Uzbek culture. "Abduhashim is a talented musician," said OM, "but his talent exceeds the limits of his worldview. Even if he were to think about the idea that maybe his ensemble isn't really necessary or desirable for the performance of *maqâm* music, he wouldn't dare to speak about it publicly, because he'd simply be replaced. The ensemble idea has been surgically implanted in people's minds. Bureaucrats, leaders, musicians, students—they all believe that you have to have a *maqâm* ensemble. It's part of the grandomania of socialist culture—the idea that national music has to be grandiose, pompous. Two performers would have been considered an anachronism for the performance of *Shash maqâm*. The authorities would have said, 'There are twenty million Uzbeks; why such a skimpy ensemble?' They wanted the *Shash maqâm* to be like a cantata, an oratorio, with voices shifting back and forth. Rajabi created his *Shash maqâm* with a huge vocal range to make the point about the need for ensemblization, where one voice would pass off to another, higher voice. His version was made expressly so that no one singer could sing the entire *Shash maqâm*.

"The ensemblization of the *maqâm* was a sin against the aesthetics of this music. But it wasn't Rajabi's fault. He wasn't some kind of evil jinni. He was a son of his epoch and believed deeply in the politics of his time. He was a Soviet man, a Communist man. He thought that there would be a *maqâm* ensemble in every school and that people would come to hear it. He spent a lot of energy trying to do it well. He had a clean soul."

A TRADITIONAL INNOVATOR

During my initial year in Tashkent, I never did come to like the performance of the *maqâm* ensemble, whose daily early-morning and late-night radio broadcasts Professor Karomatov had assigned me to listen to. Restricted to the orbit of the Conservatory, I kept imagining that there had to be musicians outside that orbit who practiced a freer approach to performing the *Shash maqâm;* musicians who, like the great performers of Indian *raga* or Iranian *dastgâh,* are as much innovators as traditionalists. The first such musician I heard was Turgun Alimatov.

One day I went to the record section of the GUM department store with Ravshan, a fellow graduate student at the Conservatory, and asked him to recommend some good recordings. Ravshan immediately picked out two records by Alimatov. One student in the dormitory had a beat-up phonograph in his room and was happy to let me listen to my new purchases. As soon as I heard Alimatov's music, I thought to myself, "I have to meet this man." But that didn't happen for thirteen years.

When I began working and traveling with OM in 1990, I asked OM to introduce me to Alimatov. OM said he was sure a meeting could be arranged, but, to my surprise, he had only a vague idea of where Turgun-*aka* lived and knew Turgun-*aka* only slightly himself. Alimatov, one of Uzbekistan's best-known musicians, was not part of the Rajabi cult at the Conservatory. In fact, OM could not recall ever having seen him around the Conservatory. For all the renown of his music, he had remained, for OM, an enigmatic figure.

One afternoon OM and I set out for the Kokcha quarter on the opposite side of Tashkent to find Turgun Alimatov. We went first to the home of an instrument maker named Usman, who knew Turgan-*aka*. After the obligatory *dasturxân,* many hours of conversation with Ustâ Usman (Master Usman), as OM called him, and a detailed tour of Ustâ Usman's workshop, the instrument maker and one of his sons finally drove us a short distance to Turgun-*aka*'s house on a quiet dirt lane lined with the whitewashed walls of adjoining houses and courtyards. We waited outside the gate while Ustâ Usman went into the courtyard to announce our arrival. After about ten minutes, Ustâ Usman returned and told us that Turgun-*aka* was home but was not prepared to see us just then. He was not dressed to receive guests and had not shaved that morning. He was doing something else at the moment and had asked whether OM and I could return the next day at 10:00 A.M.

I was taken aback. No musician in Uzbekistan had ever outright declined to see us. After making our way to Turgun-*aka*'s far corner of Tashkent and exchanging hours of small talk with Ustâ Usman, we would have to repeat the process the next day. OM was unperturbed. "Turgun-*aka* does everything in his own way, on his own schedule," he said. "There's nothing you can do about it except admire his control of whatever situation he's in."

At precisely ten o'clock the next morning, we appeared at Turgun-*aka*'s gate. We were greeted by his three grown sons, Alisher, Valisher, and Ghanisher, and led into the courtyard of the house. The courtyard was in fact a large garden plot with concrete walkways around the perimeter and a small paved section just inside the gate for parking a car. It was mid-March, and the vegetationless garden was a sea of black mud. Along one of the walkways, a denuded grape arbor loomed over a raised platform called an *aivân* where, in the heat of the summer, carpets and pillows would be laid out for relaxing and sleeping. Detached, low-slung bungalows with corrugated metal roofs ran along each of the four sides of the courtyard. Three of them contained family quarters for Turgun-*aka* and two of his married sons. On the side closest to the gate was the *mehmânxâna.*

Alisher, the oldest son, doused our hands with warm water poured from a flagon and passed around a clean towel. Then he led us to a foyer at the entrance to the *mehmânxâna* where we took off our shoes, donned slippers, and went inside to meet Turgun-*aka*.

Turgun-*aka* rose ever so slowly from his chair at the back of the *mehmânxâna* but did not move forward to greet us. He waited for us to cross the carpeted room and stand in front of him before he calmly extended his hand to mine with the hint of a smile on his face. He was a large, powerfully built man who looked as if his body had been sculpted from a single block of wood. His balding head, topped by a *doppi,* seemed to rise directly from square, stiff shoulders. Protuberant eyebrows set over deeply recessed eyes, high cheekbones, and a small nose made his face look entirely flat (his nickname among his Uzbek friends is "little nose"). At seventy years of age, he had a paunch and his hands and forearms looked spongy, but he shook my hand with viselike firmness.

Turgun-*aka* motioned for OM and me to sit at the table while he huddled for a moment with Alisher and Ustâ Usman. These two then excused themselves and withdrew. Turgun-*aka* joined OM and me at the table. We exchanged a long string of the customary phatic pleasantries, all three of us talking at once: "Are you well?" "How are things?" "How's your family?" "Your children?" "Your wife?" Turgun-*aka* spoke softly, with an almost childlike sweetness in his voice. At the end of this exchange, he fixed his eyes on me and stared with a gentle intensity. At last, he turned back to OM and asked him to introduce the *mehmân*—the guest. OM launched into what had become a set piece in our travels: "Bu kishi Amerikadan bir muzikashunas," he began. "This person is a musicologist from America. . . ."

In Uzbek company, since it is considered impolite to call or refer to someone by a personal name unless the person is already a friend, various surrogates are used: *bu kishi* (this person), *mehmân* (guest), *dâmla* (teacher), or the generic *aka* (older brother) or *opa* (mother). As a result, little attention is given to learning names. I have sat for hours with OM among a group of men and afterward asked him to help me write down their names in my notebook only to realize that he didn't know any of them.

Shortly, Alisher and Ustâ Usman reappeared carrying four bottles of vodka and one bottle of cognac and set them on the table, which was already covered with the usual trappings of the *dasturxân.* Turgun-*aka* asked me with a deadpan face, "What do you drink, vodka or cognac?" It was 10:45 in the morning.

"Tea," I answered.

He reached calmly for the porcelain tea bowl sitting in front of me and filled it to the very top with vodka. "Here's your tea."

"I never drink before noon," I protested, trying a different tactic.

"Then you can consider it not drinking, but trying vodka with us. Vodka is necessary to bring us all to the same state so that we can experience music together in the same way. Music is more interesting when you have a little *kaif*—a little buzz," said Turgun-*aka* firmly. "It's only a question of limits. For example, I consider that more than one bottle of vodka per person is too much. Why do we have one-liter bottles when we could have three-liter bottles? Because one liter is the limit. It's the same with food and music."

"But different people have different limits; limits are relative," I suggested. Turgun-*aka* smiled and pushed a plate of horsemeat sausage in front of me. "Try this after you drink your vodka, and then we'll talk about limits," he said. OM offered a toast to our getting acquainted, and we all drained the tea bowls in one gulp. Turgun-*aka* immediately refilled them. After a few minutes of conversation, the second round was drunk, and this round was followed after short intervals by two more tea bowl rounds (one tea bowl equals approximately three shot glasses) before OM casually asked Turgun-*aka* whether he'd like to play some music. Turgun-*aka* nodded to Alisher, who took a cloth instrument case from the commode in the *mehmânxâna* and handed it to his father. Turgun-*aka* untied the drawstring and took out his *tanbur,* set up the bridge, and calmly and deliberately began to tune. He tuned the five strings for a long time, setting the intervals between pairs of strings until they sounded a perfect unison or fifth, then proceeding to another pair of strings. He seemed to derive great pleasure merely from tuning his instrument.

Turgun-*aka* moved almost imperceptibly from tuning to playing a piece. As he played, he looked at the fretboard of his instrument, but his face remained impassive and expressionless, his body motionless except for his fingers and left forearm. I had requested my favorite *tanbur* piece from the recording I had purchased thirteen years earlier: *segâh*. *Segâh* is the name of one of the six suites in the *Shash maqâm* as well as the name of a mode or melody type widely found in the art music repertories of the Middle East. Turkish, Arabic, and Persian treatments of *segâh* are all based on the same core melody type, but the examples of *segâh* notated in the canonical *Shash maqâm* edition and recorded by the radio station ensemble seemed on the surface to have an entirely different melodic shape than what I came to call "International *segâh*" (that is, Turkish, Arabic, and Persian *segâh*).

When I had first listened to Turgun Alimatov's recordings, I had concluded that the slow, unmetered pieces or sections of pieces that he played on the *tanbur* and *satâ* (bowed *tanbur*)—for example, the first part of his *segâh* on the accompanying compact disc (track 4)—were in some sense improvisations rather than precisely fixed compositions like those in the *Rajabi* canon. I had no way of knowing for sure that they were improvisations except that the slow tempo, lack of regular meter, and methodical variation and elaboration of brief melodic motifs made them *sound* improvised in the way that the unmetered *alap* of Indian classical music or the *taksim* of Ottoman classical music sound improvised. But listening for the first time to a live performance of Turgun-*aka*'s *segâh,* I realized with mild astonishment that it sounded exactly the same as his performance of *segâh* on the Melodiya record that I knew from memory. Where was the improvisation that I had imagined? I asked Turgun-*aka,* "When you play *segâh,* is it one and the same piece each time, or do you change it?"

He answered, "The ornamentation changes according to my mood in the same way that someone who's giving a lecture doesn't always speak with the same tone of voice. But there's a piece, *segâh. Segâh* goes by the same path [*yol*]. I listened to *segâh* for many years. I listened for ten, fifteen, twenty years to different performers, and then I began to play. I played and played, and another ten years went by. And at last, I could play a solo. More time went by, and I played still more. I'd stop for two or three months, and then, I'd play again. The more I played, the better it got, and at the very end, I liked it, and that's when I recorded it. For each of my pieces, a lot of time goes by."

During many meetings with Turgun-*aka* for music and conversation between 1990 and 1994, I invariably asked him to play his *segâh,* and as far as I could determine, he always played it exactly the same way, changing only minor details of ornamentation, as he confirmed during our first discussion. What he was playing was very much a composition—an oral composition that, until I transcribed it, had never been written down. But Turgun had no need to commit his compositions to notation. He simply memorized them.[17]

Many studies of oral literature and of orally composed and transmitted music have focused on processes of extemporization in performance that, the studies suggest, seem broadly characteristic of orality as a creative medium. However, if extemporization-in-performance is the norm, then Turgun's music, and for that matter the entire corpus of Central Asian classical music, constitute a clear exception.[18] Conceptually, this music seems to belong to the tradition of precomposed genres found in many parts of the core Islamic world: the Ottoman Turkish *peshrev* and *sema'î,* the Syrian and Egyptian *muwashshah,* the Andalusian *nauba* of North Africa. If Turgun's elegantly crafted miniatures could not be distinguished from Rajabi's cumbersome bricolage on the basis of compositional process alone—that is, if Central Asian classical music was habitually composed in advance and then memorized down to the last detail of ornamentation—what was the essence of Turgun's innovation? And was Turgun an isolated case of an Uzbek musical prodigy, or did his brand of musical individualism—his self-selected repertory and crystalline instrumental technique (at the expense of vocal music; I never heard Turgun sing)—represent a broader shift away from the tradition of the closed *Shash maqâm* cycles canonized by Rajabi?

As a traditional innovator, Turgun was without peer in the realm of instrumental composition. But there had also been vocalists of the same generation who, like Turgun, had used the *maqâm* as a stylistic source for composing songs.[19] Their appropriation of the *maqâm* was analogous to what had occurred in other *maqâm* traditions beyond Transoxania: rigidly structured, closed repertories like the *Shash maqâm* had gradually given way to autonomous pieces performed in a relatively personalized style. Jean During, a French academic and musician who has written extensively on the music of Iran, has characterized this shift as a transformation of classical formalism to Romanticism "in which music is cleansed of its status as a sacred object in order to become recentered in the interiority of the individual." During added, "This has been achieved in Persian music over the last fifty years. The values of inspiration, creativity, originality and personality of style and improvisation have become exalted to the detriment of conformity to standards, fidelity to repertoire, and fixed composition. . . . Time becomes fragmented not only in free [unmetered] performance, but in measured (rhythmic) pieces in which long cycles as well as large compositions are abandoned. . . . Music, too, in the same epoch, became distant from text in order to develop a purely instrumental genre, yet in a way, it was still supposed to speak. Thus, it conquered its autonomy by becoming a human activity and an 'art of genius' resulting from a vocation and a communication with transcendence."[20]

The shift During described in Persia seems analogous to what has occurred tangentially in Transoxania in the music of Turgun Alimatov. But ironically, while the establishment of secular political rule and its attendant strategies for the development of secularized cultural life occurred in Transoxania decades earlier than in Iran, the old musical order in Transoxania has been far more resistant to change. In other circumstances—for example, in the Turkish Mevlevi Sufi ritual, where During also finds the persistence of a "canonical and closed repertoire"—that persistence might have come about through a heightened metaphysical understanding of music: through the notion that so-called artistic individualism is gratuitous; that external models and canons may perfectly well remain fixed, since it is in the inner process of reproducing a model or rehearsing a canon that spiritual movement or transformation takes place. But the metaphysical explanation doesn't work for Transoxania. There the old order seems to have been kept alive for patently ideological reasons— "frozen music." And Turgun Alimatov's musical innovations became the object of decades of official disdain and even persecution.

OM and I shared our fascination with Turgun-*aka* and his music. Sometimes we met with Turgun individually, sometimes together, in each case recording our conversations, which were in both Uzbek and Russian. From these recordings, OM produced his own biography of Turgun (as yet unpublished) and shared with me information from his one-on-one conversations that supplemented what I had recorded on my own.

Turgun Alimatov was born in 1922 in Keles, a place near Tashkent. His father, Alimat (a contraction of Ali Muhammad), was from a wealthy family that owned land and worked in a trading business. He was a great music lover and played the *dutar* well. Turgun, the only son in the family, often accompanied

Turgun Alimatov standing by a poster announcing his Paris concert.

his father to gatherings of friends who were also music lovers. Turgun-*aka* emphasized that his father did not teach him to play the *dutar* but allowed him to take the *dutar* and play whatever he wanted.

Aside from his father's *dutar* playing and the music he heard at gatherings of his father's friends, Turgun listened passionately to records and to the radio. Both his father and uncle had gramophones, and gramophone records became Turgun's teachers.

When Turgun was six, his father died. Turgun and his mother went to live with an uncle. His mother felt uncomfortable about adding another child to an already struggling household, and Turgun was put in the custody of one of the children's houses that had become popular in the late 1920s' spirit of socialist collectivism. But after Turgun ran away, his mother turned for help to an acquaintance, the principal of a school, who allowed Turgun to live in a small room at the school. After school, Turgun dallied in the local teahouses. "There were a lot of older *dutar* players," he recalled. "I was the youngest. They sat in the teahouses. They'd sing, eat *palav,* and listen. That all happened before 1930. Then the government started to disperse the musicians."

An amateur arts society at the school sponsored a music group open to any student who played, or wanted to learn to play, a musical instrument. These amateur societies, which still exist in schools, factories, and community centers all over the former Soviet Union, belong to the domain of *kultprosvet,* as it is known in the lexicon of Soviet-era acronyms, short for *kul'turnoe prosveshenie:* "cultural enlightenment."

As some of the most enduring policies of Soviet communism have been swept away in the post-Soviet reformist fervor of the 1990s, *kultprosvet* has remained a potent vestige of the early Communists' vision of a utopian, worker-oriented society. The idea of *kultprosvet* is credited to Anatoly Lunacharsky, the first Soviet Cultural Commissar, who sought a way to bring not only a basic education but also cultural enlightenment to the working masses. This cultural enlightenment was not disinterested but was to be used as a didactic form of socialist education that would exhort the masses to uphold socialist values and goals. "Nationalist in form, socialist in content," as Stalin had said. *Kultprosvet* inevitably absorbed the political values of Stalin's Nationalities Policies, which ensured that the artistic means through which cultural enlightenment took place would reflect the authorized "national" culture of any particular social group.

Kultprosvet has been administered by parallel bureaucracies within the Ministry of Culture and the Union of Trade Unions. The Ministry of Culture's "houses of folk arts" (*dom narodnogo tvorchestva*) were initially oriented primarily toward the cultural enlightenment of peasants, while the Union of Trade Unions' "houses of artistic do-it-yourselfism" (*dom khudozhestvennoi samodeiatel'nosti*) serviced the cultural needs of workers. These days, particularly in cities and towns, the two bureaucracies often compete head-on for culture-hungry clientele. Each runs a variety of amateur societies staffed by culture workers trained in what in the United States might be called community arts education.

Kultprosvet has been a two-edged sword in the survival of traditional expressive culture in the former Soviet Union. On the one hand, it has shamelessly put art at the service of politics. Traditional artistic forms and repertories have been skewed in the interests of political expediency in several ways. For example, in Central Asia the ideological program of cultural rapprochement and fusion with Europe imposed hybridized "national" musical theater with didactic themes, folk orchestras, and vocal choirs on non-European populations. In another bow to political expediency, *kultprosvet* made the presumptive decision that Uzbeks ought to play Uzbek music and put on theater productions written by Uzbeks, Tajiks ought to play Tajik music, etc. In other words, *kultprosvet* reinforced the national identities that, as armies of Western specialists have repeatedly pointed out, were artificial constructs meant to help the Soviets defuse the potential of pan-Turkic or pan-Islamic movements in Central Asia. Furthermore, ethnic groups that were not officially recognized as "nations" according to Stalin's definition of nation ("a historically evolved, stable com-

Turgun playing the *dutar.*

munity of language, territory, economic life, and psychological makeup [national consciousness] manifested in a community of culture") were forced into the mold of another group's "do-it-yourselfism."

On the other hand, the power of traditional art to express the very sense of national consciousness that was a cornerstone of Soviet Nationalities Policies meant that many traditional forms of expressive culture were preserved, albeit sometimes in hybridized forms. Although culture workers were guided both by broad ideological mandates handed down through the *kultprosvet* bureaucracy and by specific curricular guidelines pertaining to their artistic activities, there was little central control over their activities, at least in the early years. According to OM, it was not until the 1960s and 1970s that *kultprosvet* became standardized, unified, and unpleasantly dogmatic. But in the 1930s and 1940s, it did not bind anyone. People were free to participate or not to participate. It was, in OM's words, "a mass movement for the soul." Many culture workers returned from their training to work in the communities where they grew up and became local heroes for their commitment to preserving their community's cultural heritage.

It was one such worker who ran the arts society that the young Turgun joined in his school. Turgun played the *dutar* and, outside of going to classes and reading books, did little else in his spare time besides practice. He played for himself, simply because he enjoyed playing. "If I had had a teacher then, I might have hated music, because I would have been embarrassed to play the *dutar* for a teacher," he said. His lifelong career as a musical autodidact had already begun.

Working without a teacher, Turgun developed his own peculiar technique on the *dutar* as well as on other instruments. To play the *tanbur,* for example, he adopted the hand positions and fingering techniques that he knew from the *dutar.* As a result, many of the older players who heard him considered that he played incorrectly. But listeners liked the simplicity and sincerity of his music.

Turgun never thought of himself as preparing for the life of a professional musician, and he didn't follow the career path that had become established in Socialist Uzbekistan for young people who wanted careers as musicians: enrollment in a musical technicum or music school. He finished the tenth grade, then became a schoolteacher and directed his own amateur music society as an extracurricular activity. At the same time, he found work as a violinist at the Theater of Young Audiences, where he performed until the beginning of the war, when he was drafted and sent to the front. In August 1942 he was wounded in the leg and evacuated to a hospital in Siberia and then back to Tashkent. While he was recuperating, he learned that the Muqimi Theater of Musical Drama had announced a competition for musicians and singers. Winners of the competition would be freed from duty at the front. He entered the competition and won a place in the theater's music ensemble.

At that time, the Muqimi Theater was the center of musical life in Tashkent. The city's best singers, actors, and musicians had gathered there, and the theater enjoyed the personal patronage of the First Secretary of the Communist party of Uzbekistan, Usman Yusupov, the man who ran wartime Uzbekistan. Turgun-*aka* loved to reminisce about Yusupov. "He loved art, particularly music and theater. These days, the President doesn't have time to talk to artists. But Yusupov found time. Every week, once a week, he came to us in the theater. He watched a play, and afterward he'd offer his comments. If he didn't like the way one of the actors sang his lines, or the way the musicians played a certain song, the theater's music director would change it before the next performance. All of the actors were men. When there were women's roles, they'd be played by men dressed as women. Usman-*aka* sat with us and listened to us, and asked how he could help us, what we needed for the theater. He said that he'd help bring us good singers and musicians—he could get them released from the front." There was a story that Yusupov had phoned directly to Stalin to arrange for theater musicians who had been drafted and sent to the front to be returned to Tashkent. "How will we celebrate after the war's over if all the musicians are killed?" he is said to have asked Stalin.

Toxtasin Jalilov, the music director of the Muqimi Theater, was also a charismatic figure who had a strong influence on Turgun. Jalilov was famous for wearing a pistol to rehearsals. Turgun said that he never used it, except occasionally to fire into the air when he needed to get his artists' attention at a raucous moment. Jalilov is the only person I ever heard Turgun refer to as his *ustâz,* his teacher. He wasn't a teacher in the sense of showing Turgun how to play an instrument. Rather, Jalilov showed him how to shape music in a way that made it come alive for audiences; how to arrange popular songs for an ensemble, and how to express musical ideas with extreme conciseness. "I often remember his words," said Turgun. "'Any singer and any musician should place his listeners higher than himself.' He taught me that listeners don't serve you, but you serve the listeners. And nothing is more complicated than satisfying the soul of another person. If you look at some poorly dressed listener and think arrogantly that this person doesn't understand anything in music, then the listeners will punish you for that. If you think of any listener as one who will judge you, then you'll find happiness in your profession. The listener is a type of tape recorder that takes in impressions. You can never lie. A tape recorder and a listener—they are in essence one and the same. And both of them show what is."

After the war, the Muqimi Theater began to decline. OM and Turgun-*aka* both had their own explanations. OM thought that it was due to the rise of ideology in the postwar years: "Instead of simply making beautiful and accessible art, the theater had to contribute to the ideological struggle against formalism and traditionalism, had to stimulate the development of 'new socialist culture,'" said OM. In Uzbekistan, the chief bogeyman of the musical ideologists was not formalism, as in Moscow and Leningrad, but traditionalism. In 1951 the Chairman of the Union of Composers of Uzbekistan, Sabir Babayev, issued a decree, "About the Development of Monophonic Music," proclaiming that in monophonic music, which was to say, in the *maqâm,* no development was in fact possible. Monophonic music, said Babayev, could not "properly reflect the new Soviet reality."[21] As the life of the theater became more and more constrained by ideology, Turgun finally left it and accepted work at the radio station.

Turgun-*aka*'s explanation of the decline of the theater was simpler than OM's: "If you're giving a speech, you want people to hear it, right? At the radio you had not a few hundred listeners, as in a theater, but hundreds of thousands of listeners. It was more prestigious. And there was a lot more freedom. During the day, you'd rehearse and make recordings, and in the evening, you were free to go to weddings and earn money. Naturally, the best musicians went to the radio.

"In 1952, they disbanded all the folk music ensembles at the radio. They didn't want any Uzbek ensembles. They said it was old music, that no one needed it. They didn't allow any national music, and the theaters didn't allow it. They just played recordings made by note-reading orchestras. We went for five years, until 1957, without any pay. But that was one of the best periods of my life. I felt free, like a free bird. I did whatever I wanted."

I asked, "Wasn't there any folk music at all on the radio?"

"Folk music was presented in a different way," he answered. "It wasn't folk music, it was feudal music, Soviet feudal music, that is. There was an Armenian named Petrosants [A. I. Petrosian]. He didn't know a word of Uzbek and he didn't know a single Uzbek melody. But he directed Uzbek music and redesigned all of our folk instruments so that they could be played together in folk orchestras. That's what I mean by 'breaking a tradition.' Other countries— Pakistan, India—they didn't have a government that changed their musical instruments. Here, the musicians and singers who went to the Conservatory were ruined. They sang and played from notation. People don't like to hear music played from notation. How many years they've paid millions for music that no one wanted or needed. How much time did they lose? We have to begin again from scratch. We're beginning, but we're beginning from such an impoverished position. Opera and ballet theater—they have big buildings. Why do they have these buidings? They should be closed down completely. Who goes to hear opera and ballet?

"During the years when my ensemble at the radio was disbanded, I played at weddings with two brothers named Bâbâ Khan and Akmal Khan Sofixânov. Their father, Sofi Khan, was a famous *hafiz* [classical singer]. In those years, there were several musical dynasties which had a high calling: there was Jura Khan Sultânov, there were the Shâhjalilovs, and there were the Sofixânovs. In contrast to other singers, the Sofixânovs performed exclusively songs with a religious content. They were religious people themselves, even during the time when religion was strictly forbidden. People who rejected religion simply didn't associate with them, and for their part, the Sofixânovs stayed away from atheists. They were invited to the houses of believers.

"I've been in the company of very different *hafiz*s, but I've never seen the kind of respect I saw for the Sofixânovs. When they appeared in the distance, everyone stood up, and stood to two sides, bowing their heads and putting their hands over their hearts. Why were they so respected? First, people liked the fact that they themselves prayed. From childhood, they had been raised in that spirit. During the time I was with them, I also started to pray. They conducted themselves nobly. They had very clean souls. Second, what they sang was in a sincere religious style. In contrast to other singers, who only said the words *God, religion*, etc., they approached these words very attentively and chose the most affective texts. They completely excluded light and worldly texts. They sang almost nothing from Nawâ'i.

"Besides their singing, they performed their *zikr-samâ* [*zikr:* the repetition of divine names or religious formulas; *samâ:* mystical concert and dance—both central to the practice of Sufism, or Islamic mysticism].[22] The songs performed in the *zikr* I heard only from them. They had their circle of listeners. Rhythms such as '*ha-HU, ha-HU*' were performed exclusively on religious texts. And the listeners, as if forgetting everything around them, entered into the *zikr-samâ*. All of their greetings to one another, their discussions between themselves, were based on this rhythm [*usul*]: *HU, ha-HU, HU, ha-HU*. As the *zikr* drew to an end, one or another man began to shout. Then everyone began to shout and cry out. Someone who was seeing this for the first time, like me, also felt that he was part of the *zikr*.

"Now a lot of people do the *Hajj* [pilgrimage to Mecca]. Among those people are quite a few who do it as 'tourists.' Those who do a real *Hajj* are very few. Someone who has a lot of money and goes on the *Hajj* simply to look around told me that while you are doing the *Hajj*, you can't help but become religious. Even a person who is far from religion gradually becomes religious because everyone around him is religious. The feeling arises that the whole world is religious. When there's not another world in sight, a person doesn't notice that he's becoming religious. When everyone else cries, you also begin, unwillingly, to cry. The masses pull a person into their midst. But when you return home, you find yourself back in your familiar world and begin to live the way you lived before. That kind of retransformation happens quite quickly. In other words, I want to say that if a person doesn't have a real religiosity in his soul, then the effect of having gone into this other world will be temporary. That's why in ordinary life, every man becomes what he really is. In the same way, if you come to the *zikr-samâ,* a person begins to experience corresponding feelings. He wants to try to be religious. However, having verified his own behavior, he'll choose the life path that corresponds to his soul.

"With the Sofixânov brothers, I participated in a lot of *zikr*s. The older brother, Bâbâ Khan, played the *tanbur* and presented himself as the leader of the *zikr-samâ*. His brother, Akmal Khan, accompanied on the *dutar,* and I accompanied on the violin. Special religious meetings like a *Mavlud* were organized. Mullahs and religious people were invited to them. There was a very careful selection of participants in these meetings. Mullahs would read religious books; someone would ask a question, and others would try to answer. The conversation was mainly about the life of the Prophet. How did [Islamic] religion spread? How did people submit to it? What punishment was given to people who didn't accept it? What blessings were given to those who did? All of these questions were discussed at length.[23]

"At such meetings, the Islamic code of behavior was strictly preserved: how to greet someone, how to ask a question, how to answer, how to stand, how to sit. Precisely on time, prayers would take place. When it was time for the *zikr-samâ,* the Sofixânovs would go into the center of the circle and become the leaders of the meeting. Even well-known mullahs submitted to their authority. At that time there were teachers like Ali Khan Tura, who had a broad view of life and religion and respected the art of religious singers. From such teachers, I often heard the following aphorism: Bir gâh xudâi rasuldan, bir gâh ghamzai usuldan [Once for God and the Prophet, once for merriment (literally: "a seductive wink") and dance].[24] These two types of conversation provide man with the highest form of enjoyment. If he thinks only about religion, he'll be one-sided and boring. In order for a person to relax a bit, he has to have *ghamzai usul*—a *hafiz's* singing, or performance on an instrument. Ali Khan Tura said that 'if a singer performs a song with religious content, it's still better.' [He meant not a prayer per se, but what one might call a spiritual song; a song whose lyrics evoke religious sentiments.]

"The *zikr-samâ* was held exclusively among deeply religious people. Among the simple people, such things didn't exist."

"So you yourself participated in the *zikr-samâ?*" I asked.

"All of what I've told you about I saw with my own eyes and heard with my own ears."

If for Turgun the Sofixânovs epitomized the highest moral standards of a musical life, there were other musicians who epitomized the opposite: a musical life of moral degradation. "In order to judge the good, you have always to see the bad," said Turgun. "Only then can a person really understand who is what. I've had to perform with every which kind of musician.

"There's one category of musician that's called in slang *attarchi. Attar* means 'herd' or 'crowd.' A person who herds sheep is called an *attarchi.* Among simple people, the musicians who feed them, who give them spiritual food, are called *attarchi.* When I started to work, I went around most frequently with this sort of musician. We were *attarchi*s and called one another *attarchi.* These were not musicians who had a name, an image, who performed as a particular ensemble according to particular rules or aesthetic norms. They performed with whoever showed up. For them, there was no difference which musician, which singer, they worked with. They just had to have some work and some pay.

"Among the *attarchi*s, you could find every which kind of spiritually deformed person: people without conscience, liars, prostitutes, pimps. They were people who had no culture, no mastery. They couldn't live cleanly from their art. They had no qualms about lying and cheating, and if you exposed their lies, they'd look impudently in your eyes. But I've never seen a single dishonest person who prospered [literally: 'who received *baraka*'].

"Among real, clean artists, I never saw such people. Real artists lived honestly. They had high regard for both their art and their faith. Bâbâ Khan-*aka,* Shah Karim-*aka*—they always valued their masters' spirits, their teachers who were deceased. They prayed to their spirits; they always remembered them. They kept in contact with their families and took part in all of their family occasions. And that's the way they raised their children. Look at their children; they're following the path of their parents. I didn't want my children to become musicians. Music was put in my soul by God. All kinds of wrong behavior and ruin begin with a lack of talent. So if you have talent, you have to follow that road. If not, then you have no place there.

"Bâbâ Khan-*aka* and Shah Karim-*aka* were people who were clean not only in the soul but also in their actions. When they distributed money, they distributed it to the last kopeck. If it happened that there were a hundred rubles for the three of them, the older one gave everyone thirty-three rubles. The last ruble he'd give to Shah Karim and tell him to add it to the next day's proceeds. When I went around with the *attarchi*s, the head musician would take a hundred rubles and give the others fifteen or twenty. It was just the opposite. He had a scornful relationship with the musicians and dancer who performed with him. By the time they got around to distributing money, he'd already have hidden half of it. Since the *attarchi*s were accustomed to these sorts of things, each of them tried to steal as best he could. They'd steal bottles of vodka from the weddings where they played. The bad image of the *attarchi*s also reflects on good artists. They'd spread malicious gossip. But I repeat again and again that real art is a very high calling. After religion, there's nothing better and more dignified than art."

Turgun's work at the radio station resumed in 1957, when the Uzbek national music ensemble was reinstated. The next year, Yunus Rajabi initiated his *maqâm* ensemble, and Turgun became a member of this ensemble. But Turgun quickly became frustrated with the work of Rajabi's ensemble. For him, the *Shash maqâm* was not only a canonical musical text but also a tradition of artistic creativity. He didn't find merit simply in performing the canon.

"If a musician doesn't add something from himself, doesn't add his own soul, then the music won't go to the heart of the listener," he said. "Yunus Rajabi gave only the basis, only the text. He wasn't primarily a performer. He performed, but he wasn't a great performer. He taught musicians to play the *maqâm* who had never played it before. That should be done very slowly and carefully. But the people who taught the *maqâm* weren't creative people. Dâmla Halim—when he plays, it's alive. There's not one boring note. Everything is felt. But with Rajabi, it's not interesting. You feel like you're listening to funeral music. Musicians have to add their own souls and from that, make music. In the *maqâm* ensemble, they never found a way of working that could creatively develop the *Shash maqâm*. One of the main reasons for this failure was the collectivization of performance. I didn't become Turgun Alimatov because I sat in an ensemble with other musicians but because I found my own individual style, my own individual path. The melodies that I perform were known before I played them, but I appropriated them, added my own soul to them, my own understanding, and gave them my own interpretation."

It was Turgun's strong individualism that got him into trouble at the radio station. In addition to the daily schedule of rehearsals and performances, radio musicians had the opportunity to record their own repertory for broadcast and eventually for release on recordings produced by the Melodiya firm. Turgun made many of his own recordings; however, between 1960 and 1975 not a single recording was played on the radio. I asked Turgun-*aka* why.

"There were people there who didn't want my recordings to be played. There were jealous people. I didn't especially suffer from it. Sixteen years went by like that. They didn't play a single recording of mine. They accepted my recordings, and formally, they scolded me. 'Why don't you make recordings? Give us recordings,' they said. So I'd play two melodies. And after a week, they'd have a meeting of the Artistic Council and they'd find a reason to say that the recordings weren't done well. And for a year, I wouldn't record anything. A year would go by, and then they'd start again. 'Why aren't you recording anything?' And again, they'd refuse my recording."

"Was it connected to the style of your playing?"

"Yes. For example, I composed a piece called *Dutar Nawâisi.* It doesn't follow the path of *maqâm nawâ.* It wasn't my intent to follow the path of *maqâm nawâ.* And they'd say, 'They don't play *nawâ* that way here. They don't play *maqâm* like that.' Or they'd say that I didn't play rhythmically. I didn't argue. I said, 'Have it your way.'"

"What happened in 1975?"

"Some people left the radio and there was a new leadership. They sat with me and asked, 'Why is it that you've been here so many years yet you don't have any recordings?' I explained everything to them. The new assistant chairman said that he'd sit with me at the Artistic Council and listen to what they said to me. Later he became the head of the Artistic Council. So I played a piece on the *dutar,* a piece on the *tanbur,* and a piece on the *satâ.* I went to the Artistic Council, and no one said anything bad about me. They were afraid, no doubt. Then they said, 'You can record whatever you want.'"

I told Turgun-*aka,* "I want to write about how you took *maqâm* and, from it, created your own new music."

"I didn't create music. I took what existed, ready-made, and I played it. I listened, I played, listened, played. I didn't compose melodies. Why search for new music when there's so much ready-made music?"

"But you took *maqâm,* and what you play, your style, it's not similar to the Bukharan *Shash maqâm.* You changed something. You don't consider that you created new music?"

"No. One person builds a house and leaves that house. I come to that house and remodel it. And that remodeling will be valued for a long time. And then a still better master will come along and do another remodeling. He'll take down certain parts and build them up again in his own way. It will be still better. That's how I understand it. I'm not the one who built the house. I just did the remodeling. I can't say that it's mine. Whoever sees this house says that a workman gave it a good paint job. He doesn't say that the workman built it. If I play *segâh,* it doesn't mean that I wrote it; but people know that I play well. They know when they hear me that Turgun-*aka* is playing. And that's enough.

"The way I play *maqâm*—that's the spirit in which all *maqâm* should be played. Each *maqâm* should be taken by a musician and worked up into something beautiful. You shouldn't just make a copy of what someone else does. If you just make a copy, there won't be any growth, any progress."

I asked, "Then what is tradition? On the one hand, you say that your tradition was beaten up and broken by the Communists. On the other hand, you say that each person should find his own style of performance. If you find your own style, why do you need tradition?"

"In every tradition, there are two poles: the individual and the collective, that is, many individuals, who, through the centuries, create a direction. Tradition has its laws, its regularities. A person who wants to be in a tradition has to take account of those regularities.

"Now I go to the Conservatory and the students—they have my records at home—they listen to them, and they come to me and say, 'I want to learn to play *chahârgah*.' I play a little bit, and then I say, 'Okay, you play it.' He plays it, and then I play it again. He plays it exactly the way I play it, because he wants to learn to play the way I do on my records. So students listen to musicians who play and sing well, and they follow after them. That's also tradition. There are recordings of other *tanbur* players. They don't go to them. They come to me. People always search for the best; if students knew that there were a better *tanbur* player than me, they'd go to him. It's not necessarily that I'm good, but I'm the last. Ideally, there should be a lot of musicians like me. But the tradition has been broken."

"Do the students play exactly the way you do on your records?"

"They can't know themselves when they're playing exactly the same way."

"But do they try to imitate your recordings?"

"Yes. But if someone learns to play exactly the same way I do, all the same, I'll be the one who goes down in history, not him."

"Do you think that these students ought to be creating their own music, as you did?"

"If you plant four kinds of plum trees, one there, one five meters farther, one five meters farther, and so on, they'll live in the same weather, the same sun, the same earth and water; yet when they grow up, they'll be different. Each has its own place. But only one will be high, the others will be low. And musicians are like that."

OM admired Turgun-*aka*'s music, but even more, he admired Turgun's trenchant observations about the life of the spirit and—his special interest—its relation to music. In pondering the origins of Turgun's style of thinking, OM was continually reminded of the great Central Asian Sufi sheikhs who, like Turgun, conveyed much of their teaching orally, through didactic stories and aphorisms. The Naqshbandi tradition, for example, is full of sententious advice: Dil ba yâru dast ba kar (Soul to God and hands to work); Be zaher bâ khalq, va be batin bâ Haqq (On the exterior with people, inside with God); Safar dar vatan (Travel in your own inner world). Like the Sufi sheikhs, Turgun drew on notions such as *sâz* (harmony), *ishq* (love), *dard* (passion), *halat* (state), and *kaif* (intense pleasure or delight) to explain his views.

OM spoke at length with Turgun-*aka* about *sâz*—"harmony." "For Turgun, *sâz* is an essential part of understanding music," OM told me. "Turgun explains that music begins with *sâz*. It's like the concept of harmony among the ancients. It not only has the literal meaning of a musical instrument and a system of tuning. It's a more all-encompassing idea about proportion and relationship. For example, Turgun has a favorite expression which he endlessly repeats and varies: he says that first a musician must tune himself. Then he must tune his instrument, and only then, can he tune the listener. In practice, that means that first the musician himself has to be tuned, that is, he has to be in good form, to have a desire to make music and serve the listener. Only after that can he take an instrument in his hands and tune the instrument in a way that corresponds to the present conditions. That is, when he says 'tune an instrument,' what he means is 'What kind of listeners are there? What kind of state are they in? What do they want to hear from the musician?' On the basis of that, the musician should tune his instrument to an appropriate tuning. When he says that 'only then you can think about tuning the listener,' that is, attract him to your side, make him listen to you, in last analysis, be in harmony with you, he's speaking about the ultimate aim of music: to create harmony."

For Turgun, harmony with his listeners was created not only through music; it was also created through words. He told me, "People invite me who also like words. They like the way I talk with them at a *gap,* or the way I drink with them, like a friend. They like the fact that my character is close to theirs. What a musician plays or sings—that's secondary. What's close to the people is first words and character, then music. You don't play music right away. You talk with them, you drink a little, tell some jokes, and heart-to-heart, try to get close to them; and then, according to the mood, they'll ask, 'Can we hear something?' I like to go to places where they know me, where they know my character. If they know me, then it will be good for me there. They'll receive me well. But sometimes I go, and it doesn't work out. That also happens. Maybe four people listen to me, but the majority don't listen. They're not interested in me. They have a different character. There, I won't be in a good mood, because the others will bother me. Those who know my character and like my words, they sit with me as you do, we'll eat together and drink together, and the very last, you can ask me, 'Will you play something?' That's the way you talk with me. Some people who don't know me well, right away when I first come, before we've even had tea or sat together, they say, 'Turgun-*aka,* while they're preparing the food, play something, please. We're bored.' I really don't like that. I don't want to play under those conditions. But some people don't understand that."

I asked, "Do you prefer *gap* or *âsh?*"

"At the *âsh*, the musician sits by himself; you don't talk, you just play. That's not interesting. It's interesting when you talk with people and then drink and eat together."

"Do you ever turn down an invitation to perform at a *gap* or *âsh* if you don't think you'll like the character of the people there?"

"No, never. I've never seen a musician who refuses. If you come to my house and say to me, 'On such and such a date, we have a *toy*. We love your music very much, and we'd like to ask you to come and play, and for one singer to come with you and sing,' I don't ask you, 'Who are you? Show me your documents. Where do you work?' You can't do that. A person comes, and that's it. You ask, 'What time does it start?' And you say, 'I'll go.' And there, you find out what kind of person he is. That's how it works. Whether he's poor or rich doesn't concern me. If he respects me and asks me to come, I must go to him.

"I've never sold myself as a musician. I earned money from other channels, mostly business. I've been many thousands of times at weddings and *gaps*, and I've never once asked, 'How much will you pay me?' Sometimes they gave me many thousands of rubles, and sometimes they gave me two pieces of bread and said, 'Thank you.'"

THE AVATAR OF A MASTER

The musician Arif Xatamov was frequently mentioned when I studied at the Conservatory in the 1970s. He had made some recordings on the Melodiya label which were in the stores, and students in the Eastern Music Department at the Conservatory regarded him as one of the preeminent Uzbek musicians of his generation. Unlike Turgun Alimatov, who was known for his virtuoso instrumental technique, Xatamov was at once a vocalist and a fine performer on the *tanbur* and *dutar*. And in contrast to Turgun-*aka*'s single-minded pursuit of stylistic innovation within the framework of tradition, Arif-*aka* was an unrepentent traditionalist who bemoaned the spiritual superficiality of contemporary music.

Xatamov lived on a collective farm on the periphery of Tashkent but drove into town practically every day either for an engagement at the radio station, where he had worked for more than fifty years, or to give private lessons at the Theater Institute, where he taught three days a week. After morning rehearsals or recordings at the radio station, Arif-*aka* would come by my apartment to talk to OM and me. Arif-*aka* needed little prompting. A single question would send him into an unbroken monologue that continued until we asked him to pause so we could change the cassette in our tape recorder. During these sessions (they could hardly be called conversations, since Xatamov did almost all the talking), Arif-*aka* told us about his family background and his initiation into the life of a

69

musician, about his teacher and spiritual mentor, Jura Khan Sultanov, and about the musical traditions of the Ferghana region to which he had dedicated his artistic life.

"I was born in Jizzak, between 1924 and 1925," Arif-*aka* told us. "That was the year of the cow." Traditionally in Central Asia, it was rare to know one's actual birthday unless it corresponded to some famous date. "I'm from the lineage of the *ishân*s." *Ishân* is Persian, meaning "they"—the word is connected to the tradition of trying to avoid disrespectful direct references to first names. In Central Asia, *ishânism* might be considered the "Sufism of the village."[25] An *ishân*'s authority comes not from a formal religious post but, like the authority of a Sufi sheikh, from a reputation for spiritual mastery among a circle of disciples.[26]

"Both the tsar's forces and the Communists tried to get rid of the *ishân*s, because of the respect that people had for them and their potential to threaten the government. There were a lot of *ishân*s and their disciples [*murid*s] in Jizzak. My great-grandfather on my father's side was one of the most authoritative *ishân*s in Jizzak. But my childhood was at the time when the government was fighting against kulaks and against *ishân*s.

"The first Jizzak Rebellion was in the 1860s or so. There was a fortress in Jizzak. It had walls that were so thick that a cart could go across the top of it. The first clash with the Russians was at this fortress. Since the local Uzbeks didn't have powerful weapons like cannons—they just had rifles—they weren't able to put up much resistance against the Russians. The second rebellion was connected to the *mardikâr*—workers who were indentured to the tsar. It happened in 1916, when my mother was seven years old.[27] The local people refused to give their children to the tsar's army, and then they killed the local police officer. The Cossacks went on a rampage. They shot people like crows. My parents fled, and came back only at night to take food. There was a place where people washed, a public shower, and eight women hid there, among them my mother. The Cossacks found them and shot them. My mother was wounded but survived. She was the only one who survived. It was such horrible barbarity. If they saw children on the street, they'd run them through with their swords and hold them up for everyone to see. They did it as an example to other towns. Jizzak ceased to exist after that. Only in the 1970s did Jizzak start to come back.

"There are two kinds of *ishân*s. One kind tries to gather disciples and make these disciples totally dependent on him. That's a kind of slavery. And the other kind of *ishân* lives on his own work. The first kind takes some percent of the wealth of their disciples. Disciples paid for a prayer [*duwâ*]. There wasn't such a thing as a free prayer. My lineage went by the principle of Bahâ'uddin Naqshband, who said that people should live by their own work. There are *ishân*s who gather things from their disciples. But we never gathered, never forced people to give us things. We just lived by honest work. My great-grandfather had a lot of land, and he distributed it among his sons and grandsons, and everyone worked on the land. They were all repressed because they had land. A few of them fled, the rest were killed.

"When they started collectivization, they took away land from the kulaks. If you had a garden, they'd tax you, and if you had cattle, they'd tax you; they'd tax you to death. You wouldn't have enough money to pay the new taxes, so you'd be arrested, and no one would know what happened to you. First they fought against the *ishân*s, then they fought against the landowners.

"We had a house and a hectare of land. They gave a pig to everyone who worked in the offices [of the collective farm]. To show that you were an educated person, a Soviet person, you had to keep a pig at home [for a Muslim, especially for an *ishân,* this was blasphemous]. My mother made a special kasha for the pigs. If a pig died, you'd be accused of being an enemy of the people.

"In 1937, my uncle was repressed, with some of the first people to be repressed. He said a prayer at the home of the chairman of the collective farm that God would do away with the government, and some stool pigeon reported him, and he was arrested and sent to jail, where he was shot. My parents had to flee to Yangiyul because on both sides of the family, people had been repressed. After they moved to Yangiyul, my mother cried all the time. She wanted to return to Jizzak. Jizzak had been a flowering place. There had been a lot of *madrasah*s, a lot of enlightened people. My parents went there, but there was nothing left of it; not homes, not gardens. It had been erased from the face of the earth. So they came to Tashkent, and we've been in Tashkent ever since. In our lineage, there's not a single person who didn't suffer, and we're all spread around. We don't live together in our ancestral place.

"My grandfather liked music and invited musicians to his house. That's one of the reasons I'm in the sphere of music: because my father and my grandfather were connoisseurs of music, and we had lots of musicians in our house. One of them, a famous *nay* [flute] player, always told me that I was a good musician. I liked the *nay,* and started to play. In 1940, when I was in the seventh grade, preparations were being made to celebrate the 500th anniversary of the death of Ali Shir Nawâ'i [d. 1441]. I joined an amateur music society that was involved in the preparations. Those amateur societies have all fallen apart now, but back then they were serious.

"I sat at home and studied songs, Tajik texts, Hafiz's poetry. My mother began to correct me. She had dropped out of school at age nine, when her parents died, but she knew many *ghazal*s by memory, and she could correct me. Now ask someone who's graduated from an institute about Nawâ'i, Jami, Fizuli—they don't know these poets. You have to develop your knowledge of music and literature together. The strength of music is in its contents, in the words. Those famous poets whose words were sung were so deep, so important to philosophy and to life, that people clung to their words. People got their education through

Arif Xatamov with one of his grandsons.

those words. They knew a lot of *ghazal*s by memory and had penetrated their meanings. If you understand the words, then the music will stay in your head.

"There are two different ways of writing poetry: with open words [*achiq soz*] and closed words [*yapiq soz*]. Simple poets use open words—sometimes called "naked words" [*yolanghach soz*]. Their meaning is given directly. But deep, philosophical poets always have hidden contents which are more subtle and valuable. Sometimes when I perform, people ask, 'Why are you performing such long, complicated things?' They're already used to a lighter repertory. The fundaments of our art are falling apart. Our people have come from a tradition of spiritual learning, but they've lost themselves.

"After the seventh grade, I went to a medical high school. There was a teacher named Halim who was the the artistic director of the school's amateur music society. I joined the group as a *nay* player. In 1944, while I was studying at the medical high school, there was an announcement that the Muqimi Theater was hiring musicians. I played a bit on the violin as well as on the *nay*, and went there to try out. They told me that I'd be better off on the violin, since there were already a lot of *nay* players. So they took me as a violinist. I was given a deferment from the army to play music in the theater. I loved music so much that I couldn't get enough of it. I'd play day and night. It was a special time, when artists were really honored. There were stars like Jura Khan Sultanov and Toxtasin Jalilov. Everyone thought about trying to be like Jura Khan Sultanov.

72

"I chose Jura Khan [1912–1977] as my *pir* [spiritual mentor]. I was fanatically in love with his music. I first heard his recordings in 1936. In 1944, I met him personally, in the Muqimi Theater. That same year, I started to perform with him on the violin at *toy*s. There were four of us in the group, and we made records together that became very popular. People would sell a cow to buy one of our records. Jura Khan created new pieces from folk songs and reworked old melodies. He was an innovator by nature. He was always in search of something new, in contrast to others who just played the same repertory.

"People often wept when they heard Jura Khan sing, because his words showed the greatness of God. He sang very expressively, and he had this kind of effect. He used to sing a text from [the great mystical poet] Mashrab that says, 'Man appears on this earth in order to know God. The knowledge of God is the greatest meaning in the life of man.' People couldn't eat their *palav* after they heard those words. I was there with the other members of our group, and we also wept. Man has *dard*—passion [literally, "pain," "suffering"]. If he doesn't have *dard,* then music won't act on him. When I listen to Jura Khan, I involuntarily have tears. The main thing is the meaning of the words. The words touch a person. Certain words act on him. From a lot of words, all of a sudden, something appears that you understand.

"I'm thankful that I had a connection to people like Jura Khan. Often, Jura Khan comes to me in my dreams. I remember my teachers each day and pray for them each day. Some people have hallucinations before their death; people come to them who were close and say, 'Don't be afraid, don't be afraid; you're coming to us. Everything will be all right.' That shows that spirits are eternally alive. People who believe—it's easier for them. Nonbelievers have it very hard at the end of their lives.

"Singers like Jura Khan were among the greatest propagandists of Islam. Their main work was to agitate and educate people, not to entertain them. Of course, most of all, they agitated about God. They warned people away from evil ways and bad influences. In conditions where there were no movies or television, music was a central channel for communicating information and for education. Singers themselves had to be morally clean; if they weren't, it would get around, and they'd lose their authority. These days at weddings, musicians drink vodka and get drunk, and that has a contrary effect. That's why people's morals are being ruined, why there's a lot of crime now.

"There was a comic named Jusup Kiziq who once said to Jura Khan—I think it was in the 1930s—'You have a great talent, but you came at the wrong time. You were born too late. This generation doesn't value your art.' In the mid-1950s, I performed together with Jura Khan, and the listeners were still worse. They asked for light things; they wanted to horse around. There was little demand for serious music. At that time, Jura Khan said, 'If Yusup Kiziq had seen this, what would he have said?' And these days, I say, 'If Jura Khan had seen the way it is now, what would he say?' When Jura Khan was alive, there were still people who listened, but now there's practically no one."

Arif-*aka* spoke these words with passion and a visible sense of pain. The renewal of interest in Muslim religious practices, the increased attendance at mosques, and the opening of new *madrasah*s in post-Soviet Uzbekistan didn't seem to move Xatamov. He regarded with suspicion what he called "prayer as showing off." The tradition of Central Asian spirituality in which music and poetry played such an important part was dying, and he doubted that the mere political acceptance of public Islamic practice after decades of official repression was enough to restore that moribund tradition to health.

Despite pessimism about Central Asia's spiritual future, Arif-*aka* was an active and energetic song composer. He drew the texts of his songs from the works of his favorite poets—mostly Mashrab and the great twelfth-century mystic Yasawi—and composed the melodies himself. An ascetic philosophy of millennialism (the coming of the Day of Judgment) runs through much of Yasawi's poetry, and amid the turmoil of postindependence Uzbekistan, he has enjoyed a surge in popularity. Arif-*aka* said that listeners identify with Yasawi's pungent social commentary about the evils and hypocrisy of his time and relate them to the conditions of their own lives: not dishonest mullahs and muftis but dishonest bureaucrats and politicians. During the Soviet era as well, ideologues had presented Yasawi's works as an insider's commentary on the apparent evils of religion. Yasawi's point, of course, was not that religion should be eliminated but that hypocrisy should be eliminated. Arif-*aka* performed several songs on texts attributed to Yasawi. One of them is presented on the accompanying compact disc (track 12). Here is the translated and transcribed text:[28]

> Those who said the world is mine
> Those who wanted to gather the world's riches
> Are like a vulture
> Drowning in *haram* [filth, dirt]
>
> Those who became mullahs and muftis
> Are using dishonest means
> What's white they call black
> They'll go to *tamuq* [a cave in hell; the worst part of hell]
>
> Those who became *qazi*s and imams
> Those who gave various *fatwâs* [decrees]
> Will remain under a weight
> Like wine [being pressed]
>
> The *hakim*s who earn dishonestly
> Those who wait for bribes
> Will bite their fingers
> And remain in fear

Those who ate something very delicious
Those who dressed very beautifully
Those who sat on the golden throne
Will lie in the ground.

Dunyâ mening deganlar
Jahân mâlin âlganlar
Kargaz qushdek boliban
Ul harâmga bâtmishlar

Mullâ mufti bolganlar
Nâhaq davâ qilghanlar
Aqni qâra deganlar
Ul tamuqgha kirmishlar

Qâzi, imam bolganlar
Turli fatwa qilghanlar
Xamr yangligh boliban
Yuk âstida qâlmishlar

Harâm yegan hâkimlar
Para tama qilghanlar
Oz barmaghin tishlabân
Qorqib turib qâlmishlar

Tatliq-tatliq yeganlar
Turli-turli kiyganlar
Altin taxtga otirganlar
Topraq âra yâtmishlar

Xatamov's austere song was in keeping with a long tradition of singing or declaiming Yasawi's poetry. Anthologized by his disciples into a *Hikmat*,[29] or "collection of wisdom," Yasawi's verse has served as an abiding source for spiritual songs performed in a variety of styles ranging from simple recitative to elaborate art song. Arif-*aka* said that in the Ferghana Valley, Yasawi's poetry was often sung in the form of a *munâjât*—an appeal to God—as a part of what he called the *zikr maqâm* or *katta maqâm* (literally, "great *maqâm*").[30]

"In the mausoleum of Yasawi [in the city of Turkestan, in present-day Kazakhstan], there's a place where they held *zikr*," Arif-*aka* told us. "People would gather after prayers. They sat in a circle and the *hafiz* would begin to sing: 'I admire you, our Prophet, on the Day of Judgment, defend us.' The *munâjât* was chanted without rhythm [*usul*]. Then the *hafiz* would chant to a rhythm, 'All of my thoughts are about the desert of love' [i.e., I think only of love of God]. Under this, the people who had gathered for the *zikr* chanted 'Allah, Allah.'[31] I participated in *zikr*s. When everyone chanted together, some kind of inspiration came to me. I didn't think that there could be such an effect. My body shook from this illumination. I heard that people began to tear their clothes, their shirts;

one man even tore his pants off and threw them away; that's how much they were in ecstasy. It was said that there were cases when Sadir Khan [the famous *hafiz*] sang, and people died from ecstasy. For that reason, they called him 'Sadir Khan who killed people.'"

OM and I urged Arif-*aka* to try to reconstruct for us some of the chants, melodies, and rhythms that he had heard performed at *zikr*s in his youth, but Arif-*aka* demurred. "It was so long ago," he said, "and I've forgotten so much. I haven't practiced it, and it would be a sin for me to try to explain it." For him, the ceremonial aspect of *zikr* that has long fascinated students of Islamic spiritual traditions seemed ancillary to the essential content of the tradition itself. With his life spanning the entire Soviet era, Arif-*aka* had constructed his own private world of faith, and it had served him well. "To carry the weight of tradition has been hard for him," said OM after our last session with Arif-*aka*. "People ignored him, people criticized him. As a believer, he's seen all sorts of colossal contradictions, and if he hadn't been committed to his belief, he would have lived better, and more sweetly. But the times didn't break him. He's remained himself. And now, in so-called new times, when there's a more positive attitude toward tradition, he's become like a former dissident. He's highly respected, not only because he's a preserver of tradition but also because he's really a master creator. He's created a great deal of music. He has many students around him and devotes a tremendous amount of time to them. He thinks it's a blessing to have students. Look at all the time he spent with us. A different musician wouldn't have spent so much time. And Arif-*aka* wouldn't accept any money for doing the recording. He viewed it as an offering. I thought that maybe he needed some money, but he said, 'No, I won't take it.' He teaches his students the same values. In these times, we need people like Arif-*aka* more than ever. His is a true life of service. Thinking about him, I often recall a line from a poem by Nazim Hikmet [the Marxist Turkish poet]: 'If I won't burn, where will the light come from?'"

A CONTRALTO AND A POP QUEEN

In the United States, I lived in the perpetual world of youth that is both the blessing and the curse of a college teacher. Arriving in Transoxania, I was suddenly transported to what seemed like a perpetual world of old people. It was only natural that older people should have played a prominent role in the work that OM and I did together. "We're a society that was traditionally driven by a respect for the old," OM often said, "and after these seventy years [of Soviet rule] in which the 'struggle against the old' was imposed on our culture and threatened our traditions, we have to work overtime to try to preserve all the talent and knowledge that was shunned and ignored." The remark about working overtime was not gratuitous. During my five years with OM, many of the people who had taken us into their confidence and recounted intimate details of their lives died. Others seemed only a step away from eternity. When I returned to Tashkent after an absence of months or a year, one of the first orders of business was always for OM to update the necrology of our musician friends and liaisons.

Traditions, of course, cannot survive exclusively among the old. The act of "handing over" is central to the very definition of *tradition* (from *traditus,* past participle of *tradere,* "to hand over," "betray"), and many of the older musicians with whom we spent time had made references to working with students. The *maqâm* ensemble at the radio station employed a number of younger musicians, and the Conservatory trained entire cadres of young *tanbur* and *dutar* players all vying to be the next Turgun Alimatov or Arif Xatamov. But could the successors to these greatest of musicians emerge from the Conservatory, the epicenter of frozen music? The root notion of "handing over" is unspecific about the adaptation, evolution, and innovation that in living traditions balances custom and continuity. Where had those forces of change, or more accurately, of resistance to the status quo, come from in a society—both Soviet and pre-Soviet—in which cultural nonconformism could carry heavy penalties? Turgun-*aka* had shown that the term "traditional innovator" was not an oxymoron. For him, musical innovation seemed to have arisen from an inner vision that he nourished, whether consciously or unconsciously, by keeping himself away from conventional pedagogy, conventional standards. But in an era when formal education so dominated the Central Asian cultural world, was there any way either to circumvent it or, alternatively, move through it, and emerge as an innovator? I had become curious about that question, and my interest had led me to two Tashkent-based musicians, both around thirty years of age, both women, both preeminent in their own style of music, both in their own way at once innovators and traditionalists. One was Munâjât Yulchieva, a powerfully evocative contralto who performed classical songs; the other was Yulduz Usmanova, Uzbekistan's undisputed queen of pop.

Munâjât was a graduate of the Conservatory, but she was too young for our paths to have crossed during my time there. The story of her rise to renown was the Tashkent version of a mentor-protégée fairy tale. She had shown up at the Conservatory one day during the yearly auditions for new performance students, having made her way to Tashkent from a collective farm in the Ferghana Valley, and had tried out for the Vocal Department. The Conservatory's Vocal Department trained Western-style singers for a career in opera or concert music, and the department's instructors had summarily rejected Munâjât on the first round of auditions. Learning of her rejection, she was standing in a hallway sobbing and wondering what to do next when Shâwqat Mirzaev, a young instructor in the newly formed Department of Eastern Music, happened to pass

Munâjât Yulchieva and her mentor, Shawqât Mirzaev.

by and asked what was wrong. Hearing her story, Shâwqât invited Munâjât to sing for him, and that moment became the beginning of an extraordinary sixteen-year collaboration between mentor and student that continues to this day. Shâwqat is not a vocalist and did not instruct his student in vocal technique. What he did was to grasp intuitively Munâjât's native musical gifts and help her shape her vocal style, repertoire, and demeanor as a performer in a way that transformed both art and artist.

"Growing up in Ferghana, I didn't know classical music," Munâjât told me one boiling hot day as we sat in her small, stuffy apartment near Friendship among Peoples Square, a treeless region of wide avenues, cemented prom- enades, and massive public buildings that in the summer radiates heat with a ferocious intensity. "All we were exposed to on the *kolkhoz* was folklore. It wasn't until I came to the Conservatory and met Shâwqat-*aka* that I started to sing classical music." At the Conservatory, Munâjât focused not on the Bukharan *Shash maqâm* but on the more compact classical songs of Tashkent and Ferghana—the same repertory that had attracted Turgun Alimatov and Arif Xatamov. Working with Shâwqat, she developed a unique vocal timbre, what she calls a "Sufi tone," set low in her luxuriant alto range. I asked Munâjât how she had learned about Sufism and how she understood the place of music in Sufism. "In our time, people didn't do *zikr;* I've only seen *zikr* in films. What we [Shâwqat and I] know is an interpretation. It comes from our own understanding of Sufism. The basic idea, though, is clear: to love God. The performer should perform a song as if relating to God from inside, with an inner voice, and the

78

chest voice, or Sufi tone, shows that. It's like a prayer to God. When you sing quietly, it's more powerful than singing loudly. People who are praying don't pay attention to anything else. When I sing, I'm attentive only to my inner state. I have a kind of ecstasy." Later, Munâjât showed me what she meant, demonstrating her "Sufi tone" in a performance of the classical song "Bayât-i Shirâz Talqinchasi" (reproduced on the accompanying compact disc, track 3). The song belongs to the repertory of Ferghana and Tashkent but, as if to emphasize its classical character, was given a title that suggests that it is part of the *Shash maqâm* (in fact the *Shash maqâm* contains no such piece). Its rhythm is the "limping" rhythm (*lang* in Persian, *aksak* in Turkish) which, according to Arif Xatamov, was frequently used in the Sufi chanting that accompanied the ceremony of *zikr* in the Ferghana Valley. The poem, in Baghdadi Turkish, is by the sixteenth-century poet Fuzuli.

> O God, I beseech you, acquaint me with unlucky love
> Don't sever me for one moment from unlucky love
>
> Be generous, don't separate me from suffering
> Bring me the very greatest suffering
>
> Don't weaken my striving for suffering
> Recognize me as a friend; don't say that I'm not faithful to you
>
> Give me more suffering so that I will become weak from
>   being separate from you
> So that in the morning, I will achieve union with you
>
> Render me the honor of crying like Fuzuli
> O God, don't ever create someone like me again.
>
> Yârab balâyi ishq-la qil âshnâ mani,
> Bir dam balâyi ishqdin etma judâ mani.
>
> Âz aylama inâyatingni ahli darddan, [this couplet not sung]
> Ya'niki chox balâlara qil mubtalâ mani.
>
> Tamkinimi balâyi muhabbatda qilma sust, [this couplet not sung]
> Tâ dost ta'n edub demaya bevafâ mani.
>
> Eyla zaif qil tanimi furqatingdakim,
> Vaslina mumkin ola yeturmak sabâ mani.
>
> Naxbat qilib nasib Fuzuli kibi mangâ,
> Yârab muqayyad aylama mutlaq mangâ mani.

"Did you learn to sing like that at the Conservatory?" I asked Munâjât when she had finished.

"I learned from my teacher, Shâwqat-*aka,*" she replied, with a hint of indignation. The idea that one could have learned about Sufi approaches to

79

music at the Conservatory seemed to strike her as odd, if not perverse. And yet her teacher, Shâwqât, was an instructor at the Conservatory, a conspirator in the official conservation of frozen music. Perhaps the intensity of musical imagination that Shâwqat and Munâjât shared came purely from within, from resources that remained untrammeled by the pressures of conformity and standardization in the Conservatory and in the official music world of Tashkent.

In any event, Shâwqat had not been the only one to recognize Munâjât's talent. She had become famous in Uzbekistan. Adored by big-shot politicians and embraced by the Uzbek mass media, she became a constant presence on the radio, on television, and in official concerts. These venues, however, provided a meager income compared with the free-market world of *toy* and *gap*—a world closed to female classical singers. A female entertainer at an all-male morning *âsh* or an all-male *gap* would be regarded as an odalisque, bringing shame both to herself and to the host. The only possible venue for women entertainers is the *bazm,* and Munâjât steadfastly refused to perform the kind of light music that listeners demanded at *bazm*s.

"There's so much Europeanization around us," she said. "Young people just want to be entertained. To enjoy classical music, you have to have patience and preparation, and there's not enough of that now. A lot of the musicians who perform pop music also perform classical music. Some of them are good performers, but they're afraid to perform classical music at weddings. They're afraid people won't understand it." And so Munâjât, by all accounts one of Uzbekistan's most talented musicians, earned a modest living teaching at the Conservatory and serving as a sort of court musician to the Uzbek leadership when there was a need to show off Uzbekistan's cultural great tradition to visiting dignitaries. The majority of her income came from very occasional trips to concertize and record in Europe, where she has performed for audiences drawn by the allure of "the unknown Central Asia."

Yulduz Usmanova, like Munâjât, came from the Ferghana Valley to study vocal music at the Conservatory. And like Munâjât, she emerged from the Conservatory with a style and repertory grounded in tradition and yet entirely her own. When I had first come to Uzbekistan, and for most of the subsequent years of my work there, I had largely ignored the radio, except for the daily morning and evening broadcasts of classical music. I had lumped everything else into the catch-all category of "pop" and decided summarily that it held no interest for me, a student of "traditional" music. But Raihân, OM's sixteen-year-old daughter, had led me to have a change of heart. "Listen to Yulduz," she urged me. "You'll find her music interesting." One day Yulduz herself had shown up at the Matyakubovs to seek advice on a personal matter from Svetlana, OM's wife, who had taught Yulduz at the Conservatory. We spoke briefly, and I began to take note of her music on the radio. I liked it and phoned Yulduz to ask whether she would be willing to talk with me. She told me that she would send her driver to pick me up the following Sunday morning and take me to her place.

On the basis of Yulduz's fame in Uzbekistan, I was expecting to be picked up in an imported car and chauffeured to one of the new villas on the outskirts of the city. But as I stood in the drive outside OM's building, a battered Zhiguli—the Russian Fiat—pulled up and a pudgy middle-aged man climbed out and introduced himself as Yulduz's manager. He nursed the Zhiguli along Amir Timur Boulevard to a distant region of low-slung plain cement block apartments of the type constructed rapidly after the 1966 earthquake. A second-floor, one-bedroom, sparsely furnished space was home to Yulduz and her young daughter. The apartment's interior decorating consisted of three artificial flowering bushes and an artificial hanging plant. A cassette player and a cheap amplifier–compact disc set comprised her audio equipment.

Yulduz was an unlikely looking pop star. Her dark hair was cropped short and her mouth, set over a weak chin, seemed altogether too large for her face. She was dressed in a baggy sweater and gray slacks of an unstylish sort that made her look older, larger, and frumpier than she was in fact. But as soon as Yulduz began to talk, her slightly dubious physical qualifications for pop-star status were immediately forgotten in the wake of the extraordinary physical energy that she brought to her conversation. She spoke rapidly and practically nonstop for several hours, pausing only to leap toward the CD player to illustrate her monologue with examples from her own recordings. I had asked Yulduz to talk about how she began her musical career.

"I'm from Margelan, and the first songs I sang were traditional songs, like *katta ashula*. I hung around with old women, just listening carefully. When I graduated from teacher's college, I decided to apply to the Conservatory. They accepted me in the Vocal Department. Their orientation was toward opera singers. If you commit yourself to that training, it's no joke. You have to sing opera, and there's no money in it, no business, in Uzbekistan. You have to just do it for love of the music. I knew that I'd never have that kind of great love for opera. I was born in the provinces. I was raised in a different culture. I could never be a world-class opera singer. No one from here has ever been a world-class opera singer. So I decided to switch departments—to the Department of Eastern Music—because I liked folk music. I had a dream of being popular. I wanted to be a star. I understood one thing: you have to love classical music, but like it or not, young people the world over are not drawn to the classics. They want a different kind of music. Maybe something that's based on classical music, but that's different. I understood that with *maqâm,* I wouldn't go far.

"It took me eight years to finish the Conservatory. No one saw a future for me. I could sing one or two pieces from the *maqâm* cycles. But I started thinking about the folk songs of those uneducated women whom I'd hung around with as a child, and about what I'd gotten from them, and from other singers I'd heard.

When I was in the eighth grade, I'd worked in a silk factory. There was a man there who'd had a head injury. He couldn't speak, but he could sing. He used to walk around on the heels of the woman who was the head of the factory and sing a certain folk song: 'Qaqilaman, qaqilaman. . . .' That was the first folk music that I turned into a rock song. I took a little bit of it and put it at the beginning of my own song, and added a faster part. Listeners liked it, and so I did more things like that. I used our national instruments, too. For example, I had a *tanbur* in the beginning of one of my pieces. Turgun Alimatov played it. A German composer took that piece and made it into a rap song. He sings the rap line himself. You can hear it in the discothèques now [in Germany]. It's unquestionably a pop piece, but that little segment that Turgun Alimatov plays is so wonderful. Thanks to this new style of pop music, we can extract folk music from its source and get people to listen to it. Little by little, people get interested in the old instruments and in the music."

I asked to hear the piece, and Yulduz popped the German-made CD into her player. The song, "Schoch va Gado" (*Shâhni ham gadâni*), is reproduced on the accompanying compact disc (track 1). Here is the text:

> See the king and the beggars on the same path (road)
> The affairs of this world move along different paths
>
> We all did and do good things
> But good doesn't have a meaning; it doesn't give anything back
>
> The world is a deceptive world, in people's hands, I saw only stones
> I saw tears in the eyes of those who stood for justice and purity
>
> This world is a deceptive world, I don't know whether it's a dream or reality
> We who are guests in this world gouge out one another's eyes
>
> Shâhni ham gadâni ham bir yolda kor bir yolda
> Bu dunyaning ishlari har yoldadur, har yolda
>
> Sahâb ishni hammamiz qiladurmiz qilamiz
> Lek sahâb keti yoq tubi yoqdir, tubi yoq
>
> Dunya yalghân dunyadir, qollarida tâsh kordim
> Haqiqatning, pâklikning kozlarida yâsh kordim
>
> Dunya yalghân dunyadir bilmam tushmi ruyadir
> Mehmânlari bir-birin kozlarini oyadir.

I was struck by the moralistic message of the text and the lyrical, contemplative cast of the melody. Yulduz's song seemed like a kinder and gentler version of the fire-and-brimstone text of Yasawi that Arif Xatamov had performed for OM and me. "Yes, it's true," said Yulduz when I asked her about my perception of a resemblance. "A lot of my songs are an exhortation [*nasihat*] to love one's parents, to love God. When I perform, I sing a couple of songs in a European style and then a couple of our songs. I do that because I hope that young people will pay attention to that song and that they'll understand that song. In the beginning it was hard. It's hard to fight against people who love rock music. But now, kids are listening to these songs. They ask me to sing them at weddings."

Despite local record sales of some five million units and a yearly series of ten to fifteen always sold-out concerts at the 5,000-seat Friendship among Peoples concert hall, weddings were still the main source of Yulduz's income. "I haven't received a kopeck from my records," Yulduz said. "They [Melodiya] printed on the album cover that they'd pressed 15,000 copies, but they just keep repressing it. Okay, I don't need the money. I earn from weddings. But there are a lot of people now who are imitating me. They'll sing my songs on one side of a record and put their own songs on the opposite side. There's no authors' rights here. People just pirate whatever they want."

The commercial music business in Uzbekistan is still in its infancy, and Yulduz was the only Uzbek musician I'd met whose approach to her work resembled even a little bit that of a Western pop star. Uzbek groups had toured to the West, but in the Soviet era the bulk of their hard-currency earnings had been paid to a Moscow-based state agency such as Goskonsert, and the musicians had been given rubles, plus a tiny hard currency per diem. Hard currency from performance fees barely trickled down to the government of Uzbekistan, let alone to the musicians themselves. In post-Soviet Uzbekistan, however, Yulduz was outraged that she was still being denied access to the income streams that a Western pop musician would have received as a matter of course: recording royalties, mechanical royalties from radio airplay of her recordings, fees for television appearances, a percentage of ticket gross for concert appearances, or at least a fee commensurate with the size of halls and audiences.

Yet, even with all her talk of music as commerce and her bitterness at not earning the fees to which she felt entitled, Yulduz seemed in many ways like a traditional musician. Despite her fame and her broad exposure through mass mediation, her primary musical activity as well as her primary source of income was still the relatively intimate wedding performance. She still understood music as a form of social service whose obligation was to convey moral values. "I want to raise the level of our culture," she said impassionedly. "What Turgun does—that's our history, and people should know that history. But someone else has to raise the level of present-day culture. If everyone were concerned with history and no one thought about the future, that would be terrible.

"I'm doing a concert program now devoted to the loneliness of women," Yulduz said as our conversation drew to a close. "I'm trying to develop the idea that women should lead their own lives. Our women have such difficult, often terrible lives. Last year, when I gave my concert series in Tashkent, I heard that there was a young woman who was waiting around the stage entrance trying to meet me. Someone told me that she'd waited for three days. I went out and talked to her. She was very shy, but she thrust a notebook in my hands and said that it contained her poetry. She wanted me to compose a song to one of her poems. She gave me her phone number and disappeared. I thanked her and took the book but didn't have time to look at it until a few days later. She was more than a good poet. The texts were about the hard conditions of her own life, and when I read them, I phoned up the number she'd left because I wanted to see her again. A young man answered, and he told me that she wasn't in this world anymore. She'd killed herself the day after she gave me the poems.

"In order to feel for these women, you have to lead their lives. You can't just live like a star. I do my own washing. Yesterday someone from the Ministry of Culture was here and he laughed when he saw me doing my wash. 'How can you allow yourself to do that?' he said. A lot of people don't understand that working with your hands freshens your mind. I've noticed that great artists tend to start from bad conditions."

The renovation and recycling of tradition in the music of Yulduz Usmanova, Munâjât Yulchieva, and a host of like-minded but less celebrated contemporaries seemed a natural phenomenon amid the bustle of Tashkent. For there, just as in the West, young, sophisticated musicians have approached "traditional" music from the aesthetic distance of modernists—as a resource that could be appropriated and transformed into contemporary music or, alternatively, "authentically" revived to provide a window on the past (the appropriation or recovery of tradition by modernities is, of course, an old pattern in Western music). But beyond Tashkent, Moscow's longtime beachhead in the campaign to reorganize cultural life in Central Asia, might there still be a preponderance of music that is not "traditional" in the modern sense, but simply traditional— unaffected by conscious efforts to reject, reform, or revive it? Ma'ruf Xâja and Arif Xatamov had performed that kind of music, and, in his own way, so had Turgun Alimatov. Were such musicians still active amid the remains of long-ago greatness that had become Transoxania's provincial cities—Bukhara, Samarkand, Khiva? In Central Asia, there is an old adage: "All roads lead to Bukhara." OM and I agreed: Bukhara was where we should begin our musical travels.

BUKHARA

Bukhârâ, Qubbat ul-Islam *(Bukhara, the cupola of Islam)*

—Traditional epithet

THE IMAGINAL CITY

Bukhara is no less a city of the imagination than it is a real place, and both have old roots. The city was already old when Narshaxi wrote his *History of Bukhara* in the middle of the tenth century. In the millennium since Narshaxi, Bukhara has seen its fortunes turn more than once—although, as V. V. Barthold, the doyen of Russian Central Asianists, wrote at the beginning of our own century, "the plan of the town, in spite of frequent and devastating nomad invasions, has scarcely changed in a thousand years."[1] Under the late emirs, cultural stagnation and commercial decline reduced Bukhara, but they did not diminish the imaginal city's appeal to the chroniclers who came by turn to marvel and to recoil at Bukhara's main attractions: its mosques, *madrasah*s and palaces, its illustrious merchant trade and fervid religion, and its despotism.

European, including Russian, literary accounts of Bukhara did not begin in earnest until the nineteenth century, when the competing political interests of Britain and Russia for control of Central Asia—Kipling's "Great Game"—drew the attention of diplomats, soldiers, colonial business magnates, and adventurers-without-portfolio to one of the Game's most notorious wild cards: the Emir of Bukhara (or "Ameer," as the title was Anglicized in many writings). As the absolute monarch of a large and strategically located buffer zone that separated Britain's colonial interests from Russia's, the emir played a pivotal role in determining the regional balance of power between the two empires. He ruled the Bukharan Emirate from a walled citadel called the *ark* in the center of Bukhara city, and it was to learn more about the emir or, as the Great Game

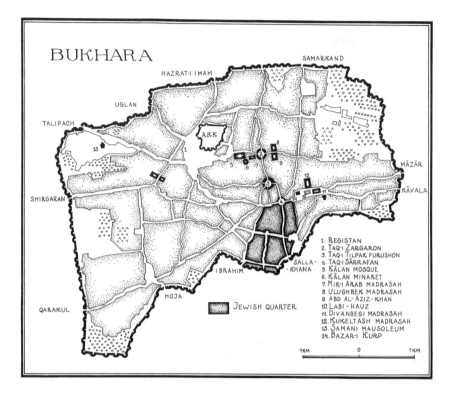

BUKHARA

HAZRAT-I IMAM

SAMARKAND

UGLAN

TALIPACH

ARK

MĀZĀR

KĀVALA

SHIRGARAN

SALLA-
KHANA
IBRAHIM

HOJA

QARAKUL

JEWISH QUARTER

1. REGISTAN
2. TAQ-I ZARGARON
3. TAQ-I TILPAK FURUSHON
4. TAQ-I SĀRRAFAN
5. KĀLAN MOSQUE
6. KĀLAN MINARET
7. MIR-I ARAB MADRASAH
8. ULUGHBEK MADRASAH
9. ABD AL-AZIZ-KHAN
10. LABI-HAUZ
11. DIVANBEGI MADRASAH
12. KUKELTASH MADRASAH
13. SAMANI MAUSOLEUM
14. BAZAR-I KURP

1KM   0   1KM

Bukhara

advanced, to conduct diplomacy with him that Russian and British emissaries
made their way to Bukhara's gates.

Between the middle of the nineteenth century and the first decade of the
twentieth, by which time the emirates had been absorbed into the Russian
Empire, dozens of books about Central Asia were published in Russia and
Britain, most of them composed in the form of travel narratives or expedition
reports. The focus of these narratives varied with the professional interests of
the writer, but they reveal a remarkable consistency of style and subject: a
dispassionate survey of geography and topography, administration and diplomatic relations, peoples and tribes, customs and occupations, all woven through
to a greater or lesser extent with personal reflection and value judgment on the
comportment and moral character of those whom the writer encountered, in
particular, rulers and their confidantes. The despotism of the emirs—whether
for its purely sensationalist punch, or out of the writers' sense of moral
indignation (or both)—comes in for fine-grained description in these narratives.

86

BUKHARA

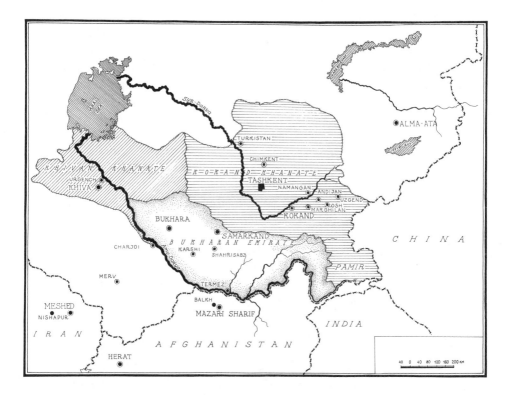

The Three Khanates of Transoxania around 1850

For example, few writers missed an opportunity to describe the pathetic demise, in 1842, of the British officer and diplomat *manqué* Charles Stoddart and his would-be rescuer, Captain Arthur Conolly. Here is an excerpt from the story of Stoddart and Conolly in the version of Demetrius Boulger, author of *England and Russia in Central Asia,* published in London in 1879.[2]

"Within three days of his arrival at Bokhara Colonel Stoddart found himself a prisoner. At first he was confined in a house, but after a short time spent there he was transferred to the Siah-tchah, or Black well"—more properly known as the *kana khâna* or, in Russian, *klopovnaya*—"bug house." Boulger now quotes from Ferrier's *History of the Afghans*: "'This horrible abode, which is in the centre of the town, is twenty-one feet in depth; and here the greatest malefactors are generally confined. The descent into it is made by means of a rope; and when Stoddart was let down he found there two thieves and a murderer, the latter having been incarcerated here for several years. With these criminals for his companions, the Colonel remained *two months in this loathsome and filthy hole,*

87

covered with vermin and surrounded by reptiles, in killing which they were constantly occupied [the italics are Boulger's]. Their food, such as it was, was lowered to them by the rope with which they had themselves descended, and much of their time was passed in smoking. When the furious caprice of [Emir] Nasrullah had been satisfied, and he thought he had humbled the pride of the Englishman and impressed him with the terror of his power, he gave an order to the chief of the police to remove him from the Siah-tchah in which he had been immured, and keep him a prisoner in his own house; but two days after this the public executioner came to Stoddart with an order to put him to death unless he consented to become a Mussulman. To this alternative, borne down by the dreadful sufferings he had endured, and the exhaustion of his mental and bodily powers, he gave a reluctant consent, repeating the Mahomedan confession of faith, after which he was taken to the public square, and circumcised in the presence of an immense crowd who had been attracted there by the novelty of the event. . . .'"

Boulger resumes the narrative: "War had in the meanwhile broken out between Khokand and Bokhara, and there were those in Bokhara who asserted that English counsel was at the root of this quarrel. The Ameer readily believed these stories, and was only biding his time to obtain a complete revenge.

"In order to obtain that, it was necessary to get the other British officer in Central Asia, Captain Conolly, who was residing at the Court of Khokand, into his power. He accordingly invited him to his Court, and Colonel Stoddart in a weak moment aided in the plot by innocently advising Conolly to come. . . . Before the month of November, 1841, closed, both officers were imprisoned. For more than six months they were kept in close confinement, and at last, having undergone torments indescribable, the most brutal treatment, and the most writhing contumely, the end came on the 24th of June, 1842. Stoddart was put to death like a sheep, in some ruins at the back of his prison, and in the presence of a few passers-by, who had been attracted to the spot by his cries and his invectives. Conolly was offered his life on the condition of his turning Mussulman; but, with that moral fortitude which is the highest courage, he refused. 'Stoddart and Yusuf (Conolly's Greek servant) turned Mahomedans, and you put them to death,' he said. 'Your proposal is a snare, for you will not spare me any more than you did them. I have no confidence in your promises; I will be no renegade. I die firm in my faith. Finish your work!' So died Arthur Conolly, as every Englishman should die, true to his country and himself, vindicating the real superiority of his race to the last by the calm resolution with which he could face death. . . ."

With lurid material like this to snare the reading public, perhaps it is no wonder that the travel narratives are all but silent about the commonplaces of expressive culture—about music and dance, ceremony and celebration, and the social contexts in which they occur. In *Turkistan,* Eugene Schuyler writes tersely of being entertained by dancing boys in Bukhara to the accompaniment of music, of "listening to two men playing on the *dutara,* accompanied by a tambourine, and singing Uzbek and Persian songs," and of hearing a band composed of "a large number of drums, trumpets, and clarionets" that accompanied the emir's entourage on a journey from Bukhara to Karshi.[3] A few more equally terse references to music are scattered through his two-volume work. But that is all. Other authors are no more forthcoming. Did these travelers not hear music in Central Asia? Did they never join a crowd gathered in a town square to listen to a *qalandar* (wandering dervish) chant a *na't* or *munâjât?* Did they never attend a *toy?* Did they feel that music was not important enough to write about, or that they were unqualified to describe its exotic sounds? (This would have been uncharacteristic, for the chroniclers were intrepid about describing a vast range of cultural minutiae about which they must have known very little.)

A half-century after the publication of Schuyler's *Turkistan,* with Soviet rule established in Central Asia and the erstwhile Bukharan Emirate folded into the republics of Uzbekistan and Tajikistan, a new kind of chronicler of Central Asian life had appeared: the Soviet ethnographer. The early Soviet ethnographers were not indigenous Central Asians; they were of European origin (Russian, Ukrainian, Jewish, etc.), most of them trained in Saint Petersburg in the classical tradition of Russian, which was to say, German-inspired, Oriental studies. They had no overt diplomatic or military mission to fulfill, but their expeditions, like those of their colonialist predecessors, were shadowed by larger political concerns: not the acquisition of empire—for Turkestan was firmly in Soviet hands—but the nourishing of empire, the deepening of knowledge about the demographics, customs, and beliefs of the newly Soviet peoples of Central Asia.

The 1920s were boom years for ethnography in Central Asia. The former lands of the Bukharan Emirate and the Khivan Khanate had been thrown open to Soviet citizens; the rear-guard attacks of the anti-Bolshevik *basmachi* had subsided, making travel relatively safe, and the Stalinist terror had yet to queer the conduct of disinterested scholarship. A pleiad of ethnographers—Andreev, Barthold, Peshchereva, Semenov, Snesarev, Sukhareva, Troitsky—fanned out through Transoxania and produced a prolific body of descriptive work that still forms the basis of ethnographic research on the region (this fieldwork did not cease at the end of the 1920s; Soviet ethnographers continued expeditionary work through the Stalin years, although much of that work was not published until the Khrushchev "thaw" of the 1960s). Among these ethnographers were the first fieldworkers trained specifically in musicology and folklore: Viktor Uspensky and Viktor Beliaev authored a study of Turkmen music (1927), E. E. Romanovskaya published a collection of Uzbek folk songs (1939) and Uzbek instrumental music (1948), and Uspensky also produced the first published transcription of the Bukharan *Shash maqâm* (1924). The Uspensky publication, however, is an oddity, and an explanation of the circumstances that led to its oddness serves as a preamble to the ideologically motivated musicological aberrations that followed and are still being produced by musical ethnographers in Central Asia—most of them now native scholars.

What is odd about the Uspensky publication is immediately apparent to anyone who knows the *Shash maqâm*. The *Shash maqâm* is a vocal repertory, and yet Uspensky's transcription included no texts. What happened to the texts? Was Uspensky not able to transcribe them, or did he have a particular reason to exclude them? Uspensky provided no clue in the publication itself, but an

A street in Bukhara's Jewish Quarter.

answer has recently been proposed by Alexander Djumaev, the current avatar of the Russian Orientalist tradition in Central Asian music historiography.[4] Searching through archives in Tashkent, Djumaev discovered a letter from Uspensky to his friend Viktor Beliaev in which Uspensky complained that Abdurauf Fitrat, the prominent Jadid who served as Minister of Cultural Enlightenment in the Bukharan People's Republic, had forbidden him to transcribe the texts of the *Shash maqâm*. Beliaev had been disturbed by the absence of texts in Uspensky's publication and had gone to Bukhara to search for them. There he discovered a manuscript copy of the very texts sung by the vocalist from whom Uspensky had notated the musical portion of the *Shash maqâm*. Almost all of the texts were in Tajik Persian, not Uzbek. Fitrat had evidently not wanted to sully a publication of "Uzbek" *Shash maqâm* with "Tajik" texts.[5]

Fitrat, despite his cosmopolitan Jadidist background, served an Uzbek government. As Minister of Cultural Enlightenment, he had overseen initial steps in the distillation of an Uzbek great tradition in the arts that promoted Uzbekness as a normative cultural value. In musical ethnography, Fitrat's censorship of Uspensky had marked the dawn of the Soviet period and introduced the so-called national question into musical scholarship. So much the worse for our knowledge of Central Asian music. The nineteenth-century chroniclers had mostly ignored it, and no sooner had their ethnographer successors come on the scene in the early part of the twentieth century than cultural commissars began to distort indigenous music; later they banished certain genres in the service of ideology.

Fitrat's Uzbekization of the *Shash maqâm* was bedeviled not only by the deep-rooted Uzbek-Tajik bilingualism of the texts but also by the fact that many of its greatest exponents were not, and had not been, Uzbeks or even Tajiks but Bukharan Jews. Persian-speaking Jewish communities seem to have existed in the larger oasis and riverine towns of Transoxania for over a millennium.[6] Documentation of the origins and early history of these communities is extremely sparse, but legends speak of the importation of skilled Jewish craftsmen from Iran by a succession of Central Asian rulers, beginning with Timur (1338–1405), and a Tashkent-based archaeologist has reported on the existence of a Jewish cemetery in Samarkand before Timur's time. Following the sixteenth-century rise of the Safavid monarchy in Iran and the ensuing cultural separation of Shi'ite Iran from Sunni Transoxania, Bukharan Jews became isolated from other Persian-speaking communities to the south and west and to a large extent assumed the cultural identity of their Transoxanian Muslim neighbors. Bukharan Jews have traditionally spoken Tajik as a first language, often in a slightly dialectical form that they call Bukhari, distinguishable to a native speaker by certain linguistic shibboleths. Many Bukharan Jews also speak Uzbek, and these days most of them also speak Russian. Within the Bukharan Emirate, particularly in Bukhara itself, Jews lived under a variety of social constraints. In Bukhara, for example, Jewish settlement under the emirs was limited to particular *mahalla*s (neighborhoods), which, as the Jewish population increased, became the most densely settled areas in a densely settled city. Jews were required to wear a distinctive sash to distinguish them from Muslims. They were forbidden to ride horses within the city, although they could ride donkeys, so as not to appear higher than a Muslim.[7] One non-Jewish resident of Bukhara told me that Jewish shopkeepers were required to make change to Muslim customers by dropping coins in a bowl of water from which the customer then retrieved them. Certain professions were forbidden for Jews, while others were dominated by them. Cloth dyers, jewelers, cobblers, tailors, barbers, money changers, and—most important here—entertainers at *toy*s were all typically Bukharan Jews.

Transoxania's Bukharan Jewish population has never been more than a tiny community compared to the Muslim population—in 1900, there were an estimated 20,000 Jews in the Bukharan Emirate and Russian Turkestan (with 4,000–5,000 living in the city of Bukhara itself), while the 1989 Soviet census recorded fewer than 40,000 "Central Asian" Jews in Uzbekistan and Tajikistan among some 20 million Muslims. This disparity of numbers makes the preeminence of Bukharan Jews as performers of *Shash maqâm* (as well as certain other genres, e.g., wedding music) all the more notable.[8]

Several Jewish family lineages dominated the performance of *Shash maqâm* and other kinds of classical, or "heavy," music in Transoxania from the late nineteenth century to the last quarter of the twentieth. Mullakand, Tâlmas, Babaxan—Russified as Mullakandov, Tolmasov, Babakhanov—were household names for the musical connoisseurs of Bukhara, Samarkand, and Shahrisabz (Tashkent's rise as the center of an academicized national culture came later). Other well-known musicians, including Ata Jalâl, credited with being the "founder" of the *Shash maqâm,* were *chala*s—Jews who converted under coercion to Islam but privately preserved elements of Jewish belief or practice. But despite the key role played by Bukharan Jews and *chala*s in the living transmission of Transoxania's art music tradition, they have been given scant attention in official accounts of Uzbekistan's national culture. Viktor Beliaev's authoritative 1962 survey, "History of the Musics of the Peoples of the USSR," which neatly correlates musical culture with then-extant Soviet political entities, makes no mention of Bukharan Jews in its survey of Central Asia.[9] During my year of study with Professor Karomatov at the Tashkent Conservatory in 1977–1978, he never mentioned Bukharan Jews in connection with the *Shash maqâm* or any other musical repertory. Other people discussed that connection in whispers.

These were the conditions in which OM and I worked when we first set out for Bukhara in the fall of 1990 to visit Ari Babakhanov and Tohfaxân Pinkhasova, both Bukharan Jews and both seminal figures in the transmission of Bukhara's musical traditions. By then, the Bukharan Jewish community in Transoxania had undergone considerable disintegration as a result of the emigration that had begun, slowly at first, in the 1970s. Through the 1980s, Bukharan Jewish emigration had continued apace, even as what was left of Jewish communities in Tashkent, Samarkand, and Bukhara came more into the open under the politics of glasnost. By the early 1990s, it had begun to seem that one could learn more about Bukharan Jewish culture in Tel Aviv or New York than in Bukhara and Samarkand. But as long as Ari and Tohfaxân remained in Central

Asia, OM and I pressed on with our fieldwork, making four visits to Bukhara between 1990 and 1993. By the end of 1993, Tohfaxân was in the United States and Ari had made plans to join other family members in Tel Aviv. Bukharan Jews were barely a ghost of a presence in Bukhara's music scene. The Uzbekization of "national" music that Fitrat covertly began in the 1920s had finally succeeded, by default.

A DRIVE TO BUKHARA

I first learned that I was going to buy a car in Central Asia late one autumn night in 1992 when I was awakened at home in New York by a phone call from Moscow. The caller was an American, a young man who had recently visited Tashkent and, at my suggestion, had looked up OM. The young man apologized for the late hour but said he had an urgent message. OM needed to speak with me right away, and would I please put through a call to Tashkent? Certain that someone we knew had died or been in an accident, I dialed OM's number.

At the other end of the phone line, OM was exuberant. "I have a great opportunity here," he told me. "Ilyas Malayev is emigrating to New York next week and he's willing to sell me his Volga for $3,000. That's a great price for a used Volga. The car will be really useful for our fieldwork. Ilyas says it's in perfect condition. What do you think? Can you pay Ilyas $3,000 when he arrives in New York?"

I was speechless. As close as I felt to OM, the tacit barter exchange that was a constant undercurrent of our work together—essentially, OM's local knowledge and contacts in return for the matériel, recording-related income, and travel opportunities that I provided him—had been a subject that we never discussed. For one of us to acknowledge it openly would have been to break a shared feeling of taboo. Neither of us had ever asked the other, even obliquely, "Can you do X for me in return for Y?"

I had in fact mentioned, in an official letter of invitation to OM that was a routine part of the visa application he was assembling to visit me in the United States, that I would pay $1,000 a month to cover living expenses during the three-month duration of his visit. OM's idea was that I would simply advance this sum of money to Ilyas for the car. He figured that he could live for three months in the States for pretty near nothing, earning a little to cover expenses by giving lectures.

I explained to OM the American principle of never buying a used car from a friend, protested that $3,000 seemed like a princely sum for a 1986 Volga, and insisted that at the very least, one couldn't buy a used car without having a mechanic inspect it. I suggested that he postpone thinking about cars until he returned to Tashkent from his visit to the United States. After all, he didn't yet have a driver's license. He could wait and see how much money he had at the end of his trip, then seek the advice of a friend who knew cars and, at his leisure, locate a good deal. There would still be time to go car shopping before our proposed journey around Transoxania.

OM reluctantly agreed, but he could barely hide his disappointment. We spoke several more times on the telephone before OM arrived in the United States, and the car was never mentioned again. I assumed he had come around to my view and put the matter to rest until his return. When OM arrived in the United States, I gave him the first $1,000 of the sum I had promised. "Don't give it to me," he said. "Send it to Ilyas. He left the Volga for us in his garage in Tashkent. I told him I'd pay him when I arrived here."

It was that Volga that was parked in the service driveway alongside OM's apartment building one morning in early May 1993 as we prepared our equipment and personal effects for the drive to Bukhara. Dadanazar, the driver whom OM had engaged for the trip (who normally worked for Rahmat, the well-to-do musician who had visited us with his patron, Xudâbergan), was wiping down the pale green exterior of the car with a greasy rag. But the car needed more than a cleaning. The windshield bore a large crack from a stone thrown up on the road, the tires lacked hubcaps, the muffler sounded as if it was falling off, and the trunk and the passenger-side rear door were jammed shut. OM was sanguine about the problems. "Everything will be fine," he said confidently. Following local custom, we sat for a moment on a nearby bench, OM said a perfunctory prayer, and then we were off. We had no road map. OM said it didn't matter. No one used maps in Uzbekistan. There were few main roads, and most professional drivers knew them. If there was a question, one could always flag down another driver.

It took a good half an hour to drive from OM's building in the center of Tashkent to the southwestern edge of the city, where the road to Samarkand and Bukhara emerged from tree-lined avenues and clumps of four-story apartment blocks into open, level countryside. Tashkent, however, didn't simply stop at the edge of the open road. Rather, it followed that road, enveloping the traveler in a cocoon of Uzbekified modernity. Sheep grazed in flower-covered fields under the spindly stalks of enormous radio antennas; a cow walked peacefully down the median strip of the four-lane divided highway past a billboard display of the Uzbek president Islam Karimov next to one of his slogans: "Independence is the historical destiny of our people." An apple orchard stretched alongside the highway beneath a dense grid of electrical lines and high-tension wires. Once there had been many mulberry trees and vineyards, but the mulberry trees had been cut down to make more room for cotton, and the vineyards had been destroyed during Gorbachev's antialcoholism campaign of the mid-1980s.

This countryside had once been "hungry steppe," but Lenin had said that the hungry steppe had to be conquered. Water was drained away from the Syr Darya and brought to new collective farms to irrigate thirsty cotton plants. The plants had flourished, and the region had become known as the region of "white gold." OM recalled being sent there as a student to pick cotton. "They didn't always take people from the Conservatory, but when there was a total mobilization, they took everyone. We would stay for twenty days, sometimes longer; sometimes for a month or two. I remember once we stayed almost until New Year's. It was in the 1970s. If someone didn't go to the cotton harvest with enthusiasm, he was considered a bad student or teacher."

The consequences of Uzbekistan's victory over the hungry steppe had more recently become a source of national scandal. As central planners had set ever-higher goals for cotton harvests and more land was turned over to cotton growing, overirrigation had severely lowered the volume of water in the Syr Darya and Amu Darya as they flowed toward the Aral Sea. The desiccation of the Aral Sea and the rivers that nourished it, combined with overuse of chemical fertilizers on the cotton plantations, had had catastrophic ecological and epidemiological consequences. Meanwhile, Uzbek collective farm officials and party leaders, desperate to meet the cotton quotas handed down from Moscow, conspired to falsify data about cotton yields and then stashed away money paid out for the nonexistent cotton. The so-called Uzbek Affair (also known as the Cotton Affair) exploded in the mid-1980s. A special team of prosecutors sent from Moscow implicated dozens of officials, right up to Sharaf Rashidov, the former First Secretary of the Uzbek Communist party. Rashidov was by then lying in his grave, but his body was exhumed from his honored place of rest in Tashkent's Lenin Square and moved to a less-exalted site. Many officials went to prison.

Following the demise of the Soviet Union, Uzbekistan had taken control of its own cotton production. The quotas had been lowered to less ecologically destructive levels, and the water level of the Syr Darya had started to rise again. As we crossed the river southwest of Tashkent, boys sniggled for eels along the muddy banks. Just beyond the bridge, a tourist bus had parked on the side of the road and a group of men was trying to stuff a huge, bloody fish into the baggage compartment.

Beyond the Syr Darya, cultivated fields gradually gave way to open steppe. As befits a language that evolved among nomads, Uzbek has different words to describe the fine gradations of terrain that English lumps together as steppe and desert. For example, there is *qir*—hilly steppe with enough vegetation to make it suitable for goat or sheep grazing; there is *chol*—thirsty earth with only the sparsest of vegetation; and there is *qum*—literally "sand," or desert. Each comes in its own distinctive shades of green, brown, or ochre.

Closer to Samarkand, the land began to heave into rolling *qir*. "Rashidov wanted to build an Olympic sports complex here," said OM as the road passed over the top of a scenic rise. "In the fall and spring, the climate is like

Switzerland. He was going to build a big highway from Tashkent. They had started work on it, and then he died." We drove through a narrow pass in the hills that is called Timur's Gate. It was there that the outermost defenses of Timur's Samarkand had guarded the approach to the city from the east. Rather than drive through the center of Samarkand, we opted for a circumferential route that took us north of the city. In the outskirts of Samarkand, the navigation became tricky, and Dadanazar headed the wrong way around a traffic circle. A policeman waved us over. Dadanazar stepped out of the car and shook hands with the policeman—an obligatory opening move in the Uzbek ritual of being stopped for a traffic violation. OM also got out and the policeman immediately recognized him from his frequent television appearances as an emcee for programs about traditional music and musicians. The policeman shook OM's hand, thanked him profusely for the wonderful music he featured on his show, and sent us on our way toward Bukhara.

West of Samarkand, the land leveled out again and became greener. The sun was falling low in a hazy sky as we transected vast fields of cotton, and OM and I were deep in a discussion about the Turkmen poet Maxtum Quli when Dadanazar pulled the car over. "I've been smelling an odd smell for a while," he said. "We'd better make sure it's not something to do with the car." I had also smelled the odd smell but had dreamily attributed it to air pollution or effluent from some unseen factory. As soon as we opened the doors of the car, however, we saw the source of the smell: the car's right rear tire was smoking badly. Dadanazar splashed the tire with water from a jug in the trunk to cool it down, then removed the tire. The brake had apparently locked, causing the ball bearings in the wheel base to spring free of their casing, and the resulting friction had come close to setting us on fire. Driving any farther was out of the question. We would have to tow the car to the nearest town and find a garage with replacement parts.

"It's *taqdir*—the will of God," said Dadanazar, a recently born-again Muslim. "You must learn to accept what God gives."

Taqdir or no, OM appeared unperturbed. "Everything will be okay. We'll flag down a car and find a mechanic," he said. "The good thing about a Volga is that you can fix anything that goes wrong with just a hammer and a wrench." OM waved down the first car that approached us, and the driver stopped. Two middle-aged men dressed in party clothes got out and looked at the disabled wheel and shook their heads. They had no mechanical skills. But they knew a man in the town five kilometers up the road who was handy with tractors and might be able to help. Though they were on their way to a *toy,* they offered to drive OM into town and search for the tractor repairman. After about forty-five minutes, they returned. The mechanic had gone to visit a relative in an outlying village and wouldn't return until the next day. There was nothing more to be done that evening. We thanked the two men, and they drove off to their *toy.* We had no food or potable water and hadn't eaten all day in anticipation of a large meal when we arrived in Bukhara. But at ten o'clock in the evening, we climbed into the car and prepared to spend the night slouched in our seats.

Two hours later, headlights illuminated the rear of the car at close range. The two men had returned. We were alone on an empty road in the middle of a sea of cotton. Having seen that I was a foreigner, were they going to rob us? We all piled out of the Volga. The men had felt bad about our plan to spend the night in the car and had left the *toy* early with the idea of taking us home with them for the night. We quickly agreed and loaded ourselves and our things into the back seat of their Zhiguli. In fifteen minutes' time, we had been installed in the *mehmânxâna* of a comfortable house, and our host, Mahmudjân, had brought tea, *nân,* and sliced tomatoes. The next morning, Mahmudjân's sons served us breakfast while our host and his companion from the night before (a neighbor, it turned out) drove off to arrange for the repair of our car. Within a few hours, we were back on the road.

"Now you've seen an example of the spirituality that's deeply rooted in this culture," said OM when we were under way again. "Where does that concern for hospitality come from? The care for travelers, the love of poetry? It's true that it's disappearing in the cities, but in the countryside it's still very strong. Millions of enlightened people worked for a thousand years to create this culture. And it's important to remember that Islam in Central Asia was built on older spiritual traditions: Zoroastrianism, Buddhism, Manichaeanism, Nestorian Christianity. Islam couldn't just erase them; on the contrary, it absorbed their spirituality. That's why Central Asians are somewhat skeptical now about Turkey and the Arab countries [and their self-interested offers of economic aid to the Central Asian republics]. Spiritually, they're not any more advanced. What are we going to learn from them? How to make money? Uzbeks are much more subtle than Arabs. They have a much older culture."

OM was fond of gently pointing out to me those subtleties when I ignored them. For example, as we had sat with Mahmudjân, the good Samaritan, consuming the midnight snack that he had prepared for us, I had inadvertently overturned the piece of *nân* Mahmudjân had given me so that the flat white bottom faced up. I had, in fact, noticed the overturned bread, and the thought had passed through my mind that Uzbeks always place their bread topside up on the table as a symbol of respect for the food they eat. But I had been too tired to reach out and turn the piece of bread over and had let it go. Without drawing attention to himself, OM had then reached across the table and set the bread right. This gratuitous gesture was a tiny expression of what OM called Central Asia's tradition of spirituality. And though he never went to a mosque and didn't consider himself religious, OM drew great pride from the observance of customs, even tiny details such as the proper handling of bread, that had defied the Communists' effort to dismantle them.

97

THE HUNDRED THOUSAND FOOLS OF GOD

A BUKHARAN JEWISH MUSICAL DYNASTY

The outskirts of Bukhara aren't what one might expect of the city known as "the Cupola of Islam." Along the busy divided highway that runs the final ten miles into town from the south are factories and industrial complexes, chemical storage tanks and railroad yards. The skyline is dotted with cranes perched atop half-finished buildings. Across the road from the industrial flotsam are the suburban enclaves of Bukhara's *nouveaux riches:* imposing brick houses enclosed in brick-walled yards plunked down on the flat, hot land (once again, architectural influences from the Mexican soap opera *The Rich Also Cry).* Closer to the center are bleak apartment blocks and unkempt avenues that slice through fragments of the old town still waiting to be transformed into more apartment blocks.

OM had arranged for us to stay in Kagan, also known as Russian Bukhara or New Bukhara. Kagan is about eight miles south of Bukhara, and it was there that the Russian-built railroad had terminated and that the tsar's political agent had resided in the later years of the Bukharan Emirate. The old chancellory building had been turned into a sports club, and young men in blue jogging suits lifted weights in a bare, two-story room that once must have been an elegant reception hall.

Our host in Kagan was Rosa, the sister of OM's closest friend from high school days in Bukhara. She was a doctor in a hospital for skin and venereal diseases, divorced, with a fourteen-year-old son. The house was large: eight rooms, including a long solarium that spanned the entire back side of the dwelling and opened onto the walled garden. Rosa cooked on a two-burner stove in an outbuilding where there was also a sink with a cold-water spigot and a few pots and pans. In the rear of the outbuilding, a homemade plumbing system conducted cold water from the municipal water pipes and hot water from a gas-heated tank to a tub with a showerhead. The outhouse was in the far corner of the garden.

Bukhara rises early. At 7:00 A.M., the small bazaar in the old Jewish quarter was a warren of activity. At a table set up next to a truck outside the gate, frozen blocks of meat were being hacked up with an ax—the local understanding of a "cut" of meat—and sold to an eager crowd of buyers. Inside the gate, a row of stocky, scarf-covered women in shabby overcoats hawked homemade tandir-baked *nân* pulled from steaming cloth sacks.

Ari Babakhanov didn't live in the old Jewish quarter. He lived in one of the bleak apartment blocks that we had passed on our way into Bukhara, but he was embarrassed to invite visitors there, especially a foreigner. He had asked us to meet him at his old family house, near the bazaar, where his brothers Boris and

98

Yuri lived. Boris and Yuri looked to be in their early fifties, but it was only a guess. Boris was tall and gaunt, with disheveled graying hair that begged for a trim. He was dressed in a rumpled and noticeably filthy blue warm-up suit. Boris had been twice married and divorced. Yuri had long ago been divorced, and his dark, deeply lined face exuded a kind of dour placidity. I never saw either brother smile, but both turned out to be gracious hosts.

For three generations, the Babakhanov family had played a central role in the musical life of Bukhara. Levi Babakhanov (1874–1926) is still revered as one of the greatest of Bukharan singers. Known as Leviche (pronounced LeviCHE), he had served as a personal musician to Emir Seyed Abdullahad Bahadur Khan, known as Ahad Khan (ruled 1885–1910), and later to Alim Khan (ruled 1910–1920), the last emir of Bukhara. Leviche's sons, Moshe (1909–1983), Yakutel (born 1917), and Shalom (born 1920), had been absorbed into the reorganized musical life that emerged in postrevolutionary Uzbekistan. Moshe had performed in the radio station ensemble, taught stringed instruments and vocal music in Bukhara's School of Oriental Music, and played in the musical theater.

"Until 1932, there had been a Jewish theater in Bukhara," Boris Babakhanov told us. "Tajiks and Uzbeks also worked there, but for some reason, they called it the Bukharan Jewish Native Theater. They had the most powerful actors and musicians. Once they went on tour to Moscow, and everywhere there were placards. There were a lot of Jews in Moscow, and the tickets were sold out ten days in advance. The first evening, they performed a program with classical songs from the *Shash maqâm*. Russian Jews had bought all the tickets, and they looked at these people and said, 'These aren't Jews. What kind of theater is this, anyway?' Half of the people got up and left and asked for their money back. It got all the way to Kaganovich. It got all the way to Stalin, that some kind of Asian people had come in place of Jews and performed things like *Nasrullâi* and *Moghulcha-i Buzruk*. They were forced to return the money they'd been paid and go back to Bukhara.

"There was a famous man among us back then, Avrâm Saidov. He was in the Central Committee. He was asked to answer Stalin's and Kaganovich's question, 'Who are these Bukharan Jews?' And Saidov had answered, 'Their language is Tajik, and their music is ours—*maqâm*.' And Saidov had been asked, 'Can they be assimilated?' 'Yes,' Saidov had answered. 'Let twenty years go by and we promise you that all the Bukharan Jews will become Muslims—Uzbeks and Tajiks.' After that, the Bukharan Jewish Theater was broken up, the actors were sent away, and they created an Uzbek Musical Drama Theater in Bukhara." Later Moshe returned to Bukhara, where his three sons, Boris, Yuri, and Ari, became teachers in the music high school. But it was Ari Babakhanov who was regarded as the real heir to the family's musical legacy.

Ari arrived at Boris and Yuri's house soon after OM and I. He was tall, pencil thin, and balding, a black *doppi* planted firmly over his pate. Attired in a dark suit and tie, he displayed a sartorial style that was at the opposite extreme from Boris's warm-up suit dowdiness. He spoke in bursts of hoarse recitative—the result of a long-ago injury to his vocal cords caused by jealous rival singers, or so the story went. The three Babakhanov brothers, OM, and I sat down to a breakfast laid out on the big wooden table in the *mehmânxâna*. Boris poured brimming tea bowls of homemade vodka and passed them around the table. "Screw this place," he said. "Seventy years of communism and look at what we have. Look at how we live. How can you blame people for leaving? It's a wonder that everyone doesn't leave. Let's drink to *Eretz Yisrael*—the Land of Israel." We raised the tea bowls and emptied them with a long gulp, grimacing and forcibly exhaling from the sour taste of the vodka. Each man grabbed for his preferred antidote: a chunk of cucumber, a pickled tomato, a morsel of cured fish, a piece of *nân*—anything to make the vodka go down with a little less burn. "*Eretz Yisrael* always seems a little closer after a good drink," said Boris, wiping his mouth with his sleeve.

I started to ask the Babakhanovs about Bukharan music, but they showed scant interest in my questions. Their minds were not on our visit. "Why do you want to talk to us?" Boris asked dismissively. "We don't know anything." In a week, their sister was to leave for Israel. When would they follow? That was the question that animated the Babakhanovs that morning.

I wanted to learn more about Leviche Babakhanov and about what precisely was meant when it was said that he had been "in the service" of the emir. If prerevolutionary Bukhara had been the forbiddingly ascetic and orthodox place that so many accounts claim it to have been, what role had there been for music and musicians? What had it meant to be a "professional" musician in Bukhara?

Leviche, we were told, had been a cobbler by vocation; his father had been a cloth dyer (two of the professions that were open to Jews in Bukhara's strictly regulated system of guilds).[10] Leviche had also worked on the side as a caterer who prepared *palav* for ceremonial events. At the same time, he was a talented singer and was often asked to perform at the *toy*s for which he catered food. As Leviche's reputation grew, he became more in demand for his music than for his food. Emir Ahad Khan heard about his vocal talent and summoned him to the *ark* to perform. Later the emir appointed him a *râtifaxâr*—the closest Bukhara had to a court musician (*râtifa* or *râtiba*: Persian "assistance," "pension," "stipend"; *xâr* from *xârdan*: "to eat," i.e., one who eats from his *râtifa*).[11] The *râtifa* was not necessarily money; often it was food or gifts, and it was assumed that the *râtifaxâr* maintained another source of income. As a *râtifaxâr*, Leviche lived with his family in the Jewish quarter of the city (he had had twenty-four children, all but five of whom had died) but was allowed to perform only for the emir and his circle, or elsewhere, only with the emir's permission.

"The emir took the best singers into his own service," said Ari. "He had both Jewish and Muslim musicians. There was good feeling and mutual respect between them. The emir often called for my grandfather to sing for him. Sometimes there would be small gatherings—just the emir and some of his friends and family. And sometimes there would be big concerts in the stone courtyard of the *ark* for guests of state. There would be four singers here, four singers there, another four over there. They would all sing the same melody, but with different words, and in different melodic variants. It was a kind of competition. The songs they sang were classical songs. The texts of these songs—they're very elegant. The poetry is from our best classical poets: Nawâ'i, Jami, Mashrab, Bedil, Hafiz. Some of the texts were in Tajik [i.e., Persian], some were in Uzbek [i.e., Chagatay]. It didn't make any difference. Everyone knew both languages. For big gatherings, the singers used megaphones to amplify their voices. At the *awj* [the melodic apogee], the voices were so powerful they could shatter glass."

Leviche's fame as a musician spread beyond Bukhara, and in 1909, representatives of one of the new gramophone companies, the Recording Cupid (*Pishushchii Amur*), based in Riga, Latvia, came to Bukhara bearing a letter of authorization from the Russian tsar and approached Leviche with a request to record his voice for a commercial cylinder. The company's plunge into Bukharan music was part of a widespread effort throughout Russia and its colonial territories to build demand for gramophones by selling recordings of local musical luminaries in local markets.

There are several versions of what happened next. Boris Babakhanov told us that when Leviche was approached by the recording engineers, he explained his special relationship with his employer, the emir, and told the men to request an audience with the emir and ask his permission to do the recording. In Boris's version, the emir diplomatically consented but was counting on Leviche not to "give his voice," as Boris put it (in fact, the emir had no choice but to permit the recording since the project had been approved by the tsar and by 1909 the Bukharan Emirate was effectively a Russian protectorate and the emir a vassal of the tsar). Boris said the emir told his grandfather, "If they record you, then anyone will be able to hear you and you will be lower than everything; your music won't have any weight." But the record company representatives insisted, and Leviche finally agreed. Boris vehemently denied other versions of the story that circulate to this day: "Those stories you hear—that the emir told my grandfather that he'd have his head cut off if he recorded—they're not true. The emir was a diplomat. He said, 'Let them record.' It was Soviet politics that tried to pit the emir against Leviche."[12]

Not long after the recording appeared, Leviche left the emir's service and moved to Samarkand. His departure was rumored to have been due to the emir's displeasure with his transformation from court musician to mass media personality. But the Babakhanovs denied this rumor also. "The emir never asked my grandfather to leave," said Boris. Later, after the death of Ahad Khan, Leviche returned to Bukhara and resumed his service in the court of Alim Khan. But in 1920, Alim Khan was forced to flee across the border to Afghanistan to escape a Bolshevik firing squad, and Leviche was out of a job. Moreover, his fealty to the former emir put him in an uncomfortable position with the new leadership. In 1923, Leviche again left Bukhara for Samarkand. Boris said, "After the Revolution, everyone knew he'd been a singer for the emir. Once the police beat him after a performance. Fitrat [the Bukharan Minister of Culture] wouldn't allow him to claim any fame for his music because he was a Jew. And he repented a lot for recording that record. He died at age fifty-two, suddenly, mysteriously. He had been perfectly healthy three days earlier. Then he suddenly got sick and died, sitting in his chair. He didn't even lie in bed. They said he died from 'Siberian ulcers' that became gangrenous. But I think he was poisoned by the 'organs' [Boris meant the security apparatus—the NKVD, the precursor of the KBG] in Samarkand who didn't want a musician going around singing about God. He sang the emir's poetry."

Leviche and his fellow performers of "heavy" songs drawn largely from the *Shash maqâm* represented the high road of artistic life in the court of Ahad Khan and Alim Khan. But there were other performers, other publics, other repertories in Bukhara. For example, popular singers provided entertainment to male company at *toy*s, working sometimes with groups of dancing boys (*bacha*s). Both singers and dancing boys belonged to a well-organized performers' guild (*ghalibxâna*).[13] *Mehtar*s played the *surnai,* a loud oboe, at weddings and civic events.[14] *Qalandar*s gathered street crowds to perform didactic spiritual songs for alms, and *maddâh*s sang Sufi-inspired verse, recited moralistic stories, and chanted *hadith*s and excerpts from the Qur'an.[15] Women had their own performers: dancer-singers called *sâzanda* entertained female guests at *toy*s, while a *guyanda* lamented the dead at funerary rites.

These performers wouldn't all have been grouped under the category "musician"—a word that doesn't have a precise equivalent in pre-Soviet Uzbek or Tajik; rather, each performer maintained a distinct nominal identity linked with a particular performance style and repertory. The various styles, repertories, and types of performers, however, were not correlated with distinctions of class, taste, or ethnicity, as is often the case in contemporary societies.[16] On the contrary, gentry, artisans, and laborers shared a largely common and consistent aesthetics and metaphysics of music that were themselves part of a broader Bukharan cultural tradition.

The metaphysics had been summed up in Turgun Alimatov's aphorism about the purpose of music: "Now for God and the Prophet, now for festivity and dancing"—the idea that humankind yearns for both a music of the spirit and a music of the flesh. Common aesthetic ideals were evident in the duplication of musical styles and repertories at all levels of Bukharan society. Differences of venue—for example, the *ark* of the emir as opposed to the courtyard of a modest

Bukharan house—would have been reflected in the level of virtuosity or sensibility of a musician, not in differences in what was performed. The poems that Leviche sang to the emir and his circle were the same poems sung by a journeyman singer at any Bukharan *toy*. The *surnai* melodies played by the emir's personal *mehtar* were the same as those one would have heard performed in the wedding processions that crowded through the narrow alleys of Bukhara's poorest quarters. OM had said once that it was this very absence of strict divisions between the religious and secular sides of life, the mixing of religion and traditional consciousness, that made it impossible for the Communists to wipe out Central Asian Islam simply by closing mosques.

The unitary musical culture of Bukhara permeated the ritual and ceremonial lives not only of Muslims but also of Jews. Like Muslims, Bukharan Jews held *toy*s to mark life-cycle events such as marriage, bar mitzvah, and circumcision, and these *toy*s featured the same entertainers and musical repertories as did Muslim *toy*s. Outside the *toy,* Bukharan Jewish ceremonial and ritual music has shown different degrees of appropriation of local vernacular musical styles. Most removed from the local vernacular is the cantillation of the Torah, which is strictly regulated by the presence of *ta'amim*—written markings that are a guide to the grouping and accentuation of words and the contour of melody.[17] Well-known prayers that are musically set to fixed pieces tend to be closer to a Central Asian melodic style. For example, OM and I recorded two versions of the sabbath prayer *Dror Yikrah* sung as *contra facta* to the melodies of two songs from the *Shash maqâm* (*Saqiname-i Iraq* and *Navruz-i Saba*). In other cases, Jews have appropriated both the melody and the text of Muslim spiritual songs or chants, changing nothing except the text's imagined symbolic references. I recorded one such song—*Ghairi Xudâ Yar Nadâram* (We have no friend but God)—from a Bukharan Jewish musician now living in Queens, New York.[18] *Ghairi Xudâ Yar Nadâram* represents a simplified folk version of a widely known *ghazal* from the *Divan-e Shams* of Mevlânâ Jalâlâddin Rumî, the thirteenth-century Sufi sheikh and sublime poet who inspired the Mevlevi, or whirling dervishes.[19] The musician who sang the song to me, Josif Abramov, ascribed the source of the text to the Torah and perceived it as Jewish spiritual poetry.

> In the two worlds, we have no friend but God
> We have no occupation except remembering God
> We're a tall, thin branch in this little corner of the world
> We have nothing to do with the good and the bad of others
> We're a modest part of this little corner of the world
> Even if someone casts stones at us, we don't pay attention

Another kind of appropriation involved whole genres, for example, the funerary chants known as *haqqâni* (from Arabic: *haqq:* "absolute truth," understood as the Absolute, or God). The purpose of *haqqâni* is to facilitate inner purification: a renunciation of the physical world and an immersion in the inner world. In both its musical style and its texts, *haqqâni* exemplifies the strong influence of Sufi ideals, and among Muslims, *haqqâni* were indeed performed in the Bukharan *xânagâhs*—dervish meeting places. But both Muslim and Jewish women perform *haqqâni* in the home of a deceased while the body is being washed and prepared for removal to the cemetery.

The idea of a unitary Central Asian expressive and spiritual culture that bound together lord and laborer, Muslim and Jew, was anathema during the Soviet era. Soviet ethnographers—whatever their personal beliefs—lashed out at the tyranny of the emir and the feudal yoke that held Bukhara's populace hostage to reactionary Islamic law and custom. "Religion in any form and in any manifestation interferes with the spiritual development of society," stated the author of a book on Sufism published in 1981.[20] It was in spite of Islam and its institutions, the ethnographers wrote, that Bukhara had managed to keep its cultural traditions alive.[21] Music had been an example of such a tradition—repressed or distorted by the emir and his circle, but zealously preserved in a purer form among "the people."

When I first visited Tashkent, I read the works of the Soviet musical ethnographers and musicologists and took for ideological posturing their swipes at Central Asia's exploitative feudal society, their insistence that the emirs had not cultivated music but repressed it, and their assurances that the true roots of the *Shash maqâm* were popular rather than elitist. Surely the *Shash maqâm*, the Central Asian incarnation of the sprawling Middle Eastern *maqâm* tradition, had served the role of court music, as had other offshoots of the *maqâm* tradition in Ottoman Turkey and in Safavid and Qajar Iran. Nourished by the patronage of music-loving monarchs (I imagined), the *Shash maqâm* had attained its highest development within a circle of professional musicians attached to the Bukharan court. But from what OM and I learned in our discussions with the Babakhanovs and with others in Bukhara who had spoken with people who were alive at the end of the nineteenth century (or who had spoken to people who had spoken to people who were alive at the end of the nineteenth century), the origins and evolution of Bukharan "court music" seemed much the way the Soviet ethnographers had described. Musical and social evidence indeed support the view that until the reign of Emir Muzaffar (1861–1885), Bukhara did not have an autonomous court music establishment and that art song was an integral part of what I have called Bukhara's unitary musical culture.

When the lengthy and complex *Shash maqâm* suites are reduced to their constituent items, these items are essentially a series of urban songs with texts by local poets, some current in the nineteenth century and some historical figures. The great tradition of the *Shash maqâm* seems to have been assembled relatively rapidly from the content of little traditions (probably in the first half of the eighteenth century on the basis of the first appearance of the term *Shash maqâm* in collections of poetic texts called *bayaz*).[22] OM suggested that the appearance of court musicians under Emir Muzaffar might have been linked to the increasing need for entertainment at social events connected to the presence of Russian diplomats and merchants and that the strictly orthodox Manghit emirs who preceded Muzaffar had, for religious reasons, simply not employed musicians.

We heard stories in Bukhara that under certain emirs, singing—that is, the singing of art song—had been forbidden. The *Shash maqâm* had been nourished not so much in the court as outside it, often in secret. People who wanted to arrange musical performances closed their windows, covered them with rugs, and put large water-filled pitchers and bowls around the walls of a room to muffle the sound of music so that it would not be heard on the street. Among Muslims, musical amateurs who sang the *Shash maqâm* (or, as it is said in Uzbek, "read" the *Shash maqâm*) were widespread, and had a different social status and image than the Bukharan Jewish singers who served the emir, and whose profession, for a Muslim, had questionable moral status, and certainly not high social status. "Muslims didn't do music as a profession; they didn't do it for money. They did it for their soul, to show their talent," one mullah told us. "My wife's grandfather," this same mullah said, "knew the *Shash maqâm* by memory. He had a circle of friends who sang the *Shash maqâm* and corrected one another."

Despite decades of unrelenting Soviet condemnation of the "feudal yoke" of Islam in Central Asia, there was nostalgia in Bukhara for the time when it was a Muslim city. The Babakhanovs, even though they were Jews, shared that nostalgia. Unlike the ethnographers, they regarded Bukhara's cultural achievement and the preservation of its musical traditions as having been linked to, not obstructed by, the patronage of the emir (they were speaking particularly of Ahad Khan and Alim Khan, the patrons of their grandfather). "The emir liked Jews," said Boris. "Jews lived well under the emir." Strolling through Bukhara's Jewish quarter with Boris while he proudly pointed out houses of near-palatial dimensions that had once belonged to Jewish merchants, I had to agree that despite coerced conversions and institutionalized discrimination directed not only at Jews but at all non-Muslims, at least some Jews had lived well under the emir. The Babakhanovs were willing to forgive the emir his seamier side—his dancing boys and his harem; there was even a kind of awe of his reputed sexual prowess: "The emir took special potions to increase his sexual stamina," Boris told us. "They'd arrange cockfights, and the cock that emerged victorious after a number of fights would be killed, hung up to dry, and then ground into fine powder, which the emir ate. A similar powder was made from dried sparrows. A legend that's popular in Bukhara has it that the emir once spat, and a man licked up his spit and had an erection for three days." Boris's eyes gleamed.

Ari was equally offended when people put down the emir. "He [Alim Khan] was a very good man," Ari said. "He was an educated man. He wrote poetry and played the *dutar*."[23]

I asked Ari, "What about the bug pit?"

Boris leapt into the discussion with a sardonic laugh. "People are always talking about that bug pit," he said. "From the whole, enormous Bukharan Emirate, there might have been two or three people in there, and a few more in the *zindân* [prison]. It was tiny. And compare that with how many prisons the Soviets built, and how many people they sent to them. There were millions."

THE CUPOLA OF ISLAM REDUX

Nostalgia for the old Bukhara is evident in the way its residents have begun trying to reimagine the city in the post-Soviet era. It is one of those places whose future—if it has one—seems to hinge on reviving its past. After years of resembling a Soviet city, the center of Bukhara has begun to look more and more like the Muslim East: Gypsy children beg on the streets, shopkeepers try to lure you to their stalls to view their mass-produced copper trays and pitchers, and the newly burnished aqua domes of the mosques and *madrasah*s are refulgent in the midday sun. A new bazaar is under construction next to the *ark,* where rows of small shops form a brick periphery around a common central vending area. Women and girls cover their heads with white shawls, and the distorted nasal twang of amplified muezzins ripples through the old city at prayer time.

One of the active forces in Bukhara's search for its past is the Naqshbandi mystical order, named after Bahâ'uddin Naqshband, the patron saint of Bukhara, who died there in 1389. The Naqshbandiya has long played a central role not only in the religious life of Central Asia but also in its politics and culture. The greatest Naqshbandi sheikh, Khwâja Ahrâr (1404–1490), cultivated a relationship with the ruling classes with the intention of serving the world through the exercise of political power. In Transoxania, this relationship continued through the Shaybanid, Ashtarkhanid, and Manghit dynasties, right down to the last Bukharan emirs, Ahad Khan and Alim Khan, who were said to be disciples of a Naqshbandi *ishân*. Even in Communist times, the mufti of Tashkent, who served as the figurehead of official Islam in Central Asia, was a Naqshbandi.[24] In the nineteenth century, the Naqshbandiya had played an active role in resisting Russian rule in parts of Turkestan, and the tsar's forces showed no mercy in fighting back against the *ishân*s and their disciples (as Arif Xatamov had described in the context of the Jizzak Rebellion). The Communists, in their ideologically ordained "struggle against the old," tried to complete the work that their tsarist predecessors had begun. The mausoleum of Bahâ'uddin Naqshband in Qasr-i Arifan[25] (recently renamed Bahâ'uddin), a village about ten miles from Bukhara that was an important pilgrimage site for Central Asian Muslims, was converted into a museum of atheism—a common fate of religious shrines in the USSR—and the Naqshbandiya went underground.[26]

106

The Naqshbandi had long maintained a somewhat inconsistent attitude toward the practice of music and poetry for spiritual ends. On the one hand, the spiritual principles of the Naqshbandiya stress strict observance of the *sharia,* and some Naqshbandi regard the mystical concert (*samâ'*) used by Sufi orders to induce ecstasy as a distraction from the spiritual path. Among Sufis, the Naqshbandiya are known for the practice of silent *zikr* (*zikr-i khafi*), which rejects the rhythmic chanting and instrumental accompaniment, or loud *zikr* (*zikr-i jahri*) that is popularly viewed as almost synonymous with Sufi practice.[27] On the other hand, many of Central Asia's leading classical poets and connoisseurs of music were associated with the Naqshbandiya—Jâmi and Nawâ'i are the most commonly cited examples. The mercurial attitudes of the Bukharan emirs toward music and musical performance might have been strongly influenced by the principles and practices of the Naqshbandiya, and to learn more about them, OM and I found our way to what we were told was the intellectual and spiritual center of the Naqshbandi revival in Bukhara.

We had first met Sadriddin and his friend Ghafurjân in 1990. A friend of OM's from Bukhara had told us about Sadriddin and his interest in the Naqshbandi order. He had said that Sadriddin was an enlightened person who could help us. Sadriddin always attended evening prayers at the Xâja-i Zina-i Din (Stairway of Faith) mosque, not far from the *ark,* and OM's friend suggested we meet him there after prayers.

A pair of small boys playing in the darkening stone courtyard of the mosque pointed out Sadriddin as he emerged from prayers with several dozen other men. Sadriddin was small and dark complexioned, with a gentle face. OM and I introduced ourselves and mentioned the name of the mutual friend who had sent us. Sadriddin invited us to join him for tea in a small building across the courtyard from the mosque. We walked through a classroom where boys were preparing for an Arabic lesson and into a modest *mehmânxâna.* In a few moments, we were joined by Ghafurjân, a young mullah with soft features and an easygoing manner who was the imam of the Xâja-i Zina-i Din mosque.

Sadriddin told us that he was an instructor at Bukhara's Institute for the Further Education of Teachers and that he used his position there to attract teachers, and later, he hoped, their students, to the Naqshbandi order. He was preparing a book on the Naqshbandiya and had created an officially registered cultural foundation in Bukhara to promote their activities. The foundation provided information to newspapers, maintained connections with Naqshbandiya centers in other countries (Naqshbandi groups exist throughout the Muslim world), and exchanged scholarly materials on the Naqshbandiya. Bahâ'uddin Naqshband had left a legacy of mystical poetry, all of it written in Persian, and now Sadriddin was translating this poetry into Uzbek in an attempt to assimilate Bahâ'uddin into Uzbek history. Though older than Ghafurjân, Sadriddin had been his *murid* (disciple). He credited Ghafurjân with teaching him about the

107

esoteric technique of "awareness in breathing" (*hûsh dar dam*), through which the Naqshbandi adept remembers God while inhaling and exhaling.

Unlike the Russian-trained native Orientalists who used Western scholarly sources and methodologies for the study of their own culture, Ghafurjân and Sadriddin were products of a largely indigenous tradition of cultural and spiritual knowledge. As a boy, Sadriddin had been strongly influenced by his grandfather, an *ishân* who belonged to the Qadiri mystical order, and by two uncles who were chanters of the Qur'an. Ghafurjân also had a grandfather, a coppersmith by profession, who had shared his extensive knowledge of poetry and religious science. Then Ghafurjân had been given to a teacher, an *âlim* named Suleiman Xâja. "There were a lot of Naqshbandis here," said Ghafurjân, "but under communism, everything was done secretly and on a small scale." When he was eighteen, Ghafurjân had joined some fifty other students who studied Muslim religious subjects as well as "scientific communism" in Bukhara's sole functioning *madrasah*, Mir-i Arab. After completing the *madrasah*, he had pursued postgraduate studies at the Imam Bukhari Institute of Islam in Tashkent. Most recently he had become a *murid* of a Turkish sheikh who had visited Bukhara two years earlier. "He's the fortieth *murshid* [spiritual guide] of the Naqshbandi *tariqât* [spiritual path or method]," said Ghafurjân. "He's a professor and an authority on four orders: the Naqshbandiya, Kubrawiya, Mevleviya, and Chishtiya." The Naqshbandi chain of spiritual transmission that had passed through generations of Central Asian *ishân*s had spread south to India, and west to Turkey. Now, through the visit of the Turkish sheikh, it had looped back to its Transoxanian birthplace, helping to reinvigorate a dormant local tradition that had just begun to emerge from a long hibernation.

In 1975, Ghafurjân had received a teaching appointment at his alma mater, the Mir-i Arab *madrasah*, and since 1983 he had been the *imam* at Xâja-i Zina-i Din. Recently he had also become the head secretary of the local Spiritual Directorate. Ghafurjân's involvement in official Islamic institutions—the *madrasah* and the Institute of Islam in Tashkent—at a time when these institutions served as a cynical and carefully supervised token of Moscow's claim of "freedom of religion" for Soviet Muslims might have called into question his credibility as a Sufi. But the Naqshbandiya's long history of affiliation with politics mollified these suspicions about Ghafurjân's spiritual authenticity. He seemed simply to be following a tradition. Drinking tea with two strangers in his intimate *mehmânxâna*, he was unpretentious and sincere, a model of the purified soul that is the goal of the Naqshbandi spiritual work.

How did a Naqshbandi think about the role of music in social life, and how might those attitudes have accounted for the guarded policies of Bukhara's rulers toward music and festivity? "The Prophet was not an ascetic," Ghafurjân began, "and by the law of the *sharia* there's no prohibition against music. There's a *hadith* about the fact that when the Prophet came from Mecca to

Medina, the people of Medina met him with *surnai*s [oboes], drums, and musical celebration. A girl said to the Prophet, 'If you go now to war and come back to Medina whole, I'll sing you a song with the drum.' And when he came back, he said to the girl, 'I have returned; now sing me a song.' Another *hadith* says that when you chant the Qur'an, you should let your voice be beautiful.[28] There's an oral legend that's not in the *hadith*s that when God created man, he ordered the soul to go into the body, and at that very moment, the sound of music was heard, and going past this music, the soul went into the body."

Ghafurjân continued his justification of music's legitimacy. "In Bukhara, a good voice has always been highly respected. If someone was noticed to have a rare voice, then this person was cultivated. There were people who were specialists in the voice, who trained the voice."

"So things connected with the open voice weren't forbidden?" OM asked.

"No, there were many different kinds of singers in Bukhara. There were *maddâh*s [from *madh:* "praise," "panegyric"] who performed *ghazal*s and *madhiya*s [odes to God]. They had their own quarter of the city and their own leader. Before the *maddâh*, a *masxaravâz* [clown-comedian] would go to the square to gather people. When enough people had gathered, the *maddâh* would appear and begin his sermonizing. They were like religious *agitprop* workers.

"*Qalandar*s also performed on large squares where a lot of people had gathered. The *qalandar*s were separate from dervishes. They had their own norms and rules. A dervish is a person who has chosen poverty and seclusion. He prays, and if he's an educated person, he can teach others. If he has a profession, then he pursues his profession, but he doesn't get mixed up in worldly things; he doesn't search for wealth. The *qalandar*s sang *qalandar* songs, and people gave them money for that.[29]

"In every mosque and in the *madrasah*s there was a *mathnawixân* who chanted a *mathnawi* [a Persian poem in rhyming couplets set to a particular meter, mainly for didactic, romantic, and heroic themes][30] and then provided an interpretation of it. One of the most famous of them died only in the 1960s. The *mathnawîxân*s were paid with money from the *waqf*, the lands belonging to mosques.

"The uses of the voice you've mentioned—they're all for ritual and prayer," I said. "What about festivity? Why was festive music not permitted?"

"Probably the emir forbade music because people were forgetting their religion. Emir Nasrullah was a very religious man. There's a story that one night, when he thought he heard music coming from some *madrasah,* he climbed onto the roof to listen. He sent people to investigate, and they said the music was coming from a *mahalla* (neighborhood), not a *madrasah*. If the music had been in a *madrasah,* the emir would have had all those people killed. Before Nasrullah, there was Haydar and Shahmurad, and they held their morality very strictly. Music had to be done secretly. With Muzafar Khan, there was gradually

109

a weakening of the strictness. Muzafar Khan had to entertain Russians, and he needed musicians. He attracted Jews to sing for him because Jews have good voices. It's natural that Jews should have good voices. They eat a lot of chicken, and they drink chicken soup, and that's beneficial for the voice. I heard that from a famous [Jewish] singer. But we Muslims also had good singers. For example, Jews weren't invited to sing at the feasts of mullahs."

Sadriddin wanted to show us the restoration work that was being carried out at the Naqshbandi mausoleum, and we agreed to meet the next day and drive out to the mausoleum together. Bahâ'uddin, the renamed village where the mausoleum was set amid orchards and mud-walled houses, lay in the flat collective farm country beyond industrial Bukhara, in what had once been Kagan Region but was about to be renamed Bahâ'uddin Region. Tractors and donkey carts were the primary users of the road, which led past a cemetery—filled, it was said, with Bahâ'uddin's descendents and pupils and surrounded by a newly restored brick wall—to a parking lot occupied by jitney buses and a few private cars.

When Sadriddin had spoken cryptically about "restoration work" at the mausoleum, I had envisioned a scene from the Soviet era: a grimy building covered with scaffolding, a few men lolling about with hopelessly inadequate tools and building materials, and a sign warning would-be visitors away from the site—preferably forever. The Naqshbandi shrine couldn't have been more different. In addition to an interior facelift of the sixteenth-century mosque of Abdullah Khan and the construction of a new *madrasah* behind the mosque, an entire tourism complex was being assembled by dozens of well-organized and equipped work crews. An enormous food-service complex was being built to process the thousands of sheep that would be brought to be slaughtered and sacrificed by pilgrims. The slaughtering was to take place in one area, and in another, huge pots were to be kept permanently boiling over open fires. A traditional water hole (*hâwuz*) was being cemented into the ground near the gnarled trunk of a fallen mulberry tree that Bahâ'uddin is said to have planted. Another large building, almost complete, was to be a reception hall for foreign visitors. Inside the hall, decorative *mirabs* spaced along the walls were painted with gaudily colored floral and arabesque designs. Sadriddin said that there had been no shortage of money for the project: the president of Uzbekistan and the mayor of Bukhara had each contributed handsomely from funds under their control, the president of Turkey had come to Bukhara with dollars, and numerous wealthy Muslims had made private contributions.

Beyond the exhibition hall, rows of identical brick shops awaited the installation of window glass. It was in these shops that the throngs of pilgrims would buy their Naqshbandi souvenirs. After a trifling seventy-year hiatus, Bukhara's centuries-old synthesis of commerce and religion was about to kick into gear again. But the renovation of the pilgrimage site seemed not to arise from a popular desire to pay respect to a great religious figure, although that desire might well have existed. Rather, the site seemed like a Central Asian version of a Disney theme park—a turnkey shrine ordered up by the government to authenticate the Muslim element in its ideological blend of secular Islamic nationalism. In fact, the neatly bricked walkways and flower gardens, the gaggles of schoolchildren on their guided tours, the roving television crew from Tashkent—all could equally well have made up the set of a Communist-era shrine to Lenin or to Soviet war heroes. In the days of the Bukharan Emirate, the Naqshbandi sheikhs had been gray eminences who had provided the ruling class a contact with an authentic spiritual tradition. But it was difficult to imagine Ghafurjân and his circle playing the same role with the present government. The persona of Bahâ'uddin had been infused with an ideology, and the shrine was being rebuilt to reflect official reverence.

MORE FROZEN MUSIC

With the revival of Bahâ'uddin, the spiritual tradition of Bukhara had been marked by the post-Soviet ethos of secular Islamic nationalism that Uzbekistan's *apparat* had created to fill the gap left by the retreat of ideological communism (even as many of the bureaucratic practices of communism seemed to become intensified). But musical tradition, by contrast, remained mired in Soviet institutions and aesthetic ideals. One of those institutions was the philharmonia. Philharmonia societies had been set up in cities and large towns across the Soviet Union beginning in the mid-1930s to provide a range of musical entertainment that wouldn't have fallen under the purview of other central cultural institutions, such as opera and ballet theaters or symphony orchestras. The philharmonias acted as clearinghouses for the activities of local profes-sional musicians and served as a venue for visiting artists on the tour circuit. In Bukhara, the philharmonia had at first tried to fulfill the function of the erstwhile *ghalibxâna* (musicians' guild) as a booking agent for wedding musicians—collecting fees and distributing salaries to musicians after taking a percentage to cover its own expenses. But musicians had soon started to go around the philharmonia and make their own performing arrangements, at least for wed-dings. Why cut the government in on their earnings? Gradually, however, the philharmonia had consolidated its hold over the organization of local musical entertainment. Part of the reason was the sheer logistical difficulty of not working with the philharmonia. A musician couldn't simply organize a profes-sional ensemble and travel around on his own doing concerts or weddings. Professional ensembles had to be approved and registered. In exchange for control of who could get approved and registered, the philharmonia took care of bookings and arranged transportation, ordered costumes, provided a sound

111

system and rehearsal space, and paid musicians a steady wage, even if it was a fraction of what the philharmonia took in from performance fees.

The director of Bukhara's philharmonia had concluded that the philharmonia needed to establish a *Shash maqâm* ensemble among the performing groups it controlled. Perhaps the director had been inspired by the revival of other aspects of traditional life—Bahâ'uddin, the new bazaar, the architectural renovations to mosques, the *madrasah*s and caravan *sarai*s that were transforming downtown Bukhara. In any event, he had come to feel that Bukhara, the birthplace of the *Shash maqâm,* had to reclaim its rights to an important element of Uzbekistan's cultural "great tradition," and he had given orders to form an ensemble of *maqâm* singers and instrumentalists.

Ari Babakhanov wanted OM and me to hear the ensemble, and one day we met him at the philharmonia's gloomy auditorium in the center of Bukhara, where the ensemble held weekly rehearsals. Thirteen men and three women sat in overcoats on the stage—it was freezing in the hall—preparing for a rare concert at Bukhara's music high school. OM and I listened silently for close to an hour. The musicians sat glued to their books of notation, Rajabi's notation published in the 1960s and 1970s by Karomatov. The lugubrious performance, with its alternating vocal solos and choruses accompanied by a small orchestra, had the same bloated quality that I had disliked so much when I had first heard *Shash maqâm* on the recordings of the Tashkent radio station ensemble.

There was a break, and one of the musicians asked OM to give his opinion of their music. He must have been anticipating high praise, but OM lit into the ensemble with an epic-length critique of their entire endeavor. The gist was that he considered it a tragedy that in the city where the *Shash maqâm* had been born, where there were still recordings of great performers like Leviche, the *Shash maqâm* should have fallen into the rut of the politicized performance tradition of Rajabi and Karomatov. OM was blunt but not mean in his criticism. Afterward he said to me, "They're all going to hate me now. But I considered it my duty to tell them. Let them think badly of me. But they know the truth. A musician like Ari understands. They've had their memories beat out of them; all they can do is look at a book and read the notes. The *Shash maqâm* is not about what's written in books; it was a living tradition. It's not just a complex of melodies but a system of creative principles that proposes a creative approach. The performer has to be in search of inspiration, which leads to the phenomenon that we call the 'eternal life' of the *maqâm*. Otherwise it turns into some kind of dead music that will be mechanically repeated. The ensemble has become like a narcotic for them. There's not a single person in it who can perform alone. They say it's easier to perform in an ensemble, but that wasn't the purpose of the *Shash maqâm*—to make it easy. And then there's the other side—there's no social demand for the *Shash maqâm*. The only thing left is the *âsh* and the

occasional special gatherings where they listen to serious music. That's the only thing that it lives on now."

I asked OM, "How is it that the *Shash maqâm* has disappeared in its very birthplace?"

"It shows that no art can be eternal if there's not a chain of tradition. One generation of musicians dies, and another generation replaces it; one generation of listeners dies, and another replaces it. But in Bukhara, there were enormous lapses. A whole generation of *maqâm* players studied a little in their youth; then

Ari Babakhanov playing the Kashgar *rabâb*. Photo by Dmitri Mikhailov.

they went to Soviet conservatories and spent the rest of their lives believing that European music was more developed. And because of that, we stand now before the dogma that the notation that's written in books is what you have to play."

I asked, "Is this really all that's left of the *Shash maqâm* in Bukhara? Might there not be somewhere a group of hidden masters, who, like the *abdâls*—the fools of God—of Sufi tradition, veiled from the world, guard the purity of the tradition?"

OM said, "Ari is an example of a hidden master. But what can a master do when there is no demand for his mastery?"

Ari had learned the *tanbur,* the quintessential Bukharan classical instrument, as a child, but he had come of age in the early 1950s (he was born in 1934) when

113

the performance of classical music was regarded as ideological heresy. He had switched to the Kashgar *rabâb,* an instrument borrowed from the Uighurs of Chinese Xinjiang in the 1920s and adapted to perform harmonized and arranged versions of popular melodies. Ari became a virtuoso technician on the Kashgar *rabâb* and, in his teaching career at Bukhara's music high school, faithfully passed on his *rabâb* technique to several generations of younger musicians. These students learned to perform not only harmonized and arranged versions of popular melodies but also Russian and Western European classics arranged for *rabâb* and piano or *rabâb* and orchestra (the latter were for the most part originally intended for balalaika). Ari was a musical professional, and performing and teaching hybrid *rabâb* music was a job that he was proud to have done well. It was only during one of our last evenings in Bukhara that he showed anguish about having devoted his entire musical career to playing and teaching a mongrelized instrument that was ill-suited to the performance of the music he most deeply loved: the *maqâm* (due to the fact that its equal temperament and low frets impeded the expressive bending of notes, ornamentation, and nondiatonic intervals that are essential to performance of the *Shash maqâm*). "Our music was taken away from us," he lamented in a hoarse whisper. "And look at what we were given in its place. What choice did I have?" That rhetorical question seemed to ricochet around our conversations in Central Asia.

I asked Ari if he would record one of the instrumental pieces from the *Shash maqâm* on the *tanbur,* in the style of his grandfather Leviche. Ari shrugged. "I'm out of practice," he said. "I haven't picked up a *tanbur* in years. It would be better if I played the *rabâb.*"

I was quietly insistent and suggested that Ari take out the *tanbur* and practice a little before our recording session. Finally he agreed. We recorded him two days later in the auditorium of the music high school. He played "Samâ-i dugâh," a piece from the *Shash maqâm* whose title conveys the image of "spiritual concert" (*samâ*) and whose austere classicism is evident in the logic of its simple melodic line and the symmetry of its phrasing (reproduced on *Asie Centrale: Traditions classique,* Ocora Radio France, disc 1, track 8). Except for the movement of his fingers, Ari sat motionless as he played, his face wrenched in concentration. He seemed completely immersed in the sound of his long-untouched *tanbur.* Observing Ari's untheatrical but obvious passion for the repertory that had been his musical inheritance, I thought of OM's description of him as a hidden master, a musical *abdâl,* and understood what he had meant.

The worker's state whose goal had been to eliminate class barriers in art had vilified the *Shash maqâm* as an elite art and tried to expunge it from cultural life. When that had failed, it had then tried to transform the *Shash maqâm* into a popular art. But Soviet cultural strategists had gotten everything reversed. In Bukhara, the *Shash maqâm* and other "heavy" music *had* been a popular art. And when they had tried to turn this music into a national "folk" art, they had inadvertently created an elite art; elite, that is, because it had all but lost its audience. No one wanted to listen to a music whose soul had been usurped by the state. It was left to Ari and a handful of fellow *abdâl*s to continue the inner tradition of the *Shash maqâm,* independent of the state and independent of an audience. And Ari would soon be bound for Tel Aviv.

TWO WEDDING ENTERTAINERS

Could one still find traditions of popular expressive culture in Bukhara that had passed from pre-Soviet times through the watershed of Sovietization and survived as popular traditions independent of any meddling on the part of the culture bureaucracy? The *maddâh*s and *qalandar*s were gone; so were the *bacha*s and *dâyradast*s. Unlike mullahs and *ishân*s, who could conduct their spiritual life in private, performers depended on a public and on public spectacle. But public spectacle tainted by association with religion had no place in Soviet culture, and as the *maddâh*s and *qalandar*s gradually passed from the scene, their chain of transmission had been broken. The gap had become too long, and even with the reappearance of popular religion like the cult of Bahâ'uddin, it was unlikely that Bukharans would again hear *na't*s and *munâjât*s chanted in the public squares.

One central Bukharan tradition of expressive culture, however, remained intact. It was a tradition that wouldn't have attracted a great deal of attention from the state culture strategists because it had been a women's tradition, practiced within the relative seclusion of women's *toy*s. This was the tradition of the *sâzanda* (pronounced "sazanDA"), the female wedding entertainer.[31] When we had first come to Bukhara, in 1990, OM had told me about Tohfaxân (pronounced Toe-fah-XAN), the greatest of the living *sâzanda*s, and we had gone to visit her and recorded her ensemble. Tohfaxân, née Yafa Taxalova (Tohfa was a nickname in Tajik that means "gift"), had seemed a pillar of Bukharan society, a woman known and loved by all of Bukhara, and I couldn't then have imagined her joining the exodus of Bukharan Jews to an émigré life in the United States or Israel. "Things are good for me here," she had told me. "Why should I leave?" But in 1992, Tohfaxân had indeed decided to quit Bukhara, and when we arrived there in the spring of 1993, she was busy settling her financial affairs and divesting herself of most of a lifetime's accumulation of household odds and ends and gifts from five decades of grateful fans.

The blue gate that led into the courtyard of Tohfaxân's house was barely visible in the long brick wall that forms an arc on both sides of a small police station just opposite the Divan Begi *madrasah*. The gate opened onto Lenin Street, a central pedestrian thoroughfare that was slated to be renamed Bahâ'uddin Street. A few meters away was the Labi Hâwuz, one of the artificial pools that had provided drinking water for Bukhara's residents. The Labi Hâwuz had been neglected—its surface covered with algae, leaves, and bits of trash, its color a ghoulish green. Still, I saw old men scoop up handfuls of water and drink from it. Around the pool's cemented perimeter, stalls dispensed tea, state *nân,* and tasteless state *palav* to occasional tourists and to pairs of well-groomed young men attired in faintly fashionable Western clothes—members of Bukhara's new merchant class who, defying local convention, quickly and dispassionately inhaled their food and disappeared back into the streets.

South of the Labi Hâwuz, behind Tohfaxân's house, were the crooked streets of the Jewish quarter. The streets were dirty, and they stank. OM remembered a time when the streets had been cleaner, but Bukhara's reputation as a malodorous place goes back at least to the medieval Arabic geographers and poets, who, as Barthold noted in his *Geographical Survey of Transoxania,* alluded to it "in the most vigorous terms."[32] The odors stemmed in part from the Bukharan custom of locating latrines just inside the entryway to a courtyard (thus expediting the removal of their contents).

Tohfaxân and her family lived in what amounted to the outer courtyard of a traditional dwelling. This outer courtyard would have been the province of male members of the household and male social life, while the women's quarters were in an inner courtyard, closed to male visitors. The various rooms abutting the courtyards came in and out of use throughout the year depending on climatic conditions. A room that got direct sunlight during the day would be ideal for winter living but uninhabitable in the summer. Cool basement rooms were reserved for the hottest portions of summer days; rooftops provided sleeping quarters for summer nights.

At the time of our visit in 1993, Tohfaxân was sixty-five, and she moved more slowly than I had remembered from the previous visit, two years earlier. She still performed at *toy*s but relied increasingly on her daughter, Gulya, to carry the show. Tohfaxân, however, had lost none of her grace and conviviality. She couldn't stop being a *sâzanda,* even in her own house. She loved guests; she loved to talk, to tell about how much she was loved by all of Bukhara, to recite popular ditties and snatches of poetry, to bestow benedictions and blessings on her visitors.

I asked Tohfaxân to talk about how she had become a *sâzanda,* and this request immediately produced a lengthy monologue. "From childhood, I loved art. My mother's sister was a *sâzanda,* and I went with her to weddings. When I was six, I started to dance in school groups. We gave concerts all over the place—for the cotton workers and silk workers, in theaters, in teahouses, in private homes. But my father didn't want me to be a *sâzanda,* an artist. My father had higher education; my mother too. They were teachers. Before the Revolution, my father had been a coach driver. After the Revolution, he became a policeman, and then he went to an evening teacher's institute. He was already

116

Tohfaxân with her troupe of *sâzanda*s, 1957.
Photo courtesy of Tohfaxân Pinkhasova.

grown, with children. He worked for two years and then became the principal of a school. It was a difficult time. The war hadn't started yet, but there was hunger. I remember in 1935—I was seven years old—they interrogated my father about gold. He spent fifteen days at the Ministry of Internal Affairs. They came and searched the house. During Stalin's time, they thought that the Bukharan Jews all had hidden gold. If anyone said anything about a person, they'd take him away and they'd say, 'Give us your gold.' My sister was eleven years old when that happened. She was terrified, and she died from that terror. They didn't find any gold, and they let my father go.

"I had one brother and one sister when my mother died. My father remarried, and my stepmother had two more daughters. We were five children. When I was thirteen, the war started and my father went to the army. Then an order came to return teachers home. He was sent to a village to get the local school back on its feet and round up students who were truant. There were ten collective farms in the rural council in his area, and each month he went around to the collective farms and arranged for the children to have a hot dinner for free. Each school bought a milking cow, and he'd go there and make gruel from milk and crushed wheat. And for that, my father was made a Merited Teacher of Uzbekistan. He was the first in Uzbekistan with that title. When we came to Bukhara, he opened a school for the blind. He built a big building for the school and hired doctors who could cure blindness. He worked until he was seventy-six. I wanted to

117

Tohfaxân at a *bazm* in Bukhara.

Three generations of *sâzanda*s: Tohfaxân with her daughter, Gulya,
and her granddaughter, Zarina.

follow in my father's footsteps, but the war got in the way. I quit the teacher's institute after the second year. I had *sâzanda* in my blood.

"Older *sâzanda*s took me on as a pupil. They'd be going to a wedding and they'd say, 'Come with us.' And I went. They didn't teach me. I just watched them dance and absorbed what they did. One of them was named Karkigi. She had danced for the mother of the emir. If the emir's mother gave her permission, she performed for *toy*s outside the *ark*. But if the emir's mother didn't give her permission, she didn't go. The mother of the emir loved to watch dancing, and most of the dancers were Jews.

"Karkigi was very beautiful. The emir's mother gave her thin silk dresses to wear all the time, so that her figure would always be apparent. She had very white skin. When she was young, she didn't go out without her mother, and she wore a veil. My mother also wore a veil. All Jewish women wore veils before the Revolution, and they wore veils for two, three, four years after the Revolution. I remember that when I was a girl, women still wore the veil in Tashkent, in Samarkand, in Bukhara. Even in the late 1940s, there were still women who wore the veil in Tashkent.

"Until the 1950s and 1960s, there were very few Uzbek and Tajik *sâzanda*s. Ninety percent were Bukharan Jews, and maybe ten percent were Uzbeks and Tajiks. Their husbands didn't allow them to do that kind of work. Now it's the opposite, because Jews are leaving and Uzbeks and Tajiks are permitted to dance. But these dancers work with men. There will be four or five male musicians and one female dancer. That kind of a dancer is not really a *sâzanda*.

"*Sâzanda*s played at weddings in groups of three or four. There were many of these brigades in Bukhara. Until 1952, we worked under the Bukhara Society of Art, and after that, under the House of Folk Arts. Then, in the 1960s, I worked in a concert brigade in the theater, and in the final years before I became a pensioner, I worked in the concert brigade of the philharmonia. But wherever I worked, I always went to weddings, and at those weddings we always had a plan to fulfill. For each wedding, we had to turn over 100 rubles to the philharmonia. At the end of the month, we got back forty percent of everything we'd given, and that was our official pay.

"*Sâzanda*s danced without music [i.e., melody instruments], and they didn't work with men—*maqâm* players or singers. That's the way it was until the 1960s. It's a tradition that men shouldn't be among women and women shouldn't be among men. Women's wedding celebrations were separate; men's wedding celebrations were separate. They used to hold them on different days. In other parts of Uzbekistan and Tajikistan, maybe fifty or sixty percent of the weddings have men and women sitting together in the evening *bazm*. But in Bukhara, the old tradition still holds. In the 1960s, I quietly took a *rabâb* player—a thirteen-year-old boy—to play among the women. I was the first one to take music among women. To this day, I don't sing or dance among men. I don't receive men. I have that rule. I've always been among women. Usually they phone me now. They ask, 'Are you free on such and such a day? Then put me down,' they say. There's no discussion about money. When we go to their place, they give a bowl of tea, and underneath the tea bowl there's some money. Guests also give us money."

The strict separation of men's and women's social events seems to have created a need among both men and women to vent sexual energy through caricature of the opposite sex. Dancing boys (*bachas*), who, as Tohfaxân reported, wore women's dresses and painted their lips and eyebrows, make cameo appearances in a number of the travel chronicles and ethnographic studies of Bukhara. Less conspicuous in these works, but far more prevalent in Bukharan society itself (as well as elsewhere in Central Asia), has been male role-playing by women. Tohfaxân described one type of women's playacting that she remembers from her teenage years during the Second World War.

"At *toys*, we used to dress up in robes and put on beards so that we looked like men. We'd play the role of *qalandar*s and dervishes. At that time, I was going around with Chirvânxân, Karkigi, Mâshkâti—they'd take a cane and do themselves up like a real dervish. They put on a man's hat and a man's belt. The women would ask us to sing something sad so they could cry, not like at a wedding, but with real grief. Everyone was in mourning, because the war was going on. And we would sing all night. We'd make little scenarios, like in the theater. When the women had cried themselves out, they'd ask the *qalandar* or dervish to make it so they'd be happy; and they'd start to dance with us. Then I'd say, 'Come on, Chirvânxân, let's make them be happy.' I'd ask, '*Qalandar,* why are you crying? Did something happen?' The *qalandar* would say, 'Yes, I lost my daughter.' 'Well, come on, let's look for her together.' And one of the women from among us would be the daughter. She'd hide herself among the women; she'd put a handkerchief over her head, hide her face so that no one recognized her; she'd hide herself, and then we'd search for this girl. We'd find her, and the *qalandar* would say, 'Why did you run away from me. What do you want?' The *qalandar* would offer to buy her slippers, earrings, a handkerchief, and so on, but she wouldn't accept any of these gifts. And then one of the women would say, 'Give her to marry, give her to marry.' So there would be a wedding. Quickly one of the guests would dress up like a bridegroom, they'd paint a moustache on her face, and they'd give the girl to the bridegroom in marriage. Afterward, they'd bring *sharbat* (white sugar and boiling water), and read prayers. Up until the 1970s, that's what we did to entertain ourselves. Then it was prohibited. Women didn't only dress up like men at *toys*. There used to be separate women's theater and men's theater. In the women's theater, women would play men's parts, and in the men's theater, men would play women's parts. That's the way it used to be, because in Bukhara, religion was strong."

By the time OM and I began our work in Bukhara, the strict segregation of men and women at *toy*s had given way to uneasy integration. The morning *âsh* remained a male bastion, but at the afternoon or evening *bazm,* men and women conducted their own parallel microcelebrations within one and the same event. At some *toy*s, embroidered cloths (*sozana*s) were hung over a rope stretched across a blocked-off street. Men celebrated on one side of the divider, women on the other. At other *toy*s, gender boundaries were less physical than imagined. For example, at one *bazm* that I attended with Tohfaxân, women sat on the ground on a section of the street that had been covered with carpets and cushions and protected by a large awning. Tohfaxân and her ensemble set up their microphones and equipment at one end of the awning, while beyond them, exposed to the sun, men were seated at long tables.

As Tohfaxân sang and danced for and with the women, groups of men stood on the margins of the women's area, watching the entertainment. At moments when no women were dancing, a few intrepid men moved into the center of the women's area and danced with one another. Later, both women and men lined up separately in front of Tohfaxân to receive a *muxammas*—a poetic blandishment traditionally bestowed upon women only.[33] Tohfaxân was a master of the *muxammas*. She glanced at the person standing before her and judged instantly what sort of *muxammas* to recite and in what language (Uzbek or Tajik). "I've been doing this for fifty years," she told me, proudly. "I ought to be good at it. Most of my material is traditional. I know a huge number of *muxammas*. For example, for a child, I might say,

> 'Let your face be in my soul
> So that when you smile, you open flowers
> Let the dream of your mother who bore you be fulfilled
> Be so sweet that I die from your sweetness.'

"For another woman, I could say:

> 'Won't you please give me a kiss with your sweet lips
> Give me a kiss
> Why only one; give two, three, four
> Give five, seven, nine. Give me an even number: ten.'

"I'm a woman, and I have a right to say this to another woman. We're accustomed to working among women, and that way, we feel free." But despite her claim that she didn't perform for men, Tohfaxân graciously bestowed a *muxammas* on each man who stepped in front of her. Later she told me that she knew that particular group of men from her work in the philharmonia, and that was why she had not felt uncomfortable with them. However, the quatrains for men were less physically explicit:

> May there be life and may you live
> May you be alive and healthy.
> In such good times
> Always be happy and dance

or:

> May God allow your height not to become stooped over
> May the joy of your heart not see any grief
> May God give you happiness day and night
> May your shadow always be on my head

Since the moment in the 1960s when Tohfaxân had diffidently brought along a thirteen-year-old boy to play a musical instrument at a *toy,* her ensemble, like her audiences, had come to include both men and women. At smaller weddings, she worked with three or four male instrumentalists and with her daughter, Gulya, who assisted her in performing the functions of the *sâzanda:* singing, dancing, reciting *muxammas,* and acting as a master of ceremonies. The instrumentalists played accordion, *tar, dâyra,* and electric keyboard. Tohfaxân rued the amplification. "It's the sound that people want these days," she sighed. "What choice do I have?"

For concerts or very large *toy*s, Tohfaxân called on her larger ensemble, Nâzanin, in which she was assisted by as many as twenty-five artists. The costar of Nâzanin was a singer equally as formidable as Tohfaxân, a portly man with a huge, deep voice, named Mahdi Ibadov. Mahdi was a *mavrigixân*—a singer of *mavrigi*s, a form of vocal suite performed at men's *bazm*s that was broadly analogous to the suites performed by *sâzanda*s at women's *bazm*s.[34] *Mavrigi* means literally "from Merv," the oasis city (now called Mari) in present-day Turkmenistan that was once a principal cultural center of Khorasan. Merv was also one of Central Asia's principal slave markets. The typical *mavrigixân* has been a descendant of the Bukharan Irani or Farsi, who trace their ancestry to slaves captured in Iran by Turkmen tribesmen and brought via Merv to Bukhara.[35] The Bukharan Irani have preserved their Shia heritage and, relative to the city's Sunni majority, are a marginalized social group. The Shia *mavrigixân*s, like Jewish *sâzanda*s, have performed work traditionally considered unsuitable for blue-blooded Sunni Bukharans.

Mahdi himself had underscored his ethnic origins. "I'm a Fars, not a Tajik," he had told us.[36] "And I'm a Shia." Unlike Tohfaxân, Mahdi had not worked full-time as a musician, and he hadn't come to music in early childhood. His grandfather had been a tax collector for the emir. His father had gone to the front during the war and never returned. Mahdi's mother, grandmother, and brother had all died soon after the war began, and Mahdi (born in 1932) had been put in an orphanage. He had finished the sixth grade and worked his entire life as a truck driver. Performing *mavrigi* was an avocation. Mahdi had started performing a little at weddings of friends and relatives and had been encouraged.

OM and I had arranged to spend an afternoon filming Mahdi's performance of *mavrigi* and other repertory. We met at a *madrasah* near the philharmonia that was in the process of being converted to a shopping arcade. The cell-like rooms where students had once lived and studied the Qur'an were to become shops and ateliers for craftsmen. The *madrasah*-arcade hadn't yet opened to the public, and with a little *baksheesh* to the foreman of the small work crew, we bought an afternoon's worth of peace and quiet in which to film and record.

Mahdi explained to us the routine of the *mavrigixân*. "We'd come to a *toy* with five or six people, and we all had *dâyra*s. We served the weddings of both Shias and Sunnis. There's no difference in the way they're conducted in Bukhara. Shias invite Sunnis, and Sunnis invite Shias. A guest is a guest. It doesn't make any difference. We'd sit near the door, which was the least-

Mahdi, the *mavrigixân*.

honored position. They'd put a mat (*korpacha*) down, and we'd sit down on our haunches. That means that you're serving; that's the way you play. You don't sit with your legs crossed—that's for relaxing. In the center of the room there would be a container for coal to heat the *dâyra*s [in order to keep the skin taut]. They'd pass around *mai* [a kind of sweet wine] and *musallas* [a strong, thick red wine made by boiling grapes for a long time, often used as a medicament]. It gives a very nice buzz. You can't find that sort of thing now.

"The first thing we'd sing was the *shahd* [Tajik: "honey"]. Whoever could perform, performed. We'd sing in turns. If there were six people, each would

123

sing a couplet or two. After the *shahd* there would be *gardân, sarxân, châr zarb,* which can have five or six parts.[37] These would make up a *pait* [performance; literally, "moment," "time"] that would last about an hour, and then people would eat and drink, and there would be a second *pait,* a third *pait.* If the *bazm* went until morning, it would be called *bazm-i Jamshidi.* Jamshid is the patron of *mavrigixân*s and *sâzanda*s." Here Mahdi explained his understanding of the ancient Indo-Iranian Jamshid legend: "Jamshid was the first legendary king in Iranian mythology who established the norms of secular life: how to observe a *bazm,* how to marry, how to celebrate *nâwruz.* That's why he's the patron of musicians. He's not a religious figure, but a worldly person."[38]

Mahdi performed for us a *shahd*—the same *shahd* that he had sung three years before when OM and I had recorded Tohfaxân's ensemble. This time, however, with more Bukharan music in my ears, I heard something different in the *shahd.* Suddenly it didn't sound so Bukharan. In place of the sturdy rhythms and expansive, open-throated vocal style characteristic of both heavy and light music in Bukhara, the rhythmic pulse of the *shahd* was irregular, the nasal vibrato of the melody concentrated within a high vocal tessitura and narrow ambitus (pitch range). The flattened second degree in the descending melodic pattern of the *shahd* (based on the scale C-B♭-A♭-G♭-F) was also anomalous for Bukharan music. In sum, the *shahd* sounded more like singing from Iran or Azerbaijan, as if it represented a musical vestige of the *mavrigi'*s cultural origins that had persisted through several centuries of expatriate life in Bukhara.[39] The beginning of the *shahd* is transcribed here, along with the text of Mahdi Ibadov's performance (reproduced on the accompanying compact disc, track 9). Since a typical *shahd* would have been too long to include on the CD, we asked Mahdi to perform an abbreviated version. The *shahd* is followed without pause by a metered *shahd-i gardân* in 6/8 time. According to Mahdi, the author of the text is unknown.

124

SHAHD

Dear one, be well, be well, be well, be well
When I turn to the blossom, the blossom points its thorns at me.
When I turn to the bud, the bud bursts open
Dear one, be well, be well, be well, be well
I experienced my fate at the bazaar of fate
If for others, hard stones turn to gold, then for me, gold turns to dust.
Dear one, be well, be well, be well, be well
I have a surprising fate: in my hands, milk turns to yogurt
But if a hawk fell into my hands, it would be turned into an eagle
Dear one, be well, be well, be well, be well, be well.
Oh my God
Oh my beloved
Consider this moment precious!

SHAHD-I GARDÂN

In the steppe, I played on the *nay,*
And from that, flowers began to burn.
What a pity, that his/(her) pure face
Became covered with dust and ash,
My bones finished burning,
My soul began to burn,
From the soul of my beloved,
My heart began to burn, pitilessly.
I knock at the door
Until midnight, no one opens it.
Midnight passes,
My beloved didn't appear.
The king of the city came out
And took me by the hand.
No one like me
Has made a fool of himself in love, pitilessly.

(Text changes to Uzbek)
I walk along the street, and my eyes always see you.
How unfortunate am I that you don't look at me
Either you stopped loving me,
Or I am bad
An enemy has come between us, and it's unlikely that we'll see each other

(Macaronic Uzbek and Tajik)
Halili has a birthmark (refrain)
Halili has a wish
That I would be a birthmark
(refrain)
In the middle of your black eyebrows
(refrain)

125

SHAHD

Yâr, âmân, âmân, âmân, âmân.
Bâ gul beshinam, gul zi man xâr gardad
Bâ ghuncha beshinam, gerebân châk gardad.
Yâr, âmân, âmân, âmân, âmân.
Man ba bâzâri tâle', tâle'i xud imtihân kardam.
Ba har kas xâk zar gardad, ba man zar xâk megardad.
Yâr, âmân, âmân, âmân, âmân.
Ajab tâle'i, ki man dâram, shiram juxrât megardad.
Ba dastam qarchigae âyad, vaiam kalxât megardad.
Yâr, âmân, âmân, âmân, âmân.
Ai, xudâii man,
Ai, habibi man,
Hamin damrâ ghanimat bedân

SHAHD-I GARDÂN

Dar biyabân nai navâxtam,
Xirmani gul dar girift.
Haif, ki ruyi beghubârash,
Chang u xâkistar girift.
Ustaxânam soxta shudu,
Maghzi jânam dar girift.
Az barâi ruhi jânân,
Shishta jânam dar girift (berahmâi).
Xalqa bâ dar mezadam,
Tâ nisfi shab dar vâz nashud.
Nisfi shab az shab guzashtu,
Yari man paidâ nashud.
Pâdshâi shahr barâmad,
Bandi dastamrâ girift.
Hech kasi bâ misli man,
Dar râi ishq rasvâ nashud (berahmâi).

(Text changes to Uzbek)
Kochadan otib bârâbman, kozlarim senga mudâm.
Qairilib bir qaramaisan, muncha peshânam yamân.
Ya, saning kongling qâlibdi, Ya, mani ozim yamân.
Araga dushman kiribdi, endi korgânim gumân (berahmâi).

(Macaronic Uzbek and Tajik)
Vâi, xâl dârad halili (refrain)
Xumâr dârad halili
Qâshingni qarâsiga-ye,
(refrain)
Xâl bâlai arâsiga-ye,
(refrain)

126

An interesting feature of Mahdi's text is the macaronic juxtaposition of Uzbek and Tajik toward the end of the *Shahd-i Gardân*. Known colloquially as *shiru shakar*, "milk and sugar," macaronic texts are commonly found in the songs of the *mavrigixân* and *sâzanda*. The metaphor comes from the idea that, like milk and sugar, each of the two languages enhances the taste and effect of the other.[40] Such macaronic texts seem only natural in the repertory of entertainers who so unselfconsciously move back and forth across boundaries of language and ethnicity in Bukhara.

At the same time, Mahdi stressed that the *mavrigixân,* the *sâzanda,* and the *hafiz* had their own repertories and melodies and that melodies did not cross over from one repertory to another, even though all three types of entertainers could frequently entertain at one and the same *toy*. Each type of entertainer presented a program organized around an identical principle of performance: progression from serious to light, from slow to fast, from meditation to dance. In effect, each type of performer, each type of music, served as a mediating link between the two essential poles of Bukharan life—prayer and festivity. And although each of the three types of entertainer performed a unique array of pieces, these pieces unquestionably displayed areas of stylistic overlap. For example, the so-called *bukharche*—the genre of dance-songs performed by the *sâzanda*—bore similarities both to the *mavrigi* and to lighter pieces from the *Shash maqâm* that would have been sung toward the end of a suite. In both *mavrigi* and *bukharche,* the antiphonal performance of soloist and chorus provided the basis of the music's texture. But the artistry of performing these suites was in linking pieces together in such a way that the progression of changing meters, rhythms, and tempos kept listeners constantly engaged, energized, and, from time to time, surprised.

An excerpt from Tohfaxân's performance of a suite of *bukharche*s is included on the accompanying compact disc (track 10). The text begins:

Solo: Between four rivers you put your platform (of boards)
   I repeat once again, don't get your hem wet, be vigilant
   Taralilalalai, taralilalalai, taralilalalai, my dear

Chorus: *Taralilalalai, taralilalalai, taralilalai, yâr eh* (my dear)

Solo: Your two eyes are bewitching, *taralilalalai, yâr eh*

Chorus: (repeats the same refrain after each solo verse)

Solo: Why don't you ask after me, *taralilalalai, yâr eh*
   Let your burning black eyes not see your sadness . . .
   Let your mother not see your sadness . . .
   Let your father not see your sadness . . .
   May your mother live to see your *toy* . . .
   May everyone live to see your *toy* . . .

127

Dar miyani châr daryâ taxtabandi karda-i
Bâz meguyam dâman tar nakun, hushyâr bâsh.
Taralilalalai, taralilalalai, taralilalalai, yâr eh.
Du chashmi jâdu dâri, taralilalalai, yâr eh.
Taralilalalai, etc. (after every line)
O, az man xabar nadâri-eh, taralilalalai, yâr eh.
O, chashmi siyâhi dâghat-eh, taralilalalai, yâr eh
O, mâdar nabinad dâghat-eh, taralilalalai, yâr eh
O, padar nabinad dâghat-eh, taralilalalai, yâr eh
O, mâdar bebinad toyat-eh, taralilalalai, yâr eh
O, hama bebinand toyat-eh, taralilalalai, yâr eh

GOING WEST

Knowing Tohfaxân's devotion to Bukhara and its traditions and the popularity that she enjoyed there, I was astonished to hear, in the spring of 1993,
that she planned to emigrate. We had talked about emigration during my
previous visits, but the talk had been loose. "Where is it better, there or here?"
Tohfaxân had asked in a formulaic question that during the Soviet era had
become almost a ritual part of conversation with an American (Soviets had
often seemed to take masochistic pleasure in the typical answer; perhaps the
pleasure arose from a confirmation of their suspicions that the Soviet state was
pulling the wool over their eyes about life in the West). Instead of offering an
unequivocal answer, I had tried to explain to Tohfaxân the darker side of life
in the United States; the difficulties she would face trying to pursue her career
as a *sâzanda*.

Tohfaxân's decision had come on the heels of what she felt had been a grave
and embarrassing injustice. "The people at the Regional Department of Culture
told me that both I and my pupil, Olyaxân, were going to be made Merited
Artists of Uzbekistan. It was in the newspapers and on the radio in Tashkent that
I was going to receive the award. The mayor of Bukhara, on the basis of
information from Tashkent, announced it in the stadium on Independence Day.
There must have been 20,000 people there. People started dropping by the house
and phoning me with congratulations. That was on September 1st. Then the
newspaper came out on September 3rd with a picture of Olyaxân, but my picture
was missing. I went to the mayor, and he phoned Tashkent to find out what was
going on. They told him, 'Yes, there had been a mistake. Tohfaxân was not
getting the award.' The mayor had figured that I had to get the award, because
there were two of us nominated, and the other woman had been my student. She
hadn't started dancing until she was forty. They couldn't give it to her and not
to me. But that's what happened. Maybe it's because Olyaxân is Uzbek and I'm
a Jew. Maybe it's because I didn't pay a bribe.

"I didn't want that award; I didn't ask for it; it doesn't give me anything. But if they didn't want to give it to me, why was it announced? Why did all the people hear it? I was ashamed before the people. It was humiliating. After that, I went to the Culture Department and handed in my working papers. I said, 'I won't perform anymore. I don't need this. I'll leave.' My children said, 'Why don't you come and live in Tashkent?' But I didn't want to live in Tashkent. I've worked here for fifty-one years. This is my homeland. I decided to go. Even if I die there [in America], I'm still going to go. What else can I do? Now people phone up and stop me on the street, and they say, 'Don't leave, Tohfaxân. We love you. We respect you.' I have a relative in Brooklyn. She sent a visa, and we were supposed to go and live there, in Brooklyn. And then, all of a sudden, they're sending us to, where is that place? Youngstown [Ohio]. They said New York City was full." (Having lived her life in a land where all citizens required a residence permit, Tohfaxân had not understood that the Jewish organization that facilitated her emigration could not place her in New York for purely internal reasons. A year after her arrival in the United States, Tohfaxân would move to Brooklyn).

The circumstances that prompted Tohfaxân to leave Bukhara were part of a broader malaise that had begun to affect the artistic life of the city after the much-touted *Mustaqilliq* (Independence) of 1991—that is, Uzbekistan's independence from the former Soviet Union. It is difficult to say whether *Mustaqilliq,* a purely formal political act, created the virulent strain of nationalism and nativism that surfaced in Bukhara in the first years of Independence or whether it had simmered there during the Soviet era, mollified by Soviet policies of "internationalism." Whatever its provenance, the new nationalism created conditions in which traditional art was forced to become synonymous with national art, and national art had to be produced by, or at least credited to, people who called themselves Uzbeks.[41] In a city where Uzbek-Tajik bilingualism had added richness to poetry and song and where performance traditions had long been nourished by ethnic diversity—in particular by the participation of Jews, Shia Muslims, and, to a lesser extent, Gypsies—in the central institution of the *toy,* the rise of nationalism and nativism could only have an adverse effect on artistic life.

In prerevolutionary Bukhara, the role of ethnic minorities in the performing arts had come about through social conventions linked to Islamic custom. After the Revolution, many of those social conventions had been sustained by the inertia of tradition, even as Soviet culture strategists undertook a massive campaign to trammel traditional beliefs and practices. Soviet culture policies that required each of the dozens of officially recognized Soviet peoples to display a "national culture" had a low tolerance for ambiguity. Music, literature, crafts had to be explained as the product of one people or another: Uzbek or Tajik, Russian or Ukrainian, not a mixture of the two, nor a product of both. But Soviet culture strategists were consumed by appearances, not essences. What mattered to them were names, labels, titles. As long as a concert, a dramatic production, an anthology of poetry could be billed as Uzbek music, Uzbek theater, Uzbek verse, thus helping to fulfill the economic plan for a certain class of cultural production, it mattered little who actually made the art. Moreover, multiethnic participation in the arts could be applauded under the ideological banner of "fraternal brotherhood among Soviet peoples." It was considered an accomplishment of the Soviet system that Bukhara, Samarkand, Tashkent, while dominated by "Uzbek" artistic institutions, could have attracted to their artistic life representatives of other peoples.

The new Uzbek nationalism *cum* nativism has little use for multiculturalism. In the new paradigm, the cultural achievements of other peoples on Uzbek turf have become a source of embarrassment, not pride. The Muslim-Jewish symbiosis, the Tajik-Uzbek symbiosis, the Shia-Sunni symbiosis—all of these complex social relationships that fulfilled the mutual needs of different groups living in close proximity have begun to disintegrate under new ideological pressures. The forces of provincialism and ethnocentrism in Bukhara come not from religion but from politics. They represent not Islamic fundamentalism but Uzbek nationalism. At present, those forces seem confined largely to an ideologically engaged elite. As Tohfaxân had said, "Among the people, I'm still the star of Bukhara."

On our last day in Bukhara, OM and I went to Tohfaxân's for a farewell lunch of *palav*. We made small talk about the logistics of the move, and Tohfaxân gave me a ring to take back to the United States and hold for her arrival. She was afraid that it would be confiscated by Uzbek customs inspectors, who, it was said, paid particular attention to the personal effects of emigrating Bukharan Jews, just as Stalin's secret police had singled them out in the quest for gold in the 1930s.

When it was time to say goodbye, Tohfaxân walked us outside. We stood at the gate to her courtyard across from the Divan Begi *madrasah*. The sky had clouded over and the air had become paltry, intensifying the scent of outdoor toilets. Even in the middle of a Friday afternoon, it was quiet on Lenin/Bahâ'uddin Street. Teenage girls in silk *iqat* dresses held hands and strolled slowly; groups of children in school uniforms dawdled on their way home from classes. Tohfaxân and I shook hands. "See you in Youngstown," I said.

THE SOUTH

SURXANDARYA & QASHQADARYA

KARSHI

Weeks in Bukhara and months in Tashkent spread over a period of years had nourished friendships with remarkable musicians, and as our conversations and musical experiences together had grown more intimate, I had been drawn into their private worlds of reflection and reminiscence. How different they were one from another—those worlds of the spirit, each a crystallization of its maker's creative search within the bounds of a tradition. And yet, beneath evident differences of form, style, and content, all the music I came to know in Tashkent and Bukhara shared an urban sensibility. Tohfaxân, Mahdi, Arif Xatamov, Munâjât—all of them performed music geared to the social sophistication, literary tastes, and spiritual aspirations of city dwellers. But Transoxania contained other musical realms as well whose center was not the city but the countryside and the small towns where herders, farmers, merchants, and trades-men all crossed paths—and musical repertories. Surxandarya and Qashqadarya, in the south of Uzbekistan, promised an eclectic mix of oral epic—the quintes-sential musical art of the countryside—and rural-based folk song that had remained solidly on the periphery of the "great tradition" music of Bukhara and Tashkent despite the modest distances and old cultural ties between urban and rural populations, between oasis and steppe.

Driving south from Bukhara toward Karshi after a week on the road in our pea-green Volga, I began to understand why OM had summarily dismissed my idea that I could handle all the driving and had recruited Dadanazar. In Central Asia, a driver is not simply a person who drives but someone who coaxes and nurses a vehicle, constantly attending to its various ills, washing and dusting it, discussing its defects and advantages with other drivers, negotiating for fuel from local black marketers when the gas stations have run out, making arrangements for repairs, and standing guard against the theft of windshield wipers, side mirrors, and hubcaps (for starters). Sharing meals, sleeping quarters, and endless rounds of tea, Dadanazar and I had begun to develop a close relationship that became quite independent of our liaison, OM. Dadanazar had gotten the sense that I was open to his newfound religious faith, and when no one was near us, he would offer brief homilies and observations about how I could improve myself and better please God. But he held his comments until a moment when OM was absent; he had only recently become a practicing Muslim and didn't like to talk about his religion in the presence of Uzbeks who he suspected were nonbelievers.

What had attracted him to Islam? I asked him once. "Nothing in my life was going well," said Dadanazar. "I had come back from the army and worked as a driver. I was kind of a hooligan. My father was in jail, in Khorezm. Because of our family conditions, I couldn't study. My mother had nine children; five survived; two were sons. My brother graduated from the Teachers Institute, and I came to Tashkent and got a job driving a bus. For a long time I had this feeling that nothing was working out for me, and I started to think about God. Then I got sick and spent a long time in the hospital. There I met a man who prayed, and I began to go to someone and learn prayers. I went after work. I've learned something. I've become different now. I used to be careless, negligent in everything—even in simple things. I didn't study well in school, but when I started to read, I realized that there was a lot that one could learn from books. I can hold myself better now. Religion gives patience; it gives you something to learn about and be interested in which I never had when I was young. There's a kind of peace and calm."

Dadanazar's tranquillity, which sometimes seemed so exaggerated as to border on catatonia, was still barely enough to counter the skittish energy of Sabirjân, the frenzied young culture bureaucrat who served as our host during a week-long visit to Surxandarya and Qashqadarya. Sabirjân was Director of the Regional Scholarly Methodological Center of Folk Creativity and Cultural Enlightenment Work in Karshi, a city of some 200,000 situated a little over a hundred miles southeast of Bukhara. Karshi, formerly called Nasaf, had once been the center of a province (*vilâyat*) within the Bukharan Emirate. Alim Khan, the last emir, had ruled the province as a young *beg* in the years immediately following his return from studies in Germany, and even after he became emir, Alim Khan often visited Nasaf, where he maintained a palace, later demolished by the Bolsheviks. Following the Revolution, Nasaf had been renamed Beg Bude, after a well-known Jadid, and later, when the Jadids fell out of favor, the name had been changed once again, to Karshi.

Karshi has long occupied a position on the political and cultural periphery of Bukhara. Its very provincialism had facilitated the preservation of a rich musical folklore, OM said, whose focus was not the classical *maqâm* but older

132

forms of song, instrumental music, and dance. Some of these forms contained vestiges of what were assumed to have been Zoroastrian practices. In a village scarcely five miles from the center of Karshi, we would record and videotape a group of elderly women who showed us how small bonfires were lit before a wedding ceremony and the bride was marched around the fires to purify her before marriage. From Karshi, we would proceed south, to the rolling steppe and low hills beyond the cotton plantations, where, among the historically nomadic Qongrad Uzbeks of Qashqadarya and Surxandarya, epic singers are still an active part of community social life.

Karshi had the feeling of a provincial place that had known better times. A broad avenue swept grandiosely past government office buildings, shops, and the walled gardens of large private homes, but the only traffic consisted of beat-up dump trucks and a few tired-looking Ladas and Zhigulis. A single aging yellow bus plied the avenue, up and down, listing feebly to one side and spilling a trail of dense black exhaust fumes.

Karshi had grown rapidly in the 1970s as the surrounding steppe land had been irrigated and transformed into cotton plantations. The First Secretary who had masterminded the transformation was Rozmat Gaipov. As a student who had relatives in Karshi, OM had greatly admired Gaipov. "He was a simple person and a decisive person. He'd swear at anyone he wanted, but he was a good person. He loved art, and he was very musical. He planted gardens and made Karshi flower. Gaipov fell in the first wave of the Cotton Affair. They thought that what he'd created was a luxury. But it wasn't luxury for the benefit of one man. He did it for the people. I'll never forget when my aunt died in Karshi. Of course, we had to bury her in Khorezm. We asked ourselves how we were going to manage that. It was going to be very complicated and expensive, and then my aunt's husband said, 'Let's go and ask Gaipov.' We phoned him and he said, 'Hold the line,' and on another phone he called [First Secretary] Rashidov. Within an hour, there was a special plane to take her body to Khorezm. That's what kind of person he was. People like Gaipov weren't really the guilty ones in the Cotton Affair. They were the soldiers of bigger politicians. What they did was to find a way to make use of unused capital made available by Moscow. They built things with that money. Look at the houses and orchards here. This was once all steppe." OM recounted how when the security forces had come to arrest Gaipov for his part in the Cotton Affair he had said, "Okay, I'm ready to go, but I want to wash first." He had gone to the bathroom and washed and prayed, then slit his own throat.[1]

OM rarely visited Karshi and didn't have close friends there among the cultural *nomenklatura*. Though we had our own contacts among musicians, it was our custom to pay a courtesy call to the local regional authorities, explain our project, and let them feel that we were working with their support rather than behind their backs. We had gone first to Mr. Rajabov, the head of the Culture

Directorate in what had been in Soviet times the Qashqadarya Regional Party Committee but had been renamed in independent Uzbekistan the Provincial Mayoralty (*Vilâyati Hakimiyat*). Rajabov had four telephones on his desk in addition to a large switchboard. He was a man of action. After hearing our story, he had immediately picked up two phones at once and begun barking orders. Within a few minutes, we were on our way to the office of Sabirjân.

Sabirjân's responsibility for our program in Qashqadarya was not to be restricted to bureaucratic formalities. When we appeared at his office late in the afternoon, he had immediately invited us to spend the night at his house. This, it turned out, was to be more than a trifling inconvenience for him, but the protocol of hospitality dictated that Sabirjân had to extend the offer and that we had to accept it, even though both host and guests would have been happier had we bunked down in the local hotel. When we were safely inside Sabirjân's gate, he explained to us that it was his wife's birthday and that the house was already full of family members, some of whom had come from afar to celebrate. "Make yourself at home," he said. Sabirjân was used to living in close quarters, for he had been raised in a family of fourteen children. He set up a separate table for OM, Dadanazar, and me on a small patio area next to the driveway, brought us food and drink, and through the entire evening, shuttled back and forth between our table outside and the company inside. Our outdoor party, it was clear, was intended to be separate from the birthday party going on indoors. Perhaps Sabirjân thought that we preferred it that way, but in any event he never asked.

Many of the out-of-town guests were planning to spend the night at Sabirjân's place, and their things were strewn around the house's three rooms. Sabirjân's sense of protocol, however, dictated that our group should be given a separate room. Trying not to let us see what he was doing, he removed his guests' personal belongings from one of the rooms and freed it up for our use. The birthday guests were crowded into the remaining two rooms—one for men and one for women. Sabirjân's insistence on offering hospitality in the face of daunting obstacles was in one sense an example of the Central Asian "spirituality" of which OM was so proud. In another sense, however, it became a feat of endurance for both host and guests aimed not at making either party comfortable but at mechanically serving the principle that, as one Uzbek aphorism summed it up, "the guest is higher than one's own father." In the service of that principle, hosts tend to view guests not as individuals with personal needs and personal preferences but as anonymous tokens of the abstract category "guest" who required a conventionalized, ritualized treatment. How many unwanted bottles of cheap vodka had been mindlessly opened in defense of that imperious principle? How many sheep needlessly slaughtered?

Sabirjân was a choir director by training. He had completed a five-year course at the local Institute of Culture that prepared students to be "culture workers" within the Ministry of Culture or Union of Trade Unions network of culture clubs and houses of culture. Sabirjân had studied piano, score reading, vocal conducting, solfège, harmony, and music history. He had also taken humanities courses, as he described them, in subjects such as the history of the Communist party and of the USSR, and methodological courses in how to organize activities within a house of culture, how to lead what was called "club work." I asked Sabirjân whether his institute's music curriculum had focused primarily on European composers or Uzbek composers.

"We studied both," he said.

"Which European composers did you study?" I asked.

"There were a lot of them. I don't remember their names. That was ten years ago," he replied.

I asked, "Did you ever work as a choir director?"

"No, I never had the chance. Karshi is eighty-five percent Uzbek, and you can't just gather twenty or thirty people together and create a choir. People aren't interested in choir music. In schools you can do it, and there are one or two choirs functioning. But in Karshi there are ten or fifteen people like me. Outside the schools, people don't have any use for European vocal music. They don't want to hear it." And so Sabirjân had gone to work within the culture club system. The seventeen collective farms in the Karshi District had twenty-seven clubs, which employed 120 people in the organization of culture. There were libraries, reading halls, and chess circles, girls' dance ensembles and ensembles of elderly women. Sabirjân managed this whole club network.

It was to one such culture club in the town of Baysun, southeast of Karshi, in the neighboring region of Surxandarya, that OM, Dadanazar, and I made our way with Sabirjân. Two years before, a group of dancers and musicians from Baysun had appeared at the spring *nâwruz* festival in Tashkent, and I had been impressed with their reconstructions of pre-Islamic music and dance. I had spoken briefly with the director, a gracious, friendly man named Abduxaliq, and he had invited me to visit him in Baysun. OM and I had tried to go to Baysun soon afterward, but it was impossible for a foreigner, we had been told at the Office of Visa Registration. There were defense installations nearby—missile sites, it was said—and the whole area was off-limits. By 1993, however, the missile sites had mysteriously become a nonissue and my request for a visa was quickly granted.

A "TRAVELER" IN BAYSUN

Sabirjân knew the narrow, twisting road between Karshi and Baysun intimately, and insisted that he drive our car instead of Dadanazar. I was leery of the form his nervous energy might take behind the wheel of a car, but since neither Dadanazar nor OM objected to his driving, I held my tongue. Within moments,

I knew I had made a mistake. Sabirjân immediately floored the gas pedal, and our creaky Volga whizzed along bumpy straightaways, insouciantly overtaking lumbering tanker trucks as we approached blind curves, slowing slightly before hairpin turns, and screeching to a halt when obstacles such as fallen rocks or trucks bearing down on us from the opposite direction momentarily blocked our route. I asked Sabirjân whether he wouldn't mind slowing down so that we could savor the magnificent emptiness of the surrounding steppe. Sabirjân couldn't understand why we preferred to look at scenery instead of reaching our destination as quickly as possible. OM tried to explain. "Life's more enjoyable if you do things with *kaif*," he said, invoking the local term for the feeling of well-being that comes from drinking wine or smoking opium (the Uzbek-Tajik term has also entered Russian slang: *kaifovat'* means "to get a high from something"). But Sabirjân clearly did not catch on. Within minutes the car had accelerated to its former terrifying pace. "Pull over," I ordered Sabirjân. "I am going to change places with you." Meekly, Sabirjân sank into the back seat while I put the car in gear and drove away at a *kaif*-inducing thirty miles an hour. To the end, Sabirjân never understood what I found so enticing about motoring slowly through the vast, silent steppe of Surxandarya, sixty miles north of the Afghan border.

Baysun is an ancient town. Local people told us that in Soghdian times it had been called Basant. Approaching it from the northwest, we drove across a narrow pass cut through rock striations known as Timur's Gate, just like the Timur's Gate east of Samarkand. An older Timur's Gate lay about 100 yards away, where, before the invention of dynamite, the road had zigzagged through a strategic dip in the southwesternmost spur of the Zaravshan Ridge that guarded the shortest route between Samarkand and the great cities of northeastern Khurasan: Balkh, Mazar-i Sharif, and Herat. Sabirjân assured us that not only Timur but Babur and even Alexander the Great had passed along the same road and looked down at Baysun and its gardens, set on high, flat land at the very edge of the mountains.

Baysun's cosmopolitan history is evident in the intermingling of Turkic and Tajik groups that have long cohabited the region. A chance conversation with two men building a clay wall along the road made the point. They were Tajiks, the men told us, but they spoke perfect Uzbek. "Here, all the Tajiks speak Uzbek and all the Uzbeks speak Tajik," they said. "Everyone in Baysun is bilingual." The "Uzbeks" of Baysun and its surroundings were themselves a mixture of different clans, tribes, and patterns of settlements, many of which still maintained their own identities. Local people gave as an example the Taghchi, a Turkic tribe that is thought to have inhabited Transoxania long before the appearance of the nomadic Qipchaq Uzbeks in the late fifteenth century. Besides the Taghchi, there were Qongrads and Kenagas, Katagans and Munka (a subgroup of the Qongrads).[2]

136

Unlike Transoxania's great oasis cities, Baysun does not betray its long history through a legacy of architectural monuments. Perhaps because of the scarcity of water, the town never achieved a size large enough to attract major wealth and big-time religion. Mosques and *madrasah*s have come and gone; gone even is the modest country house where, in 1920, Emir Alim Khan stayed on his flight south from Bukhara across the Amu Darya to self-exile in Afghanistan. Baysun had been a *basmachi,* a counterrevolutionary stronghold, we were told; Enver Pasha—one of the most famous of the *basmachi*—had operated from there; Ibrahim Beg had maintained a field camp nearby.[3]

We found Abduxaliq, the founder and director of the Baysun Ensemble, in Baysun's House of Culture, a pleasant, glass-fronted building whose sun-drenched lobby was filled with potted tropical plants. Two years had passed since our chance meeting in Tashkent, and he gripped my hand firmly and held it for a long time while fixing his eyes directly on mine. He was a smallish man with unruly, greasy hair, dressed in the most innocuous of Uzbek working-class clothes. It was his eyes that betrayed the inner fire.

The Baysun Ensemble had created a sensation in Uzbekistan in the early years of perestroika. Rejecting the well-trod path of "national" folklore glorified by Soviet Russian groups such as the Moiseyev Ensemble and the Piatnitsky Choir and later cloned into a variety of non-Russian "national" forms through-out the USSR, in which authentic folk music was choreographed, arranged, or simply composed by academically trained musicians, the Baysun Ensemble had offered an alternative vision of how to represent ethnographic tradition on the concert stage. Like revivalist folk musicians in Europe and the United States, Abduxaliq and the young members of his ensemble had sought out the sources of local musical tradition among old people and painstakingly reconstructed their songs and dances. Abduxaliq described this work to us. "We'd go to someone and find a musical phrase—maybe several words or a few strophes of a song. Then we'd start to search for other pieces of the song. We'd speak with old people, and gradually we'd reestablish the song, then we'd test ourselves. We'd invite old people, we'd sing, and we'd ask, 'Do you remember this?' And they'd give their comments: 'I think something's not right here,' or 'It's supposed to sound like this,' 'It didn't sound like that,' etc. There wasn't any other way to work except what we did. There aren't any people left who know a whole ritual in its entirety. They all know pieces. For one song, we spent two years putting it together. We found one phrase, then we spent two years finding the rest of the song."

At first the Tashkent television station had refused to televise concerts by the Baysun Ensemble. "They said that what we did was wild, crazy," said Abduxaliq. But later the television bureaucrats had come around, and Abduxaliq's seemingly iconoclastic approach to representing Uzbek musical traditions had been vindi-cated. What was the inspiration that had led Abduxaliq beyond the glitzy

137

Abduxaliq

superficiality of Socialist Realist folk kitsch to his search for something authentic in music? I asked him whether he could explain that to me. Abduxaliq said that it was a long story but that if I had the time, he would tell it. As I turned on my tape recorder, we settled into uncomfortable chairs in the bare, green-walled room that served as his office in the House of Culture.

"I was born in 1945. My father had fourteen children by two wives. I'm the sixth, the oldest from the second wife. My father's first wife died shortly after the birth of her fifth child. We lived not badly. My father knew how to work. He was a simple man, and he had a particular trait: he always liked to work alone. He worked on the land and herded. He was a capable man and a good storyteller. Our lineage has a long connection to art. My father's father was a talented singer. He played the *tanbur* and *dâyra*. He was invited to live in Bukhara and for several years served the Bukharan emir as a singer. They called him Ustâ Qurbân Tanburi.

"I finished school in Baysun, studied in the teachers institute in Tashkent, then served for three years in the army. After the army, I continued my studies in Tashkent. While I was a student, I was arrested and sent to jail for eight years. In 1969, I'd written a short story that was published in a journal. It was about the civil war—about an old woman who found a wounded Russian soldier. He was with the Red Army. The old woman didn't understand anything; she was a simple, good woman, and she wrapped his wounds so he wouldn't die. And she said to him, 'What do you want, anyway? You have a homeland. Why don't you just live in peace instead of torturing yourself like this? Why are you fighting? What will it bring?' That idea—that there wasn't a reason to fight—was treasonous. After that, they began to look askance at me. In those days, they applied only two articles [of law] against all undesirable people. If someone were in a position to be set up, they'd set him up as having accepted a bribe; if not, they'd accuse him of rape. The rape law isn't the way it is in other countries. If a woman points to a man and says, 'He raped me,' that's enough to put someone away. Maybe that article was specially intended for Central Asia. It's absurd. There's no role for any kind of proof. Eight students were accused, and two of them were freed. Their parents were wealthy, but the children of simple people were sent to jail: sixty-six years in all for the six of us.

"There was a lot of talk about this in Uzbekistan. Many teachers wrote letters. It was all a brazen lie. It was all rigged. The first day of the trial, the judge said to us, 'Listen, fellows, don't think that you're going to get out of this. I know you're all clean; I know, but I can't let you go. Once you come here, you don't leave clean. If you admit your guilt, even though you didn't do it, I'll lighten your sentence to the minimum term. That's the only way I can help you.' He wasn't a bad person, that judge, for those times.

"I had an interesting relationship with the warden of the prison. I saw very good people there, perhaps because they understood that there's a lot of injustice. When the warden of the Karshi camp died, I was sad. I went to his funeral. He was a good man. When we came to the camp, there were ten of us accused of breaking various laws. He spoke with each of us; he said to me, 'Son, I know that you're not guilty, but be a man. God tests good people; be patient. If you get mixed up in any sort of dirty business here, my conscience is going to suffer from it.' I served seven months in the Tashkent jail, then five years in Karshi, then I was sent to Zaravshan, to a penal colony. I worked there and paid twenty percent of my salary as a fine. I was released a year-and-a-half early. I worked as a dispatcher, a brigadier of construction. I saw real evils. My soul burned. I could have killed people then. But when that warden said that I couldn't change the system, that I had to be patient—that's when I started to study Sufism."

I asked, "Did you have books?"

"The interesting thing is that in prison you can find all sorts of prohibited books. They didn't forbid books in the camp. You could receive ten thousand books a year and they wouldn't be forbidden. The people who worked there, the guards, half of them were very good people. They saw evil and they were revolted by it. And they became good people from that. The other half of the people were for sale. You gave them something, and they wouldn't see what you were doing. And between the two halves, you could quietly do your business. The prison was supposed to buy books, but they took the money they were given for books and put the lion's share in their pockets. With the rest, they bought old books that people brought to them or that were confiscated or removed from circulation in libraries. They bound the books, and they became better than new ones. There were books from 1918 and from 1937. There were books from tsarist times. I was amazed. I never found those kinds of books in the public library. There were books about Islam, about history, and about psychology. Books on parapsychology, on human potential, were forbidden. They [the authorities] said that the limitations of the human body wouldn't allow the kinds of things described in those books. Sufism, however, isn't only about the cultivation of the soul but also about the cultivation of the body, the cultivation of physical forces."

"Do you consider yourself a Sufi?" I asked.

"To become a Sufi is very difficult. I consider myself a traveler (*yolavchi*). A person who wants to go on this path is called a *yolavchi.*"

"Do you have a sheikh?"

"He died. He was an *ishân*. His name was Pir Muhammad Ishân. He lived in Tajikistan. He died a long time ago. We had an interesting relationship. When I went to him, he knew that I was going to come, and when he needed me, I felt that in Tashkent. We never spoke in advance about my visits. When I would go to him, unexpectedly, of my own will, there would always be *pelmeni* (dumplings) ready. I like *pelmeni*. He'd bring the *pelmeni* and he'd look and smile. He lived outside of Ghissar Region in a village. He worked in the fields. He knew a lot about religion, but he didn't have a lot of *murids.* He didn't want them. He was so modest that the people who lived around him in the village didn't know that he was a great man."

"How did you find him?"

"After finishing the first year of my institute, I was traveling on a train from Tashkent to Karshi together with a young woman from Baysun who was the daughter of an *ishân*. She said that her father, the *ishân,* knew someone who was a great man. Her father was a lot better known than that man, but the young woman said that when her father met with him, her father was usually silent. So I took the man's address and I went there. He was fifty-nine when I met him, in 1963. He died at age sixty-three, in 1967. I consider that man my teacher."

"Was he literate?"

"Yes. He could read Cyrillic; he could read Arabic. I always had tears in my eyes when he read the Qur'an. We didn't read books, though. We had conversations. Usually I listened. Or sometimes he'd force me to talk. To talk logically. He taught me to think abstractly; he taught me to connect facts and arguments. He taught me to feel intuitively. Those sorts of things. He'd talk, and for some reason, I'd understand him; not only his words but an entire understanding. He'd always say to me that people don't think in words. They think in blocks of understanding. He taught me to read quickly. He said that good people can learn good both from good people and from bad. 'Every younger person is your younger brother; every older person is your older brother,' he'd say. 'Every old man is your father; every old woman is your mother.' Only in that way can a person find himself. The rest is all nonsense. He felt sorry for evil people. He was full of good. I was young, and I knew how to fight. But he would look at someone and say, 'I feel sorry for that person, that he won't become a man. May God help him to become a man.' He ate only from his work. He didn't accept gifts. I used to go in the spring and help him in the fields. I'd be gone for a month at a time."

"Was the *ishân* connected to a *xânâgah?*"

"No. A person who has achieved a certain level of intellect, of education, likes solitude. The most interesting is that the more he understands, the more he'll move away from groups. For example, dervishes go in groups—that's the beginning of the path; but *qalandar*s don't go in groups. An attraction to perfection exists in everyone. It's the nature of man. It's especially developed in the East, and it existed before Islam. When someone goes along that path, he reaches a certain state where religion doesn't exist for him in the usual sense. He himself becomes religion. That happens in Islam, in Christianity, in the synagogue, the mosque, the church. The person understands that everything is a unity."

"Do you connect that philosophy to music?"

"Of course. No single philosophy, no single scientific understanding, can describe the state of man's soul. We can never understand why we are walking along and suddenly we have a clear image of our childhood. It's something mechanical. But in that mechanism there's also a thought. So music is consonant with man's soul, with intellect. And intellect without soul isn't intellect. My teacher had an expression: 'mind is power, but sensitivity is a miracle' [*aql qudrat, farâsat mu'jiza*]. So music is great, inexplicable, incomprehensible in the way it works on the soul and intellect of man. In my understanding, music *is* soul itself.[4] I don't know how to explain it. But you can qualify and distinguish different types of music, because every kind of music arises according to types of people. For example, why is European music polyphonic and in Central Asia it's monophonic? When I was in England giving concerts, I sat in that concert hall and had the idea that maybe in Central Asia the stage of polyphonic music has already passed, that polyphonic music is the first step in the understanding of music. When I hear a single violin playing one of our [Central Asian] classical pieces, it seems that I supplement what I hear. The music becomes polyphonic in my soul. For example, *Chol-i Iraq,* played only by a violin, maybe accompanied by a *dâyra* or maybe without a *dâyra*. But when I hear the Appassionata, or a requiem, or *Chol-i Iraq,* it's one and the same. A person's soul fills in the places that need to be filled in, because for this [Uzbek] nation, polyphony is a stage that's already been passed through, and it's a part of the soul. When you play any individual instrument, the soul fills it out. I started to listen to European music about fifteen years ago, as an experiment. I tried to understand it. And it seems to me that Europe has also begun to listen to solo instruments; it's becoming popular. They're getting through the stage of polyphonic music." Abduxaliq was suggesting, in so many words, that perhaps the Orient was more musically advanced than Europe.

"How do you apply your philosophy to your practical work as a musician?" I asked.

"It's not my philosophy. I'm just one of its transmitters. I try to understand more deeply what I'm doing; to take things to their completion; to understand the songs that we learn; to put myself in the place of the people who sang them. For example, *Sus Xâtin,* about the patron of rain. That song is 3,000 years old. The words might have changed, but the ceremony could be that old. It's a primitive understanding, but to find reason in this primitiveness, a striving toward reason, is interesting. You have to put yourself in the place of those people who are waiting for rain, from God. Only God can help them. *Sus Xâtin* can help them. You have to feel that. That philosophy has helped me a lot to feel the world, to feel my work."

"Your ensemble performs not only traditional ritual music but also contemporary music," I said.

"Islam doesn't like pomposity. That's true in general about religions, but in order to preserve our national culture, in particular, national music, there appeared this form, the *toy.* Our national music was preserved in *toys.* No ministry of culture did anything to support the *toy.* They could oppress you, but they couldn't create anything. I say that thanks to our rituals, our songs have been preserved. Take the Yakuts, the Khakas; they were wiped away as nations, because they didn't have these kinds of *toys.* Here, people would sell their trousers if they had to, but they'd always put on a *toy."*

"Are you disappointed that your ensemble uses amplifiers and loudspeakers when you perform at *toys*?"

"There's an aphorism, 'If the mountain won't go to Muhammad, then Muhammad has to go to the mountain.' What can you do, when that's the way it is? What people understand now by the word 'tradition' is not tradition; it's some kind of stupid current. It will stop sometime; and those who value real music will listen without amplifiers. When we go to weddings with the ensemble, I always try to give something to the audience; I try to let people feel the music. But I can't change the world alone. It seems that in the world, evil can never be conquered; it just recedes. Evil always has nothing to lose, and good always perishes."

My questions had begun to seem banal and academic in the presence of this deeply thoughtful man who had bared his soul to me. I fell silent, and Abduxaliq and I sat together and shared that silence for what felt like a long time. Abduxaliq was a living example of what OM had described after our overnight stay with the good Samaritan of Samarkand as "a thousand years of work by millions of *ishâns*." His suffering-onto-mindfulness, his clarity, and his almost exaggerated modesty had stemmed not from immersion in a high religious science of Sufism but from the pragmatics of daily practice that was characteristic of Central Asian *ishânism*. In a sense, religion and music in Transoxania had moved along parallel trajectories through the post-Timurid centuries that both Soviet and Western historians had so often described as a period of stagnation. While the great medieval tradition of indigenous *ilm*—"science"—had withered and died and the resulting vacuum had been filled by European learning disseminated through the institutions of Russian colonialism, a vast orally transmitted tradition of both musical and religious praxis had flourished. For music, the key to continuity, as Abduxaliq had pointed out, had been the enduring presence of the *toy*. For religion, it had been the work of the *ishâns*. Seventy years of communism had secularized the *toy* and cast a pall over the work of the *ishâns*, but Abduxaliq's example added to the evidence that the populist spiritual energy that nourished those venerable institutions had not completely dissipated.

My reveries were interrupted by Abduxaliq. "Come, I will show you our ensemble," he said. The ensemble had been rehearsing in the auditorium of the House of Culture, and Abduxaliq brought OM and me there. I wanted to hear *Sus Xâtin,* the song about the patron of rain, and Abduxaliq asked the group to sing it for us (see the accompanying compact disc, track 8). Here is a transcription of the text:

> Soften [the ground], woman, woman full of water [refrain]
> Woman of wide embrace
>
> Let it rain, let everything get wet
> Let the whole earth become a lake
> Let grasses grow
> Let there be a lot of milk and yogurt
>
> Refrain
>
> Let there be rain, so that everything will turn green
> Let there not be drought
> Let millet and wheat stalks fill out
> Let the *kaivânni* [female master of ceremonies] serve all the food
>
> Refrain
>
> Let it rain, let everything get wet
> Let us get wet together
> Let us be merry together in the spring
> Let us be merry and strong
>
> Refrain

"It's raining!"

Rain came, it became wet
All the land has turned into a lake
The peach trees have sprouted leaves
The world is filled with flowers

Refrain

Soloist: refrain
Sus xâtin, suzma xâtin
Kolankasi maidân xâtin

Ensemble: refrain

Soloist:
Yâmghir yaghdir hol bolsin
Eru jahân kol bolsin
Maisalar qulok yaisin
Sutu qatiq mol bolsin

Ensemble: refrain

Soloist:
Yamghir yaghdir kok bolsin
Qurghoqchilik yoq bolsin
arpa-bughdâi bâsh târtsin
Kaivânilar âsh târtsin

Ensemble: refrain

Soloist:
Yamghir yadir xol bolailik
Bizlar senga jor bulailik
koklamda oinab kulib
Ham shuxu, ham zor bolailik

Ensemble: refrain

Yamghir! [shout]

Soloist:
Yamghir yaghdi hol boldi
Eru jahân kol boldi
Shaftâlilar barg yazdi
Dunya tola gul boldi.

Ensemble: refrain

The ensemble's nineteen singers, most of them in their early or mid-thirties, had dressed in their costumes for this informal performance before an audience of two. The group sang *a cappella,* with nicely modulated dynamics and clear articulation of the text. Their reconstructed archaic songs were declaimed in a

144

syllabic style without the melismas, extended cadences, and complex ornamentation characteristic of art song. "Their music is like wildflowers," OM said to me between songs. "Its wealth is in its diversity. The songs are simple, but it's not a primitive simplicity. There's a great variety of rhythms and themes, from magical to lyrical, tragic to joyous. Men and women sing together; you don't find the gender distinctions that pervade urban music. And they can sing as long as they want and won't run out of songs. We may not think of their music as part of a great tradition, but in its own way, that's what it is." (In a nod to the cultural politics of musical revivalism in Uzbekistan, almost all of the ensemble's "authentic" songs were sung with Uzbek texts, although Abduxaliq freely acknowledged that when the group performed at weddings, they mixed Tajik and Uzbek texts in whatever way seemed appropriate for a particular audience.)

Members of the Baysun Ensemble demonstrating an old form of men's dance.

What the Baysun Ensemble showed us was in every sense of the word a performance. What about their "own" folk music? What did they sing when they were not fulfilling the role of revivalist musicians? "Pop songs," said one of the singers. Even in a place as remote from centers of popular culture as Baysun, indigenous musical tradition was a choice, not a necessity. To live, it had to be revived; it wasn't simply "handed down." And that revival had been problematic and unwelcome in the beginning. The culture authorities had wanted kitsch—a Soviet-style song and dance ensemble, not ethnographically informed demonstrations of pagan customs. Even after Abduxaliq and his ensemble had become successful cultural revivalists, their bread-and-butter work

145

still consisted of performing at weddings, and wedding guests in Baysun liked amplified pop music. Ethnographic performances were a kind of public service sideline. Learning these intimate details about the life of the Baysun Ensemble, I had once again asked myself a recurring question: was there any place left in Transoxania, even in this sparsely settled corner of Surxandarya, where local musical traditions had not been overrun by Sovietized pop influences whose origin was in the West? Our meeting with Shâhberdi *baxshi* was to provide a tentative answer.

BAXSHI CHIC IN SHIRABÂD

Shâhberdi's sobriquet derived from his profession. He was a *baxshi*—a reciter of oral poetry. The occupation of *baxshi* in Transoxania has for some centuries—how many is hard to say—been split into two subspecialties, each centered on a distinct social activity. The first subspecialty, practiced only by men, is artistic entertainment. *Baxshi* entertainers like Shâhberdi are musician-poets (analogous to the *ashug* of Anatolia and Azerbaijan) whose primary artistic work is the musical performance of oral poetry at *toy*s. The second subspecialty, practiced more commonly by women than men in Transoxania, is healing with the aid of music. At some point in the past, the two subspecialties seem to have been linked both socially and psychologically in the work of one and the same individual (the prototype of such a figure is identified with the Korkut of Turkic legend).[5] That is, the recitation of musically heightened poetry was understood to have a magical and potentially therapeutic effect on listeners. This therapeutic effect could be intensified through an individual séance performed by the *baxshi* that included special incantations to facilitate contact with the spirit world and exorcise evil spirits from the body of a sick person.

Shâhberdi was one of the busiest *baxshi*s in Surxandarya.[6] He had been called to perform at a *toy* in a village beyond Baysun, near the border of Tajikistan, and when we met him over lunch at Abduxaliq's house, he was on his way home. He lived in a small settlement of herding families near Shirabâd, a town about two-thirds of the way from Baysun to the Afghan border. Why didn't we come with him? Shâberdi proposed. In fact, OM and I had planned to visit a different *baxshi* who lived farther to the northwest, along the route back to Karshi, but Shâhberdi persisted with his invitation, and after the ritual three declines, we accepted it.

The drive to Shâhberdi's place took us through a dramatic countryside of pristine grassland and craggy hills, framed by the distant snow-covered crest of the Zaravshan Ridge. Shortly after we left Baysun, the skies darkened with rain clouds, and rippling pulses of sheet lightning punctuated by vast, panoramic lightning bolts moved toward us rapidly from the west. The clouds produced only modest rainfall, but I had never seen such violent lightning. I became terrified that our car would be struck as we made our way across the flat expanse of grasslands, but OM, Dadanazar, and even Sabirjân were nonchalant.

Emerging from the storm, we passed a plaque forty feet long by twenty feet wide featuring a frontal view of Lenin's face assembled from thousands of variously colored stones built into a hillside on the edge of a small town. "The Party is the Mind, Honor, and Conscience of the People" said an inscription in Russian below the plaque. Sabirjân, appearing embarrassed when I asked about the plaque, explained that the local rural council wanted to rearrange the stones to represent a different face but hadn't yet come to agreement on whose to substitute for Lenin's.

At first glance, Shâhberdi's place gave the impression that he lived in the sort of *baxshi* chic that would not have been out of place in Aspen or Taos: a long, wood-beamed adobe ranch-style house with a veranda overlooking a spectacular vista of canyon, river, and barren hills stretching to the horizon; a sauna bath, a patio with a barbecue pit, two magnificent horses tied up in a barn; a pasture of dark green rye grass bordered by an impeccably masoned stone wall. It was only the details that suggested to a visitor that he was in Central Asia: aside from the barbecue pit, there was no other place to cook; there was no indoor plumbing; the entrance to the sauna building traversed a dribble of foul-smelling sewage running out the end of a pipe that wasn't quite long enough to reach a hole dug into the ground, from where it continued its downward journey, presumably to the river.

Shâhberdi had a shaved scalp, a long, aquiline nose, and prominent ears set very low on his head. He spoke rapidly in a stentorian voice whose cadence and tempo seemed to change not at all whether he was speaking Uzbek or Russian. Shâhberdi's lineage was from the Qongrad tribe of Uzbeks, and it was the Qongrads who had traditionally provided both the largest audience for *baxshi* music and the greatest number of *baxshi*s in the Surxandarya (Qongrads we met invariably emphasized their ethnic distinctiveness from "Uzbeks"). From Shâhberdi, I hoped to get a sense of the present status of the *baxshi* tradition: Was it a living tradition in which the traditional heroic *dâstân*s came alive for their audiences and new poems were being added to the repertory? Or was it a frozen tradition like the *Shash maqâm,* or a reconstructed one, like the Baysun Ensemble's performance of old Turkic songs? I asked Shâhberdi to tell us about his professional life as a *baxshi.*

"People started to call me *baxshi* when I first went to a wedding to sing. It was difficult. I was very shy and I knew just one *terma* [a short, orally composed poem, often improvised in the course of performance; *terma* is the antipodes of the long narratives that comprise the *dâstân,* or heroic epic]. I had been trained as a teacher, but at the Teachers Institute in Termez there had been a *baxshi* who was studying in a different department, and he became my teacher. He taught me

147

texts—where to say what. At present I know seven *dâstân*s that are my own and another eight that are printed in books.

"Just about every day I sing at a *toy*. Mostly it's rural people who like *baxshi*s—particularly in Qashqadarya and Surxandarya. They wouldn't have a wedding without a *baxshi*. Sometimes I perform for the old people and there's a different singer for the younger people."

I asked, "How far in advance are you booked?"

"As much as forty or fifty days. There are more than thirty *baxshi*s in Surxandarya and twenty-eight in Qashqadarya; there are also five in Samarkand—but they don't sing like us. Sometimes I sing until four o'clock in the morning. There's a lot of people to serve. Suppose someone from the leadership, the secretary of the District Committee, or the mayor has a wedding. You have to go. If you're the secretary of our region and you want to have a wedding, you won't come to me and ask, 'Shâhberdi, when can I book my wedding? Tell me the date.' *He'll* tell *me* the date. And maybe I already have a wedding scheduled for that day. So I'll go to the person and I'll explain that the secretary is having a wedding and I'll say, 'How about if I sing for two hours?' and he'll say, 'Okay.' So I'll sing for two hours, and then I'll go to the secretary's wedding. Sometimes that happens. When I have one, two, or three weddings a day, I don't make any money. What can you take for two hours' work, for an hour's work? It's not nice. You sing for five or ten hours, and you've earned your money."

"Do you have a fixed agreement?"

"No, no, no. I never have an agreement. People give money to my students, and I tell the students to put the money in the trunk of my car. I don't even take it in my hands or put it in my pocket. When I get home, of course, I count it."

"Is that a custom among *baxshi*s?"

"No, it's just what I do. Some have an agreement. They say, 'If you give such and such a sum, I'll sing; if you don't, I won't sing.' But that's not right. It's not good."

We stayed up late with Shâhberdi as a nearly full moon rose over the steppe and turned the stone-filled river below a splotchy silver. In response to a query about whether he actively composed his own material, Shâhberdi performed for us a recent composition—an erotic *dâstân* that recounted the exploits of a sex-starved herder with young donkeys. When Shâberdi had finished, OM remarked with great scholarly detachment that collectors of oral epic had paid scant attention to the erotic side of the *baxshi* repertory. Like the religious-to-lyrical paradigm of art song, the *baxshi* repertory also displayed a range of expression that extended from heroic to erotic, and Shâberdi's poetic creation had left no doubt that the art of the *baxshi* was a living one, at least at the erotic end of the paradigm. But despite Shâberdi's busy schedule and widespread renown, OM judged his poetic talent to be inferior to that of the *baxshi* whom we had originally intended to visit. So rather than hunker down with Shâhberdi to learn more about the performance style of the *dâstân* and *terma,* we thanked him for his hospitality, signed his guest book, and made our way north toward Dexânâbâd, to the tiny settlement of Xâja Mahmud, the home of Qahhâr *baxshi* (pronounced "kaHAR").

XÂJA MAHMUD

I had first traveled to Xâja Mahmud in the spring of 1991, when OM had suggested that we invite Qahhâr *baxshi* to join a small group of Uzbek musicians who were to give a series of concerts in the United States under the auspices of the Asia Society. Qahhâr was thirty-three when we met, and though he had been performing *dâstâns* for only five years, he had grown up in a household steeped in the bardic tradition. "Nomadic people should know seven generations of their ancestors," Qahhâr had said, "and all seven generations on my father's side were *baxshis*." The last of them had been Qahhâr's father, Qâdir *baxshi,* who died in 1986 in an automobile accident. Qahhâr had begun to sing after his father died. "I was very wounded by my father's death," Qahhâr told us. "A lot of people were saying that his craft had died with him, and the people who used to come to our house and share our food started to stay away. I didn't want our house to lose the spirit that our father gave to it, and in order to turn that around, to convince people that his art hadn't died, I started performing. Before, I had played and sung mainly for myself, but through the recollections of my father's friends and through the many recordings of my father [on cassettes], I began to learn his repertory and to follow in the footsteps of my father. I started going to local *toys*, people started passing the word around, and that's how my reputation grew. We had a lot of distant relatives who lived in different regions, and they started inviting me. I've been in Tajikistan and in Turkmenistan. In our region, I've been everywhere. I know more than thirty *dâstâns*. My father knew sixty-five *dâstâns* from memory."

Xâja Mahmud lay isolated at the end of some ten miles of bumpy dirt track that stretched over a rocky, treeless landscape where sheep grazed on a gossamer covering of parched grass. The settlement itself consisted of fifteen squat, clay-plastered houses with corrugated roofs facing one another across a muddy field on which cows, sheep, and chickens mingled randomly with dozens of small, shaven-headed children. Qahhâr *baxshi* was the sole teacher in the local primary school. When we had appeared unexpectedly in Xâja Mahmud, his wife had sent word to the school, and Qahhâr *baxshi* had dismissed his students, returned home to greet us, and ordered a sheep to be slaughtered and butchered in preparation for a feast.

Three walls of the *mehmânxâna* in Qahhâr's house were painted in an abstract design in which pink rose blossoms were clustered into ethereal,

Qahhâr *baxshi* holding his *dombra*.

cloudlike blotches. The fourth wall was devoted to a painted mural that featured Qâdir *baxshi*, Qahhâr's deceased father, sitting before a backdrop of mountains and a yurt clutching his *dombra*—the small, fretless lute on which the *baxshi*s of Surxandarya and Qashqadarya accompany their singing (technically, the *dombra* may be described as a short long-necked lute). The mural was done in a primitivist style that called to mind the Russian artist Nikolas Roerich's mystical Himalayan landscapes. In a corner of the *mehmânxâna* opposite the mural was a refrigerator and a table with a television set and a VCR. The floor was covered with kilims and a felt rug around whose perimeter mats and pillows had been neatly laid out. As we were making ourselves comfortable in the *mehmânxâna,* more guests arrived. The mayor of Dexânâbâd had heard about our visit and had driven out to Qahhâr's place in his jeep, together with the director of the Dexânâbâd house of culture and a few friends. The presence of the local officials all but guaranteed that what we had hoped would be a musical working session with Qahhâr *baxshi* would instead be a bacchanal.

While the butchered sheep cooked slowly in a sealed tandir oven, I claimed an hour of free time and slipped away for a hike amid the herb-drenched aromas of hilly open rangeland behind Qahhâr's house. When I returned, the sheep had been removed from the tandir oven and the feast was in full swing. Sabirjân was pouting because the sheep's testicles had been thrown to the dogs instead of set

150

aside for his consumption. He had been looking forward to eating the "light bulbs," as they are called in the local slang. During the period that encompassed my travels with OM, I was in various stages of commitment to vegetarianism, and at the time of our trip to Xâja Mahmud I had adopted a strictly meatless regimen. The concept of not eating meat was difficult to explain to our host. There is no word for "vegetarian" in Uzbek. The closest one can come is "grass eater." A quizzical expression had come over Qahhâr's face when I cited a line popular in certain vegetarian circles, to the effect that humankind will gradually evolve toward a higher state of noncarnivorous consciousness in which vegetarianism will become the norm. "What about us herders?" asked Qahhâr. "What will happen to us?" I didn't have an answer.

Among Transoxania's myriad social groups, it is the Qongrad Uzbeks, with their legacy of herding and stockbreeding, whose music seemed most strongly linked to an archaic Inner Asian Turkic sound world.[7] At the center of this sound world is the singing of epic poetry by bards who accompany themselves on a stringed instrument (the choice of instrument—which may be plucked or bowed—varies from one region to another, sometimes from one type of epic singer to another). Complementing the epic singing of the bard is a vast practice of homemade solo instrumental music played on jew's harps, single-reed end-blown pipes, and a variety of bowed and plucked lutes. This quintessentially Turkic sound world extends from northeast to southwest across the heart of Inner Asia, linking the shamanistic cultural milieu of Altai peoples such as the Tuvans and Khakas with Islamized Turkic groups such as the Uzbeks and Turkmens.

Several aspects of Qahhâr *baxshi*'s performance of both *dâstân* and *terma* were remarkable for what they suggested about the Qongrads' vestigial links to the pan–Inner Asian Turkic musical idiom. These characteristics were clearly evident in a short *terma* that we recorded in Qahhâr *baxshi*'s *mehmânxâna* (reproduced on the accompanying compact disc, track 15). Qahhâr *baxshi* extemporized the *terma* on the theme of our reciprocal visits: his to America and mine to Xâja Mahmud. Here is the transcribed and translated text.

1. *Ha, hai, yâr, eh . . . , hai, yâr, ai, eh*

2. Let no one be left with an unfulfilled wish
3. A valiant man takes spiritual strength from the land of his people
4. If God is looking after us, he'll take command of our fate
5. **I want to say something brief, my spirited one** [i.e., my *dombra*]
6. Look, in this circle [of people], I'll recite a potpourri of a *terma*

7. Let every person's head be healthy [i.e., let everyone be healthy]
8. The valiant man always has a lot of relatives around him
9. **Now I want to say something brief, my spirited one** [my *dombra*]
10. From another country, most honored relatives came

151

11. In the sky, the moon gleams
12. Let there be prosperity throughout this world
13. God gave me the chance to drink tea in different places
14. **Now let my *dombra* say a brief word**
15. Some of the most distinguished Uzbek people have
    gathered in this land

16. It was said that a valiant man would come
17. To hell with a bad person; he'll never be a native of this land
18. If there will be rivers, everything will blossom
19. If that person who came is good, *aq sakal* [literally,"white beard";
    Qahhâr is referring to the author]
20. Now's the right moment to say good words.

21. **Speak, my *dombra*, sing, my *dombra***
22. Show the whole world what you can do, my *dombra*
23. A guest has come to us today, sing, my *dombra*
24. Tell me everything that's in your soul, speak, my *dombra*

25. Let him have a lot of wealth, let his height be like a mountain
26. Say a few words, friends, in honor of these brothers

1. (Ha, hai, yâr, eeeeh . . . , hai, yâr, ai, eeeh . . . .)

2. (Hai) Qâlmasin (yârâna) har bir bandani armâni
3. (Hai) Eli khalqinnan keladi (ai) mard âdamning dârmani
4. (Hai) Himâyam bolsa kelar (a) bir xudâyimni farmâni (ai)
5. **Yakka âghiz aitar boldim jânivar (eeeh . . .)**
6. (Hai) bu davrada qâra deiman(a) termani (eeeeh. . . .)

7. (Hai) âmân bolsin har bandaning bâshlari (hai)
8. (Hai) mardning bolar karangga qarindâshlari (hai)
9. **(Hai) yakka âghiz (ai) soile deiman jânivar (eeeh . . .)**
10. (Hai) ozga eldan keldi bâshine qarindâshlari (eeeeh . . .)

11. (Hai) âzman bitda yarqilaidi âilari (hai)
12. (Hai) âbâd bolsin (a) bu dunyâning jâilari (ai)
13. (Hai) atâ qildi (yârân ai) ozga jâining châilari (a)
14. **(Hai) yakka âghuz aitsin deiman dombram (eeeh . . .)**
15. (Hai) bu elâtga birikdi ozbek eldning baîlari (eeeeh . . .)

16. (Hai) mard bir âdam gelatirgan gap bâr edi.
17. (Hai) jaman korsin, elidan darrâv quridi (eeeh)
18. (Hai) âgha daryâ bolsa gar bizning kokdagilar saridi
19. (Hai) hai, yâr ai, yaxshi âdam kelgen bolsa, âqsaqal (eeeh. . . .)
20. (Hai) aitarga bugun hâl qizib bâr êdi (eeeh. . . .)

21. **(Hai) soile deiman dombram, kuile deiman dombram**
22. (Ha) jâhanga kilighing taila deiman dombram
23. (Hö) mehmân kelipdi shu bugun, kuila deiman dombram
24. (Hai) juragingdagi dardingdi soile deiman dombram

152

25. Katta bolsun davlati, tâghdai bolsin sâvlati
26. Ikki aghiz dostlar aiting shu akalarning xurmati.

Qahhâr's verse exemplified the prosodic form known as *barmak,* a common genre of Turkic folk poetry, which in its canonical form is organized into quatrains with the rhyme scheme AABA or AAAA. In a classic *barmak,* each line would contain an identical number of syllables—most commonly seven, eleven, or fifteen—divided by caesuras into three or more segments. Qahhâr's extemporized poem, however, rides roughly over the classical *barmak* form. For example, line 5, which ought to be the final line of the first quatrain (the initial line of vocables is an independent introduction) becomes a poetic refrain that provides a kind of deceptive cadence to the previous four lines. (In the transcription and translation, the refrain line, continually transformed in the course of performance, appears in boldface.)[8] According to both the rhyme scheme and the meaning of the text, the final word in line 5 ought to be *termani.* But Qahhâr withholds *termani* until the end of line 6, and in its place at the end of line 5 sings a long, held pitch on the vocable "eeeeh." The timbre of this held note is noticeably colored with an intentionally amplified overtone. The overtone never reaches the clarity or intensity of the articulated harmonics in the widely known Tuvan and Mongolian *xöömei* style, but it is nonetheless an unmistakable presence in the *baxshi*'s sound world.[9] Qahhâr adds a brief, overtone-enriched vocable coda to the end of the penultimate and final lines of each of the first four strophes. In each case, the vocable is the sound "eeeh" (as in "cheese"), a sound rich in high overtones.

The remainder of the extemporized *terma* is formally uneven. The syllable counts of successive lines don't match up, the quatrain structure is repeatedly violated, and the rhyme scheme differs from one quatrain to the next. Nonetheless, the flow of the music covers the formal inconsistencies of the poetry. OM commented on the relationship between text and music as we analyzed our recording and transcription. "It's not good poetry when you read it, but it sounds good. Music is the main thing for Qahhâr, and he's a good musician. In the *terma,* it's as if he works out a musical structure and then adds the poetry [his *dâstâns* were poetically more polished]. There are other *baxshis* who are better poets but less-talented musicians. But a great *baxshi* must be both a great musician and a great poet."

Qahhâr's method of oral composition contrasted starkly with that of Turgun Alimatov, who carefully works out and memorizes his instrumental compositions before bringing them to performance, where the spirit of the moment may alter details of the musical surface. Of paramount importance for Qahhâr and his listeners is the mimetic narrative quality of the *dâstân* and *terma:* the fact that every performance comprises the telling of a story that may provide new information and fresh insights, even about a well-known theme.[10] Qahhâr's singing and *dombra* playing rounded the rough edges of his poetry, and the imperfections that remained brought a liveliness to his performance.[11]

In both musical style and metaphysical referents, *dâstân* and *terma* contrast sharply with *maqâm*. Unlike the *hafiz,* whose voice reaches upward toward the transcendent God of Islam and whose renown stems from his ability to sustain almost inhumanly high pitches, the *baxshi's* voice reaches downward, toward the earth spirits of earlier shamanistic times, to which the *baxshi's* art is connected.[12] The *baxshi's* guttural, raspy vocal timbre presents an immediate contrast to the normal speaking and singing voice, thus creating an artistic and magical distance between everyday experience and the heroic world in which the *baxshi's* stories take place. Qahhâr told us that the special, laryngeally tensed voice in which the *baxshi* performs is called *ichqi avaz,* "inner voice," in distinction to *tashqari avaz,* "outer voice." The timbral quality of the "inner voice" remains unchanged throughout an entire *dâstân.* Changes of mood or emotions among the characters are conveyed through changes in the tune or melody type (*name*) performed on the *dombra.*

"If you perform *dâstân* with 'inner voice,' then your whole essence *(wujud)* focuses on it, and with the help of the *dombra,* there's a complete fusion with your listeners," said Qahhâr. "But if you sing in 'outer voice,' your thoughts can wander elsewhere, and you can cut yourself off from what you're doing." I had brought along a cassette of Tuvan overtone singing, and listening to it together with Qahhâr, I asked him whether he sensed a similarity between the "inner voice" of the *baxshi* and the Tuvans' guttural throat singing. "Yes," said Qahhâr. "We sing the same kind of long, drawn-out notes." What particularly struck Qahhâr was the wide, pulsing vibrato of the Tuvan singers' fundamental pitch, which he called *tolqillantirish,* literally, "movement like a wave." Qahhâr imitated the Tuvan sound, showing how it would be performed in the Qongrad style. Qahhâr assured us that this way of singing was very old. "Our craft has come down to us through thousands of years. We inherited this way of singing from people who sang in the same way at the very beginning of music. It's been passed down across time from one generation to the next: my father sang like that; his father sang like that."

Qahhâr's antediluvian *terminus a quo* for the "inner voice" style of *baxshi* singing was of course a poetic one. No trace of evidence exists that could suggest how long humankind might have sung in such a way. However, the prominent place of intensified overtones in Qongrad vocal style suggests an old relationship to the music history of other Inner Asian Turkic peoples. A widely accepted, if schematic, account of Central Asian historiography holds that beginning in the early Islamic era and continuing roughly until the beginning of the sixteenth century, numerous nomadic Turko-Mongol groups migrated to Transoxania from regions farther to the northeast. With the breakup of the Timurid Empire, the rise of the Iranian Safavids, and the division of Transoxania into the territories of the three khanates, the Uzbek nomads who had established themselves in the grasslands north of the Amu Darya were largely cut off both from their Altaic forebears and from the cultural influence of Khurasan, to the south. It is likely, then, that if there is indeed a genetic relationship between stylistic features of the Qongrad *dâstân* and the Altai *khöömei,* this relationship was molded at least half a millennium ago.

The "inner voice" of the *baxshi* is not the only element of Qongrad music that shares aspects of the musical aesthetics and metaphysics of a larger Inner Asian Turkic cultural realm. The same inclination toward narrativity that shapes the musical style of the *baxshi* is also present in instrumental music. During our stay at Qahhâr's, I had an unusual opportunity to experience the narrative powers of two instruments commonly played by the Qongrads: the *sybyzyk* and the *chang-qobuz.*

The *sybyzyk,* a short, single-reed pipe made from cane, is often used either to represent animals or to make contact with them. "Representing" animals in this case means not only conveying their stereotypical sounds through onomatopoeic resemblance (although it may mean that) but in addition representing their persona, their manner of being, through a sound image. One of the men who had arrived at Qahhâr's house with the mayor of Dexânâbâd turned out to play the *sybyzyk,* and during a break in the vodka drinking and sheep eating, he took out his instrument and demonstrated a series of animal representations. The "lament of a young camel" (*bâtabâzlar*) consisted of a plangent series of slurred high notes that slowly descended at the end. The "melody of a horse" (*ât kuii*) focused on the rhythmic clopping of the horse's hooves. A nightingale was represented by a sweet timbre and delicate ornamentation, while a goat was sonically rendered in a loud, gruff timbre.

I found the *chang-qobuz,* or jew's harp, more subtle and expressive than the *sybyzyk*—or perhaps it was simply the circumstances in which I heard it. As the vodka-driven festivities in Qahhâr's *mehmânxâna* were reaching a raucous climax, I noticed that a woman had entered the house and was sitting by herself in the room adjacent to the *mehmânxâna.* Qahhâr asked her to come into the *mehmânxâna* so he could introduce her to OM and me. She was his aunt, the sister of his late father, Qâdir *baxshi.* Her name was Xushvakt, and she was fifty-three years, although she looked much older. Qahhâr told us that she was an excellent player of the *chang-qobuz.* She was holding the instrument in her hand, and I asked whether she would perform a melody. Xushvakt didn't want to play in front of all the men but agreed to go into the adjoining room and play for me alone.

Xushvakt's music was extraordinary. Delicate and subtle, even amid the isolated austerity of Xâja Mahmud, it conveyed the feeling of having been delivered there from a world still more distant. I asked Xushvakt if she wouldn't mind playing the melodies again and telling me a little about them. Portions of the first and third melody are reproduced, with a cross-fade between them, on the accompanying compact disc (track 17). Here are Xushvakt's descriptions of what she represented in the melodies.

1. "I played while imagining a rocking chair and drew this picture [i.e., it was a lullaby]."

2. (Not on CD.) "This is an old melody called *tuya kairish* [make the camel stoop]. I'm using this instrument to call a herd of camels to return home."

3. "I performed this melody remembering my dear brother, Qâdir *baxshi*. Seven years ago he died. I performed this melody to call him to me. I performed this melody filled with sadness; in my body sits tremendous sadness which doesn't give me peace. I can only express it with tears, and with my soul [i.e., with my jew's harp]. When I played the melody, I imagined that he stood here, next to me; I remember his thoughts, his feelings, what kind of man he was."

In each melody, Xushvakt used her *chang-qobuz,* as she put it, to "imagine" an image or a brief narrative program. Strictly speaking, her melodies comprised a kind of program music. The example of Xushvakt's *chang-qobuz* suggests that the old Inner Asian Turkic predilection for musical narrativity is found not only in oral poetry but in instrumental music as well. Indeed, in many parts of Inner Asia it is common for instrumentalists to perform pieces in which their instrument is said to be telling a story.[13] The performer assumes that an enculturated listener can follow the story and respond emotionally in the proper places, just as a Western classical music lover might be expected to follow and respond to instrumental program music such as Berlioz's *Symphonie Fantastique*. In Inner Asia, however, the program may also be closely held—intended more for the performer than for listeners. OM had commented that music for *sybyzyk* and *chang-qobuz* is personal, intimate music, not communicative music. "That's why there are so many different forms and styles. There's not a 'tradition' in the sense of a lot of people sharing songs that are performed for audiences who know and recognize them. But of course every player has heard another player who came before."

It was over in no more than fifteen minutes. Xushvakt said that she had to get back to helping her five daughters-in-law and ten grandchildren, and with a slight bow, rose to leave. I thanked her, accompanied her to the door, and watched her walk away across the muddy field, clutching her precious jew's harp. Reentering the *mehmânxâna* to rejoin the boisterously drunk male company sprawled on the mats and pillows, I felt that in those fifteen minutes I'd been thrust through a time warp to a moment near the beginning of music, as Qahhâr had put it in his description of the genesis of "inner voice."

KHOREZM

Qarzing mingdan âshsa, har kun yumurta barak ye
(If a thousand debts are overflowing, ignore them and have a party
[literally, "eat egg ravioli every day"].)

—Khorezmi aphorism

ACROSS THE KARA-KUM

I had a vague feeling of foreboding on the hot, hazy morning in mid-May 1993 when we left Bukhara to make the 260-mile drive northwest across the sands of the Kara-Kum to Khiva, in the oasis on the Amu Darya known since antiquity as Khorezm. Khorezm was not only the home of a unique performance tradition of oral epic, spiritual poetry, and music for women's *toys* but also the birthplace of OM. From our first days of working together, OM had spoken exuberantly of Khorezm's unique cultural role within Transoxania and of the inordinate influence that its musicians and musical styles had on those of Tashkent—particularly in the arena of what might be called traditional popular music. OM drew pride from the notion of province—his province—influencing center rather than, as is more typical, the other way around.

Our journey to Khorezm had started out routinely, but I had become concerned with Dadanazar's driving—the way his attention seemed to wander at times, as if his newfound Muslim peace of mind was leading him on momentary visits to some other plane of existence unburdened by roads and traffic. Once, in the middle of a broad, straight highway, our car had gradually slowed until we were creeping along at fifteen miles an hour. At first I had assumed that Dadanazar had intentionally decelerated in order to check out some aspect of the car's performance. But after a few minutes of tortoiselike travel, I called his name sharply, and he roused himself with a startled look on his face. He had been daydreaming, he said, and had lost track of how fast we were going.

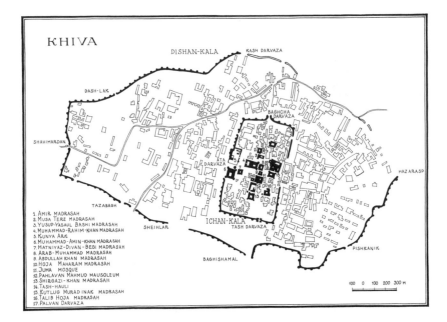

KHIVA

DISHAN-KALA

KASH DARVAZA

DASH-LAK

SHAHIMARDAN

BASHCHA
DARVAZA

HAZARASP

DARVAZA

TAZABAGH

1. AMIR MADRASAH
2. MUSA TERE MADRASAH
3. YUSUP-YASAUL BASHI MADRASAH
4. MUHAMMAD-RAHIM-KHAN MADRASAH
5. KUNYA ARK
6. MUHAMMAD-AMIN-KHAN MADRASAH
7. MATNIYAZ-DIVAN-BEGI MADRASAH
8. ARAB-MUHAMMAD MADRASAH
9. ABDULLAH KHAN MADRASAH
10. HOJA MAHARAM MADRASAH
11. JUMA MOSQUE
12. PAHLAVAN MAHMUD MAUSOLEUM
13. SHIRGAZI-KHAN MADRASAH
14. TASH-HAULI
15. KUTLUG MURAD INAK MADRASAH
16. TALIB HOJA MADRASAH
17. PALVAN DARVAZA

SHEIHLAR

ICHAN-KALA
TASH DARVAZA

PISHKANIK

BAGHISHAMAL

100 0 100 200 300 M

Khiva

For the trip to Khorezm, OM, Dadanazar, and I had been joined by a fourth traveler, a Tashkent-based photographer, Dmitri Mikhailov, who had come along to make a photographic record of our work. Dmitri had taken the train from Tashkent to Bukhara, where we had picked him up on our way north from Baysun and Karshi. Leaving Bukhara behind us, we could look back at the blue domes of the Great Mosque and the Mir-i Arab *madrasah* rising above the residential districts of the old city. Those domes must have provided inspiration to centuries of pilgrims and merchants slowly making their way toward Bukhara from the steppe. Now they were dwarfed by Bukhara's television tower—the central visual landmark from afar. At times, even the television tower was obscured by clouds of dust and exhaust fumes swirling around the stream of heavy trucks with which we shared the ribbon of road through parched *kolkhoz* fields. Twenty-five miles north of Bukhara, the land was still cultivated, but a little beyond, the irrigation ended and cultivated fields gave way to clumps of sagebrush. We were in the Kara-Kum.

It was there, literally in the middle of the desert, that Dadanazar had fallen asleep behind the wheel. No one had noticed his drooping eyelids until the car began to arc to the left onto the narrow dirt shoulder. Dadanazar had awakened with a start and pulled the wheel hard to the right, then hard to the left. The car had skidded back and forth twice across the sun-softened asphalt before

158

careening off the road into the sand, bumping along for several hundred feet, and finally crashing into a large clump of sagebrush. We were shaken up but unhurt. The scenario that ensued had been a vintage Central Asian example of brute manpower overcoming paucity of equipment and infrastructure. While I had naively proposed an American-style solution to our predicament—hitching a ride to the closest town, sixty miles away, and searching for someone with a flatbed truck and a hoist who could ferry the battered Volga to a repair facility—my companions knew better. In less than an hour, the car, whose right front wheel had been twisted around so that it dangled pathetically at almost a ninety-degree angle to its normal position, had been pulled out of the sand by a passing truck with a tow rope, and a brigade of truck drivers had gently lifted the Volga off the ground and tipped it on its side while one of the men bashed away at the axle and wheel base with a sledgehammer, bending the offending parts back into proper alignment.

The accident had cast a pall over our little expeditionary force. On the one hand, the outcome had been almost an undeserved gift of fortune in a situation that could just as easily have ended catastrophically. On the other hand, I had lost faith in Dadanazar and, by illogical extension, in OM, and in our work itself. There seemed to be a hex that had queered my efforts to learn about music in Khorezm. We had come to Khorezm twice before, OM and I. When we had started working together, OM had been particularly eager to show me his native region and to have me understand the distinctive features that set its traditions apart from those of other parts of Transoxania. But perhaps it was in part OM's very rootedness in Khorezm that hindered us. He was, in fact, a well-known public figure there, a favorite son who had gone off to Tashkent and achieved a certain fame yet had never forgotten his small-town origins. When he came home to Urgench, his social obligations began to pile up as soon as he stepped off the airplane. After attending to friends and family and taking care of various personal business matters, OM seemed physically and emotionally used up, and our work had suffered from that.

There were also the logistical difficulties of doing musical fieldwork in Khorezm. Musicians were not concentrated within a compact urban area, as in Bukhara, but spread out among the sprawling suburbs and collective farms that filled the fifteen miles between Khiva, the old seat of the Khivan Khanate, and Urgench, the Russian-built city closer to the Amu Darya that became the center of the Khorezm region of Soviet Uzbekistan after the downfall of the short-lived Khivan Republic in 1924. The local telephone system worked so poorly that it was next to impossible to call Khiva from Urgench or vice versa, let alone any of the settlements that lay between them. People who had a telephone tended not to use it as a practical tool. When OM wanted to find out whether a particular musician was home and willing to meet with us, he visited the musician's house. The Khorezmian sense of hospitality often made such visits into epic events, and several days could be used up simply arranging appointments.

Spontaneous social invitations, however, could also result in unusual encounters. For example, shortly after arriving in Urgench in 1991, we had run into a casual acquaintance of OM's, and he had invited us to a birthday party in a *madrasah* recently converted into a bar and grill. I didn't want to go, but OM hinted that he had something to discuss with his acquaintance and said that I'd be amused by the *madrasah*-to-grill renovation.

Inside a dark, cavernous room, an enormous U-shaped formation of tables had been set up. About sixty men sat on two sides of the U and a small group of women sat on the third side. A separate table outside the U provided places for children. The brick walls of the *madrasah* ricocheted the distorted voice of an emcee, which boomed out through cheap loudspeakers mounted on poles. Artificial reverb in the amplification system further magnified the resonating cacophony. I was seated at the head table and, over the din of the emcee and his music, started to chat with a patrician elderly gentleman seated to my left. "Hello, my name is Levin," I said to my neighbor.

"Good evening," the man replied. "I am Madyarov, Abdurasul Madyarovich. My grandfather was Feruz, the last khan of Khiva."

I put my fork down, took a deep breath, and looked intently at Madyarov (whose erstwhile title was Abdurasul *Tora*—Prince Abdurasul). He stared back at me. He was wearing an overcoat to ward off the chill of the unheated room and a brown fedora pulled down low over his forehead. His face was lined, but the skin held tightly against his high cheekbones. He sat ramrod straight and his movements betrayed not a trace of unsteadiness.

"This is my first visit to Khiva in seventy-one years," Madyarov yelled above the music. Seizing upon occasional lapses in the evening's entertainment, we managed to carry on a conversation over the next several hours in which Madyarov recounted the story of his life. Yielding sometimes in mid-sentence to the onset of the music or the glad-handing emcee, Madyarov would resume at the first available moment precisely where he had left off.

Madyarov spoke in unaccented Russian. I asked him whether he knew Uzbek. "How could I know Uzbek?" he exclaimed with annoyance. "I was sent away from Khiva when I was eighteen years old. I've lived all my life in the Ukraine. I haven't spoken Uzbek for seventy years, and I've forgotten every word I knew." To be precise, Madyarov had been sent away from Khiva on July 12, 1920, when the Bolshevik "Commission for the Affairs of Turkestan under the All-Russian Central Executive Committee of the Congress of Soviets and the Council of People's Commissars" decided to get rid of the khan and his family.

Madyarov's father was the second son of Said Muhammad Rahim Khan, popularly known as Feruz II. Feruz ruled for forty-six years and eight months, from 1864 until 1910, when he died at the age of sixty-five. He was not literally the last khan of Khiva, but Madyarov's description of him as the last khan was in keeping with the exalted image of his long rule that has survived decades of Soviet slandering and is presently undergoing an active renaissance in Khorezm.

When Feruz died, his fourth son, Isfendiyar, Madyarov's uncle, succeeded him. Isfendiyar ruled until 1918, when he was assassinated by Djunaid-khan, a rival Khivan and the real power in the khanate. Isfendiyar was succeeded in turn by his brother Abd Allah. Historians may have their own views of these two rulers, but Madyarov was clear about what he thought of them: "*Babniks* [womanizers, skirt-chasers], both of them," he said, with distaste. "And they had no interest in music." On the other hand, Feruz Khan, despite his harem of 130-odd members and his eleven wives, is remembered not as a womanizer but as a poet, a connoisseur of the arts, a lover of flowers. Many stories tell of how he personally examined and corrected the musicians who served in his court.

Along with seven other members of the khan's family, Madyarov was put on a train and taken to Lubyanka Prison number 2 in Moscow, where he spent twenty days. The former khan died shortly afterward, in a prison hospital. Between 1920 and 1923, Madyarov was incarcerated in a series of monasteries that had been converted into concentration camps. Finally released, he was forbidden to return to Khiva. He worked as a guard and at other menial jobs, married, and had three children. Then, in 1990, through a casual dinner-table conversation at a Ukrainian spa where he was vacationing, Madyarov had made the acquaintance of a wealthy man from Khiva, who, upon learning his identity, promised to send him a ticket to visit Khiva for *nâwruz,* the New Year's festival.

"How do you find it here after seventy-one years?" I asked.

"The air's good, I feel at home. I kissed the earth when I got off the airplane, and I visited my parents' grave [his father had been allowed to return to Khiva in 1935]. I had a good life here. We lived outside the court but visited the khan every few days. I attended *madrasah* in this very building eighty years ago. I'm almost ninety years old. I've spent half of my life in jail and in exile, and for what? Two hundred grams of butter, a half kilo of sausage, three kilograms of sugar," Madyarov said bitterly. A few months later, OM heard that Madyarov had died.

KHOREZM REIMAGINED

The respect for Feruz that had inspired the wealthy Khivan to send Madyarov a ticket to Khorezm was in the spirit of the historical and cultural reawakening that has been gathering strength there since Uzbekistan's independence. The figure of Feruz has undergone a radical facelift that has peeled away decades of Soviet-inspired antikhan sentiments and revealed (or recreated) the image of a benevolent and cultured despot—a leader to whom present-day Khorezmis can proudly trace the origins of their own peculiar brand of Transoxanian modernism *cum* traditionalism. A Feruz wall calendar produced to mark the 150th

The summer residence of
the Khan of Khiva.
Photo by Dmitri Mikhailov.

anniversary of the khan's birth in 1845 displays the portrait of a mandarin-looking gentleman in his mid-forties dressed in a Karakul hat and a richly colored, patterned robe. The facial expression mixes resolve with contemplativeness; the eyes are more soft than stern. OM said that Feruz became a legend after his death. "In the 1950s, there were still many people alive who remembered him, and they could talk endlessly about Feruz. But the Soviets turned him into an evil, lazy, good-for-nothing who exploited the peasants. It was only with perestroika and Independence that they started to resurrect him. Samarkand had Timur, Ferghana had Babur, Bukhara had Bahâ'uddin. Khorezm needed its own heroic figure. It was an opportunistic game.

"They've published two books of Feruz's poetry. Almost every day they read his poems on the radio, early in the morning. Literary scholars are saying now that he was a good poet. He also played the *dutar* and *tanbur* and loved classical music. Feruz personally supervised the affairs of his *maqâm* players. His devotion to music is captured in many stories and legends. In one story, for example, the leader of the *maqâm* ensemble, a man named Xudek who played the *bulaman,* a wind instrument, choked from a sip of water in the middle of a performance. When the performance was finished, the musicians were all paid, as usual, and went home. The next morning, Xudek arose to find that two men were standing on the roof of his house tearing it apart. 'What are you doing?' he cried. 'We're fulfilling the orders of the khan,' the men said. 'He told us to destroy your roof.' Xudek requested an audience with the khan, and when he was received, he said, 'Your Highness, these men have come and ruined my roof.' 'Ah,' said the khan. 'You don't like it when someone ruins your house. And who allowed you to destroy my house?' 'Your Highness, I won't be a musician any more,' said Xudek. 'I am truly guilty.' When Xudek came home, the roof was already back on his house. The point of the story is that if someone didn't play well, the khan took it personally—like the destruction of his own house." The khan was evidently quite a punster, for the word for house (*xâna*) that he used in his reprimand of the musician is also a musical term that refers to groupings of new melodic material introduced episodically in the instrumental pieces of each *maqâm* cycle. Thus the khan was saying simultaneously, and more or less literally, "Who allowed you to destroy my house?" and "Who allowed you to destroy my music?"

The edifice of classical music and poetry over which Feruz presided has to a remarkable extent survived as a living tradition in Khorezm. Unlike the Bukharan *Shash maqâm*—all but dead in Bukhara and exploited in its mummified form mainly to fulfill the role of a national cultural symbol—Khorezmian classical music remains a strong presence at *toy*s and at intimate evening gatherings of men. "It's a music that still fulfills a popular need," said OM. "There's still a strong predisposition toward local tradition in Khorezm that probably has to do with its location on the periphery, relatively speaking. It was on the periphery of the Islamization of Transoxania, just as, centuries later, it was on the periphery of Russification. Khorezm wasn't affected as much as Tashkent, Samarkand, or Bukhara by the Soviet 'struggle against the old.' If it had been the center of attention, they would have tried harder to modernize it." But Khorezm's embrace of tradition also has a contradictory side, for there, more than anywhere else in Uzbekistan, communism found a receptive audience. As one musician put it, "We believed. We were close to communism. We believed that you had to change people's consciousness. Moreover, religion wasn't strong here the way it was in Tashkent, Ferghana, and Bukhara. We didn't go to the mosque on Fridays."

OM's own father, a well-known traditional singer, had been a Communist Party member since early adulthood, and I asked OM how his father had dealt with the seeming inconsistency of supporting an ideology that lashed out against the very traditional culture of which he was a prominent exponent. "No Communist leader here ever had anything bad to say about traditional culture," said OM. "On the contrary, they publicly supported the notion of 'tradition.' The 'struggle against the old' was aimed at what they called 'vestiges'—vestiges, that is, of superstitious, antirational ideas that stood in the way of progress. It sounded good. People accepted Stalin's slogan that art should be 'national in

The unfinished minaret (*Kelta Minâr*) of Madamin (Muhammad Amin) Khan, in Khiva.

form and socialist in content.' It was only later that the full scope of the 'struggle against the old' became apparent." The members of one amateur ensemble we recorded in Urgench recounted to us how this struggle had been carried out. Every musical ensemble that gave public performances had to be registered within some institution: the philharmonia, a theater, a house of culture, etc. Singers in these ensembles kept notebooks with the texts of their songs, and these notebooks had to be submitted to a censor within the institution whose job it was to ensure that they contained no religious texts. Approved notebooks received a stamped seal of certification. If an ensemble was found to be performing texts that hadn't been approved, it could lose access to the stage. This system stayed in place until the mid-1980s.

Perhaps it was Khorezm's compliant attitude toward Communist authority that encouraged Soviet planners to hatch the idea of turning the entire city of Khiva into a museum—and, they hoped, a cash cow. Beginning in the early 1970s, inhabitants of the central area within the old city walls were moved out, mosques, *madrasahs*, and caravaran *sarais* began to undergo renovation, a hotel was built, and the city was made ready for Intourist, the Soviet foreign tourism monopoly. But throngs of tourists never came. Foreigners, it seemed, wanted to visit not a dead city but a living city. And so it was decided to move the former

164

inhabitants back inside the walls and make Khiva live again. The revivification of Khiva has been going on for close to a decade, yet Khiva does not yet seem to have made up its mind what sort of revivified city it wants to be. Entering one of the crenelated gateways set into the city's reconstructed outer walls, a visitor walks along antiseptically clean, cobbled streets past newly renovated homes and others still awaiting renovation. Beyond the small residential district, *madrasahs* and mosques, one after another loom austerely behind sand colored brick walls. According to an old mullah with whom I spoke, there were ninety-six mosques and 136 *madrasahs* in Khiva before the Revolution. Many of them have by now undergone renovation, but the renovations are for the benefit of tourists, not the religious. Open religious practice on a large scale has not yet returned to Khiva, and it is not clear that it will anytime soon.

Nearer the central open *maydan* (square) of the museum-city, virtual silence was coarsely interrupted by the slashing beat of rock music. Closer investigation revealed that a tape of the band Modern Talking was being piped through speakers set atop a video- and audiocassette rental shop built into the walled courtyard of a mosque. Across from the shop, a kneeling camel and his photographer-owner awaited tourists susceptible to Oriental blandishment. The blandishments came not in English, the universal language of tourism, but in heavily accented Russian, the closest that the local Uzbek tourist-wallahs seemed to get to a European language. The vigil for tourists, however, was in vain. As I learned from a plainclothesman working for the Ministry of Internal Affairs who asked to see my documents ("Just checking to make sure your visa is in order," he had said cheerily in German, the language in which he spoke to all foreigners, whether or not they understood it), Khiva had two other foreign visitors that day. The idlers in the antiseptic central square were not tourists but the local *hoi polloi*.

Down the pedestrian mall that transected the *maydan*, the seedy fluorescent lights of another shop appeared through the carved wooden doors of a *madrasah*. As a visitor entered the shop, the young owner turned on a recording of Western disco music at top volume. The shop's few shelves offered candy bars, assorted electronics parts, tawdry housecoats, and cans of beer. A separate alcove surrounding a small stand-up bar was wallpapered in pinups of bikini-clad European women. When the visitor departed through the carved wooden doors, the disco music was turned off. Khiva, the city of Feruz Khan, the connoisseur of classical *maqâm*, was once again silent.

Unlike Bukhara, with its effervescent Naqshbandism, Khiva is not striving to reinvent itself as a place of pilgrimage for the religious. Rather, in perhaps too literal a way, the Khivan revival mixes the religious and the worldly; it bows to tradition while at the same time mocking it. OM attributed the confusion to the complex process of de-Sovietization. "We're in a transitional period now from the old tradition to something new, but no one knows yet what it is. People are searching."

165

TWO EVENINGS OF CLASSICAL MUSIC

OM and I returned to Khorezm in the fall of 1994. The postaccident bad spirits that bedeviled us during the previous year's visit had, I felt, adversely affected my ability to get emotionally inside Khorezmian music and understand the source of its apparent power—power apparent, at least, to OM and his circle of music enthusiasts. OM had spoken frequently and with awe of his Khorezmian musical idols, and I had developed a reverent image of men devoted to the practice of a music that seemed truly to unite broad popular appeal with the message of a traditional spirituality. I was eager to meet those men, and OM had set about arranging opportunities for conversations and recording sessions for a compact disc of Khorezmian music that we had agreed to produce together.

The greatest living exponent of Khorezm's classical music, OM said, was a singer named Rozmat Jumaniyazov. Rozmat had been a student-apprentice (*shagird*) of the legendary Xâjaxân Baltaev, who himself had been apprenticed to a musician who served in the *maqâm* ensemble of Feruz Khan. Rozmat sang both *maqâm* and *suvâra,* a Khorezmian song genre that has much in common with *maqâm* but is less musically formalized. Before Soviet cultural reforms clamped down on religious song texts, the *suvâra* had been one of the principal vehicles for the expression of spiritual poetry. Unlike the vocal pieces of the *maqâm,* which begin in a low tessitura and ascend gradually toward the *awj,* the point of culmination, the *suvâra* moves quickly toward the *awj* and stays there, sustaining a state of spiritual tension in which the singer's voice strains to reach upward, toward heaven, with all its power.[1] In the *suvâra,* the entire focus of musical attention is the voice, and the vocal quality most celebrated in a performer is the ability to belt out the high pitches at the peak of an *awj* and hold them for what seems like an impossibly long time—what is known locally as a "wild voice." There is nothing subtle about the performance of *suvâra*—none of the filigree-like ornamentation of Bukharan *maqâm* singing. Rather, *suvâra* is performed in an open, straightforward style that seethes with raw emotion and an almost ruthless vocal power. Directness, plainness, intrigue with power— these are qualities that seem to run not only through Khorezm's music but also through much of its cultural life. They are qualities evident in the design of houses—huge graceless rectangles built of thick, unwhitewashed clay—and in the entertainment that seems most to captivate Khorezmian males: animal fights. One afternoon, OM and I sat for hours in a stadium with five hundred or so men and boys who watched with apparent fascination as pair after pair of sheep were sent rushing on a collision course to butt their horned skulls together with a resounding thud. OM attributed the extroverted and direct Khorezmian temperament, the worship of physical strength and power, in art as well as in

166

life, to the effects of Khorezm's extreme continental climate: frigid winters and scorching hot summers.[2]

We had met Rozmat one afternoon over lunch at the home of Ibadullah, a friend of OM's. Rozmat was a stout man in his early sixties with a bulging neck and a large bald head covered by a faded *doppi*. He looked as if he had once been as strong as a camel but had become flabby with age and drink. Indeed, Rozmat drank. He drank so much that for days at a time he might be incapable of performing. OM had warned that there could be no guarantee what kind of shape we'd find Rozmat in on the day when we'd agreed to meet to record him. Rozmat had become a kind of unofficial court musician to the Governor (*Hakim*) of Khorezm Region, a blunt man with a rough, red face that looked as if it had been chopped out of stone, named Marx Jumaniyazov.[3] Jumaniyazov was a contemporary version of an old-style charismatic leader—the sort of leader who brought to Uzbekistan a form of honest totalitarianism that many Uzbeks seemed to miss. Like his feudal predecessor Feruz, Jumaniyazov loved art. He acted as both a patron and a guardian of his namesake, Rozmat, and when Rozmat started to drink, the Governor would try to settle him down and get him off the bottle.

I had assumed that OM and I would be alone with Rozmat and our host at the lunch in his *mehmânxâna,* but Ibadullah had invited about a dozen friends to join us, and by the time we had finished our vodka and *palav,* Rozmat was already showing signs of fading. He had brought along some accompanists, but the ensemble was unrehearsed, and after a few desultory attempts at a *suvâra* and a piece from the Khorezm *maqâm,* Rozmat gave up. His voice was cracking on the high notes, he was having trouble remembering song texts, and the simple accompanying line that he plucked out on his *tanbur* meandered aimlessly. "He's having a bad day," OM acknowledged. "We'll have to try again another time, and set it up so that there's no *palav* and vodka before."

After the failed recording session with Rozmat, OM had mentioned another great exemplar of what he called the old style of performing *suvâra* and *maqâm,* a violin player named Alanazar. OM had said, "You must hear Alanazar," and so we had gone to his crumbling apartment block, hoping to find him at home. Alanazar lived alone in a room that was bare except for an iron cot with a filthy blanket, a stained red rug, and a television set perched on top of its cardboard box. When we walked in, Alanazar was sitting in the middle of the floor eating something that looked like dog food out of a metal basin. He was wearing a gray T-shirt and striped trousers of which one leg was ripped open half of the way down the length of the seam. He was not an old man, but his hair had turned completely white, and he had a square face with deep lines that ran from his nostrils to the corners of his mouth.

Alanazar was a heavy drinker and smoker. He wheezed as he spoke. Singing was out of the question, but he was willing to play us some classical instrumental pieces. Before he played, however, he wanted OM to pour him a glass of home-brewed pure distilled spirits from a bottle that lay just beyond his reach. OM complied. Alanazar picked up his violin, holding it upright on his thigh, and began to saw away. The tone was scratchy and the bowing sloppy, but the music conveyed the sense that he had once had a considerable technique. Putting down the violin, Alanazar reminisced about the old days when he had played with Xâjaxân Baltaev, and asked for another drink. OM complied again. The cycle of music, conversation, and pure spirits was repeated several times. After four or five glasses, Alanazar's condition worsened, and asking for more music seemed pointless. We thanked Alanazar and left. Outside, I asked OM why he had given Alanazar alcohol. "It's hopeless," he said. "He'll keep requesting it, and it's humiliating to ask him to play first before he drinks, or to have him repeatedly plead for alcohol."

For all of OM's advance buildup of the "old style" of Khorezmian classical music and its legendary exponents, the tradition had seemed to be one held together by safety pins. Or perhaps we had just been down on our luck to have visited Rozmat and Alanazar on a bad day. And that is why we had returned to Khorezm.

In the fall of 1994, we arranged to meet Rozmat one evening at the home of a well-to-do businessman who was also a music lover. The businessman assured OM that he would organize the evening so that Rozmat remained sober and we could get a good recording. To increase the likelihood that the music would reach a level of inspiration, the businessman invited not only Rozmat but another musician named Azad Ibragimov. The evening thus took on a traditional Khorezmian form of unarticulated but fully cognizant competition between the two vocalists and their accompanists.

We arrived at Mahmad's house just after 7:00 P.M. and were led to his *mehmânxâna,* located in a separate building in back of the main dwelling. The *mehmânxâna* had the look of a prosperous Khorezmian businessman's place: along the length of the room, a table large enough to seat twenty-four guests; against the back wall, a wood-paneled cabinet with imported stereo equipment; and next to it, an oversized imported television. The floor was covered with new Turcoman rugs, and atop the wood-paneled cabinet, dark portraits of Mahmad's father and uncle, the musicians Nurmamat and Xâjaxân Baltaev, added a somber formality to the space. The table was set with the usual trappings of a *dasturxân,* including numerous bottles of vodka. There was a brief discussion about whether or not to open the vodka. The host had promised, after all, to deliver a sober Rozmat. But the discussion about abstention was perfunctory, and after a few moments, bottle number 1 was opened and the vodka poured into tea bowls. Rozmat proclaimed loudly that he did not want to drink, but the host insisted, and Rozmat acquiesced after briefly feigning resistance. An hour or so into the drinking and small talk, chairs were set up for Rozmat and the three musicians who were to accompany him on *dâyra,* violin, and accordion. The evening promised to be a great musical event, worthy of documentation, and one of the dozen or so guests set up a video camera in front of the musicians. I prepared the microphones of my digital tape recorder.

As soon as Rozmat began to sing the first *suvâra,* my heart sank. Rozmat himself was in good form, but the accordion player—his son—couldn't follow the vocal melody. At the same time that he was losing his way melodically, he added tasteless bass chord harmonies that thickened the musical texture into a confusing, gooey mass of sound. Recording Rozmat would be useless with the accordion accompaniment. OM tactfully asked Rozmat whether he wouldn't mind suggesting to his son that he hold off on the accordion for a few songs, but Rozmat took offense. He wanted his son on the recording.

After Rozmat had performed several *suvâra*s and songs from the *maqâm,* it was Azad's turn. Could Azad sing a higher, longer, and louder *awj?* The competition was not a particularly friendly one. The two musicians did not sit attentively and listen to one another's singing. Rather, as one performed, the other stepped outside to smoke and banter with his own entourage. Azad sang well, but the violinist, who first accompanied Rozmat and then Azad, had drunk far too much vodka. His playing was weak and uncoordinated, and once again the effect was to make the whole of the ensemble unsuitable for presentation on a compact disc.

The level of attention to the music went steadily downhill as more vodka bottles were opened. Rozmat and Azad traded off two more rounds of performance. The musicians' chairs had been set up in front of the large-screen television, which was connected to a satellite dish (an uncommon appliance in Uzbekistan). As each set of musicians played selections from the *maqâm* and *suvâra* repertory, sitcoms and detective shows from the BBC World Service provided a silent visual backdrop. Fifteenth-century Sufi texts about the ecstasy of metaphysical love collided with the television images of police chases and seduction scenes. For both musicians and listeners, the television seemed an absolutely normal part of the evening—as traditional as the music and vodka.

After the music ended and the musicians retreated to the table for a late-night bowl of mutton broth with noodles, the drunken violinist asked me to make a toast. I gathered up my courage. "Did Xâjaxân, your teacher, drink?" I asked the violinist.

"He drank until he was forty, then he gave it up completely," the violinist answered.

"And did his teacher drink?"

"No, he never drank. He was a religious man."

"Then why do you drink?" I blurted out in vindictive desperation.

Later, OM offered his own answer. "There's a real social sickness here. People are exhausted. They're beat up from living such hard lives. The material position of musicians is getting worse. I can guarantee you that none of the musicians who were at that evening are training their children to be musicians. Musicians used to be a middle class, but now they're a lower class, and getting lower. And they're all running to and fro trying to make ends meet—buying, selling, trading. More and more in these evenings, the repartee (*askiya*) ends up turning to vulgarity. It's the easiest way to have *kaif.* They don't want poetry or music—the high road to *kaif.* They want the low road: *askiya* and vodka. They're good people, my friends, but the times are making them into people with no *qadriyat*—no spiritual values. There's nothing saintly, nothing spiritual, for them. Spirituality is when people value friendship, relationships, the difference between good and evil. But for that, you have to have some sort of inner morals, and you can't have them when you're indifferent, when nothing matters."

"Where are the fools of God?" I asked OM.

Again the Khorezmian paradox. OM replied, "If you ask Turgun Alimatov or Arif Xatamov, 'Where are the most serious musical listeners, where are the best singers, where is the musical tradition holding most strongly,' they'll say, 'In Khorezm.' I've had many evenings in Khorezm with my friends that have been different. We've sat until two o'clock in the morning listening to wonderful music and talking about poetry. You can't measure the *qadriyat*—the spiritual values—of Khorezm by what you saw at Mahmad's."

I pushed OM. How was it, I asked, that the measure of an entire musical tradition seemed to rest on the sobriety, or lack of it, of two or three musicians?

"There are hundreds of musicians who can sing *suvâra,*" OM said. "You can hear them anytime you want on the radio or at *toys.* But they're journeyman musicians, not masters in a technical sense, let alone musical creators." OM was right: the standards of an artistic tradition always come from the top, from those who give shape or sound to a society's highest aesthetic aspirations. It was as Turgun Alimatov had said: students came to him, not to some other *tanbur* player, because they wanted to learn from the best. He was not being immodest but realistic. And if the artists who embody the highest standards of a tradition cease to maintain those standards, however the actual form of their work may evolve, or if they pass from the scene without training replacements of the same quality, the tradition must inevitably decline.

It was back in Tashkent that my luck with Khorezmian classical music finally improved. OM had invited Azad to come to Tashkent the day after our departure from Khorezm to participate in another of his television programs about musical traditions. The television program was to be taped in the afternoon, and the same evening, OM said, we had all been invited to the house of a friend of his. The guests would be mostly Khorezmians living in or visiting Tashkent. Among them would be Xudâbergan, the musical connoisseur and patron whom I'd gotten to know the previous year. I was eager to see Xudâbergan again and readily agreed to go along with OM, Azad, and Azad's two accompanists.

The host of the evening gathering, Arslan, taught martial arts at a physical education institute and was himself a karate champion. OM had met him through Xudâbergan. It was Arslan who supervised the early-morning workout sessions that OM had started attending with Xudâbergan. Some of the guests were also members of the workout group, while others were businessmen or drawn from Arslan's karate circles.

Arslan lived in a detached house in Tashkent's Old City. The house had originally been quite modest, but he had built a two-story addition that made it into a comfortable place in which to entertain. The *mehmânxâna* was on the second floor. An L-shaped table with sixteen settings occupied more than half of the room; the space that was left was filled with mats and pillows set out in front of the television set. When we arrived, the evening had obviously been under way for some time. The table was covered with the detritus left by one shift of diners, and we had no sooner taken off our coats than Arslan poured us full tea bowls of vodka. An inauspicious beginning. But I liked Arslan. Our discussion deepened, and the evening began to take on an intimate character. When OM felt the moment was right, he proposed to Azad that he perform. Mats were arranged for the musicians on the floor, and Azad and his accompanists tuned their instruments. Arslan and his businessman and karate-practicing friends listened quietly to the slow, tensed singing, occasionally emitting a spontaneous *"akh"* or *"yaxshi"* (good) after a particularly high, piercing *awj* or a particularly poignant line of poetry. Some had tears in their eyes. The song lyrics consisted of direct, accessible spiritual poetry, for example, the following verses of Xazini:

> For Mustafa (the Prophet) the world deceived
> For Zakaria the world deceived
> For the holy ones the world deceived
> For the saints the world deceived.
>
> Abu Bakr, Umar, Osman, Ali
> Zahrâ and Hasan, Husein Wali
> Death swallowed all these prophets
> For Murtazâ (Ali) the world deceived.
>
> What happened to the thirty-three thousand companions (of the Prophet)?
> They appeared in this world to suffer and weep
> This world is an impermanent hovel
> For he who has given his whole life to this world, it still deceives.

As Azad sang and played, the listeners approached him one by one and stuffed wads of bills into the breast pocket of his shirt. Azad never made the slightest acknowledgment of the alms—no bow of the head or smile in the direction of the donor. That would have been inconsistent with the moral rectitude of a fool of God. The performance wasn't exactly a concert in the usual sense. Men came and

171

went from the room, retreating to the balcony to smoke and descending the stairs to the courtyard where *shashlik* was being grilled over charcoal.

OM perceived the performance of *suvâra* as creating a kind of trance. "The music exists mainly to focus the listener's attention on the words; and when you've taken in those words and the music ends, you can't immediately go back to conversation. There's a moment afterward when you can't talk. You've gone to another state and you need time to come back to yourself. In vocal style, the *suvâra* is very much like the reading of religious books, except that such readings don't have a melodic apogee [*awj*]."[4] Two or three generations of singers working within the constraints of the Soviet "struggle with the old" had secularized the *suvâra*. Azad's personal chrestomathy of texts included many lyrical *ghazal*s from poets such as Nawâ'i, Hafiz, and Agâhi, but he had religious texts as well—the majority from Mashrab, the mystical poet popularly known as Diwana-i Mashrab—(Mashrab, the Holy Fool) because of his eccentric displays of otherworldliness.[5]

The performance of a full *suvâra* is longer than what could sensibly be included on the accompanying compact disc, and I thus asked Azad to create a three-minute version of one piece (*sawt*) that normally took around six minutes to perform.[6] He did so by eliminating repetitions of certain of the couplets and shortening the melodic interludes that he normally adds between couplets. The abridgement made the rondolike character of the melody all the clearer: the melodic theme of the first verse line serves as a kind of *ritornello* that returns episodically throughout the short song. The *awj*—the ascension of the voice to the melodic and poetic apogee—begins with the third couplet and reaches a climax in the penultimate line (see the accompanying CD, track 14).

The text of Azad's *sawt* was a well-known *ghazal* of Nawâ'i. It is a lyrical poem in which the metaphysical dimension exists at a level of abstraction far enough removed from the literal meaning of the text not to have created problems for the singer whose notebook would have been submitted to Soviet censors. Here the poem is translated and transliterated.

> The melancholy and sadness of my soul isn't like it was before
> Even the melancholy for that moon [i.e., beautiful girl] isn't like it was before
>
> Whatever suffering she used to cause me was concealed
> But the suffering she causes me now isn't like it was before
>
> For what she did, she took offense at me and started to love another
> I'm dying from that pain, but it's not like it was before
>
> In love, don't compare me with Farhad or Majnun*
> Since my shame isn't like it was before
>
> When you take to the road [to God], do
> For [along the road] to him there is not pleasure [literally, "the
> sweetness of the harem"] like it was before

Oh, Nawâ'i, don't sing the praises of Jamshid and Faridun
The good feeling toward Shah Ghazi** isn't like it was before

---

* Farhad and Majnun: the idealized male lovers of Sufi legend and parable.
** Shah Ghazi: the literary pseudonym of Sultan Husein, the fifteenth-century Timurid ruler of Herat under whom Nawâ'i served as vizier.

Konglim ichra dardu gham avvalgilarga oxshamaz
Kim ul âyning xajri ham avvalgilarga oxshamaz

Ne sitam kim qilsalar maxfi erdi zimnida
Endi qilsa ne sitam avvalgilarga oxshamaz

Javridin ermish alamlar endi tutmish ozga yar
Olmisham kim bu alam avvalgilarga oxshamaz

Ishq ara Farhâd ila Majnunga oxshatmang mani
Kim bu rasvâi dejam avvalgilarga oxshamaz

Kuyini ehramidin konglimni man etmang yana
Kim anga azmi haram avvalgilarga oxshamaz

Ey, Nawâ'i qilma Jamshidu Faridun vasfi kim
Shâh Ghâziyga karam avvalgilarga oxshamaz

A *BAXSHI* AND HIS PUPIL

The Khorezmian musical life to which OM had first introduced me was solidly grounded in urban traditions—in repertories that had once comprised the local court music and in the elevated spiritual poetry that singers of *maqâm* and *suvâra* drew on for texts. But Khorezm had another side to its musical life that existed in close proximity to the classical urban tradition yet had its base in the irrigated and thickly settled countryside beyond the city walls, where, before its transformation into cotton plantations, farmer-herders had worked small plots of land and grazed cows and sheep. The leading musical figure of this more rural sound world was the *baxshi*—the reciter of *dâstân,* or oral epic. Farther north along the Amu Darya, in the region now known as Karakalpakstan, the reciter of *dâstân* was called *zhirau.* The Khorezm *baxshi* and the Karakalpak *zhirau* each had his own repertory and performance style of *dâstân* distinct from that of the Qashqadarya and Surxandarya *baxshi*s to the south, across the geographical and cultural divide of the Kara-Kum.

The most-renowned *baxshi* in Khorezm was Bâla *baxshi.* Bâla *baxshi'*s official name was Qurbannazar Abdullaev, but like many performers, he'd picked up a nickname. Bâla means "child," and Bâla *baxshi* had been given the name at the age of seven, when he first performed in public. By age twelve, he was already performing on his own. Bâla *baxshi,* however, was no longer young.

Bâla *baxshi* and OM.

Born in 1899, he was an alert ninety-two-year-old when I first met him at his small house in a rural settlement near Khiva (he died in 1994). Attended by a swarm of flies buzzing around his face, he was sitting ramrod straight on a mat in his *mehmânxâna,* nattily dressed in a pink shirt, a button-down knit sweater held together with a safety pin, a red wool hat, and army fatigue pants. His face was imposing: a huge white moustache drooping over a mouth that showed no signs of any teeth, large ears, and what could only be described as beady eyes. Bâla *baxshi* had married three times and had twelve children, the oldest of whom was seventy-eight and the youngest, seventeen. He thought he had around seventy grandchildren. He still maintained an active physical life that included a daily horseback ride. After our conversation, Bâla *baxshi* invited us outside to observe his equestrian skills; with a little help from a young boy, he hoisted himself into his horse's saddle and rode proudly up and down the street.

Bâla *baxshi* told us that he had been the first Khivan *baxshi.* What he meant was that before him, *baxshi*s had come to Khiva from other places to perform, then left Khiva to return to those places. He, by contrast, had lived near Khiva and performed regularly both in the city and the suburbs. "For the khan," Bâla *baxshi* said, "the main thing was *maqâm.* But if a very interesting *baxshi* appeared, the khan listened to him, or even invited him to perform at the court."

174

Bâla *baxshi* had performed at the *toy*s of members of the khan's family, and he recalled to us his three-day stint at the *toy* of the brother-in-law of Isfandihar Khan. But he complained that among the men at the *toy,* not a single person had asked him to sing; no one was interested in his music, and so he had been taken to perform for the women. By contrast, the audience that appreciated Bâla *baxshi*'s art was a country audience. After the Revolution, Bâla *baxshi* had lived for eleven years in a small settlement where he served the circle of a local rogue hero named Nurjan Batir. Nurjan Batir had made a name for himself fighting the Turkmens who constantly harassed Khiva, and had won the favor of the khan. When the Turkmens launched a raid and stole Khivan horses, Nurjan Batir would hunt down the culprits. Bâla *baxshi* told us, "He'd sneak up on the Yomuds [Turkmens] at night, pull a man out of bed, say a prayer over him, and slit his throat. The next day, he'd bring the head to the khan."

From 1930 into the 1960s, Bâla *baxshi* worked in the theater. "For seven years, the performance of *dâstân*s was forbidden. It was considered to be adherence to the old, to old traditions. I didn't have any other craft, any other way to earn a living, so I went to the theater and worked there as the director of a brigade [a small ensemble]. Fifty percent of the theater's income came from my work. People paid money to the theater for me to perform at concerts and at *toy*s. We'd come to a *kolkhoz* for an evening and the directors of the *kolkhoz* would force us to stay for a second evening. They'd pay another 1,500 rubles and force us to stay. I did twenty-five or thirty concerts a month. They took us from *kolkhoz* to *kolkhoz* in a camel-drawn cart. People particularly respected me in the Turkmen regions. We'd be taken to the *kolkhoz*s to play official concerts, but at the same time, we'd do *toy*s. We'd be paid money, and then on the way back, before we reached the city, we'd find an abandoned place, and I'd distribute the money to the musicians, depending on how they had played. We earned good money. If we went illegally to *ziyâfat*s, people would follow us. The Internal Affairs people and the police—they liked me. They felt sorry for me. If someone was going to come after me, I'd get a signal, and I'd disappear. I'd live for several months at a time by a lake in the desert and go hunting."

Bâla *baxshi* had stopped singing by the time I met him, in 1991, and it was to the most successful and popular of his students, Qalandar *baxshi,* that OM and I turned to hear a performance of *dâstân* in the so-called Shirvani style for which Bâla *baxshi* was renowned.[7] The Shirvani performance style made clear the consanguinity of the Khorezm *baxshi* to the bards of the Western Oghuz Turks (Azerbaijani, Turkmen, Turkish), called *ashug* or *ashiq*. A number of the heroes of the Khorezm *dâstân*s are themselves called *ashiq,* which suggests that in earlier times this title was also used in Khorezm to designate the performer of *dâstân*.

Ashiq means literally "one who is in love" (from Arabic: *'ashiqa*—"to love," "to be in love"). The object of the *ashiq*'s love is traditionally understood to be God, and the *ashiq*'s musical performance is considered an expression of that

Bu dunyâ deganing bir bebaqâdir
Manga siz yâr garak dunyâ garakmas
(Akh yârai jâningnan)

2. My name was Gharib, but they called me "the one with bald spots"
Whom should I tell about the pain that I have in my chest
My angel, listen to my soul's groaning
I don't need riches, I need you, my beloved one
(Oh my beloved, my soul)

Gharib adim (ai) kal qoydilar âdimni
Kima aytay siynamdagi dâdimni (ai)
Parizâdim san eshitgil zârimni
Manga san yâr garak, dunyâ garakmas.
(Ay yârai jâningnan)

3. Let everyone's wish be fulfilled by his beloved
Let every person be happy and laugh with his beloved
If someone looks at cloth (i.e. another woman's clothes),
  let him hang himself with it
I don't need riches, I need you, my beloved one
(Oh, my beloved, my soul)

Har kimning murâdin oz yâri bersin
Har kim yâri bilan (ai) oinasin kulsin
Kishi matâ gorsa âsilsin olsin
Manga siz yâr garak (ai) dunyâ garakmas.
(Akh yârai jâningnan)

4. Those who are true in love always groan and suffer
Day and night their thoughts are with the thoughts of their beloved
Why does one who's really in love need riches?
I don't need riches, I need you, my beloved one
(Oh, my beloved, my soul)

Chin âshiqlar chakar âh bilan zârin
Kecha kunduz fikri yârni hayâli
Chin âshiq naylasin dunyâning mâlni (ay)
Manga siz yâr garak (ay), dunyâ garakmas
(Akh yârai jâningnan)

5. Ashiq Gharib says, "these words are the truth" (Oh, my soul, the truth)
What we call this world doesn't exist only for a single day
Who can be my friend except my God (Oh, who can be my friend)
I don't need riches, I need you, my beloved
(Oh, it's not necessary, Oh, my beloved, come my beloved, my darling one)
I don't need riches, I need you, my beloved
(I don't need riches, be well, you be well, I'll die for you)

(Ay) Ashiq Gharib aitur bu sozim râstdir (ay jân râstdir)
Bu dunyâ daganing bir gun amasdir (ay amasdir)

178

Khudâyimnan ozga kim manga dostdir (ay kim dostdir)
Manga siz yâr garak, dunyâ garakmas
(ay, garakmas, âkh yârai gal yârai, nâzanin)
Manga siz yâr garak, dunyâ garakmas
(garakmas, ay, âmân ay, âmân, senai, adâingman)

The poetic sections of the text are composed in the same syllabic *barmâq* style—in the present case, with strict adherence to an eleven-syllable line—as the *dâstân*s and *terma*s performed by the Qashqadarya and Surxandarya *baxshi*s. However, in contrast to the chronicle-like narrative style of the Qashqadarya and Surxandarya *dâstân*s, "Ashiq Gharib" is more introspective. As in a typical numbers opera, plot is carried by recitative, while set pieces dwell on the sentiments of the characters, sometimes illustrated through trope, as in the following line from the third strophe: "If someone looks at cloth, let him hang himself with it." "Cloth" is used as a metonymy for "woman" to suggest the meaning, "If a man looks at another woman besides his beloved, let him perish." The idea is that one should be content with one's own beloved. The lyrical theme of the *dâstân*—the trials and tribulations of an *ashiq*—is the epitome of *ashiqlik,* and gives rise to a different kind of poetics than the more martial exploits of the *batir*s (heroes). "Ashiq Gharib" is rich with the traditional mystical imagery of Sufism: the deceptive world, the figure of the "friend of God," the dual understanding of the "beloved"—on one level earthly, on another level heavenly. This Sufi-inspired content is brought to life in Qalandar *baxshi*'s vocal style—in what OM had described as the plangent sound of his voice.

Not only does the vocal style of "Ashiq Gharib" contrast sharply with that of the Qashqadarya and Surxandarya *dâstân*s. The musical form also arises from different principles. For example, Qahhâr *baxshi* had told us that for him, the choice of a melody type (*name*) was determined by the need to show the various moods of the main hero of the *dâstân*. But once a particular melody type had become established, Qahhâr could repeat a basic melodic configuration as many times as were called for by the requirements of the narrative. For Qahhâr, melodic form evolved from narrative structure. By contrast, the sung portion of Qalandar *baxshi*'s "Ashiq Gharib" comprised a rounded musical form in the pattern of a typical Khorezmian art song in which the tessitura of the melodic line ascends in successive strophes to the *awj,* then descends to a well-prepared cadence. A diagram of the musical form would look as follows:

strophe:		1		2		3		4	5
description		instrumental	vocal	instrum.	vocal	instrum.	vocal	instrum.	vocal	vocal
of music:	overture	"A"	reprise	"A"	reprise	"B"	reprise	"C"	"D"
								AWJ	coda

179

In performance style and musical form, "Ashiq Gharib" shares many of the features of Khorezmian art song. Not the least of these is the presence of the *dâyra,* which provides not simply a passive *usul* but also an active rhythmic counterpoint to the *tar* and violin. The close relationship between *dâstân* and art song is in turn evidence of abiding cultural patterns on the territorially circumscribed Khorezm oasis—the constant intermingling of city dwellers and the inhabitants of the *yavâh,* the cultivated land that lies between the end of the city and the beginning of the desert.

SEARCHING FOR A *ZHIRAU*

Khorezmian culture looks not only west to the Oghuz Turks, with whom it has such strong links through the poetry and music of the *dâstân,* but east to the herders of Turco-Mongol stock who still range over the semiarid lands northeast of the Amu Darya. One of these herding groups is the Karakalpaks. Their name derives from the men's shibboleth of dress—the black (*qara*) wool hats (*qalpaq*) made from the wool of their famous sheep. Groups of Karakalpaks are thought to have migrated from steppe lands around the Aral Sea and along the Lower Volga (north of the Caspian) to their present territory on the east bank of the Amu Darya in the sixteenth and seventeenth centuries. They were absorbed into the Khivan Khanate, and as part of the 1873 treaty that made the Khanate a Russian protectorate, the east bank of the Amu Darya, the home of the Karakalpaks, was annexed to Russian Turkestan. After the creation of Soviet Uzbekistan, this territory became the Karakalpak Autonomous Region (*Oblast'*) of Uzbekistan, with its capital at Nukus, a Soviet-built city. With the breakup of the Soviet Union, the Karakalpak Autonomous Region officially became the Sovereign Republic of Karakalpakstan within Uzbekistan, as it is oxymoronically called. Ethnically, the Karakalpaks consider themselves close relatives of the Uzbeks, but also different from them. Their dialect of Turki is closer to the more easterly centered Kazakh language than to Uzbek, and as part of the Soviet effort to reify a distinct "national" culture for the Karakalpaks, the Karakalpak "language" came to be written in a Cyrillic orthography slightly different from that used for either Uzbek or Kazakh.

The distinctiveness of Karakalpak musical culture from that of present-day Khorezm needs no artificial illumination from cultural strategists. After an immersion in the urban, Iranian-influenced instrumentarium, poetics, and performance style of Khorezmian oral poetry and art song, Karakalpak music readily suggested its more purely rural Turkic roots. Like other Turkic herding cultures, the Karakalpaks developed an extensive oral poetry, and this poetry comprised the repertory of the *zhirau.* The *zhirau* accompanies his singing on the *qobyz,* a two-stringed fiddle that also serves as the traditional instrument of

Karakalpak and Kazakh shamans (*baqsy*), thus suggesting the same ritual consanguinity between oral poetry and healing that must once have existed among the Uzbeks. It was in hope of hearing and recording a *zhirau* that OM and I set off from Urgench toward Nukus.

OM knew of two *zhirau*s in Karakalpakstan. Jumabay, a well-known performer, lived on a *kolkhoz* fifty miles north of Nukus. In the ailing Moskvich that belonged to OM's brother and served as our only means of transport in Khorezm (this time we had left the green Volga in Tashkent and flown to Urgench), a trip across 200-odd miles of barren steppe seemed a bit of a gamble. The second, lesser-known *zhirau* lived in a tiny farming and herding settlement of reclaimed steppe land about a two-hour drive from Urgench. OM had never been to the settlement nor met the *zhirau,* but someone had said that he was talented. As always when we went to a rural place, OM enlisted the aid of the local district authorities in making our initial contact. He knew a man who was head of the Culture Department in Ellik Qala District, where the *zhirau* lived. OM phoned his acquaintance and received assurances that we would be welcomed.

Arriving in Bâstun, the small town that served as the district center, we met OM's acquaintance. It was lunchtime, and the acquaintance had thoughtfully ordered "tea" at the crumbling and seemingly empty hotel in the middle of town. OM said that he knew someone else in Bâstun, and phoned him with the hope that he could join us for lunch. Fifteen minutes later, I was introduced to Erkabay. He and OM had met through mutual friends in Tashkent. They'd hit it off and seen one another several times since. OM didn't know Erkabay's last name nor any details about the work he did (it turned out that he was a lawyer). In a social setting, it is considered banal to ask a man about his work. Work is one thing, life is another. But Erkabay and OM had discovered that they had similar tastes in poetry and had enjoyed reciting their own compositions to one another. Erkabay had written poems for many years, while OM had taken it up only the year before our trip to Khorezm, during a period of hospitalization. We explained our plans to Erkabay, and he decided to take the afternoon off and join us on our search for the *zhirau*. The head of the Culture Department explained where he thought the *zhirau* lived, on a *kolkhoz* some distance from the district center, and having fulfilled his ceremonial role as official welcomer to Ellik Qala District, left us to fend for ourselves.

The rest of the afternoon was taken up with the kind of feckless adventure that the anthropologist Lévi-Strauss (in the opening of *Tristes tropiques*) disparagingly called one of the "bondages" of anthropology: a vain search for the elusive *zhirau* punctuated with long waits and gratuitous meals, and in the end, the realization that the *zhirau* we had sought was not a *zhirau* at all, but a rather amateur *baqsy,* who played not the *qobyz* but a *dombra*. Disappointed, we set our sights on Nukus and a meeting with Jumabay, arguably the best-known *zhirau* in Karakalpakstan.

We departed for Nukus the following morning. Erkabay, obsessed with our search for a *zhirau,* had decided to drive us there himself. The route took us northwest, parallel to the Amu Darya, past the last irrigated cotton fields and into sun-drenched, lumpy steppe covered with tumuli and tiny sage-covered mounds of sand. In the midst of this desolate landscape, a herd of camels passed in the opposite direction, bobbing along slowly next to the road. I asked Erkabay whether they were wild camels. No, domesticated, he said, the property of a collective farm that raised them for their milk and meat. The steppe land might have appeared empty, but it was not unused. Beyond the camels, a range of vegetationless hills appeared to the east and, set against the nearest of the hills, what looked like an enormous glistening white field reflected sunlight off the sand. As we drew closer, the white field resolved into hundreds of densely packed tombstones and vaults. We were approaching a major site of *ziyârat*—pilgrimage to the tomb of a saint. The saint was Sultan Uways al-Qarani, known locally as Sultan Bâbâ, and around a tomb reputed to contain his remains, a domed brick mausoleum rose tentatively out of the sand adjacent to the cemetery.

Karakalpakstan is not the only place that lays claim to the tomb of Sultan

The mausoleum of Sultan Uways in Karakalpakstan.

Uways, the legendary contemporary of Muhammad who is said to have communicated with the Prophet by telepathy and gave rise to the Uwaysi mystical tradition in which a Muslim mystic "looks for instruction from the spirit of a dead or physically absent person."[9] The mausoleum, according to local tradition, was first built by Sultan Muhammad Khorezm Shah, one of the pre-Mongol Iranian rulers of Old Khorezm, and was destroyed by Chingis Khan.

Rebuilt in 1805–1806, it was soon destroyed a second time, by an earthquake. The structure that stands today dates from 1837.[10] OM recalled making a *ziyârat* to the tomb as a thirteen-year-old in 1959. "I went with my father and my father's uncle, a man named Qâri Bâbâ, who read the Qur'an in our settlement. The place was jammed with people. They came on donkeys, on horses. There was a sort of stable there. Near the mausoleum was a huge *aivân* where two or three hundred men sat, talked, ate, and slept. They must have slaughtered forty or fifty sheep a day. Everyone wanted to slaughter a sheep. They kept several big pots boiling, and people were constantly preparing *shurpa* and *shavla* [a watery *palav*]. There was a sheikh who sat and read the Qur'an for each person who came, and people threw packets of money into the alcove where the tomb is— it was covered with bills. Twenty years later, during the time when the fight against religion was strong, I read in the newspaper that people had done something with the money. The article was probably some kind of provocation. I'm sure that no one would have touched that money. They closed the mausoleum for a long time, but people visited it all the same. Maybe not in the same quantities, but all the same, they came."

Now the mausoleum was open again, but during our visit it remained nearly empty. The only other visitors were three elderly women who prostrated themselves and prayed as we walked in and took our bearings. They quickly ended their prayers and left. The mausoleum and adjacent cemetery were immaculately maintained; there was evidence of new masonry work, new electric lamps had been installed, and the parking lot had been recently paved. Yet in all the immaculateness, something was missing. In a moment of *déjà vu,* I was transported back to the Bahâ'uddin theme park outside Bukhara. Like the Bahâ'uddin site, the Sultan Uways mausoleum seemed a kind of spiritual confection. But perhaps in that confection was some poetic justice, for the Sultan Uways mausoleum, after all, was a monument to a saint who, in all likelihood, no one had ever seen.

Jumabay *zhirau* Bazarov was sixty-seven years old, with a lined but virile face, a thick white handlebar mustache, and a full set of gleaming false teeth. He was not a tall man, but he stood straight and proud, his head covered by a karakalpak wool hat. Jumabay told us that he had completed four years of formal education and had then gone to work on a *kolkhoz*.[11] He had driven a tractor and done carpentry work while at the same time learning the *zhirau*'s craft from a master *zhirau*. Jumabay's entire repertory of epic poetry had been learned through oral transmission (in contrast, for example, to Shâhberdi *baxshi,* in Surxandarya, who had learned epics from printed transcriptions in books as well as from living oral tradition). More recently, he had become a kind of national cultural treasure of Karakalpakstan. We met at the home of Karakalpakstan's Minister of Culture, Najimaddin Muxamed-dinov, an energetic composer who had become an equally energetic bureaucrat and

Jumabay *zhirau* Bazarov

had good-naturedly given up a free Saturday afternoon to host our recording session. I had never heard a *zhirau* sing, and my interest was to locate the performance style of the *zhirau* within the larger context of the Inner Asian oral poetic tradition.

The *qobyz,* the two-stringed fiddle traditionally played by the *zhirau,* had once been a common instrument in Khorezm. Even in Bukhara, the very center of urban Persianate cultural influence in Transoxania, the *qobyz* was said to have been played for the enjoyment of the emir.[12] Its popularity among the later Bukharan nobility served as a reminder of the ruling Manghits' Turco-Mongol origins and of the importance to them of cultural vestiges of those origins. "It would have been natural for the Bukharan emirs to listen to the *qobyz,*" OM had said. "They were Manghit Turks. It was in their blood." Musicians, however, preferred the greater technical possibilities and brighter timbre of the *ghijak*—the Persian spike fiddle—and the European violin. Relatively quickly, the *qobyz* yielded to the violin in Khorezm and to the *ghijak* in Bukhara. Even earlier, the *qobyz* had disappeared almost completely in Kazakhstan, where performers of oral epic switched to the strummed *dombra.*[13] Encouraged by the Minister of Culture, Jumabay had taken on pupils, and his style of epic performance was being resurrected among a younger generation of musicians in Nukus's music high school. But Jumabay and his *qobyz* represented the oldest surviving contact

with a musical tradition that had once been widespread, linking the settled Uzbek cultural realm to the south and west with the nomadic Kazakh cultural realm to the northeast.

We asked Jumabay if he would sing for us. Before launching into a fragment from the epic repertory, Jumabay wanted to perform some shorter songs. One of them was a setting of a poem in honor of Maxtum Quli, the eighteenth-century Turkmen poet.[14] The song appears on the accompanying compact disc (track 16). Here is the transliterated and translated text:

> When you turned twenty years old
> You began to search for a teacher
> On a donkey you arrived at a *madrasah*
> The imam despised you, Piraghi [the literary pseudonym of
>   Maxtum Quli].
>
> You were a person who didn't have an equal in the world
> You were a wise poet, a man with a *pir* [spiritual teacher]
> You searched for a scholar, a teacher who would give you knowledge
> You looked around in all four directions, Piraghi.
>
> At last you found a friend enlightened by God [i.e., the Prophet]
> Experiencing the pain, the pleasure, of travel
> Sitting together with my grandfather, Kunxâja
> You stayed on the banks of the Syr Darya, Piraghi.
>
> Traveling through India, Afghanistan, Crimea,
> Turkistan, Georgia, Bolghar (on the Volga), Turkey
> Wandering the whole earth, the seven regions of the world
> You looked around in all four directions, Piraghi.
>
> In the *madrasah,* I saw you
> Each of your steps is like *surma* [eyeshadow] for my eyes
> Aqmurad Axun gathered together all of your words
> And I learned them from him, Piraghi.
>
> Yanga yashin yigirmaga kirganda
> Axbâb yaka safar tarjing gurganda
> Eshak minib madrasaga kelganda
> Imâm sizni yermâq qildi Piraghi.
>
> Jahânda tengi yoq bir âdam eding
> Dâna shâir eding pirdân eding
> Ta'alim berar âlim ustâz izlading
> Châr tarapa nazar sâlding Piraghi.
>
> Axiri dost tâlpidi ul nuri xazân
> Sayaxatning tartib azâbin xazi
> Men babam Kunxâja minin bir bolib
> Sir boyinda qonib qâlding Piraghi

THE HUNDRED THOUSAND FOOLS OF GOD

Axtarib Khindistân, Afghân, Krimni
Turkistân, Gurjistan, Bulghar, Rumni
Kezib jumla jahân yetti iqlimni
Châr tarapa nazar sâlding Piraghi

Madrasaga kelib kurdim ozingni
Kozga surma qildim basqan izingni
Aqmurad Axun yighnab bârliq sozingni
Men sundan organib âldim Piraghi.

Jumabay's vocal style clearly had something of the Qashqadarya *baxshi*'s laryngeally tensed "inner voice," although it was less pronounced than in the singing of Qahhâr *baxshi*. OM asked Jumabay whether he thought his own singing sounded like that of a Qashqadarya *baxshi*. Jumabay responded poetically: "It would be shameful if a hunting dog barked or a workhorse bolted, and it would be shameful if someone sang like a *baxshi* who considers himself a *zhirau*." There was more than a hint of disdain in Jumabay's voice as he said these words. He clearly considered the art of the *zhirau* to be not only different from that of the *baxshi* but also more powerful and sophisticated.

Jumabay used his *qobyz* not so much to accompany his voice as to fill in the space between poetic lines and strophes and to carry forward the strong tonic accent of the recited verse. In its turn, the recitation was not so much sung as chanted in a kind of metricized intoned speech, or *sprechstimme*. Like the performance on the jew's harp (*chang-qobuz*) that I had heard at Qahhâr *baxshi*'s house, Jumabay's ode to Maxtum Quli seemed like a musical anachronism; it was literally the last vestige of a sound world that had come to within a hair's breadth of extinction. Thanks to Jumabay's tenacity and the enlightenment of the Minister of Culture, it had been given at least a temporary reprieve.

As the centerpiece of the afternoon's program, Jumabay performed a fragment from the epic *Yedigei* (or *Idige;* there are many variant pronunciations). The performance began with a brief instrumental prelude that introduced a long section of unaccompanied narrative. This narrative was followed by a briefer section of chanted melody accompanied or interspersed by *qobyz*, performed in much the same style as the ode to Maxtum Quli. Unaccompanied narrative and accompanied chant alternated throughout the rest of the performance. A plot summary of the fragment Jumabay performed is as follows:[15]

> A long time ago, during the reign of Toxtamysh, a descendant of Chingis Khan, there was a beautiful lake where three doves came to bathe year-round. Once a man named Bâbâ Tughul stole the clothes of the doves and hid them.[16] The doves pleaded with the man to give them back their clothes, but before he would agree to do so, he set a condition: one of the doves had to become his wife. Since the two older doves were already married, he took the youngest one. The dove also set a condition. She said, "If you will observe four conditions, I'll be a faithful wife until death. First,

186

don't look at her armpits [she used the third person]. Second, don't look at her heels. Third, don't look at her when she washes after menstruation. Fourth, don't look at her when she combs her hair." After some time, Bâbâ Tughul's curiosity got the better of him, and he looked at her armpits, and saw wings. When she walked, he looked at her heels and saw that they didn't touch the ground but that she walked on her toes. Then he looked at her while she washed and saw that she took out all of her intestines and washed them in a copper basin. Finally, on Fridays, she removed her human head and combed her hair. But discovering that Bâbâ Tughul had observed her, she changed herself into a dove and said, "My husband, since you violated our agreement, our marriage is annulled" (*haram*). She flew away and told him that she was six months pregnant. She said that she would give birth underneath a tree that was called *talai*. Time passed, a boy was born, and he was named Yedigei. When he turned fourteen, the khan of this place gave his daughter to Yedigei.

King Toxtamysh had two daughters. Their names were Kanikei and Yenigei. In order to keep Yedigei from trying to marry one of his daughters, Toxtamysh started to think of a way to kill him. He decided that Yedigei had to be killed in a roundabout way; if he were killed openly, the people would be upset. He had to be given a task that in the process of being performed would cause him to die. The task was the following: the enemy continually disrupted and stole from the land where Yedigei lived. In particular, they stole Aq-Belek, the fourteen-year-old daughter of Alp-Bâbâ, a descendant of Timur the Lame. They gave Yedigei the task of finding this girl. He went to search for the girl, and he returned to Chalpak [a place in Karakalpakstan]. In Chalpak, there is a mountain called Karategin; the first thing that Yedigei saw was the tracks of a demon. And there lay the monsterlike demon himself, with a head like a *tandir* oven, feet like a plough, hands like a pitchfork, and a mouth like a curved river. Yedigei saw this demon and became scared. The demon was the guardian of Aq-Belek. Aq-Belek's father, Alp-Bâbâ, had an arrow eighty yards long. He could cut down trees with it and cut right into rocks in the mountains. He gave this arrow to Yedigei. The demon was such that he could not be killed with an arrow or a sword. Nothing could kill him. The demon took Aq-Belek away with him, and Aq-Belek left a note that said that the demon could not be killed or injured. Then Yedigei said to Aq-Belek that one had to be cunning in order to subdue the demon. But Aq-Belek said that she had never been cunning in her whole life; then Yedigei said, "Every woman has so much cunningness that it would be a heavy weight for forty donkeys and a mule." And he said to her, "Make him some delicious tea, and put some opium into the tea. And don't just put him to sleep, but coax out of him how he can be killed." She did this, and tenderly said to him, "I often see you after a fight; if you should ever be injured, I should know what your strength is and how I can serve you." Then the demon said that he could not be killed, and that if he were to lie on a rock, an arrow would have to come directly at his heart and smash his heart, and then go through his body to the rock and smash the rock. After drinking the tea, the demon lay down to sleep on the rock. Yedigei took the eighty-yard-long arrow that Alp-Bâbâ gave him and approached the sleeping demon. He felt some sentiment—he felt sorry to kill the demon. He started to doubt; but he had no choice, because he had to perform his task and free the girl. He shot straight into the heart of the demon, and the arrow went into the rock. The demon started to bleed, and the blood went into his eyes. He couldn't see anything; the demon started to move his arm around in a circle in front of him. He caught the hand of Yedigei and took it, and began to lament. He said, "I'm going to leave this world with an unfulfilled wish. In the city of Kobrul lives my brother—his name is Yedigei—and he will take revenge for me." And Yedigei said, "If Yedigei were around you now, what would you say to him?" The demon replied, "If he were around me now, I would shake his hand and say that we are relatives; that he was born from a younger dove, and I from an older one; that our mothers were sisters; that if we were to work together, we would be able to conquer Toxtamysh, and free the people from the Mongol yoke." Yedigei felt bad and said, "I am Yedigei." "If you are Yedigei," said the demon, "I will not swear at you. But I will foretell your fate: you will have a son and that son will kill you."

Jumabay's telling and singing of the Yedigei tale had been a spirited living creation. Drawing on his skill as a performance artist—his sizing up of the social situation in which we all found ourselves and the length of our collective attention span—Jumabay had stitched together a half-hour version of *Yedigei* consisting of a summary of the beginning of the epic and an episode from somewhere in the middle. What most interested OM was the way Jumabay seamlessly melded human characters, history, and actual toponyms with fantasy and magic. "We need to understand that for people who listened to this epic and who listen to it still, there's no dividing line between the natural and the supernatural," said OM. "For them, the demon is as real as any human." No wonder the *baxshi* and *zhirau,* like the shaman, had ended up on the blacklist in the Soviet "struggle with the old." A more antimaterialist worldview would be hard to find than that represented in the epic. Its metaphysics indeed represented a vestige of the old that had been carried from a pre-Islamic era through Islamization and Communist rule down to the present. But in the cultural and political conditions of *fin-de-siècle* Karakalpakstan, where (as I waited for the Minister of Culture outside his office building in downtown Nukus) a young consultant from an American accounting firm specializing in evaluating state assets for privatization auctions drove off in his chauffeured car, would the epic survive another generation as a living art form? Or to put the question more precisely, would a popular demand for the *zhirau's* art continue to exist? Demons might have endured the resistance of Islam and communism, but how would they fare against Price-Waterhouse and Exxon (Karakalpakstan is said to be sitting on large oil reserves)? As we said goodbye to Jumabay and to the well-intentioned Minister of Culture, the question lingered in my mind.

XALFAS

Of all the regions of Transoxania I visited, it was in Khorezm that women's lives seemed most separate from men's (this generalization does not apply to the social world of Slavs, Ashkenazi Jews, or native Central Asians who have adopted a Europeanized social identity). In Bukhara, or at least in the part of it that I came to know, women did not shun men's company. For example, Rosa, the quasi-Europeanized doctor who was our Bukharan host, remained a constant presence during our stay with her. She sat with us in the *mehmânxâna,* greeted us each morning, and wished us goodnight in the evening. At Tohfaxân's, even though the household was arranged in traditional Bukharan fashion with separate areas for men and women, there was a free and easy exchange back and forth across the courtyard that divided the two areas. Tohfaxân never displayed any discomfort about inviting me to sit with her in her room, and I never felt any. At both the Jewish and Muslim *toy*s that we attended, men and women had always appeared together in one and the same place and time, even if their social interaction was limited. Among certain rural groups with nomadic roots—Qipchaqs and Karakalpaks, for example—the conventional gender divisions of urban Muslim life were not as strong. The rigors of life on the steppe enforced more of an equality between the sexes.

Khorezm was different. I am sure that part of the feeling of strangeness and alienation that always overcame me in Khorezm was due to my complete removal from contact with women. Khorezmian men saw women and spoke with women in the intimacy of their private family lives, but as a guest, even of people whom I considered friends, I was kept away from women, and women, for their part, kept away from me. On our last visit, for example, OM and I had stayed at the house of OM's youngest brother, Batir. Batir is in his mid-thirties, married, with three children. He teaches accordion at a music school and earns extra money playing at weddings. In a Khorezmian way, he is a thoroughly contemporary person. His wife is a nurse who works sixteen-hour shifts every other week so that she can spend long stretches of time at home with her children. During our ten-day stay at Batir's, the children were a constant presence, but I only once saw Batir's wife. I was never introduced to her and never told her name. We ran into one another at the telephone one morning when there was a moment of confusion about registering my passport. She said hello to me, spoke on the phone, then disappeared. I don't know how she managed to navigate around the house without ever passing me. When OM and I departed for Tashkent, she stood far away from the front door, in the kitchen, and bowed her head slightly in response to my shout of thanks for her hospitality. At the many Khorezmian evening gatherings of men that I have attended over the years, I have caught only fleeting glimpses of women while being marched in and out of the *mehmânxâna*. Food is always carried from the kitchen and served by sons or male friends of the host. Sometimes at the end of a ribald evening, as groups of men linger on the street, smoking and waiting for sober drivers to take them home, I have peeked inside the door of the host's house and watched as the women of the household enter the *mehmânxâna* to begin their cleanup. During the men's bacchanal, they would have been sitting up in their own part of the house, talking or watching television, waiting for the men to finish.

In the privacy of their own quarters and celebrations, however, women in Khorezm have also maintained their own musical world. The figure who presides over this world is the *xalfa*. The term *xalfa* derives from Arabic *xalifa,* rendered in English as "caliph," and means, literally, "deputy," "vicegerent," or "assistant." The early caliphs who served as both the religious and temporal rulers of the Sunni *umma* were understood to be God's vicegerents to human-kind. The notion of *xalfa* as deputy turns up in Sufi practice: a *xalfa* is a man whose level of spiritual knowledge places him between *pir* and *shagird* or between *murshid* and *murid,* i.e., between master and pupil. On a more worldly level, the term *xalfa* is commonly used among members of craftsmen's guilds to designate an apprentice craftsman.

In Khorezm, a *xalfa* is always a woman. At present, *xalfa*s can be divided into two classes, one whose primary function is religious and another whose primary function is musical. The religiously oriented *xalfa* fills the role of a mullah among women. She reads or recites the Qur'an and other religious texts, offers her own commentary, and leads prayers. No matter how great her knowledge, the *xalfa* must remain a kind of "deputy" mullah who fills an intermediary position lower than that of a mullah or imam, for the *sharia* forbids a woman from standing in the front row of worshippers in a mosque. OM's guess was that the meaning of the word *xalfa* simply expanded to include not only women who read the Qur'an and said prayers at ritual events but also women who provided music at *toy*s (called *xalfa sâzi*). The distinction between the two kinds of *xalfa*s was not based on a distinction between a sacred function and a secular function. Everything having to do with *toy*s and any other ceremonial event was guided by an understanding of *sharia*. It often happened that a woman would be a musical *xalfa* in her younger years and, as she grew older, would gravitate toward reading or reciting religious texts. This synthesis of entertainment and religion distinguished the *xalfa* from the Bukharan *sâzanda,* a wholly secular figure in Bukharan life. With no Jews in Khorezm to assume the morally ambiguous role of the wedding entertainer, Muslim *xalfa*s had fashioned that role in a more limited sense—both dramatically and musically.

Like the Bukharan *sâzanda*s and *mavrigixân*s, *xalfa*s have most frequently been drawn from the ranks of socially marginalized groups. In overwhelmingly monoethnic Khorezm, marginalization has not been based on religious or "national" identity, as in Bukhara, but on family background, lineage, and physical appearance. Many *xalfa*s have been blind or crippled. Others have

190

*Xalfa*s Shirin and Dilbar.

come from poor families or an undistinguished lineage (*avlâd*). "A girl from a good lineage would never become a *xalfa*," OM told me. The profession of *xalfa* traditionally had a low social prestige, but nonetheless it was a profession; a woman could earn money from it and help support a family.

More recently, the image of the *xalfa* seems to have taken a turn for the better in Khorezm. OM said, "If you compare the number of presently active *xalfa*s with the number who were active in the 1920s, you'd find an enormous increase. In the 1920s, only well-to-do people could afford weddings with music. These days it's the norm. Over the shorter term, another factor has to do with the revival of religious weddings. There was a time in Khorezm when there were a lot of Soviet-style 'Komsomol' weddings, or *qyzyl toy*s [red weddings] in which bride and groom, men and women, would sit together and eat. I had one of the first in Khorezm in 1971. It was a scandal in my family. My father didn't want it, but I insisted. Men and women sat together, but quickly they went to their own separate places. They didn't feel comfortable."

At the Tashkent Conservatory, OM had taught a student who had become a *xalfa*. Her name was Shirin, and she had become a teacher in the music school in Khiva. OM arranged for us to meet and record her. *Xalfa*s normally perform in groups of two, three, or four, often including a dancer, and Shirin brought along one of her *xalfa* companions to the recording session. Shirin was twenty-nine, married, with one child. "Thank God, my husband allowed me to be a *xalfa*," she said. She had a full schedule of bookings and had taken on several

191

younger pupils who assisted her during performances by singing backup and playing the *dâyra* and *garmon,* a small accordion.

The *xalfa's* performance program, like that of the *sâzanda* and *mavrigixân,* is normally divided into blocks of songs (*dawr*) that gradually progress from slow tempo to fast through the course of a *toy,* although with less rhythmic intricacy than in the performance of the *sâzanda.* One of the key songs at any wedding is *yâr-yâr,* which exists in many melodic and textual variants all over Transoxania. *Yâr-yâr* is performed in a slow tempo and solemn style at the beginning of a wedding, as the bride waits quietly to be led away from her parents' house, and again as the bride leaves her parents' house. Later it may be sung in a boisterous spirit at a fast tempo as the bride is met at the home of the bridegroom. There are many verses, of which Shirin sang the first four for the accompanying compact disc (track 11). Normally she would have accompanied her singing with a simple *usul* on the *dâyra,* but I asked Shirin to sing *a cappella* to best display the richness of her solo voice.

First of all, we think of God
We celebrate the spirit of the prophets

First of all, God, the pure and saintly Prophet
Who created us with one stroke

My dear child, let your companion be from the line of the king
Let the straight road show you pure people

192

The scissors on the shelf began to rust
The bride is anxious about the wedding.

Yâr-yâr is a little gem. Using the simplest of melodic means and sung in an austere, sparsely ornamented style that contains none of the vocal pyrotechnics of the *suvâra* or *maqâm,* it conveys a pure spirituality in which the personality of the performer recedes to the background. It is the sound that matters. The *xalfa* repertory is folk music in the most classical sense: a largely anonymous body of songs and texts transmitted through oral tradition within a community of listeners. If communities of listeners throughout much of the world are increasingly divided by age, education, and ethnicity, in Khorezm they are still overwhelmingly divided by gender. Men's music and women's music exist side by side in the same households, the same *toy*s; but like men's and women's social lives, they have largely gone their own separate ways. "Women's music has remained more conservative," said OM, underlining an important characteristic of women's music not only in Khorezm but in many other cultures as well. "There's more of a sense of following tradition, of respecting the past. That's not to say that *xalfa*s don't compose new songs; they do, but more often than not, these songs make their way into the repertory without attribution. Compared to the innovations that you see in genres like *suvâra* and *maqâm,* women's music is changing much more slowly."

Both musically and socially, *xalfa*s work within a more confined space than men. OM's view was that Khorezmian women didn't interpret this confinement as an injustice. "They understand it simply as the fate of women in an Islamic society," he said. "They're not about to become feminists."

Back in Tashkent, Svetlana, OM's wife, joined the conversation. "Communism made things worse for women here," she said. "Not only did women have the responsibility of managing a household, but they had to become breadwinners as well. That wasn't natural for an Islamic society, where men are supposed to deal with money and women with the household. Many people are going back now to a more traditional family life, but for women it's still no better, and very likely getting worse."

OM didn't see it that way. "People are going back to a more traditional family life, but in a more modern way. It's not just fundamentalism. A man with means naturally does all he can to make his whole family comfortable. You could see that in the houses where we were received, for example, at Mahmad's, the nephew of Xâjaxân Baltaev." That had been the evening of the unsuccessful recording session, when I had lashed out at the drunken violinist. The *mehmân-xâna* had indeed been lavish, but all I could remember of the rest of the house and household was being hurriedly rushed through the entryway and out the back door while the women stared curiously at an errant American and his sack of recording equipment, knowing only that because of his presence they would be up late that evening.

THE UPPER ZARAVSHAN & YAGNÂB

Har kas ki binad yâ kohi baland, yâ shahri azim
(Every person should see either high mountains or a great city.)

—Tajik aphorism

A MYSTERIOUS VALLEY

"If you worry about rocks, don't go to the mountains," the Deputy Chairman of the Aini District Executive Committee advised matter-of-factly after I asked about the danger of avalanches on the trek into Yagnâb. "But if you're sure you want to go," he added with a hint of annoyance, "we'll take you there. You'll leave tomorrow after breakfast."

OM had first mentioned the idea of visiting Yagnâb in 1990. One of the new cultural organizations sprouting up throughout the USSR in the wake of glasnost, a group in Tajikistan called the Tajik Culture Fund, had set about trying to organize a long-term, multidisciplinary study of Yagnâb. The Yagnâb project had been the inspiration of Oleg Panfilov, a young Russian archaeologist, journalist, and cultural activist who had become a central figure in the Culture Fund and had envisioned a group of specialists drawn from a variety of disciplines—linguistics, ethnography, botany, architecture, folklore—conducting research projects from a permanent base camp in Yagnâb. Through an intermediary, Panfilov had sent word to OM that we would be welcome to join the research effort by undertaking a survey of musical life in the Yagnâb Valley.

For more than a century, philologists and Orientalists—mainly Russian—have ventured into Yagnâb, attracted first by the peculiarities of the local language, which residents of Yagnâb call Yagnâbi. Yagnâbi differs markedly from Tajik (or Tajiki), the eastern dialect of Persian spoken in Transoxania, and

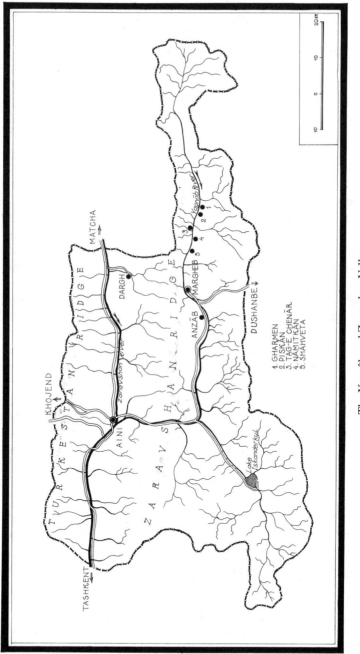

The Yagnāb and Zaravshan Valleys

1. GHARMEN
2. PISKĀN
3. TĀG-E CHENĀR
4. NĀMITKĀN
5. SHAHVETA

195

some of the first philologists who studied Yagnâbi classified it as an Indian or Pamir language. But the provenance of Yagnâbi turned out to be far more mysterious: it is the last vestige of Soghdian, an otherwise extinct middle Iranian language once spoken in ancient Soghdia (linguists now classify Yagnâbi as New Soghdian). Yagnâb's atavistic language is only the most noticeable of its cultural archaisms, each of which over the years has attracted its own constituency of scholar-adventurers and anthropological curiosity seekers.[1]

Travelers from afar have not been the only ones animated by Yagnâb's unique cultural artifacts. In the folklore of Bukhara and the Zaravshan Valley, Yagnâb represents a "personification of the magical," as OM put it to me. In this folklore, Yagnâb is a land of mysterious herbs, of fakirs who perform miracles of healing, of secret incantations that have the power of life and death. The aura of mystery that surrounds Yagnâb has only been enhanced by the survival of Soghdian, which for Tajiks is a key to their past that evokes special awe and respect.

Yagnâb is just the sort of place that one might expect to find mystery, magic, and an otherwise extinct language. Flanked by the snow-covered 15,000-foot peaks of the Zaravshan Ridge to the north and the Gissar Ridge to the south, the Yagnâb River winds through a pristine alpine valley accessible only by an ancient footpath that once served Chinese traders traveling to Samarkand and Bukhara. From November until the end of May, deep snow makes the footpath impassable. Yagnâb's air is delicately perfumed with the bouquet of dozens of varieties of herbs that grow profusely on the mountain-sides. According to hunters, snow leopards, wild goats, and wolves inhabit the upper elevations, while marmots and foxes live closer to the bottom of the valley.

Though Soviet authority was finally established in Yagnâb in the mid-1920s after seven years of resistance by the *basmachi,* that authority remained tenuous. Lenin's promise of electrification for the entire Soviet Union was never fulfilled in Yagnâb. There are no electrical or telephone lines, no shops, no mail delivery, no polyclinic. Medical care is in the hands of local healers; a few ad hoc primary schools operate in dark, barren rooms with unimaginably meager resources.

In the spring of 1991, Tajikistan's factious politics were just beginning to slip into the catastrophic disarray that would ultimately lead to a devastating civil war. Oleg Panfilov, the highly visible organizer of the Yagnâb Project, became one of the first victims of those politics. Accused first of being a Russian nationalist and later a Tajik nationalist, he was forced out of the Tajik Culture Fund and ultimately had to flee for his life to Moscow. When Panfilov left the Culture Fund, the Yagnâb Project was canceled. Meanwhile, OM, his wife, Svetlana, and I had become so intrigued with the idea of visiting Yagnâb that we decided to go by ourselves. If Yagnâb had preserved an otherwise extinct language, might it also have preserved an otherwise extinct music? Perhaps Yagnâb would provide clues about an older layer of musical tradition in the Upper Zaravshan region that predated the Tajik song forms common there today.

The Aini District Executive Committee had been asked to furnish OM, Svetlana, and me with a jeep and driver to take us to Anzâb, the headquarters of the collective farm that has jurisdiction over the settlements in the Yagnâb Valley. The very morning of our arrival, the request had been telephoned to Aini from the office of the Regional Party Committee in Khojend (formerly Leninabâd), the administrative center of the region in which Aini District is located. OM had a friend in Khojend, the Vice-Rector of the Khojend Pedagogical Institute, who owed him a favor (OM had helped his son gain admission to the Tashkent Conservatory). In the spirit of barter exchange that became a principal form of currency in the Soviet Union and has remained a principal form of currency in post-Soviet Central Asia, the Vice-Rector asked a friend at the Regional Party Committee who owed *him* a favor to call Aini and order the District Executive Committee to assist us. Considering the short notice on which they'd been told to produce a jeep, a driver, and the most precious of commodities, gasoline, the functionaries at the District Executive Committee were unreservedly gracious in their welcome when the Vice-Rector's driver dropped us at their doorstep just before lunch. We were fed at the party cafeteria and installed at the party hotel, a concrete bungalow behind the party headquarters building that contained a sitting room painted with arabesques of birds and flowers in an irridescent pinkish purple and two bunk rooms, one for men and one for women.

Aini is a picturesque spot as district centers go, situated on the north bank of the Zaravshan River about a hundred miles upstream from Samarkand. The starkness of its largely postrevolutionary concrete block architecture is mollified by well-manicured parks, rose gardens, and large shade trees and by the spectacular alpine scenery on both the north and south sides of the Zaravshan. To the north, the view over the mountains is marred only by a large billboard set into the cliffs high above town. From the left side of the billboard, Lenin glowers down at pedestrians on Aini's main street, and to his right, immense lettering proclaims in Russian (a language that most of Aini's overwhelmingly Tajik population barely knows), "Lenin is eternally alive." As of June 1994, when OM and I once again passed through Aini on the way to Dargh (our first trip to Yagnâb and Dargh was in June 1991), the Lenin billboard was still in place.

Until the Revolution, this region of the Upper Zaravshan Valley was known locally as Fâlghar (Persian: "light mountain"). Like other territories incorporated into what became Soviet Tajikistan, Fâlghar was once a princely state ruled by a *mir* (Uzbek: *beg*) loyal to the Emir of Bukhara. The local population is overwhelmingly Tajik, but in the tradition of these parts, the local inhabitants called themselves, before the Soviet era, not after an ethnicity but after their place of residence, thus Fâlghari.

Aini itself used to be called Varzimonor but was renamed after the writer Sadraddin Aini, one of the demigods of the Bolshevik Revolution in Tajikistan. The renaming was not without an ironic twist, as Aini is only a short distance from the little settlement of Zasun, the birthplace of Naqibxân Tughral Axrâri, the other great name in early twentieth-century Tajik literature. Tughral (as he is known) was from an aristocratic family but had welcomed the Revolution and taken part in the Red Army's struggle against local *basmachi* guerrillas. Despite his official Bolshevik sympathies, however, rumors had been spread that he was secretly collaborating with the *basmachi*s. In 1919, on the basis of these rumors, he was arrested and executed without a trial or an investigation (he was "rehabilitated" in 1960). Aini is now considered to have been a much inferior writer to Tughral, and Tughral supposedly detested Aini. Some local people consider it blasphemy that the main town in the region of Tughral's birthplace should have been renamed after his arch-rival.[2]

THE YAGNÂB AFFAIR

These days Yagnâb is probably best known in Central Asia for the so-called Yagnâb Affair, an episode of impudent and imprudent central planning that has come to epitomize Soviet Central Asia's sinister "cotton politics" of the 1960s, 1970s, and early 1980s. The Yagnâb Affair involved the forced resettlement of the Yagnâb Valley's entire population in less magical but, according to the officials who ordered the resettlement, socially and seismologically more propitious surroundings. The cultural and medical disaster that followed the resettlement became a scandalous *cause célèbre* in Tajikistan.

The resettlement of the Yagnâbis, which began in 1970, was conducted under the guise of official concern both about Yagnâb's lack of social amenities and about the danger of landslides in the valley triggered by seismic tremors. Fear of earthquakes was especially high in Central Asia in the years following the devastating quake of 1966 that destroyed large parts of Tashkent. However, an unofficial and more cynical explanation of the resettlement also circulates in Transoxania. This explanation is corroborated in a series of newspaper articles published in Tajikistan in 1990 by Oleg Panfilov, who gained access to official documents pertaining to the resettlement and interviewed some of the individuals responsible for carrying it out.[3] In the unofficial explanation, the primary motive for the resettlement was not concern for the safety and welfare of the Yagnâbis but a need for laborers on Tajikistan's newly created cotton plantations.

In the late 1960s, the cotton politics that had gripped Uzbekistan and ultimately brought down its leadership spilled over into the north of Tajikistan. In order to meet ever higher goals set out in the yearly economic plans handed down from Moscow, more cotton had to be planted, more cotton had to be picked, and thus more workers were needed on the cotton plantations. In a prearranged display of socialist solidarity, Uzbekistan's First Secretary, Sharaf Rashidov, presented Tajikistan with 55,000 hectares of steppe land north of Ura-Tyube that was to be irrigated and turned over to cotton growing. Summer temperatures on this part of what Russians call the Hungry Steppe can reach 120 degrees. Uzbekistan's gift became the district of Zafarabâd. *Zafar* means "victory," and *abâd* most commonly means "town," although it also means "flowering"; thus Zafarabâd literally meant "victory town" and symbolized the flowering of victory over the steppe. In the cynical explanation of the Yagnâb Affair, the Yagnâbis were resettled in Zafarabâd to provide the labor that would bring about this victorious flowering.

According to accounts we heard in Yagnâb, it was in March 1970 that helicopters began to land in the small settlements built along the steep slopes of the valley. Men with bullhorns gathered residents together and announced that there existed an imminent danger of landslides and that the residents were to gather what belongings they could carry and prepare for evacuation within three or four days. Families were compensated (at rock-bottom prices) for their herd animals, and the animals were left behind. The official version of the resettlement has it that the Yagnâbis left voluntarily, frightened by the physical danger of remaining in their valley and convinced that their material needs would be better provided for in Zafarabâd. However, our conversations in Yagnâb and Zafarabâd, as well as Panfilov's investigative journalism, provide overwhelming evidence that the Yagnâbis were coerced into leaving. "Everyone wept and wailed when we left," one man told us. "Some people tried to run away rather than board the helicopters, but the women were forced into the helicopters, and after that, the men had to follow."[4] During the spring and summer of 1970, some three thousand people from over five hundred families were airlifted out of the Yagnâb Valley, the bottom of which is about two miles above sea level. The Yagnâbis were taken by helicopter to Aini, then loaded in trucks for the ride to Zafarabâd, where they were transformed instantly from mountain herders and subsistence farmers into cotton plantation workers. Soon after their arrival in Zafarabâd, Yagnâbis began to die in alarming numbers from disease, many from tuberculosis. We were told that in the first weeks after the resettlement, as many as ten people died in a single day.

Conditions on the Hungry Steppe were so intolerable that over a period of years, some Yagnâbis abandoned Zafarabâd without authorization and made their way back to the empty settlements of Yagnâb (Yagnâbis, like collective farmworkers throughout the Soviet Union, were not issued internal passports until the 1960s and thus could not legally travel away from their place of residence). By 1978, hundreds of Yagnâbis were once again living—illegally—in the Yagnâb Valley, and a helicopter-borne roundup was organized to return them to Zafarabâd. This time the authorities brought along police with automatic weapons.

The 1978 roundup was only a temporary setback for the Yagnâbis, who once again began to return to their mountain settlements. After a while, the authorities gave up. The Yagnâbis managed to reestablish their herds of sheep, replant their gardens, and rekindle the spirit of their subsistence life on the periphery of Soviet power. They carried no internal passport, no *propusk* permitting them to live in a particular region, no military card. In 1994, there were about 380 residents spread out through the Yagnâb Valley.

During the Gorbachev years, the Yagnâbis' plight was taken up by several journalists in Dushanbe, Tajikistan's capital. A Committee for the Defense of Yagnâb was established, and a Yagnâbi was elected a deputy in the Tajik Supreme Soviet. Finally, in September 1990, the President of Tajikistan, Kahar Maxkamov, flew up to Yagnâb in a helicopter and announced that he would help the Yagnâbis reestablish their original settlements. Yagnâbis from Zafarabâd would be allowed to return to their valley, and money was appropriated for the construction of a jeep track into Yagnâb. The Aini District Executive Committee was told to send representatives to Yagnâb to register residents for passports and residence permits, and a team of medical personnel was assembled to assess the Yagnâbis' medical needs. Our visit took place as these efforts to resuscitate Yagnâb were getting under way.

TREKKING FOR MUSIC

The good-natured functionaries at the Aini District Executive Committee produced a driver and jeep, as promised, to take us to Anzâb, fifty-odd miles to the south, over a twisting but well-constructed paved road that lies along the most direct route between Tashkent and Dushanbe. In Anzâb, the chairman of Kolkhoz Ordzhonikidze was expecting us. He had already arranged for his jeep driver to run us the remaining few miles to Margheb, the gateway to Yagnâb, along a terrifying dirt track that consisted solely of a series of steeply ascending and descending switchbacks. The driver, an elderly man who sat barely high enough to see over the steering wheel of the jeep and squinted through thick glasses, seemed to have the track memorized. I held up a video camera to record the dramatic scenery and closed my eyes tightly.

At Margheb, our jeep driver introduced us to Xâlmurâd, the village librarian, an avid hunter who often went up to Yagnâb to shoot wild goats, foxes, wolves, and, if he had an especially good day, a snow leopard. Xâlmurâd was thirty-three, tall, thin, dark, with deeply set, intense eyes and thick black hair. He had no warning of our arrival, but in the inimitable way in which authority is handed down from center to periphery in Central Asia, the jeep driver, on authority from the Chairman of Kolkhoz Ordzhonikidze, at the request of the Chairman of the Aini District Executive Committee, on orders from a bureaucrat in the Khojend

Crossing the Yagnâb.

Regional Party Committee (who was exchanging favors with the Vice-Rector of the Khojend Pedagogical Institute, who was exchanging favors with OM), ordered Xâlmurâd to close his library for a week or two, assemble two donkeys, and take the three visitors to Yagnâb. The twinkle in Khâlmurâd's eyes as he loaded the donkeys and strapped his rifle on his back suggested that he was not unhappy to be packing off for another Yagnâbian adventure.

We rose at 4:30 A.M. the day of our departure from Margheb. Khâlmurâd's wife brought breakfast—tandir-baked bread and a bowl of fresh, hot milk. When Xâlmurâd noticed I was avoiding the milk, I explained that I hadn't drunk milk since childhood, but liked milk products. Xâlmurâd nodded knowingly and after a few minutes returned with a large bowl of melted butter. "Drink this," he said. "You'll need energy for the trail." What could I do but comply?

Our party of two donkeys, one guide, and three musicologists tramped out of Margheb under threateningly overcast skies, but as we reached the upper boundary of the terraced fields that extend beyond the village, the clouds broke, and an arrow of sunlight illuminated the snowy crest of the Yagnâb Wall, a massive rock cliff that guards the entrance to the valley. An hour's march from Margheb took us to the end of the new jeep track that Kolkhoz Ordzhonikidze had started to blast and bulldoze into the valley, and after another hour of steep climbing, we were already high above the river in a level saddle between the mountain peaks pocked with mangy grass and knee-high shrubs. From the midst of the rock and scree grew an ancient juniper tree with a bulbous trunk where travelers stop to pray and, after their prayers, tie white ribbons to the tree's branches to bring good luck on their journey. Xâlmurâd recounted a legend about the tree. Long ago, God had sent a baby in a cradle to a holy man who lived below, in the valley. The woman who raised the baby had foretold that he would become a saint. The child did become a saint, and when that saint grew older, he frequently walked to Yagnâb, where many other saints lived. At the very spot where we stood, a small tree had been in the process of drying up and dying. The saint had stopped and prayed that the tree would grow into a giant juniper, and the juniper before us had been the result of his prayer.

Yagnâb derives from Persian *yax* ("ice") plus *âb* ("water"), and the temperature of the Yagnâb River was true to its name. Above Margheb, the river is never terribly broad—perhaps fifty feet at the widest point—but it is extremely deep and flows with a strong current through narrow gorges and around dramatic curves from which grassy fields slope gently upward. Above the fields are stony escarpments that recede to a backdrop of cone-shaped, snow-covered summits linked by serrated ridges. The trail into Yagnâb zigzags up and down the sides of the valley, hugging the river where it is convenient and climbing steeply to bypass gorges that are impassable on foot. Snaking along cliff-bound ledges hundreds of feet above the river, the trail is sometimes little wider than a traveler's body. In these spots, Xâlmurâd mounted one of the sure-footed donkeys, nonchalantly strumming a *dombrak* that he kept in one of the sidepacks and singing in a full-throated tenor voice. Though Xâlmurâd assured me I was wrong, I felt safer choosing my own footing.

Every few kilometers, the trail passed through another of the silent little colonies of tumbledown stone and clay dwellings built into the walls of the valley. Some of these settlements were empty. Roofs had caved in, doors and window glass had been carried away by herders from the next valley. In other settlements, only one or two among dozens of houses were occupied. The stillness of these crumbling villages was not the uplifting stillness of a mountaintop or a deep forest; it was the uneasy, unnatural stillness of civilization abandoned, of once-flourishing communities gone to seed.

Shortly after we passed the settlement of Xushârtâb—population: one family—Xâlmurâd spotted a fox peering out from behind a rock on the opposite side of the Yagnâb River, about a hundred yards distant. In a single, swift motion, he rotated his rifle sling so that the rifle hung in front of him, raised it to eye level, aimed at the fox, then fired. He missed, and fired again. Apparently unhurt, the fox disappeared into a hole under the rock. I asked Xâlmurâd, "Why did you shoot at the fox when you knew you wouldn't be able to retrieve it?" (the river could not be forded at that point).

"I just wanted to see if I could shoot that far," Xâlmurâd answered, slinging his rifle back to its aft position. The "take nothing but photos, leave nothing but footprints" philosophy of wilderness trekking has yet to hit central Tajikistan.

Approaching the eleventh hour of our first day's hike, we noticed a young man careening down a path in our direction from a group of houses set high above the trail. The young man scrambled over some rocks and jumped onto the trail, blocking our route. We exchanged greetings, and with unusual forthrightness, the young man immediately invited us to spend the night in his house. He told us that as he herded his sheep, he kept a pair of binoculars trained on the trail in the hope that a traveler would appear with whom he could pass the evening in conversation. We had planned to reach a settlement a few kilometers farther along, but after the young man told us that his father played music, we agreed to follow him up the slope, through brush and scree, to the settlement of Shâhveta (Yagnâbi: "Place of the King"). On the way up the slope, Xâlmurâd confided to us that the jeep driver from Anzâb, on instructions from the Chairman of Kolkhoz Ordzhonikidze, had told him to warn the Yagnâbis we encountered in the settlements not to complain about their living conditions or about how the government had treated them.

As soon as our small caravan came abreast of the settlement, the sidepacks on the donkeys were unpacked and the donkeys were taken to a pasture, where they were tied to poles and allowed to graze. A single extended family inhabited Shâhveta. There had once been eighteen families with some three hundred people. Svetlana was led to a house where the women in the family lived, while OM, Xâlmurâd, and I were taken next door to the men's house. We didn't see Svetlana again until we were ready to depart the following morning.

The men's house was about fifteen by eight feet with smooth walls plastered inside and out with clay. Light came from one small window, about a foot square, and from an open door less than five feet high. The floor was covered with straw, on top of which were layered, in turn, felt mats, a felt rug, and cotton *korpacha*s. At one end of the room was a stove made from a square iron box with a gasoline jerry can fastened horizontally to the top so as to extend over the side of the box. A length of stovepipe connected to a hole cut in the jerry can ran straight up through the roof. The roof was made from log beams set perpendicular to a row of sticks and smaller logs crudely hewn to fit over the beams. Hay covered the logs, and rocks and dirt topped off the hay. In the middle of the floor a low table was set over another iron box recessed into the floor, called a *sandal*. In the winter, hot coals were placed in the *sandal* to warm the legs of those sitting around the table. The room was cozy but not particularly warm in the chilly evening air, and dried dung was put in the stove and lit.

Our host, a man in his mid-fifties named Sattâr Adinaev, offered tea, followed by greasy fried mutton and potatoes prepared by the women in a separate cooking house which the Yagnâbis call *âtashgâx* (place of fire). Contemplating the mutton and potatoes, I thought of an Uzbek aphorism: "With enough grease, you can eat even dirt" (Yagh bilan, tuprokni ham yeyish mumkin). The main

203

course was washed down with *katiq,* a sour kefir, and followed by an offering of *airan,* fermented sheep's milk poured from a bladder made from a sheep stomach. While we ate, Sattâr showed off his only appliance, a battery-operated radio that could pick up the radio station in Dushanbe. After supper, at our prompting, Sattâr took out a crudely made *dombrak,* an unfretted long-neck lute with two strings, and started to play. The sun had gone down, and Sattâr lit a kerosene lamp. When kerosene was unavailable, he used homemade cow-fat candles. I unpacked my digital tape recorder and set up the microphones. The batteries would provide six hours of recording time before needing a recharge, which would be impossible in electricity-less Yagnâb.

Sattâr was a competent musician but complained that he was out of practice. "I don't take out my *dombrak* much, because there are practically no occasions here that call for music," he lamented. He strummed a *mashq,* an instrumental etude, then sang several songs whose melodies he said he had made up himself.[5] One of them was a setting of a mystical *ghazal* called "Afarid" (literally: "God Created"), the melody of which had been composed by Sattâr's uncle (see the accompanying compact disc, track 18). OM and I translated the text and transcribed the beginning of the melody.

Ân xu-dâ-van - dâ ki av-val nur-î i-mân âf-a-rid ___

Bin ki dar aw - ji fa-lak xur - shid-î tâ-bân âf-a-rid _____

This God, who first created the light of faith,
Look at Him who at the very height of the universe, created the radiant sun.

We, suffering ones, were given our place in these changing heavens,
[God] sowed us among the flowers of the desert and turned the desert
    into a garden.

[God] brought a sheep to the Prophet,
A swarm of worms came out of the body of Ayub Sâbir.

By his will, Jesus made the dead living,
Look at how much divine strength He gave to Jesus the Prophet.

He put Holy Moses close to him,
Following God's command, he turned His world into a garden.

From the rocky mountains He made a flowing spring,
If He dives in the river, He turns it into a gold mine.

To Holy Yakub, He gave good children,
Among them, He created Yusuf the imprisoned one.

When Ibrahim came among the nonbelievers, they tortured him,
The fire of Namrud [in which Ibrahim was burned] was turned into a garden.

To the people, He showed Ismail to be a Prophet,
For that faith, He created Idi Kurbân [the Feast of the Sacrifice].

He said to his angels, bow down to the dust of man,
In the two worlds, He sent to the devil the necklace of the cursed.

Ân xudâvandâ ki avval nurî imân âfarid
Bin ki dar awji falak xurshidî tâbân âfarid

Mârâ dard nishiniyân charxî gardân jâi dâd
Kârd dar sahrâi gul, dar gulistân âfarid.

Barrarâ bar farqi dihiyâyi paighâmbar nihâd.
Az tani Ayubi Sâbir quti kirmân âfarid

Hazrati Isâ ba hukmash murdarâ zinda kunad
Bin ki dar Isâi paighambar chi hurân âfarid

Hazrati Musârâ dar fasli nâi jâi dâd.
Olami dunyâyi dumbâli vai dar gulistân âfarid.

Mekunan az sangi xârâ chashmaî âbi ravân.
Gar ba daryâ gharqi gardâd zar dar kân âfarid

Hazrati Yâkubrâ dâdast farzandâî xub
Az miyânî Yusufî zindân âfarid

Xamchi Ibrâhim ba dasti kâfirâ bud dâdan azâb.
Atâshi Namrudra bar vai gulistân âfarid.

Pirrâ bar xalqi Ismâili Paighambar nihâd
Az bârâî etiqâdash Idi Kurbân âfarid.

Bâ malâik guftan khâki âdamirâ sajda kun.
Tâwqi lanat dar du âlam bahri shaitân âfarid.

OM found the *ghazal* interesting for several reasons. "It shows that in the not-so-distant past there was a high level of spiritual culture in Yagnâb. The text is mystical and sophisticated. It reveals Sufi inspiration in the poetic imagery, in the very notion of such a personal glimpse of God.[6] The music is also sophisticated. It's more than a simple folk tune. The melody ascends to an *awj* in the middle, then begins again with a *darâmad* [introductory section in low register]. At the same time, it's not a song that requires great vocal mastery of the singer. There's little of the melodic ornamentation that you find in the *maqâm,* and the melodic range is relatively limited." I noted that the *ghazal* was in Persian, not Yagnâbi, and asked Sattâr whether he also knew Yagnâbi *ghazal*s.

"I heard them from older singers," he replied, "but people here have always known Tajik as well Yagnâbi. We've always known Persian poetry."[7] Sattâr's comment made me wonder to what extent the concept of a musical subculture or microculture made sense in Transoxania. Even a region as physically isolated as Yagnâb had a tradition of strong connections to other parts of the Upper Zaravshan Valley, to Samarkand and Bukhara, and through these citadels of Persianate culture to the larger world of Greater Persia. Other recording sessions and musical conversations in Yagnâb also suggested that a long tradition of travel and pilgrimage, not to mention the exile to Zafarabâd, had made for an almost seamless musical connection between Yagnâb and the Tajik-speaking Upper Zaravshan region. While Yagnâb had indeed preserved local traditions pertaining, for example, to aspects of language, architecture, and nutrition, music in Yagnâb, or at least that which we were able to hear in 1991, fell into a different, more international category of Transoxanian tradition.

Sattâr played a few more songs, the last of them "Yak Dâna Gul," a Tajik folk song that had become widely known in arrangements by pop singers (see the accompanying compact disc, track 19).

> One single flower, two single ones, a pomegranate with single seeds
> In our garden, we have peaches, apples, and pomegranates
> We gather a lot [of fruits], a lot of apples, a lot of peaches
> I went to a faraway place and brought back from there the stems of flowers
> Where are we going to plant that flower? In Mirza Gul's yard.

> Yak dâna gul, du dâna eh, anâri dâna-dâna (refrain)
> Dar bâghi mâ shaftâli, sebi anâri dâri
> Dâman-dâman bechinim eh, ham sebi, ham shaftâli
> Raftam râî durâ-dur, âvardam nihâli gul.
> In gula kujâ kârem eh, dar havliî Mirzâ Gul.

Then he put down his *dombrak* and shrugged his shoulders. "I don't remember any more songs," he said softly. The recording session by kerosene light had come to an end.

The following morning, Xâlmurâd rose to pray a little before 5:00 A.M. A light rain was falling. We had tea and a bowl of mutton broth for breakfast, and Xâlmurâd brought the donkeys up from their pasture to load the sidepacks. As we prepared to depart, Svetlana was delivered from the women's house. A little girl held her hand and cried. She didn't want Svetlana to leave.

Another day's hike brought us to Tag-e Chenar, which means "underneath the plane tree" (Tajik: Taht-e Chenar). The plane tree, some four feet in diameter at the base and said to have been 1,700 years old, was no longer standing, but lay on its side at the edge of the settlement. A mosque had been built next to it, at the burial site of a legendary saint, Eshan Abdurasul Wali. Shortly after the residents of Tag-e Chenar had been taken away to Zafarabâd, the tree had dried up and died, falling on the mosque and crushing it.

Tag-e Chenar was set high above the floor of the Yagnâb Valley, on the bank of a glacier-fed stream that ran down the mountainside to the Yagnâb River. Approaching the settlement, we were overcome by the pungent, mustardlike smell of *rovak,* a cruciferous alpine weed that is fed to cattle. Everything and everyone in Tag-e Chenar smelled of *rovak.* A robust, heavyset man attired in a faded orange skullcap and the tattered remains of a brown suit that perfectly matched his bronzed complexion, introduced himself as the brigadier (*avaz*) of Tag-e Chenar—the Soviet equivalent of the traditional *âqsâqâl,* who served as a village elder. The brigadier, who might have been in his early sixties, was the single representative of Soviet power in Yagnâb. He had two years of education, had served in the army in Moscow, and spoke some Russian. The first thing the brigadier told us was that he had the only electricity in Yagnâb. Drawing on knowledge he'd gained as a radio operator during his army service, he had cobbled together a simple hydroelectric generator powered by the rushing water in the stream that ran by Tag-e Chenar. The generator produced enough electricity to power an electric light bulb in the brigadier's house as well as a two-way radio given him by the *kolkhoz* in Anzâb to use in the event of a medical emergency. In such an event, a helicopter could be called from Dushanbe, a twenty-five-minute flight from Yagnâb.

Tag-e Chenar had been a much larger settlement than Shâhveta—we were told that there were once a hundred families there—and a correspondingly larger number of residents had returned from Zafarabâd. Most of the houses were still uninhabited, but we saw many children, and the muddy streets were animated by a feeling of activity. When we explained our business to the brigadier and asked whether anyone in Tag-e Chenar was a musician, he immediately shook his head, "no." "You will be my guests," the brigadier said firmly. Could he have been concealing the presence of musicians simply to promote his own offer, or better, command, of hospitality? Once again, Svetlana was led off for the night to the house occupied by the women and girls in the brigadier's extended family.

The brigadier had a severe case of verbal incontinence. He talked loudly and lubriciously in monotonous sentences. As he spoke, no one answered him or even looked in his direction. His talk seemed most of all a way to make noise, to break the silence. The gist of the brigadier's prattle was that in the morning, he planned to radio the *kolkhoz* in Anzâb and order a helicopter to fly in and meet us at the end of the Yagnâb Valley so that we wouldn't have to spend another week retracing our steps to return to our starting point at Margheb. This theme dominated the evening's conversation. After several hours of the brigadier's monologue, OM faded out and began his Wagnerian snoring while the brigadier and male members of his family slurped their soup with what seemed like

207

exaggerated loudness. What a counterpoint of sounds! When we agreed that it was time to sleep, I waited for the brigadier to turn off the electric light, but it became clear that he had no intention of doing so. He was so proud of the light that he wanted it to be on all night. In the end, I decided that his feelings would be hurt if I requested that he turn it off, and we slept with the dangling bulb burning brightly in our faces.

Through the night, a thick snow fell. It was the tenth of June. In the morning, OM, Svetlana, and I went out in the snow to walk around Tag-e Chenar. The snow had begun to melt and had turned the ground into a cold mud. The houses were built in a terrace arrangement along the stream, and the main byway of Tag-e Chenar was a long dirt concourse that ran between the stream and the houses. Midway along the concourse was a freestanding, doorless outhouse set adjacent to the river.

A group of three small boys approached us. One had no shoes. He shared a pair of shoes with his brother, he told us, and it was the brother's turn to wear them at that moment. We met the father of the boy without shoes. He was sixty-three years old and had had twenty children by three different wives. When I asked him, jokingly, what his secret was, he said with a serious face, "The most important thing for a man is to eat meat and fat. I drink two cups of sheep fat and I feel great. If I didn't do it, my cock wouldn't work right." Unfortunately, the sheep fat hadn't done much for his children's health once they were born. Thirteen of them had died, along with the first two of his wives. His first wife and all four of her children died in Tag-e Chenar. His second wife and her five children died in Zafarabâd. The third wife, still alive, bore eleven children, four of whom died. The remaining seven were in Tag-e Chenar, including the boy with no shoes.

There is a *mektab*—a school—in Tag-e Chenar. It had opened not long before our visit, and the brigadier was proud of it. The teacher was a Yagnâbi from a different settlement who had finished middle school in Zafarabâd. He had applied twice to the Pedagogical Institute in Khojend but had been rejected, and so he had come to Tag-e Chenar. The school occupied a tiny, low room, half underground, whose entryway was through a hatchlike door. With the door closed, the only light came from a single square window built high into one wall. The school's educational materials consisted of a blackboard and a box of miscellaneous primers and textbooks, no two of which seemed to be the same. The students were of different ages, although age was only casually related to level of education. One fourteen-year-old boy was in his second year of school. Yagnâbis had never had access to much formal schooling. We were told by an official in Zafarabâd that at the time of the resettlement, there were six people in Yagnâb with "higher education," which included high school, yet at least in local folklore, Yagnâb had once boasted a high level of cultural literacy. Mullahs and *ishâns* provided instruction in Islamic law and custom; the works of the great Persian poets circulated in oral tradition, if not always in writing; music, too, had occupied a place in this system of traditional knowledge. But school-age children in postresettlement Yagnâb were caught in a hiatus between cultures. The old culture was moribund, while Soviet culture had barely established a beachhead. The result was that at the time of our visit, Yagnâb seemed to be moving, at least among younger people, toward universal illiteracy, as a generation of children born after the return from Zafarabâd grew up with little or no schooling.

We were relieved when it was time to leave Tag-e Chenar. Svetlana was aghast at her experience in the women's house. "They asked me whether my husband beat me. They all said that their husbands beat them; they were beaten if they didn't stand up when their husbands looked at them, and they were beaten if a child cried. They age so quickly here. I told them I was thirty instead of forty to make them feel better. The women barely sing," she reported. "They have no time, and their life is too hard. Or they are constantly in mourning for children who have died. There was one woman who knew some songs, but she refused to sing because her daughter had died in Zafarabâd and left four young children, and these children were now in Yagnâb. Her daughter-in-law didn't know any songs. She was twenty or so but didn't know anything. A neighbor came in, but she also said that she didn't sing. None of them even knew a lullaby."

Piskân, set in a sunny alpine field that overlooked enormous cliffs flanking the north bank of the Yagnâb River, was a happier place than Tag-e Chenar. Or so it seemed from the men's side of the household where Xâlmurâd had sought out an old hunting acquaintance and where we unloaded the donkeys and arranged our things for the night. As the sun fell low behind the mountains, we were invited to walk up to the vast open field behind the settlement to watch some expert Yagnâbi horsemanship. During weddings, the boys and men of Piskân galloped around this field playing *buz kâshi,* in which a goat is beheaded and the goat carcass set in the middle of the field while men on horseback try to grab it and carry it to a designated position. The game can be played by teams, by one group of men, or by a single man. The point is to show strength, stamina, and dexterity.

Xâlmurâd had brought along his *dombrak,* and as we watched the horses, he began to play. One of the herders standing with us danced to the rhythm of the *dombrak,* using a wooden walking staff as a prop. He held the staff tightly against the nape of his neck, and then angled it against his back, the lower end held by his left hand and the upper end levered in the crook of his right arm. Then he raised his hands over his head, the staff in one hand, and twirled it gently, all the while gracefully turning his torso and shifting his weight from one foot to the other in time to the lilting *dombrak* rhythm. Xâlmurâd explained that it was a herder's dance that expressed the basic elements of the herder's life. The hand motions symbolized rounding up or driving a herd and counting the animals; the foot movements, the peregrinations of the herder as he moved with his animals. After the counting had been completed, the herder relaxed, and the dancing became more active and joyous. In another dance, the curvilinear motions of the

Xâlmurâd and OM.

stick represented a falcon in flight. Musical accompaniment was provided by a comb with paper placed over the teeth, which sounded like a kazoo. Neither the dance nor the music revealed a sense of progression from a beginning to an end; rather, they represented a kind of pure presence in the moment.

Piskân's name was connected to its history. In Yagnâbi, *pis* means "knowledge" and *kân* means "source," thus Piskân: "source of knowledge." There had been a mosque in Piskân that, as local tradition had it, had once been the holiest place in Yagnâb. An eighty-one-year-old mullah still lived near the site of the mosque. "He's a wellspring of information," we were told. "You must talk with him."

After a breakfast of stewed wild mushrooms and fresh potatoes, we were taken to meet the mullah. He was sitting on the flat roof of his house, a red bandanna tied around his grizzled, fully bearded face. Behind his profile, the snowy peaks of the Zaravshan Ridge stretched toward the horizon. It seemed like the perfect setting for words of ancient sacred wisdom to pass from the mouth of the mullah to the young seekers who had made their way to this remote Shangri-La. But the old mullah was ailing, and his eyes stared blankly. His memory was gone. "Go to the mosque," he mumbled, when we asked whether people in Piskân had been religious.

The small mosque was in the process of being disassembled piece by piece. Wooden posts and beams had been ripped out to be used in the reconstruction of houses or burned as firewood. Stones from the walls had also been carried away for home improvement projects. The raw materials of old Piskân, "source of knowledge," had been reassembled to build a new Piskân, and as the mosque

210

The mullah in Piskân.

Piskân

was transformed piece by piece into houses and barns, the religious practice of old Piskân had disappeared without a trace. In Yagnâb, religion, music, and other forms of traditional knowledge seemed no longer grounded in the physical territory of communities and the collective experience of their inhabitants; rather, tradition had been reduced to a tenuous existence in the deracinated lives of particular individuals. One of these individuals was Nur Bâbâ.

We met Nur Bâbâ in Gharmen, a settlement near Piskân. Nur Bâbâ was seventy-eight years old. He lived in Zafarabâd and had ridden a horse up the Yagnâb Valley to Gharmen to find his daughter and take her back with him to Zafarabâd. The daughter had been married but hadn't borne any children, and her husband had married again. For a while, the husband had lived with both wives, but he had grown weary of bickering between the two women and finally had told the first wife, Nur Bâbâ's daughter, to pack her things and leave. As if to make his point, he had beaten her. Nur Bâbâ's daughter later told us that she had lost her memory from this and other beatings.

Nur Bâbâ was a mullah. His father and grandfather had been mullahs, and both had studied in a *madrasah* in Bukhara. The *madrasahs,* however, had been closed by the time Nur Bâbâ was old enough to attend, and he had been educated at home. In the mid-1920s, when Soviet power came to Yagnâb, Nur Bâbâ's father had put his religious books in a box and sent the box floating down the Yagnâb River.

Nur Bâbâ explained that when he said he was a mullah, he was using the term in a general sense. There were different levels of mullah. For example, a *maxsum* [*maxdum*] was like a "quarter of a mullah" and had only a partial knowledge of religious science. An *âxun* was someone who was "halfway enlightened," while a *taqsir* was a mullah who had reached the highest stage of knowledge.[8] For Nur Bâbâ, being a mullah wasn't only a matter of knowing the Qur'an. More broadly, a mullah relied on acquired rather than inspirational knowledge—on books and on *ilm* (knowledge or science)—to solve people's problems. Nur Bâbâ not only was familiar with the *ilm* of the Qur'an; he also commanded a special kind of *ilm, ilm-e Kashmiri:* "Kashmiri science," or magic (in this sense, Kashmir was synonymous with India). In Zafarabâd, he had worked officially as a night guard at the hospital, but in the evening, after the doctors left, Nur Bâbâ held his own clinic, and patients frequently came to the hospital to be treated by him rather than by the medical staff.

Unlike the old mullah on the rooftop in Piskân, Nur Bâbâ displayed both an exuberant energy and a polymathic knowledge of Islamic law and tradition, local history, the poetry of Bedil, Mashrab, and Hafiz, magic, and music. He played the *dombrak* for us, out of politeness, he said later. He hadn't played in thirty years but didn't want to refuse our request. It was Nur Bâbâ's understanding that God did not forbid the playing of musical instruments but that with the exception of drums, they should be played in the home rather than outside—in essence, a rationalization of local tradition.

Nur Bâbâ

Nur Bâbâ spoke at length about healing and about the basis of healing in a knowledge of the hot and cold natures, or temperaments (Arabic: *mizaj*) of people, animals, and foods. The theory of *mizaj* has its origins in ancient Greek teachings about the humors and, like other aspects of Greek learning, was codified in Central Asia in the writings of the early eleventh-century physician and philosopher Ibn Sinâ (Latin: Avicenna).[9] Nur Bâbâ's understanding of *mizaj* was a much-simplified version of Ibn Sinâ's scheme, which included not only hot and cold natures but also dry and wet, as well as combinations of hot, cold, wet, and dry. Nur Bâbâ gave us a brief inventory of the hotness or coldness of various common foodstuffs.

Hot	*Cold*
butter	sour milk (*qatyq*)
sheep	calf
black tea	green tea
boiled sugar (*navat*)	granular sugar
pepper, garlic	most herbs
soup with meat fat	bouillion
egg yolk	egg white
palav	bread, noodles (flour)
vinegar	forage (*yachmen*)

213

For Nur Bâbâ, the art of healing involved correcting a loss of equilibrium between cold and hot temperaments. This kind of healing was not an abstraction locked up in ancient sources of esoteric wisdom but an aspect of his daily practice as a mullah. Nur Bâbâ explained that three different approaches to healing were represented by three categories of healers, all of whom shared the same goal of correcting a loss of equilibrium between the temperaments. The *baxshi* healed with a drum, i.e., with sound, the mullah healed with books, and the *tabib* healed with herbs. The techniques of the *baxshi* and the mullah were mutually exclusive, but both *baxshi* and mullah could draw from the healing arsenal of the *tabib*. In his healing practice, Nur Bâbâ employed several options: he could recommend changes in diet; he could recite a prayer, fingering his prayer beads and then blowing in a sick person's ear; or he could recommend herbal treatments. He acknowledged that music could be used to warm a cold temperament or chill a hot one. Obese people, he said, have a cold character and often need active music to be healed. Thin people have a hot character and need peaceful music. But Nur Bâbâ did not practice this kind of music therapy himself.

OM was full of admiration for Nur Bâbâ. He saw in him the last gasp of a cultural and spiritual elite that had otherwise disappeared in Yagnâb. "Nur Bâbâ is living proof that Yagnâb was once an enlightened place," said OM. "His name is appropriate: he's an example of a *nurani,* an enlightened person. This kind of enlightenment doesn't have a pragmatic character; its goal isn't to make one's life easier or to accomplish something. It's spiritual enlightenment. We encountered Nur Bâbâ in an extraordinary situation, but he never debased himself; he never asked for anything, he never lost his dignity. Even the way he sat on his horse was dignified, the way he played his prayer beads through his fingers was dignified. He's a model of faith and belief. If all the mullahs were like him, I'd worship Islam, I'd love Islam. Nur Bâbâ could have lived anywhere and been a millionaire, because he's a talented man. He could go from house to house and read the Qur'an; he could heal people. But he doesn't do those things. For him, living in Zafarabâd is a kind of service."

OM and I saw Nur Bâbâ again a week later, in Zafarabâd, where we stopped on our way back to Tashkent (Svetlana skipped Zafarabâd and returned directly to Tashkent by bus after our visit to Dargh). It was early morning when we arrived, but it was already miserably hot. A cloud of haze hung over immense level fields of cotton that stretched toward the horizon, at some indiscernible point metamorphosing into uncultivated steppe. Through the haze, the mountains from which we'd come traced a faint blue contour, like a distant, uncertain mirage. After Yagnâb, the air in Zafarabâd felt oppressively heavy and dirty. Pesticide odors rushed at us through the open car windows as we drove past mile after mile of scrubby cotton plants.

Nur Bâbâ's house was at the end of a street lined with low-slung, tin-roofed cinderblock bungalows. The design of the bungalows couldn't have been less

214

suited to Zafarabâd's desertlike climate, for compared to the largely shadeless street, the interior of Nur Bâbâ's place felt like an oven. Eight people inhabited three tiny rooms: Nur Bâbâ and his wife, his son and daughter-in-law and their three children, and his divorced daughter, recently returned from Yagnâb. Inside the house was the accumulated flotsam of twenty-one years in Zafarabâd. Cabinets with garishly painted flowers contained a jumble of teapots, tea bowls, trinkets, and mass-production Soviet souvenirs. A cloth panel with machine-embroidered flowers and a bright yellow tasseled fringe was draped across the top of one cabinet. A three-year-old calendar provided the only wall decoration.

When we arrived, Nur Bâbâ was installed in the backyard on a grapevine-shaded *aivân* covered with pillows and cushions. In the middle of the *aivân* was a tablecloth set with tea bowls, a plate of raisins, and a bowl of sugar cubes. Nur Bâbâ sat cross-legged amid a dense swarm of flies that swirled, like a cyclone, above the raisins and sugar.

We tried to pick up the conversation about Yagnâbi traditions that we'd begun in Piskân. For two days, OM and I sat, ate, and slept on the *aivân* with Nur Bâbâ. But Nur Bâbâ had become a different person in Zafarabâd. The savage heat had sapped the striking physical energy with which he had moved, gestured, and spoken in Gharmen, and the intensity of his eyes had slackened into lethargic dullness. Our conversation was punctuated with long silences. Nur Bâbâ wanted to speak not about Yagnâbi traditions but about their loss. He feared for the rising generation of Yagnâbis in Zafarabâd who had never known the Yagnâb Valley. "They get used to it here, and they give up the fight; they lose the desire to return to Yagnâb. And that is the worst that can happen."

"I miss Yagnâb," Nur Bâbâ said wistfully, as we were preparing to leave. "I had a house there with six rooms. Twice I ran away to Yagnâb, but they brought me back here. I've lost three sons and a daughter in Zafarabâd. I've lost eighteen years of my life to this place."

OM, ever willing to extend the benefit of the doubt, even to politicians, had described the creation of Zafarabâd and the resettlement of the Yagnâbis as an example not of evil but of stupidity. "The problem was, once they started in with that kind of politics, they had to take it to the end. They couldn't say, 'no, we made a mistake.' No, they had to keep stirring the kasha." I couldn't agree with OM. Perhaps it was simply the effect of the incapacitating heat, the dirt and disorder, the flies and ubiquitous latrine odors, but I saw Zafarabâd as an evil place.

A WEDDING IN DARGH

Ever since passing through Margheb, at the entrance to the Yagnâb Valley, we'd been hearing about the village of Dargh. For the Yagnâbis, Dargh seemed to represent everything that Yagnâb, in its desuetude, lacked. Dargh, we were

215

told, was a place where traditions had been preserved. It was a musical place, it had several working mosques, and people still did things in the old way. What could account for the difference between the moribund traditionality of Yagnâb and the living, evolving traditionality of Dargh?

Dargh was not in the Yagnâb Valley itself. It lay to the north of Yagnâb, over the top of the Zaravshan Ridge and down the other side, along a tributary of the Upper Zaravshan, which at this point is called the Matcha River, after the area's largest town. As the crow flies, Dargh is only a day's trek from Tag-e Chenar. We had entertained the thought of ascending the Zaravshan Ridge from Tag-e Chenar and then following a half-built jeep track used by herders down the other side into Dargh. But the pass over the top of the ridge had been blocked by snow. The only way to reach Dargh was to retrace our path from Anzâb back to Aini, then to follow the Zaravshan eastward for forty miles along a dirt road toward Matcha. Before reaching Matcha, another road forked to the south, over a bridge that spanned the Zaravshan, and continued on up into Dargh. In place of an eight-mile trek over the mountains, we'd be making a trip of more than one hundred miles through the river valleys.

In Aini, on our way to Dargh, we bedded down again at the party hotel. Nur Bâbâ and his daughter had traveled with us for the first stretch of their trip to Zafarâbâd, and we asked the ever-cooperative functionaries from the District Executive Committee if they would mind putting up our two friends for the night as well. The hotelkeeper groused about the two extra guests. "Those Yagnâbis, they're dirty people," he said. "I didn't want to take them in, but the party secretary asked me to do it, as a Muslim."

To ensure that we made the proper contacts in Dargh, the head of the Culture Department at the District Executive Committee, Mirzâ Avedov, had promised to accompany us on our visit. We received this news with some consternation. Even though the culture departments and their programs of "do-it-yourselfism" (*samodeiatel' nost'*) have shed the *agitprop* spirit that characterized their early years, official culture workers are still viewed as the front-line troops of the *vlast'*—the "power"—and having a culture worker as one's traveling companion tends to formalize relationships with musicians that might be less constrained in different company. But we were traveling to Dargh under the auspices of the District Executive Committee, and the offer of companionship from the head of the Culture Department was one that we could not easily decline.

We would travel not by jeep but in what was known in the lexicon of Soviet motor vehicles as an *ekspeditsionnaya*, an expedition vehicle. The *ekspeditsionnaya* is a bit like a paddy wagon with picture windows—it has a cab in front and a raised passenger cabin in the rear with a single door and a large glass panel on each side. Passengers in the rear communicate with the driver through an intercom or, if the intercom system is broken, which it has always been in my experience, by banging on the glass pane set in the metal divider between the cab and the passenger compartment. The *ekspeditsionnaya* must have been designed by engineers from Russia's polar region, for the only parts of the rear compartment that can be opened to let in air are a small sliding panel above the left picture window and a not terribly effective vent in the roof. In strong sunlight, the sealed, glass-enclosed rear compartment turns into an oven.

About a half hour out of Aini, our driver stopped to pick up a hitchhiker dressed in a suit and tie who flagged us down in a wooded glade along the Zaravshan. He was traveling to Dargh, and the driver told him to climb in the back. The head of the Culture Department greeted the hitchhiker warmly. He was a cheerful, outgoing man of indeterminate middle age who spoke not only Tajik but also good Russian. He told us he had worked for three years as an interpreter in Afghanistan and that at present he was the principal of the school in Dargh. His name was Nur Muhammad.

The head of the Culture Department seemed relieved to have Nur Muhammad join us. When we stopped some way down the road to take tea with the chairman of the local *kolkhoz,* the head of the Culture Department told us that we couldn't have found a better host to show us around Dargh. In fact, he had such confidence in Nur Muhammad that he would leave us to continue on together with our new guide while he returned to Aini to take care of urgent business. OM, Svetlana, and I bid goodbye to the head of the Culture Department with a collective sigh of relief. Nur Muhammad listened attentively as we explained the goal of our expedition and, when we were finished, told us with considerable excitement that he knew just how to help. He would organize a display of music and dancing for us in the square in the center of Dargh. We could turn on our video camera and tape recorder and document whatever we wanted.

Forty miles up the bumpy dirt road that meandered from Aini eastward along the Zaravshan, we spotted the bridge that marked the turnoff to Dargh. From the south bank of the Zaravshan, the approach to Dargh was along a rough track that hugged the contours of bleached rocky precipices on the east side of the Dargh Sai (a *sai* is smaller than a river but larger than a stream). As the road climbed high over the *sai,* dramatic, long-range views of the Zaravshan Valley opened to the west. From that distance, the valley appeared barely inhabited. Only a few small horizontal strips of green along the river marked areas of cultivated land amid the overwhelmingly vertical landscape of gray and ochre slopes.

At the outskirts of Dargh, the road came level with the *sai,* passing small fields planted in potatoes and tobacco, and, still following the water, turned sharply into the bottom of a large, U-shaped alpine bowl. The western side of the bowl consisted of a series of steep, scree-covered slopes and ledges, but to the east were high pasture lands mottled by the whites and blacks of grazing herds of sheep, goats, and cows. From certain vantage points along the village's narrow alleys, snow-topped peaks atop the Zaravshan Ridge burst out from between the seams of the hills. At an elevation of around 9,000 feet, Dargh was lower than the settlements of Yagnâb, but even in the summer midday sun the air was dry and not unpleasantly hot.

As we drove into town in our *ekspeditsionnaya,* pedestrians ducked into doorways along the walled street and stared. Women and girls were in traditional garb, loose-fitting shifts made from silk fabric that hung over baggy pantaloons (*lâzim*), heads covered with white shawls. Men and boys wore black *doppi*s on their heads. Some, like Nur Muhammad, were in European clothes; others were dressed in a robe (*chapan*) belted loosely over baggy trousers and a shirt. A narrow, fast-moving channel of water flowed along one side of the wall-lined street, and women were washing clothes in the greenish water. Dargh's streets were in fact pedestrian malls; our own motorized incursion aside, we never saw another vehicle in the central part of the village. Nur Muhammad directed the driver to an open square dominated by a whitewashed school building with oversized square windows; opposite it was a large, glass-fronted teahouse set in a shady corner. In front of the teahouse was an *aivân* covered by carpets. Knots of men in *chapan*s slouched on the *aivân,* sipping tea, conversing, and observing the procession of pedestrians through the square.

Our arrival in the square caused all activity to come to a dead stop. Conversations on the *aivân* broke off, and pedestrians stopped in their tracks. Nur Muhammad approached the men on the *aivân,* greeted them, and explained our business. The men listened quietly. As soon as Nur Muhammad finished, the *aivân* erupted in a cacophonous surge of sound. Everyone was talking at once. Nur Muhammad's idea was to recreate in the square the various elements of a wedding that would illustrate the sorts of dances and songs performed in Dargh. We would stand in the middle of the square with our digital tape recorder and video camera and record away. Before we could express any reservations about the notion of staging a wedding on our behalf, the *aivân* had emptied out and Nur Muhammad had slipped through the crowd to round up actors for the performance.

Within minutes, the square quickly began to fill with people. A horse bearing a red caparison was led in, and a "groom" dressed in a white turban and silk wedding *chapan* mounted the horse. Nur Muhammad stood in the middle of the square and shouted instructions. While women and girls clustered to one side, the several dozen men and boys milling in the square formed a phalanx around the mounted groom. At a command from Nur Muhammad, the procession began to move slowly around the square, led by two young men beating a lilting rhythm on *dâyra*s. The group of men and boys began to chant a wedding song, or *naqsh,* each gesticulating with one arm as if to mark accents at certain moments in the text. In front of the *dâyra* players, several teenage boys in striped green *chapan*s performed a desultory dance, rotating and twisting their torsos, pushing arms out from shoulders in swift, karatelike motions that bled into

218

Dâyra players.

swooping turns of the wrists. Neither dancing nor chanting seemed to bear any relationship to the *dâyra* rhythms. Rather, dancers, chanters, and drummers were intently focused on their own roles in the ceremony. As the procession slowly circled the square, the volume of the chanting grew to a roar and the gesticulating became more energetic. What started as a simulacrum of a wedding had become transformed into an event that conveyed real emotion. Nur Muhammad was pleased with his production. The chaotic sound generated by the throng of chanters, drummers, and dancers was completely authentic, he assured us with a grin.

After some fifteen minutes of marching, Nur Muhammad ran in front of the procession and waved his hands. The marchers halted, and Nur Muhammad shouted more instructions from the center of the square. Next we were to be shown the women's procession, in which dancing girls lead the bride and her wedding train from the bride's house to the home of the groom. Nur Muhammad moved to organize the crowd of women and girls who had been observing the men's procession from the front of the school building. Two elderly toothless women wearing white shawls took the *dâyra*s that had been used in the men's procession. They were joined by a third drummer, who played a smaller *dâyra*. The "bride," her face and entire torso covered by a transparent white veil, walked in front of the *dâyra* players, each arm supported by one of her young friends. A dozen or more teenage girls preceded the bride, dancing as they moved slowly forward. The girls held a handkerchief in each hand, and these were swept and waved in precise, angular movements that, in contrast to the

219

men's dancing, were perfectly coordinated with the *dâyra* rhythms and with the limping forward progression of their feet.

Once again, Nur Muhammad shouted instructions, and the girls reassembled to show us a different kind of dancing. To the same *dâyra* rhythms beaten out by the toothless women, lines of six girls stood facing one another some fifteen feet apart. Then, with handkerchiefs waving, each line moved slowly forward, passed through the opposite line, turned 180 degrees, and passed back through to its starting point. The effect was like that of a slow-motion Virginia reel. The hand and arm movements had none of the liquescent, wavelike motions associated with what is performed these days as traditional Uzbek and Tajik dance—which, in any case, is presented as a solo art. Rather, the movements consisted of concise and abrupt shakes of the handkerchiefs accompanied by foot movements carefully coordinated among the dancers in each set. This was set dancing, the sort of dancing commonly associated with the traditions of rural Europe. What was it doing here in the middle of Tajikistan?

Nur Muhammad explained that what we had been shown was an ancient dance, called *Astin Bâzi,* and that the waving of the girls' arms represented the flight of birds, which, even as fledglings, were able to fly. Young brides, like young birds, must prepare themselves for life, and the symbolism of flight connoted this stage of preparation. The dance was done only by unwed girls during the wedding procession, but once the procession has reached the groom's house, married women could join in as well. "It's very strict, very measured," said Nur Muhammad. "You see a kind of pride and determination among the bride's friends. There's no gaiety, no emotion. They hold their emotions inside, because, like birds learning to fly, they're just learning to deal with emotion. But there's also another kind of dance that girls do at weddings that's freer, where they can express whatever they want to express. We call it simply *toyana* [wedding dancing]."

Later, Nur Muhammad described the entire sequence of a typical wedding in Dargh, putting the processions and dancing in the context of a multiday event. He also arranged for three singers to perform the men's wedding chant we'd heard from the cacophonous throng in the square so that we could accurately transcribe the melodies and texts.

"These days, weddings are arranged by parents, but not without consultation with the young couple," said Nur Muhammad. "Now the bride is asked in front of witnesses whether she wants to marry the groom. If she says no, then by Muslim law, it's forbidden to marry her. If she's silent, the silence is interpreted as a yes. It used to be that she wasn't asked.

"There are ten to fifteen clans (*avlâd*) here and no restrictions on marriages between members of any of these clans. First cousins can marry, as in other Muslim societies; only marriages between brother and sister are forbidden. A second and third wife are officially allowed now if a man can't have children

220

with his first wife. During Soviet times, multiple wives were prohibited, but men had them anyway. A couple would officially get divorced, but the wife would stay in the man's house. Divorces are rare in Dargh. There's only been one divorce here in the last few years.

"Every quarter of Dargh has an elder (*âq sâqâl*) who is in charge of weddings. He decides which days they'll take place and ensures that families have the supplies they need to conduct the festivities. You could say that there are six stages of activities connected to a wedding. These stages usually happen on successive days, although this is not obligatory. Sometimes there are gaps between the various stages, and sometimes two activities might happen on the same day." Nur Muhammad explained the stages as follows:

Step 1: At the house of the groom, a small group of close relatives gathers to prepare food for a larger group of guests that will participate in the next step.

Step 2: This larger group—perhaps twenty to thirty relatives and neighbors—gathers to prepare food, extend personal invitations, and distribute jobs to a still larger group that will include people from the whole quarter (*guzar*).

Step 3: The people of the quarter are invited to a meal at the home of the groom. That evening, the bride and groom gather their friends separately at their respective houses for food and conversation.

Step 4: In the early afternoon, there is an *âsh-e kalân* (devotional meal of *palav*) for the men at the groom's house. In the evening, there is a *bazm-e gap* at the home of the groom—a sort of bachelor's party. At the same time, the bride's family holds a *duxtarxâna* for the bride's friends.

Step 5: The bride's family holds an *âsh-e kalân* for men; the groom's family holds an *âsh-e zanân* for women. The actual marriage ceremony, which includes both civil and religious components, takes place in the evening. The wedding is recorded by a representative of ZAGS—the Law of the Act of Civil Registration—and then, as the sun is setting, the groom is put on a horse and accompanied to the home of the bride. It is during this procession that the groom's male friends sing a series of *naqsh,* or wedding songs. The *naqsh* are sung only for the procession of the groom. The groom is called the *shâh* (king), and his closest friends or relatives are called viziers.[10] From the bride's house, the bride and groom make their way separately to the groom's. That's when the women's procession takes place. Once at the groom's, men and women split up into different parts of the household. In one room is a mullah. The bride and bridegroom are invited to do *nikâh* (the religious act of marriage). At the end of the *nikâh,* the bride and bridegroom are taken to a separate room. The bride is attended by two older women, called *yanga*s, one from her own family and one from the groom's family. The *yanga* may be the wife of a brother, a cousin, or an uncle. The *yanga*'s job is to explain to the bride how to behave with her husband, what to do. The following morning, the *yangas* examine the bed covering to ensure that there is blood on it, and the bed covering (*sozana*) is hung up for public inspection in the groom's yard. It's important for the prestige of the groom's family that there is blood; it shows that his bride was chaste. Thursday and Sunday nights are considered the best for the consummation of the wedding.

Step 6: Friends and relatives come and congratulate the bride and groom— separately. This is not considered mandatory. Then, for three days, the bride holds a *chilla:* she doesn't go out and doesn't receive visitors while she gets acclimated to her husband and her new home. The groom can go out, but the bride stays home. (*Chilla* means "forty days" and commonly refers to the forty hottest days of summer (June 25–August 5), the forty coldest days of winter (December 25–February 5), or a forty-day period after the birth of a child when visitors are not allowed to come near the newborn. Nur Muhammad used *chilla* in the more generic sense of "quarantine.")

WEDDING SONGS

The *naqsh* sung during the wedding procession represent a song genre that was once widespread in Central Asia and the Middle East.[11] They are typically sung in cycles of three to seven songs performed *a cappella,* in unison, by groups of men. The number of songs depends on the length of the procession from the groom's house to the bride's. Even if bride and groom live next door to one another, however, the groom's friends still go into the bride's yard and sing a few *naqsh*.

Naqsh means literally "decoration" or "ornament." Stone carvings, for example, are called *naqsh*. In the *naqsh* songs, the metaphor of decoration seems clearly to refer to the melodic and rhythmic decoration of the word in a sacred context. The particular songs that comprise a *naqsh* cycle may vary, but the organizing principle of the cycle itself is always the same. Like the song cycles of the *Shash maqâm,* the *naqsh* progress from solemn religious texts sung at a slow tempo to lighter, dancelike songs with amorous and humorous texts; that is, from sacred to worldly. The cycles of *naqsh* are thus like miniaturized versions of a *maqâm* cycle and, like the *maqâm,* exemplify Turgun Alimatov's aphorism about the dual purposes of music: "Gâh Allâh rasul, gâh ghamza usul" (Now for God and the Prophet, now for merriment and dance).[12]

The first song in the cycle of *naqsh* that we recorded in Dargh is known as *naqsh-i mulla*.[13] It is an austere devotional song whose text gives thanks to God, to the prophets, and to particular saints for bestowing grace on the wedding that is taking place. The melody and text are transcribed here. The full transcription

222

of the text is given without the repetitions of phrases that figure in the singers' performance. Brief excerpts from all three *naqsh* in the cycle we recorded are reproduced on the accompanying compact disc (track 20), with cross-fades between them.

Av - val zi xu - dâ   gu - yam u   du - yum zi Ra - sul

1. At first, we say the name of God, and second, [the name] of his Prophet
2. The name of that very Muhammad became known to the whole world
3. From impatience, man does not achieve his place [in heaven]
4. From patience, the patient Ayubi Sabur achieves his place [in heaven]
5. Oh, our wonderful and all-powerful Lord
6. In all things, take me [God] by the hand
7. I'll go to Shâhi Zinda [cemetery] and bow my head down
8. On the smooth face of our Master are many jewels
9. Oh, you magnificent one, be in everyone's soul
10. We'll follow in your good deeds; you are in all of our acts
11. Everyone who comes to your world will become your friend
12. We can't appear twice in this world
13. I'm in love with the beauty of Mustafa [Muhammad] the Arab
14. Out of respect for the sixty-fourth generation of the tribe of the Prophet
15. Don't shame us while we're alive
16. I'm yours until the Day of Judgment comes
17. I'm yours, I'm yours, say I
18. When I see your face, you can build the walls of my grave
19. The angel of death brings the burial cloth by the will of God
20. As long as my tongue moves, I'll ask God to affirm my belief [in Him]
21. So that I can die with faith
22. Woe to him who dies without faith
23. The sword of retribution of Ali and the two-headed lion
24. Our Prophet sits on a throne
25. The key to the lock [of the path of faith] of Hasan and Husein is with Haidar [Ali]
26. The six prophets revealed the magnificent nature of God
27. Oh, I repent, oh, my friend [i.e., God]
28. Oh, let my two eyes not tire of crying, my friend
29. Oh, I want my eyes to see your beauty, my friend
30. You are always, always, always, my friend
31. Oh, your name will be eternal, our creator.

1. Avval zi xudâ, avval zi xudâ guyam u, duyum zi Rasul (each line is
   repeated twice)
2. Yak nâmi Muhammadash rafta ba âlam mashhur
3. Az besabri kase ba jâîi narasad
4. Az sabri ba jâîi rasidi Ayubi Sabur
5. Ay, qadiri zul jelâllu sultani Karim
6. Dar mândaiyi kâri ashtum dar dastam gir
7. Man rafta ba Shâhi Zinda sar memânam
8. Bâ ruhi ravâni Xâja durdâni basi.
9. Ay, servi tu dar sinayi har sâhebi xân
10. Paivasta dar in rahmat u, tu dar hama kâr
11. Har kas ki ba dargâhi tu âyad bari yâr
12. Mahrumi zi dargâhi tu bargarda du bâr
13. Yâram ba jemâli Mustafâi Arabi
14. Az hurmati shastu chârum avlâdi nabi
15. Sharmanda ma sâz u marg u yâbat mârâ
16. Ruzi ki hisâbi bandarâ metâlabad
17. Vâyat man u, vâyat man u, vâyat guyat
18. Devâli lahad gerifta peshi ruyat
19. Ayandu farishta jâma farmâni Xudâ
20. Amma ba zabâni xâlu imân talabat
21. Imân ki ba mâ tu margi marâ (yarâ) tuyat
22. Taziya ba ân kas ki imân nabarat
23. Shamsheri Ali u kavza yak sheri du sar.
24. Paighambari mâ nashasta bâlâî minbar
25. Qulfash Hasanu Husayna kalitash Haidar
26. Didâri Xudâ shafâat shash paighambar
27. Hâi tawba, yâri man eh
28. Hâi baraki du chashmi surat, yâr eh
29. Hâi du nazar xush namâi, yâr eh
30. Tu hamân, hamân, hamân, yâr eh
31. Hâi, tu hamân nâmi rabbâni

None of the singers knew the author of the poem, but Nur Muhammad
assured us that it was a "classical text."[14] The mention in line 23 of Ali, the
cousin and son-in-law of the Prophet, whom Shias venerate as the Prophet's true
successor, underscores Ali's popularity in Sunni Transoxania. OM emphasized,
however, that this popularity should be understood not as an echo of Shi'ism but
as admiration for a saint who many believe had a real presence in Transoxania.
For example, in Khorezm, Ali was said to have jumped on his horse from one
bank of the Amu Darya to the other. In Chimgan there is a place where he is said
to have put his hand. Shahimardan, in the Ferghana Valley, has a site that is said
to mark his grave. The Shia martyr Husein and his brother, Hasan, the sons of Ali

and Fatima (mentioned in line 25 of the poem), are also popularly regarded as helpers and protectors in Transoxania.

The circular and asymmetrical rhythmic pattern of the melody, with its abrupt pauses and strong accents, seemed to bind the singers together as they sang *naqsh-i mulla*.[15] The rhythmic playing with words, the use of repetition and unexpected accents, was the source of the artistry of this type of singing; it was what held the singers' interest through myriad repetitions of a simple tune. "There's a kind of dissonance that's created in these *naqsh*," OM said, "but it's not melodic dissonance; it's rhythmic dissonance."

The text of the second *naqsh* in the cycle is less austere and more lyrical than the first, yet in its own way it is no less religious. Its imagery is grounded in the extended metaphors common to so much Sufi-inspired poetry: the object of love is at once human, cosmic (e.g., the moon, lines 9–13), and divine, and Layla and Majnun, the idealized lovers, make a cameo appearance.

Na cha - man, na gul, _na bo stân Ki ku - nad gul az gul - i - stân ki ku - nad

1. Not a lawn, not a flower, not a garden
2. He who picks a flower from the garden
3. Doesn't know that a new flower has already grown
4. If you don't know about me [your lover]
5. You'll come early in the evening
6. Let the door be open
7. A night without memory of my beloved
8. Let this night be long
9. On this night, let the moon [my beloved] appear
10. Let my moon come to the door
11. My moon is like a huge bouquet of flowers
12. Let [my loved one] come to my bosom
13. In my bosom is the expanse of the steppe
14. In my bosom is Majnun's steppe [land]
15. I became a friend of Majnun
16. I became [a friend of Majnun] from one wish of Layla
17. I don't have a greater concern
18. Than to raise my loved one over my head
19. Her spirits will feed on his tears
20. Spirits, help me to quench my thirst for love. . . .[16]

1. Na chaman, na gul, na bostân,
2. Ki kunad gul az gulistân
3. Xabarest, ki nav rasidast

4. Tu magar xabar nadârî
5. Tu biyaî avvali shab
6. Dari subhu bâzu bâshad
7. Shabi âshiqâni bedil
8. Chi shabast darâzu bâsha
9. Chi shabast ki mah barâyad
10. Mahi man zi dar darâyad,
11. Mahi man zi xirmani gul
12. Ba kanâri man darâyad
13. Ba kanâri dashtu xâshu
14. Ba kanâri dashti Majnun
15. Shudayam rafiqi Majnun
16. Ba juz az surâqi Laîlî
17. Ghami bâl u par nadârem
18. Sarashân nahâda bar sar
19. Ruhâshân ba âbi dida
20. Tu gazi du mâri ishqat. . . .

The third *naqsh*, "Guftam duxtar," moves into solidly secular ground, both in form and content. It is humorous and amorous, and the text is not a classical *ghazal* but an example of a universal folk genre: a refrain song with a motoric sequential pattern in which the end of one couplet provides the beginning of the next. The first couplet is translated here in full; in successive couplets, repeated words and phrases are eliminated (these include, besides the refrain, the last phrase of the second line, which is always a repetition of the first phrase in the line, and the expressions "dear one" and "eh, princely one").

1. I told you, girl, I told you, girl [refrain], let me kiss you, dear one
Kissing costs money, eh, princely one, kissing costs money

2. Give me money
Money in a purse

3. Give me a purse
A purse in a beautiful robe

4. Give me a beautiful robe
A beautiful robe in a knapsack

5. Give me a knapsack
A knapsack in a trunk

6. Give me a trunk
A trunk on a camel

7. Give me a camel
A camel in a herd

8. Give me a herd
A herd with a caravan leader

9. Give me a caravan leader
A caravan leader with a caravan

10. Give me a caravan
A caravan in the steppe

11. Give me the steppe
I'll take that steppe

1. Guftam duxtar, guftam duxtar, busa ba mâ deh âzâda jâne.
Busa ba tanga, eh shâhi jâne, busa ba tanga

2. Tanga ba mâ deh âzâda jâne
Tanga ba kisa

3. Kisa ba mâ deh, âzâda jâne
Kisa ba jâma

4. Jâma ba mâ deh, âzâda jâne
Jâma ba buxcha

5. Buxcha ba mâ deh, âzâda jâne
Buxcha ba sanduq

6. Sanduq ba mâ deh, âzâda jâne
Sanduq ba ushtur

7. Ushtur ba mâ deh, âzâda jâne
Ushtur ba qatâr

8. Qatâr ba mâ deh, âzâda jâne
Qatâr ba sârbân

9. Sarbân ba mâ deh, âzâda jâne
Sârbân ba kârvân

10. Kârvân ba mâ deh âzâda jâne
Kârvân ba â'ul

11. A'ul ba mâ deh, âzâda jâne
A'ul ba qâbul

POETRY IN THE AFTERNOON

Commenting on the intimate connection in the *naqsh* between poetic form and musical style, OM said, "This music can only be understood in a context where people know poetry. And in Dargh, they know poetry. People on the humanities faculty at the University [in Tashkent] don't know classical poetry like these people know Nizâmi, Hâfiz, Firdawsi, Dihlawi, Kamâl Khâjendi, Bedil." And indeed, while we were sitting one afternoon with Nur Muhammad and a group of his friends in his *mehmânxâna,* OM and I had an opportunity to see an impromptu example of what has come to be called *Bedilxâni. Bedilxâni* means, in the strictest sense, a communal commentary and interpretation (*tafsir*) of the poetry of Bedil (1644–1721), who lived in India and wrote in Persian; but these days the term has come to be applied more generally to any sort of a poetry circle devoted to the recitation of classical verse.

The *Bedilxâni* took place during our second visit to Dargh, in June 1994. The weather had turned bad in the mountains that week. The welcoming alpine sun that we'd remembered from our first visit had vanished behind a solid layer of gray cloud that lopped off the tops of the snow-covered peaks on the Zaravshan Ridge. A cold rain had begun to fall, and it was a good time to be indoors, sipping green tea and making slow conversation in Nur Muhammad's spacious *mehmânxâna.* Nur Muhammad had summoned a group of his friends to celebrate our return to Dargh after three years. Among them were several men, teachers in the local school, whom we'd gotten to know on our previous visit.

The men seemed genuinely glad to see us—touched, in fact, that we'd made the arduous trip from Tashkent to pursue our interest in their traditions—but the spirit of celebration was muted by a palpable weariness. Since our 1991 visit, shortly before the breakup of the Soviet Union, Tajikistan had been engulfed by a catastrophic civil war. The war had been ostensibly a struggle for political power that pitted the old-guard Communist leadership, traditionally from the relatively prosperous north of Tajikistan, against an ad hoc coalition of Western-style democrats, secular nationalists, and Islamic revivalists, the latter with a large constituency concentrated in the much poorer south and southeast, where they were supported by Afghan guerrilla fighters who smuggled themselves across Tajikistan's mountainous borders. The political struggle, however, had been fueled by much deeper and older rivalries: north against south, richer against poorer, clan against clan. Apocalyptic statistics circulated in whispered voices: a million people killed, injured, displaced—a fifth of Tajikistan's prewar population.[17] Could these statisics be verified? Who could add up the carnage of thousands of savage rural bloodlettings and intimate vendettas in which whole families were eviscerated and hung from trees beside their houses? This war had few outside observers. It had been purely a family matter.

The fighting had taken place mainly in the south and center of the country. Dargh and the surrounding Zaravshan Valley had been spared. With military assistance from Moscow and neighboring Uzbekistan, the Communists had won the political struggle. That was why Lenin still glowered at the residents of Aini from his vantage point on the huge billboard above town, why his portrait still hung in Dargh's schoolrooms, and why the red flag still flew over government office buildings. But the Communist victory had been truly Pyrrhic. Tajikistan was in economic shambles; government salaries had not been paid for as long as seven months, there was no local currency or even coupons, and a large infusion of rubles provided by Moscow after the war had immediately disappeared. Food stores sold basic commodities—when they were available— on credit, but most people lived on what they could grow or raise and on what they could obtain by barter.

It was in the context of the ubiquitous postwar shortages that Nur Muhammad apologized for not having any vodka to offer us. "One unfortunate result of our present conditions is that we can't even drink a toast to distinguished guests," he said glumly. OM and I both gave silent thanks for at least this one consequence of Tajikistan's turmoil. But the turmoil had done nothing to reduce the population of sheep in Dargh, and Nur Muhammad had ordered one to be slaughtered in our honor. While his son was dispatching the sheep, Nur Muhammad brought a large television set into the *mehmânxâna* and set it up on a recessed window ledge. The World Cup soccer match was being televised on the Moscow channel, and Nur Muhammad thought we'd surely want to watch it. The volume was turned up loud enough to hear but not loud enough to make conversation in the room difficult.

The men in the *mehmânxâna* didn't give the impression of being soccer fans. The game, taking place in the United States, was between Saudi Arabia and Morocco, and Nur Muhammad and his friends watched the television screen with voyeuristic detachment. During the commercials—they were Russian commercials—the voyeurism turned bemused. There were sexy ads for a candy bar new to the Russian market called Sweet Marie, a brand of dog food, and an investment scheme promising an annual 300 percent return on ruble deposits. The slashing disco beat of the ad music and the stroboscopic images of scantily clad women munching candy bars and feeding dogs seemed to affect the men in the *mehmânxâna* in a way contrary to what the ad producers had intended: the men's interest slipped away from the television screen. Gradually, conversation in the *mehmânxâna* began to pick up, and the World Cup match and commercials became a backdrop to a discussion about the poetry of Hâfiz, the fourteenth-century literary luminary of Shiraz. Not far into this discussion, a disagreement that I couldn't follow arose about some lines in Hâfiz, and a few of the men went home to get their books of poems. The men returned with small, worn printed copies of Hâfiz and well-thumbed manuscript notebooks into which they had copied by hand, in Cyrillic script, a chrestomathy of their favorite verses.

The disagreement was quickly resolved, and the recitation and discussion—actually, several small recitations and discussions—moved on to other works of Hâfiz. An elderly gentleman sitting at the far end of the *mehmânxâna* collared OM and turned him into a captive one-man audience for a melodramatic reading and run-on exegesis of a long poem. OM gracefully complied. At my end of the room, the Chairman of the Executive Committee of the local Rural Council, which oversaw the operations of several collective farms in the region, an attractive man in his late thirties named Shadikur, wanted to know whether it was true that Americans worked very hard. He approved of hard work, he said, but reminded me, in a Tajik way, that people don't die wishing they'd spent more time at the office. To illustrate what he meant, he recited a *rubâ'i* from a poem:

> Stand up and pour in this golden cup the wine of joy
> Before your skull is filled with dust [literally, "Before your
>   fire pan is filled with ash"]
> In the end, we all come to the silent valley
> Before it's too late, pour wine, and riot, so that the noise
>   will rise to the very heavens!

> Xezu dar kâsan zar âbi tarabnâk ansâz
> Peshtar z'ân, ki shavad kâsai sar xâkandâz.
> Aqibat manzili mâ vâdii xâmushân ast,
> Qâliyâ ghulghula dar gunbadi aflâk andâz!

Shadikur used Hâfiz's six-century-old Epicureanism to support his own point of view: that amid all of life's obstacles, one had to remember the cleansing powers of celebration and revelry. Shadikur's driver from the Executive Committee nodded his head vigorously in agreement. He was a man of early middle age, a graduate of a professional technical high school, a lover of poetry, and at that moment a full participant in the *Bedilxâni*.

Someone in the room started to talk about his parents, about the importance of respect for parents; and to illustrate more precisely what he had wanted to say, he recited a classical poem about parents. OM started to write the poem down. This poem served as a bridge that brought the various discussions in the room together. It wasn't recited as a way of showing off or offering a demonstration of erudition. It came naturally, in the flow of the conversation. And so it went, the conversation moving from one topic to another, poetic recitations interspersed at appropriate moments in the men's badinage.

Later, OM reflected on the impromptu *Bedilxâni* and its link to traditional values. "If these people had lived in Tashkent, they'd be thinking about how to build a big house, how to earn a lot of money, how to buy a car. But here it's different. They're better off with a donkey than with a car. They earn money from selling their tobacco in Samarkand. They live on their pay and on what they grow and raise; if they need money for a wedding, they sell animals. They don't read newspapers, and you can see that they're really more interested in poetry and conversation than in television. It's living contact, hospitality, that nourishes them. They crave contact with people. Their hospitality is made interesting by discussions about philosophy, and philosophy is inseparable from poetry: poetry recited and poetry sung. This tradition once existed through all of Transoxania, but we didn't see it in Bukhara. We had to come to a remote place to see what had once also flourished in the center."

STRANGE POLYPHONY

After the wedding processions and dancing in the square, Nur Muhammad had wanted to show us another of Dargh's musical traditions: a kind of field holler performed antiphonally by groups of women or men as they scythed wheat at harvest time. Again Nur Muhammad busily moved among the crowd in the square that had become his all-purpose production space. He formed two groups of eight girls, each group standing in a tight cluster several yards from the other. The toothless women drummers, lingering in the square, began to beat out a simple, steady rhythm on the *dâyra*s: da-da-da-DA, da-da-da-DA, da-da-da-DA. To this rhythmic background, the two groups of girls took turns shouting out a recitativelike couplet, drawing out the final pitch in the second verse of each couplet with a brilliant wash of dissonance. While the chant had a dominant reciting tone, some of the girls sang the reciting tone a bit flat, creating a rich body of beating tones.

The singing went on for a long time, growing louder and more raucous as the girls became energized by the raw power of the music. Two groups of men joined in the antiphonal exchange, and men's and women's antiphonies continued simultaneously back and forth across the square, turning the singing into high-spirited cacophony. The toothless *dâyra* players ceased their playing, unable to find a rhythm in all the noise. Nur Muhammad yelled to us across the din that during harvest time, both work and singing became a form of competition. One work brigade would sing from one part of the field, another brigade from somewhere else, trading couplets back and forth, each trying to sing the loudest. If one group finished their work first, they'd help another group. "This custom is being lost," Nur Muhammad shouted, "because now we're growing only tobacco here; families all have their own small plot, and there's no one to compete against."

Later, Nur Muhammad helped us translate some of the couplets sung by the girls. Each couplet had its own end rhyme, but no narrative thread linked one couplet with the next. Rather, each was independent, dredged up at the moment of performance from a seemingly endless stock of verse known by all the singers (see the accompanying compact disc, track 21).

1. From far away I came running [to you]
2. I paid three hundred rubles before I came.

3. When you come to the door, let the room be filled with light
4. Let our friends all be glad, and enemies become blind

5. In Farzâd, there are lots of tulips
6. On the four high mountains, there are beautiful places

7. I want to sing today only for you
8. I'm willing to sacrifice my soul for you

9. A *kolkhoz* was created, and I became a *kolkhoz* worker before anyone else did
10. Even if you were an angel in paradise, I wouldn't be your neighbor

11. Today we are guests in this world, and tomorrow we leave it
12. [Therefore] play the *dâyra* loud, so that we can make merry

13. If you know the law, I also know it no worse than you
14. Because I study with educated teachers

15. On this summer night, we began the wedding
16. And began to dress the much-vaunted bride

17. We go to gather wheat, but the harvest was small
18. Let's boil tea, because it's tea time.

1. Az râhi dur dav-davân âmada'am
2. Sesad suma pul dâdemu ba'd âmada'am

3. Az dar, ki darâyad xâna pur nur shavand
4. Dostân hamma shâd, dushmanân kur shavand

5. Farzâd ba muram chi lâlazârhâ dârad
6. Châr kuhi baland jâîi tamâshâ dârad

7. Imruz dilam bari shumâ baitguî
8. Yak jâni azizama kunam kurbâni

9. Kolkhoz shudu kolkhozchi shudam az hama pesh
10. Hurâni bixisht shavî namesham ba tu xesh.

11. Imruz musâfirim pagah meburavem
12. Dâyra garm kuned, ki xursandi kunem.

13. Qanuna tuham dâni, manam medânam.
14. Dar baini muallimâni safdil xânam.

15. Imshab shabi tâbistân ba toy sar kardem
16. In bachaî ta'arifiya shah râst kardem

17. Lalmâbe barâmadam, ki lalimhâ nâshud
18. Chai jushe biyâr jura, ki vaqti châi shud

Nur Muhammad hesitated at line 9. He didn't want to transcribe the verse about a *kolkhoz* because he considered it politically inspired and hence inauthentic, the vestige of an era of ideological meddling in poetry and music that would be better forgotten. We urged him to transcribe the line anyway, explaining that our aim was not to sift out and discard poetry and music that wasn't authentic—whatever that meant—but to document what people performed.

The singers made it clear that their dissonance was not accidental and not the result of an inability to tune a unison. We had heard other songs in which a unison was kept well tuned. On the contrary, judging by the gusto with which they put their faces close together and shouted out the antiphonal couplets, they clearly reveled in their collective dissonance. Nur Muhammad, a graduate of a specialized music school, agreed. "They love seconds here," he told us. "But try to sing that kind of dissonance through solfège. You can't do it; it's very difficult."

The dissonant antiphony of the field hollers couldn't help but bring to mind the intense dissonances present in certain kinds of Slavic folk song. Could there be a connection? Was it possible that the dissonant antiphonal singing in Dargh was a fragment of an old Turanian musical substrate that at one time had stretched from Eastern Europe all the way to Central Asia? Musical maps of the world conventionally mark Central Asia as a bastion of vocal monody or monophony, while polyphony is clearly expressed in a variety of instrumental genres.[18] But the Dargh field hollers are not the only recorded examples of vocal music in Transoxania that shuns the unison. Tajik folklorists had recorded a dissonant, multivoice performance of *naqsh* in Ura-Tyube, and V. S. Vinogradov's compendium of music of the Soviet East includes a transcription of a polyphonic wedding (*yâr-yâr*) song.[19] Several of the performances we recorded in Dargh had also exhibited various forms of polyphony (or, if not exactly full-fledged polyphony, then at least "nonmonophony"): the dissonant field hollers; the *naqsh* that we'd heard on our second trip to Dargh, when eight singers insisted on singing in parallel octaves rather than in the unison that is typical

Singing polyphony
in Dargh.

elsewhere; and the *zarb* (described in the following section), with its parallel thirds, fourths, fifths, and octaves.

In Transoxania, polyphony is very likely older than monody and monophony—a likelihood that might seem counterintuitive to a listener grounded in the history of European art music. In Europe, polyphony evolved out of medieval liturgical chant to dominate the art music tradition. But in Transoxania, monody became the preeminent style of urban art music while polyphony, particularly in instrumental repertories, flourished in rural-based folk musics whose roots are most certainly older (in Europe, too, folk polyphonies with seemingly old roots have long existed independently of developments in art music).

Nur Muhammad added that vocal style wasn't the only aspect of culture in Dargh that seemed linked to pre-Islamic times. There were many customs as well, and some of these he explained to us. "People put certain special herbs on their houses to keep away bad spirits. Or they nail up the horns of a sheep or bull or the skull of a donkey on a tree near their home. People also put the horns of a wild goat on graves. When a man is married, a triangular talisman is sewn on the outside of his clothes in a place that won't be noticeable—often in the armpit. It's called *bâzuband*—armpit band. It's sewn from cloth, and in the inside of the triangle there's a little piece of paper with an incantation written on it, or perhaps something from the Qur'an. It's worn for three days before the wedding. This three-day period before a wedding is called *tag-e târ*. During this period, the bride isn't allowed to go out. She sits at home [as she does during the three-day period of *chilla* following the wedding]. In some places, the groom also sits at home for three days, and if he goes out, even to the toilet, one of his relatives accompanies him to make sure that no evil spirits gaze at him and that if he has any enemies, they won't injure him. There are special women, called *suqmol*— a Turkic word—who cure people from the evil eye.

"We've also preserved certain Zoroastrian customs here. Until not long ago, on the last Thursday of a particular month, people lit fires, and as a form of cleansing, they jumped over the fire. They also lit candles around a large tree and at gravesites. In Islam, it's forbidden to light candles. The mullah said that it's forbidden because it's a vestige of Zoroastrianism. People prayed to trees or to rocks. That's forbidden. There's only one God. All you have to do is believe in God. God created the rest. What's the point of praying to a tree or a rock?"

THE *ZARB*

In our conversation with Nur Muhammad about multivoice singing and the dissonant field hollers, he had mentioned another practice that attracted our attention. This practice he called *zarb*. "In the *zarb*," he told us, "there are two voices. Some sing at the octave, and some sing beneath. I've also heard it sung with three voices." We asked more about the *zarb*. Nur Muhammad explained that *zarb* was like what was called in other places *zikr*. *Zarb* (Arabic: *ḍarb*) means "stroke" or "beat" and, by extension, "accent" or "force." Later we learned that when *zarb* is used as the name of the ceremony that Nur Muhammad had described, it is short for *châr zarb* (four accents), a reference to the four accents (*lâ, lâ, il,* and *llâh*) in the textual formula that is its ritualistic essence: *lâ ilâha illâ' llâh* (There is no God but God). The *zarb* was performed in the mosque every day after *bâmdâd,* morning prayers. We asked if we could attend. "No problem," said Nur Muhammad. "It begins around 4:15 A.M."

The next morning, OM and I arose before sunrise and joined the *zarb* at the mosque. From the outside, it was an unremarkable building, with no visible exterior ornamentation or calligraphy, that dates from the end of the nineteenth century. One could have walked along the narrow lane past the mosque and easily missed it, hunkered down as it was behind a blank wall at one end of which was a low, narrow gate leading to a tiny yard. Inside the mosque, sixteen men sat on their haunches in a semicircle that filled almost half the mosque's floor space. The area where they sat was covered with a white sheet laid over the Soviet-produced Oriental rugs that covered the floor. Only the intricately painted ceiling and expertly carved interior wooden pillars and plinths betrayed

235

the high level of craftsmanship that had once been available even in provincial places like Dargh.

Morning prayers had already concluded. Nur Muhammad introduced us to the mullah, who sat midway along the semicircle, and, with the most minimal of explanations of our business, asked whether it would be all right if we set up our tape recorder and video camera. The mullah had no objection. We quickly arranged ourselves just outside the semicircle as the mullah began to chant the opening lines of the *zarb*. At the appropriate moment, the men joined the mullah in a chorus that at first sounded heterophonous and disorderly, as though each chanter had begun from his own starting pitch without regard for the other chanters. But a structure quickly became apparent: some of the men were holding more or less accurately the interval of a fifth below the reciting tone and moving the fifth in parallel to the melody as it rose and fell. As they chanted thirty-three repetitions of *lâ ilâha illâ' llâh,* and a hundred repetitions of *illa' llâh,* they nodded their heads gently from side to side. The harmony that had begun as a fifth reemerged as a third, a fourth, a seventh, and, still later, an octave. An excerpt from the *zarb* is reproduced on the accompanying compact disc, track 22.

The *zarb* lasted about half an hour, and throughout it was measured, con-trolled, emotionally contained, with an almost humdrum sense of routine. Except for the slight sideways nodding of heads, the men sat utterly motionless. During the formulaic repetitions of the name of God, the chanting displayed neither the strong accentuation nor the trancelike quickening of tempo and hyperventilation customary in many *zikr*s. If the goal of *zikr* is to lead participants to a state of immersion in God, then the men in the mosque betrayed none of the outer signs of that immersion frequently associated with Sufi rituals. But after-ward, the mullah assured us that there had been *wajd:* spiritual ecstasy, "a tranquil kind of ecstasy," he added emphatically. "In some places, people beat themselves when they hear the name of God, but our people do the *zarb* with peace [*ârâm*]."

As the men filed out of the main chamber of the mosque, the mullah invited Nur Muhammad, OM, and me to follow him to an adjoining room. It was cold inside, and we hunched in overcoats and *chapan*s on the thinly carpeted floor. The mullah's name was Shamsiddin, and he was fifty-two years old. He had finished the seventh grade, and that had been the end of his formal schooling. After that, his father had taught him the Qur'an at home. He was proud that his eight children (four girls and four boys) had all received a religious education and could read and write Arabic letters. In addition to fulfilling his religious duties, Shamsiddin had a worldly profession: he was a farmer.

Mullah Shamsiddin knew the names of his patrilineal ancestors seven generations back, as was customary in Central Asian tradition. Qahhâr *baxshi* had attributed this custom to "nomadic people," but it existed among settled populations as well. Shamsiddin's ancestors had lived in Yagnâb, and all had been mullahs. His father had been orphaned and had gone to Bukhara to study in a *madrasah*. In 1922, with Bukhara in Soviet hands, he had come to Dargh and stayed. Later the repression of religion came to Dargh as well. Mullah Shamsiddin told us that the large mosque had been closed for many years—it was converted into a library and storeroom—and had been reopened only in 1991. A smaller mosque had stayed open, but for eight years Shamsiddin's father, the *imam* of the mosque, had been prohibited from entering it. He had led Friday prayers in secret. Holiday prayers were recited at a cemetery above the town, and the last prayer for the dead was recited in a secret mortuary (*janâzaxâna*), where a guard was posted to keep out informers. Even in this small place, there had been informers.

We asked about the origins of the *zarb,* and Mullah Shamsiddin produced a small, worn book handwritten in Arabic letters. The text, composed in Yagnâb, was a compendium of prayers with commentary in simple wording on Muslim law and custom. The text of the *zarb* came from that book.

Was the practice of *zarb* related to a particular *tariqa,* or school of Sufi teaching, we asked? Mullah Shamsiddin didn't use the word *tariqa.* He said that the practice stemmed from the *suluk* (path) of Mirza-e 'Abd al-Qâdir Jilani

Mullah Shamsiddin (second from left) and fellow worshippers at the *zarb*.

(1077–1166), who gave his name to the Qâdiriya Order. He also mentioned Bahâ'uddin Naqshband as a *pir* of their practice—an example of the fusion that was widespread in Central Asian Sufism. Mullah Shamsiddin had learned the *zarb* from his father and grandfather. The rhythm of the *zarb* imitated the hammering of a blacksmith and was meant to drive the devils out of one's body—that's what he had been told. But the mullah could tell us no more about al-Jilani, as he called him, nor about the Qâdiriya Order, nor about the relationship of *zarb* and *zikr*.[20] He knew nothing (or at least admitted to knowing nothing; given his overall ingenuousness about his religious practice, I have no reason to believe that he was withholding information) about the esoteric work with breath that is an important part of the Qâdiriya practice, in which the name *Allâh* circulates through the body, facilitated by rhythmic breathing, a particular posture, and coordinated movements of the head. We asked about the parallel harmony we had heard in the chanting: did the men always divide their voices, with some chanting higher and others lower? Mullah Shamsiddin said that each man chanted where it was comfortable for his voice. But that didn't explain the presence of the consistently tuned intervals we had heard in the *zarb*.

Frustration. But what right had we to think that Mullah Shamsiddin, living as if in an oasis of religious practice, sustained only by memories of his father's teachings and by the contents of his worn Islamic primer, should have been a font of esoteric knowledge about Sufism and its litanies and rituals? On the contrary, it was remarkable that Shamsiddin, cut off for decades from an authoritative living line of spiritual transmission and surrounded by his tiny band of followers, had been able to preserve anything at all of an esoteric religious practice. It was only in 1991, at the age of fifty-two, that he had met the man whom he considered his *pir* and had become a *murid*. The *pir* lived in Dushanbe—they had met when the *pir* visited Dargh—and Shamsiddin had gone three times to Dushanbe to receive from him a spiritual task. Before that, Shamsiddin had been, spiritually speaking, on his own.

Perhaps Shamsiddin sensed our reluctance to part with so much about the *zarb* and its tradition still unclear, for as our conversation fell off and we began packing away our things, he seemed to be searching for a kind of summary valediction. Finally, as he was standing to leave, his dark, creased face momentarily brightened. "The essence is to remember the name of God," he said triumphantly. And having imparted to us the essence of his creed, Mullah Shamsiddin stretched out upturned hands, recited a prayer to wish us health, and walked out the door.

We strolled back to Nur Muhammad's house through a misty rain. In the household's outdoor kitchen area—a *tandir* oven and a firepit set into a low semicircular clay wall—four generations of women and girls were preparing *lagman* (noodle, vegetable, and herb soup) in an immense iron wok suspended over a blazing fire. The rain had turned the ground around the cooking area to mud, and laid out on a towel on the mud were long thin noodles, each individually cut from a sheet of dough, that would be added at the last minute to the soup stock. Stoking the fire, stirring the soup, and preparing bunches of herbs for flavoring, Nur Muhammad's mother, wife, daughters, and granddaughters seemed oblivious to the rain that was soaking their clothes.

I asked Nur Muhammad, "On a day like this, why don't they cook in the

Nur Muhammad with four generations of his family.

indoor kitchen [where the single appliance was an electric hotplate]?" Nur
Muhammad laughed. "I wanted to serve you our special *lagman,* and you can't
make *lagman* on a hotplate. You have to make it in a *kazan* [the large wok].
Women have been making *lagman* in the rain here for a thousand years, maybe
two thousand years. Why should they do it differently now, just because the
Soviet *vlast'* [power] gave us hotplates?" That answer, I thought, explained a
great deal about why Dargh was as it was, and about why people still did things
in the old way, as the Yagnâbis had put it when they first told us about Dargh. It
wasn't that Dargh lacked modern ways and modern things. There were hotplates
and behemoth television sets, and if not private automobiles, then at least trucks
belonging to the *kolkhoz.* Men like Nur Muhammad smoked Marlboro cigarettes and dressed for work in jackets and ties. The local pop music ensemble
had microphones and amplifiers to service wedding banquets (although, unlike
their city cousins, no synthesizer or electric bass; they still used indigenous
instruments, plus an accordion). One young man had a Japanese video camera
and VCR and two videotapes. But more often than not, these modern ways and
things seemed like a sideshow to the main business of Dargh: the television set
ignored while men recited poetry; the hot plate sitting idle while women
huddled around an outdoor fire pit cooking *lagman* in the rain.

Yet traditionalism in Dargh was far from monolithic. Traditional ways and
things were deployed selectively, at times out of cultural preference and at times
as a result of economic necessity. Modernity is expensive, and Dargh could not
always afford modernity. People rode long distances on donkeys rather than in
trucks not because they preferred donkeys to trucks but because gasoline was
scarce. Men had turned from smoking fashionable American-brand cigarettes to

chewing the local green tobacco because a smoking habit had become unaffordable. The local *tabib,* or herb healer, did a booming business because sick people had ceased seeking treatment in the polyclinic in Aini. The doctors there had no medicaments; in many cases, the best they could do was to refer patients back to local healers.

Nur Muhammad and his friends felt both pride and anger in Dargh's increasing isolation from the post-Soviet world beyond the Zaravshan Valley. The anger came from a sense that many of the economic accomplishments of the Soviet years were slipping away from them (Nur Muhammad once made a dark joke about living out the reality of Lenin's famous description of building communism, "One step forward, two steps back"). But there was more pride than anger. The pride was in Dargh's collective ability to cope with isolation and austerity. For Nur Muhammad, that ability was grounded in Dargh's strong sense of tradition and community. "Everyone knows everyone else here," he had said. "Everyone's related to everyone else. It's impossible that there would be someone you don't know or to whom you're not related. People help one another. They live peacefully. No one allows himself to take anything extra, and no one gives anything extra to anyone else. If someone exceeds the limits of our customs, then people will look at him in a way that will make him not want to live here. Even if people don't physically drive him away, they won't come to his weddings, to his funerals. He'll live like someone who's been singled out for punishment."

"Have there been these sorts of cases?" I had asked.

"Yes, but very few. People grow up with the idea that neighbors are neighbors and relatives are relatives. That's a tradition that we've had for centuries that's been preserved until now. And that explains the freedom that you see here, because people don't do anything that they're not supposed to do."

For Nur Muhammad—by local standards a worldly and contemporary man (and, one had to remember, a Soviet man; he had served, albeit in a civilian capacity, in the Soviet war in Afghanistan)—freedom came from tradition, with its simple elegance, its clear social models, and its regimen of self-regulation. A Westerner might consider Nur Muhammad's a primitive freedom: not freedom *to,* but merely freedom *from*—from the moral and technological complexities of the modern world and from the adverse effects of its rampant social disorder. But Nur Muhammad was no Luddite and no fundamentalist. It wasn't simply old customs or Islamic customs that provided the pillars of what Nur Muhammad meant by tradition. His rendering of tradition was a synthetic one formed from a congeries of local practices, some rooted in Islam, others with pre-Islamic roots, and still others Soviet-era modifications of older practices (for example, the marriage ceremony that included both civil registration and a prayer from the mullah). He exemplified the middle ground of rational, secularized traditionality typical of men of his position in Transoxania: he grumbled about the unavailability of vodka to toast his guests but chatted amiably with the mullah in the

240

mosque. He could talk politics with the First Secretary of the local District Executive Committee as well as he could talk Islamic spirituality with his neighbor just back from the *hajj* to Mecca.

Back in Tashkent after almost three weeks of travel to Dargh, Yagnâb, and Zafarabâd, I calculated our expenses for the expedition. They came to the equivalent of eight dollars, which I had paid out on the first day for a hundred-mile taxi ride from Tashkent to the home of the Vice-Rector of the Khojend Pedagogical Institute. Everything else had been provided us as an offering. When I remarked to OM how strange this seemed to an American, he replied with resignation, "Well, that's socialism for you." He hadn't said, "Well, that's Islam for you." But perhaps, in all that had been given us, there had been a little of each.

SHAHRISTAN

A FORBIDDEN VOCATION

In June 1994, OM and I traveled to Shahristan, in northern Tajikistan, for the third time. Our aim was to learn more about the *baxshi* healers who use drumming and chanting as a central element in their healing rituals. For reasons not clear to us, Greater Shahristan has a profusion of practicing *baxshi*s. We both knew of *baxshi* healers elsewhere in Transoxania—presumably the vestiges of what had once been a widespread tradition—but we had never heard of a place where that tradition has been as actively preserved as in Shahristan.

Shahristan's *baxshi* healers represented the "road not taken" by *baxshi* entertainers like Qahhâr *baxshi* and Shâberdi *baxshi* after the presumed separation of *baxshi* subspecialties once united in the activities of a single healer-entertainer. The technology of present-day Transoxanian *baxshi* healers draws heavily on an inventory of beliefs broadly associated with shamanism, yet the *baxshi* healers do not derive their powers solely from contact with the spirit world. They are Muslims, and their ritual practices syncretize Islamic prayers and postures with shamanic beliefs about spirits and the etiology of illness.

Shahristan lies 140 miles south of Tashkent in the foothills of the Turkestan Ridge, which is one arm of the mountainous massif that slices horizontally across Transoxania from the Tien Shan range in the east all the way to Samarkand. Despite its name (in Persian, *shahr* means "town" or "city"; *shahristân* is the old name given to an inner town, like the Arab *madina,* to distinguish it from its suburbs), Shahristan doesn't look like much of a metropolis when you first drive into town along the meager north-south asphalt road that links Tashkent with Dushanbe during the summer months (from late October to early June, the road is closed by snows). The ubiquitous institutions of a Soviet-era district center are spread out almost casually along the road: the RaiKom, or District Party Headquarters, its bust of Lenin (for this is Tajikistan) rising from the midst of a feral rose garden, a monumental, graceless sculpture celebrating the Soviet victory in the "Great Patriotic War," a public cafeteria, a tiny and nearly empty department store, an equally barren housewares store, a police station.

Before Shahristan became a district center, it was not really a town but rather a dense concentration of *qishlâq*s (*qish:* Uzbek "winter"; *qishlâq:* "a place for spending the winter"). The area's residents still seemed to identify more with their own *qishlâq* than with the Greater Shahristan district of 30,000 people. The three collective farms that formerly employed the district's entire population had been cloned into fourteen so that each *qishlâq* could manage its own affairs. Most everyone we met both worked a plot of land and kept livestock—sheep, cows, and goats—that grazed on the open rangeland beyond the *qishlâq*s. At an elevation of five thousand feet, the climate was too cool for cotton, but potatoes, onions, and carrots grew particularly well. A modest tobacco crop was exploited for local use.

OM and I had visited Shahristan together in 1991 and again in 1992 to look up contacts that OM had made years before on an expedition dispatched by the Conservatory under the leadership of Professor Karomatov. Karomatov wasn't particularly interested then in *baxshi*s. He was simply looking for vestiges of old musical traditions in the vicinity of Ura-Tyube, an ancient trading city about fifteen miles north of Shahristan that is still well known for its enormous Sunday bazaar. OM recalled that during the Karomatov expedition they had met a man named Raxmanqul, whom one local source had identified as a *baxshi*. But Raxmanqul himself had denied any knowledge of *baxshi*s. "What's a *baxshi?*" he had asked Karomatov disingenuously. Neither Karomatov nor anyone else on the expedition had tried to penetrate Raxmanqul's ploy. "It was because of politics," OM told me laconically. "Everything about the *baxshi* went against the grain of Marxist thinking. They were supposed to be one of those vestiges of religious superstition that would die out under communism."

Our first two visits to Shahristan had been only partially successful. On the first visit, we had found Raxmanqul, and he had gruffly invited us into his house. He was seventy-five years old then, with a huge, rough face, crew-cut hair that grew halfway down his forehead, and heavy whiskers. He turned out to be little more forthcoming with us than he had been with Karomatov fourteen years earlier. After serving tea and dodging our questions, Raxmanqul finally took down his *childerma* (frame drum) from the wall and held it in front of us. (A *childerma* is the same as a *dâyra,* but calling it *"childerma"* identifies it as the instrument of a *baxshi* and imbues it with the *baxshi*'s magical power). Understanding that he wanted me to try playing it, I took it in my hands, tapping on the skin head a few times. Raxmanqul's hedgehog-like face grew red. He told me angrily that I had sinned because I had touched the drum without washing myself or saying a special prayer. The *childerma* would have to be reconsecrated. He took it back from me and refused to give us any more information. OM and I left his house in a slashing rain that mysteriously began shortly after my sinful handling of the drum.

After being sent away by Raxmanqul, we drove to the home of another *baxshi*, a fifty-five-year-old woman named Nasri-oi. Friendlier than Raxmanqul, she told us in some detail about her activities as a *baxshi*. But when we asked whether she could perform for us a *koch*, or, as it is sometimes called, a *koch-koch*, the ritual in which the *baxshi* strives to heal a sick person, Nasri-oi demurred.[1] "I don't have a *koch* scheduled," she said, "and I can't do an imitation séance. It wouldn't do you or me any good."

We returned to Shahristan a second time and recorded interviews with Nasri-oi and with a woman named Turdijân *baxshi*. Once again, however, we were unsuccessful in witnessing an actual *koch*. Returning for our third visit, we resolved to stay in Shahristan until we succeeded in seeing a *koch*.

In 1994, it was no longer as easy to visit Shahristan as it had been two and three years earlier. The Uzbekistan-Tajikistan border, once all but invisible, had begun to sprout customs posts and checkpoints manned by Ministry of Internal Affairs troops. A foreigner wishing to cross into Tajikistan was required to possess a separate visa (in the old days, a single Soviet visa sufficed for entry into any point in the USSR as long as the point was indicated on the visa). OM had heard stories that vehicles with Uzbek license plates were likely to be stopped and searched in Tajikistan. The police were trying to stem a flourishing cross-border trade in everything from gasoline to onions, with particular vigilance directed at small-caliber weapons and poppies. Rather than take our own car, we would ask a Tajik friend living in Tashkent to drive us over the border to Shahristan and leave us there to fend for ourselves.

At the Uzbekistan-Tajikistan border, a yard-high concrete barricade extended halfway across the road with a hexagonal red stop sign fixed to the middle. Police and Ministry of Internal Affairs troops with automatic weapons surveyed the road from an observation post beside the barricade. As we approached the checkpoint, I began to sweat. Salaxiddin, our driver, maintained a steady thirty-five miles per hour; when we were almost upon the barricade, he swerved into the left lane, missing the concrete slab by inches, and kept going. The police and armed troops, occupied with another driver, seemed barely to notice our passing. Nervously, I asked Salaxiddin why he hadn't stopped. "I travel this road often. They know my car. They don't need to check it each time I go through," he said with smug self-assurance, as if my question had been utterly gratuitous.

Our host in Shahristan was Qurbanbay Ataev, who had been the director of the House of Culture when we had first come searching for *baxshi*s. By 1994, he had quit his job and become the manager of a shaky Tajik-Chinese joint venture that was trying to establish a tourism and recreation center in the foothills of the Turkestan Ridge, south of town. Qurban-*aka*, as we called him, was a handsome, slightly built man with wavy, graying black hair and a stubbly mustache that looked as if it could have grown simply from his having neglected to shave for a couple of days. He lived with his wife and eight children, ages three to eighteen, in a modest compound on a dirt track a few minutes' walk from the asphalt road. One cool summer night we stayed up late together sitting on the pillow-covered *aivân* in his yard, chatting, drinking tea, and gazing at a distant row of gangly poplar trees silhouetted against a nearly full moon. Qurban-*aka* chewed *nâs,* a preparation of finely chopped green tobacco mixed with lime and the ash of cotton stalks. While chewing, he talked with his mouth closed, making his speech slurred and hard to understand (when I first came to Shahristan, I thought all the men had a speech defect; it turned out that they were simply chewing *nâs*). Every so often he'd spit out the *nâs* and pronounce a few undistorted sentences before packing in another wad. Qurban-*aka* seemed self-conscious both about what he considered his diminished ability to extend hospitality—the result of Tajikistan's precipitous economic decline—and about what he perceived as his lack of worldliness. In the middle of our conversation he suddenly asked me, "Can you tell from the way I answer your questions that I've only received a middle-level education?" Earlier he had apologized for the *dasturxân* that he offered us—a loaf of dark bread from the store, cucumber spears, sour cream, and tea. The sour cream had been provided as a special ration by the Shahristan Executive Committee because he was entertaining a foreigner. His family of ten survived on milk from their cow, vegetables from their garden, and store-bought loaves of bread. Flour was generally unavailable, and the centuries-old tradition of baking puffy *nân* in clay tandir ovens had temporarily come to an end. Families were entitled to a certain amount of monthly credit at the local stores; beyond that, food and goods could be acquired by barter or with Russian rubles or dollars.

CALLING SPIRITS

The morning after our arrival, Qurban-*aka* took us to the home of Turdijân, one of the two female *baxshi*s whom we had met on our previous visit to Shahristan. She lived on the outskirts of town in a settlement called Qipchâq after the tribal lineage of the Uzbeks who had settled there. Turdijân *baxshi* welcomed us into her small, darkened *mehmânxâna* and offered tea. She was a large woman with nothing delicate about her features but an unusually expressive, doleful face and a soft voice. A long white shawl covered the scarf tied around her hair and fell over the shoulders of her purple and green flower dress. As we sipped tea, the obligatory exchange of pleasantries was short. OM got right to the point: we had returned to Shahristan with the hope of witnessing a *koch* and wondered whether Turdijân had one scheduled and would be willing to allow us to come along.

Turdijân replied that she had nothing against our being present at a *koch,* but that only the family of the ill person receiving treatment could extend permission for us to attend. The prime times for doing a *koch* were Tuesday and Saturday evenings, and so far she had no booking for the coming Tuesday. However, while she waited for a client to turn up, she agreed to explain what takes place in a *koch*.

Preliminary to any *koch* is a diagnostic ritual called *fâl* (Arabic: "fate"), conducted by a *fâlbin* (*fâl* + *bin*, from Persian *didan* "to see": "fate-seer," "fortune-teller"). The *fâlbin* must also be a *baxshi*. The *fâl* shows whether or not a sick person needs a *koch*, and if so, which *baxshi* should perform it and what kind of animal should be sacrificed. Turdijân said, "Most of the people who are sent to me, I take. But sometimes I don't take them. I can't help everyone. If my spirits accept a person, it's clear from the first moment that the person enters my house. If my spirits don't accept him, I'll send him to another *baxshi*, very politely. All the attributes—what kind of treatment you need—are given by the *fâl*. The *fâl* tells you what kind of an animal you have to sacrifice—a white sheep or a red rooster, or a black bull. And you have to do that."

OM asked Turdijân whether she could perform a *fâl* for us and volunteered to be the subject of the diagnosis. He was, in fact, feeling a little blue that day, and perhaps Turdijân could explain the cause. Turdijân agreed. She spread out a small white cloth in one corner of the room and placed on it four ritual objects: a mirror, a knife, a short braided cord, and a string of beads. The mirror, she explained, was used to see the state of a sick person. The knife served to fend off illness. The cord was for beating, and the beads for "finding words," that is, to aid concentration. She took her *dâyra* and positioned herself on a white sheet on the floor so that she was facing southwest toward Mecca, the ritual objects before her. She explained that she used the *dâyra* to call the spirits. "When I see a sick person, the spirits come like jewels on a string. The spirits give me the sound. They tell me how to play, and what to play."

Closing her eyes, she began to beat a rapid, regular rhythm on the drum. After the rhythm was well established, Turdijân began to chant in a tuneful alto voice.

> *Bismallah-Hu, Bismallah, Bismallahdan bashlailiq*
> In the name of God, in the name of God, we begin with *Bismallah*
> My spirits, give me the road
> I always cry when I say "God"
> Let the one without children have children
> Give healing to the humble Muslim
> From the very beginning, I am on your road, God
> My spirits, give me the road.

The chant continued with a series of supplications to saints (*avliya*) and relatives to "give the road" or "open the road" so the spirits could speak. Turdijân's eyes remained tightly shut, the *dâyra* bobbing in her hands as she held it upright in front of her and struck the head of the drum with her fingertips.

After a long series of supplications, Turdijân addressed the condition of her "patient," OM, extemporizing her text to slight variations of a single melodic pattern that repeated in each line.

> My dear, your head hurts
> Sometimes your heart is nervous
> From time to time something squeezes you from both sides [of your
>   abdomen]
> You have a lot of concerns
> In your home, everything is fine
> There's one hateful person
> From time to time, he's the reason that you're nervous
> You have friends, and enemies who hate you, my brother
> Sometimes you want to leave all of your work
> I don't know why your work doesn't move forward
> You wanted to go somewhere
> But for some reason, things changed.
> Did the road turn for you?
> Or maybe you yourself didn't want to go
> Dear brother, your heart told you not to go
> In the name of the *chiltan*s
> If God wills, your road will be happy, dear brother
> However, there's one person, dear brother
> He hates your roads
> Otherwise, everything else is fine
> Your hand reaches to any place
> Your soul is healthy
> Sometimes your head hurts a lot.

The diagnosis: the white spirits were mad at OM for drinking vodka and eating sausage (i.e., pork). OM had something unclean in his head, connected not to his psyche but to the fact that he had a cold. The remedy: stop drinking. The good news was that no *koch* would be necessary. OM conceded that yes, he had had a headache. How had Turdijân been able to divine that? "I gaze at the back of my *dâyra* and I see something dim inside the *dâyra*," she said. "I see not with my eyes, but with my soul. I close my eyes, and in my imagination, like a dream, a picture is formed. The action circles around inside the *dâyra*. But it's dim, like a television when the picture tube is ruined. I can do a *fâl* at a distance, too. If a sick person can't be moved, someone can come and say his name and his age, and I can do a diagnosis."

After the *fâl,* Turdijân told us about the *koch* itself. "First, you have to slaughter some kind of animal." (We learned later from a post-office worker who moonlighted as a butcher for *baxshi* rituals that *baxshi*s are particular about the color of the animal that must be sacrificed and about whether or not the animal has spots.) "I take the fresh blood and rub it on the patient—usually on

247

the person's back. Sometimes I rub a lot, sometimes a little. It's clear to me how much blood to use. Then I unroll my white flour cloth [*surpa* or *âqliq*] made from a sheep skin or goat skin and put it on the floor and prepare forty-one candles (made from cotton dipped in oil) for the forty-one *chiltan*s, or evil spirits. [Again, echoes of Zoroastrianism in the lighting of candles, a breach of Islamic practice]. I make forty-one, because there are forty-one *chiltan*s that you have to overcome or suppress. Besides the forty-one, I do a few extras in memory of the spirits of people who have died from the house where I'm doing the *koch*."

Turdijân's use of the word *chiltan* for "evil spirit" drew my attention. In Islamic mythology, *chiltan* refers to forty supernatural spirits who assume the form of men and, preserving their anonymity, influence the course of events in such a way as to protect other people from misfortune (these same supernatural spirits were also called *abdâl,* or "fools of God"). The cult of *chiltan*s most certainly predates Islamization in Transoxania, and Islam seems to have stood the *chiltan*s on their heads, turning evil spirits to good.[2] Turdijân had counted forty-one *chiltan*s instead of the canonical forty because it was customary to add one *chiltan* to represent the totality of the group.

"I put some flour, candles and a mixture of flour and ash on the flour cloth and light the candles," Turdijân continued. "Then we begin the *koch*. We eat some of the meat from the animal that has been sacrificed. I blindfold the sick person, and then I begin to work. Besides me, there are four or five helpers. After we begin to work, it sometimes happens that the sick person goes out on the street and goes to the very place that the illness came from. And when he finds that place, he falls on it. Sometimes the sick person doesn't find the place that's the source of the illness, and then I take the person back into the room and do another *halqa* [circle, ring]. If I feel that the sick person hasn't found the source, I do another *halqa*. I work until I feel that the person has found the source. And it happens sometimes that we don't find the source. It turns out that the illness is something else; then I say, go to the doctor, or treat it by some other means. There are sick people who don't go out on the street. The sickness is inside them. Then the spirits tell me to send them to people who practice magic [*amal*] or to a mullah. The spirits can be driven out of the sick person either through [intestinal] gases or through the mouth."

For Turdijân, the essence of healing was not treating symptoms but establishing the etiology of an illness: finding the spirits responsible for the illness and clarifying the cause of their anger. Once the spirits and their physical source had been identified, they could be appeased through a process of transference in which the *baxshi* lured them away from the flesh and blood of the sick person to feed on a surrogate, such as the meat of a slaughtered animal. Turdijân had been frank about the sorts of illnesses she could hope to cure: not endogenous illnesses but exogenous ones. And she had a sober, straightforward view of her therapeutic procedures that cast them as empirical and mechanistic compared with the incantations of magicians or the prayers and Qur'anic amulets of mullahs.

We asked Turdijân how she had become a *baxshi*. Her story was typical of other stories we'd heard: her calling had arisen in the aftermath of her own illness. "I was sick for a whole year. I lost a lot of blood. I went to the doctor, and he gave me a shot in my hand, but my hand swelled up. My body didn't accept the shots. The doctor said that I should go and see a *baxshi*. 'If a *baxshi* can't cure you, I'll take you myself to Dushanbe,' he told me. I went to Mexri *baxshi*. When she did a *fâl* for me, she said that the *dâyra* that belonged to my husband's mother—she was a *baxshi*—was broken, and that it was having a bad effect on my livestock and on the health of my children. I said, 'Yes, I did have some animals that died.' She told me that until I accepted the responsibility of being a *baxshi*, this bad luck would continue. Then my husband went to buy a three-year-old yellow calf. There was a *baxshi* named Xaljan *baxshi*—he's dead now—and Xaljan *baxshi* did a *koch*, a cleansing. Xaljan *baxshi* ordered me to do a retreat [*chilla*] at home. I didn't see anyone; I'd go out only in the evening, completely covered up. I didn't speak to anyone. After I did the *chilla*, I started to get better, and I started to live completely differently. It was the will of the *jinn*s. If they give a road [*yol*], we can do something; if they don't, there's nothing we can do for ourselves.

"My son was against my becoming a *baxshi* in the beginning. He came back from the army and said that people would tease him about it—that it would make him uncomfortable with his friends. And I said to him, 'Okay, I won't do it.' But that very evening, he got sick. I said to him, 'Evil spirits have fallen on you. Let me do *sadqoq* for you'" (literally: "a hundred beatings"). *Sadqoq* is a ritual in which the *baxshi* beats a sick person with a fist, a short, knotted rope, or a chicken. Turdijân explained the chicken treatment as follows: "I take a chicken and cut off the crest with a scissors [the chicken is still alive]. I take the blood from there and rub it on a person—on the ribs, on the head, on the groin—and then beat him with the chicken. *Sadqoq* is for illnesses connected to the head—when you have a pale face or problems with blood circulation. I beat people with the chicken, then whirl it around the person's head three times and throw it away. I wait for three days, and during that time it becomes clear whether the chicken is going to get sick or remain clean [*halal*]. If it remains clean, then after a month or so, you can eat that chicken. If the illness [of the sick person] is very serious, the chicken can take the illness into itself and die. After I did *sadqoq* [on my son], he got better. And my son realized then that I had to become a *baxshi*. Thank God, everything's turned out well. I have nine children."

How had the work of *baxshi*s been able to continue during decades of Communist rule, when shamanism and spirit healing were subject to the same persecution as other forms of religious activity? "It continued illegally," said Turdijân. "There were people who wrote anonymous letters about such and such a *baxshi*. The police came and investigated people. We're still afraid. When you first came, I was also a little afraid. I thought that maybe someone had complained that I was doing this kind of work. We were accused of lying to people and taking their money. But here there's practically no money. People would give five or ten rubles. We don't do it for the money. Sometimes people give us flour. You could give one onion. If people give me an onion, I'd never say, 'No, give me such-and-such an amount of money.' That's not done."

THE *BAXSHI*'S DANCE

Since Turdijân had no clients waiting for a *koch,* we promised to stay in touch with her and went off in search of our other *baxshi* acquaintance, Nasri-oi. Nasri-oi had been the most forthcoming of the *baxshi*s we had met on our previous trips, and we held out hope that she would allow us to witness a *koch* if a client appeared. Nasri-oi was an attractive and energetic woman, not quite sixty, who greeted us with a broad smile and a strong handshake; the handshake was almost unheard of for a woman greeting men. Nasri-oi was expecting us. She'd heard that OM and I were in Shahristan and wondered why we hadn't come immediately to her. Nasri-oi said that if a client appeared, she would be happy to invite us to witness a *koch.* And if no client appeared, she would organize a demonstration *koch* with a stand-in patient so that we could record and transcribe the text of the *koch.*

Nasri-oi told us the story of her initiation as a *baxshi,* and the parallels to Turdijân's story were clear. She called her healing powers a "sickness." "This sickness began when I was twelve years old," she said. "It came to me—so it was the desire of God. I was sick for a month. I couldn't sleep. I had no appetite, and I suffered a lot. One night I was taken away by spirits to Kaarabchi [a place]. Kaarabchi is to the southwest, in the direction of Mecca. And there a river appeared. A man came up to me from the twenty-seventh heaven. The upper part of him was a body that was held up by two long legs. This man lay across the river, and a woman pulled him out of the water. The woman took him to the school. From the school, she took him to my house. Those spirits frightened me, and then they ascended to the sky. They appeared to be red and white, blue and black. My mother then said, 'My dear child, you've been frightened.' She did all the Muslim customs for when someone is frightened: a *koch,* a prayer chanted by a mullah. But nonetheless this sickness stayed in my body. The sickness became my friend. Gradually I became better. I grew up and became a woman. My parents gave me in marriage, but it wasn't a good household. They married me to a man who had been married once before. He lived sixteen days with his first wife. For two years, I didn't have a child. After two years, I gave birth to daughters, and then twice I had twins. First a girl and a boy, then two girls. All four of them died.

250

"I lived six years with that husband. His first wife lived practically next door. She didn't give us any peace, and we had to go to Dushanbe. My husband worked as a veterinarian's assistant. We lived in Dushanbe for two years. I had an uncle nearby who worked as a public prosecutor. My uncle died, and my father also became ill. My husband didn't tell me that my uncle had died or that my father had become ill. When I found out, I was in shock. I lost a lot of weight. I kept seeing my uncle and my father in my dreams. I told my husband, 'You stay in Dushanbe, and I'll go to my family.' Then, after some time, my husband gathered his things and came back to Shahristan. He started to fool around. He was working on a farm, and there he found a new wife, a widow, and he brought her home. After that, I left the house. She gave birth to a son. That had a deep effect on me. I was deeply depressed. I was taken to my relatives in Aini, and my relatives gave me to be married to an old man. He was seventy years old. He was an *ishân,* and that *ishân* healed me. He read prayers. I lived nine years with him. He was a widower. He had four children, two sons and two daughters. I had my two daughters, and I raised six children. *Ishân* Bâbâ, my husband, died when he was seventy-nine. After that, I came to Shahristan and bought the house where I live now. I got sick again and went to have a *fâl.* The *baxshi* foretold that at age fifty I would become a *baxshi* myself. And indeed, at age fifty, I became a *baxshi.* Thank God, I've been doing it for eight years, and I'm very happy. God gives me some income, and that's what I live on."

Was it not odd that Nasri-oi, a *baxshi,* had been married to an *ishân,* a Muslim spiritual teacher? I asked Nasri-oi whether she didn't feel a contradiction between performing a *koch* and reciting Muslim prayers. "They're different things," she said. "Prayers are for my own personal use. Prayer is belief. It's for your own cleanliness. The *baxshi* is connected to the road of the jinns. Mullahs are stronger than *baxshi*s. They can close the road for us or cancel our actions. But we *baxshi*s can't stop the road or the actions of a mullah. If a mullah closes my road, there's nothing I can do about it. I become ineffective. I lose contact with the spirits; they don't come to me. If a mullah closes my road, I won't even be able to do a *fâl,* no matter how much I pray to God." Perhaps out of respect to the mullahs, *baxshi*s do not perform the *koch* during Ramadan, Nasri-oi told us. In a different discussion, however, Nasri-oi considered the powers of spirits to be stronger than the power of God. "If God punishes someone, he can still live; if the spirits punish him, he'll definitely die," she said.[3]

While we were sitting on a pillow-covered *aivân* under the portico of Nasri-oi's modest house, a young woman appeared, wrapped in a black veil and overcoat, her face a study in worry. Nasri-oi motioned for her to sit on the *aivân.* The woman held out her left hand and showed Nasri-oi a festering abscess on her index finger. She had already been to a doctor, and the doctor had sent her to Nasri-oi. "They frequently refer patients to us," Nasri-oi said. "What can they do? They have no medicines, nothing to treat people with." Nasri-oi excused herself for a moment, went inside, and returned to the *aivân* with the instruments she would need for her treatment. First she took wads of cotton and moved them back and forth above the abscess, never touching it. Then she belched loudly—to frighten the evil spirits, she later explained—and hit the woman on the shoulders and head with small branches of wood while she murmured an incantation. Finally she hit the woman on the back several times with her fists. The treatment took about two minutes. The young woman thanked Nasri-oi profusely and gave a broad smile as she left. No money changed hands. After the woman had gone, Nasri-oi said to us sadly, "That's an example of how people get sick. They cause it themselves. That woman's abscess was on the hand that had borrowed a pail and not returned it. It was her own fault."

Nasri-oi had become committed to the idea that OM and I should see a *koch*. Since she had no clients lined up that week, she decided to ask her women helpers to come by that very afternoon and show us at least the central part of the ritual. What would be missing was the preparations: the sacrifice of an animal, the consumption of its meat, and the baking of the special bread.

Nasri-oi during a *koch*.

We set up tape recorder and video camera in Nasri-oi's *mehmânxâna* while she went out in search of helpers. Nasri-oi returned after a few minutes with three women and a young girl, who was willingly blindfolded and served as the sick person. Before a real *koch*, Nasri-oi said, she would light the candles and bake the thin bread (*kulcha*) of ash and flour that Turdijân had described, so that the spirits could feed on its smells. The meat from the slaughtered animal would be consumed and the bones thrown in water or buried far away so that they would not be eaten by dogs. It was very important, Nasri-oi said, that dogs not get near the meat and offend the spirits.

Nasri-oi began the *koch* alone, seated in front of her white cloth and beating lightly on her *dâyra* while singing to a repeated melodic pattern, much as Turdijân had done during the *fâl*. After a few minutes of singing and *dâyra* playing, the three helpers joined in with hand clapping and sharply accented vocables, *Hai, Hai, Hai, Hai,* which became longer and more drawn out, *Haaaaaa, Heeeeeee, Huuuuuuuu*. Both Nasri-oi and the helpers stood and began to dance about the room, Nasri-oi in the middle, the helpers around her. The *koch* progressed to a section of energetic rhythmicized eruptions chanted in unison—*Errrr-ha, Errrr-ho, Hai-hu, Allah hai, Ya-erei, Ooooooo-haqq*—that sounded much like the rhythmic chanting of a Sufi *zikr*. The three helpers clasped hands around one another's shoulders, dipping and rising rhythmically to the *dâyra* rhythms.[4] After some ten minutes, Nasri-oi belched several times and brought the first *halqa* to an end. A second and third *halqa*, separated by short pauses, followed much the same melodic pattern as the first *halqa*, but with different texts. Both ended with the same *zikr*-like chanting and dancing, which grew most intense at the end of the third *halqa*. Following the third *halqa*, Nasri-oi performed *sadqoq* on both OM and me. She didn't beat us with a chicken but rather, belching continuously, hit us hard on the shoulders and back with her open palms in an effort to force evil spirits from the body. *Sadqoq* seemed like a kind of mechanical shortcut to the more complex and symbolic procedure of the *koch*. An excerpt from the *koch* is reproduced on the accompanying compact disc (track 23).

After the third *halqa*, Nasri-oi and her helpers quickly left the highly wrought state (was it trance?) that they had entered through the chanting and dancing, and Nasri-oi began an earnest explanation of the various kinds of spirits (*pari* or *qizlar:* "girls," as she sometimes called them) in the pandemonium of the *koch*. The spirits come in three colors: black, white, and yellow.[5] Black spirits are the most negative, white are positive, and yellow occupy a middle position between the two. If a black spirit touches a person, it leads to death. Yellow spirits (*sariqiz*) can paralyze a leg or an arm. White spirits (*âq pari*) don't cause any harm; they are the protectors of the white flour cloth (*surpa*) that brings good to people. Clean or pure spirits are called *pari pâk*. If this kind of spirit grabs someone, he will always live in cleanliness and have pure thoughts. But if someone with *pari pâk* does something dirty, he will become ill, for he is going against the will of the spirit that is inside him. Besides these three kinds of *pari*, the text of Nasri-oi's *koch* revealed an extensive inventory of spirits, angels, furies, figures from the Bible and the Qur'an, mythical personages, and local saints. There were yellow *Juhûd pari* (Jew spirits) that looked like monsters and *ilân pari* (Uzbek: "snake spirits"), which were snakes with wings like a dragon; there were vengeful *xunxârlar* (Persian: "blood drinkers"), *su pari* (Uzbek:

"water spirits"), and *âtash pari* (Persian: "fire spirits") that performed incantations with fire. Luqmân Hakim, a mythical doctor who heals with pomegranates, turned up alongside Moses and Jesus, Fatima and Abu Bakr. In Nasri-oi's *koch,* the spirit world merged seamlessly with the Islamic world—or at least with a version of the Islamic world, as illustrated, for example, in the following sequence from the third *halqa.*

> One God, dear God
> Give my belief to my helpers
> Don't leave me without you
> You yourself, show mercy
> I love you, my dear God
> I love you, soldiers of fire
> White furies
> Merciful furies
> Fire furies
> Regal spirits
> Jewish spirits
> *Hai-hai*
> Yellow girls
> White spirits
> Blood-drinking spirits

The shamanic-Islamic syncretism was evident not only in the text of the *koch.* It was even more starkly apparent in the form of the ritual itself. For example, the dancing and rhythmic chanting at the end of each *halqa* that seemed so similar to a Sufi *zikr* were indeed known as *zikr* among the *baxshis.* Turdijân defined *zikr* simply as the part of the *koch* where "people stand in a circle and clap and say, *'Ablâ Hu'"* (i.e., "Allah Hu"). Neither Nasri-oi nor Turdijân could tell us anything about Sufi orders or the Sufi practice of *zikr.* The Sufi-*baxshi* connection had been made, had existed, and had already dissolved at a time that predated the reach of present-day cultural memory. When exactly the connection had been forged can only be a matter of speculation. The *zikr* might well have been integrated into the *koch* as a substitute for a more archaic form of shamanic dancing that had disappeared, possibly under the pressure of Islamization.[6] If such was the case, then the relationship of shamanic ritual and Sufi *zikr* would have come full circle, for there is wide speculation that the ecstatic body movements and dancing that occur in many forms of *zikr* were themselves inspired by shamanic dancing.[7]

Since the Sufi *zikr* is overwhelmingly associated with the religious practice of men, it might seem odd to find *zikr* performed by female *baxshis* and their helpers. However, Sufi *zikrs* performed by women have been documented in Transoxania for many centuries and were still a presence in the religious life of Tashkent as late as the 1920s.[8] The funeral ritual called *jahr* or *jar* (from Arabic *jahara:* "to speak loudly"), commonly performed by rural women at the grave of the deceased, particularly in the case of the death of a child or young adult, seems also to be related to the *zikr* (*zikr-i jahri,* or *"zikr* with loud voice," is a common description of one kind of *zikr*). During the *jahr,* groups of women put themselves in a highly emotive, trancelike state through violently loud and accented chanting accompanied by forceful body movements. A women's ritual analogous to *jahr,* called *sadr* (or, in Shahristan, *samâ*—another loanword from Sufism), is performed at the home of a relative of the deceased.[9]

MORE SYNCRETISMS

Shamanism and Islam are the antipodes of one kind of syncretism in the *baxshis'* life and work. Tajik and Uzbek ethnicity are the antipodes of another. Soon after we arrived in Shahristan, I had asked our host, Qurban-*aka,* to help compile a list of all the *baxshis* in the Shahristan area, along with their age, sex, and ethnicity—which Qurban-*aka,* in the Soviet tradition, called nationality. Qurban-*aka* knew of thirteen living *baxshis* and wrote down the names of another five who had died in recent years. Of these eighteen *baxshis,* twelve were women and six were men. And even though roughly ninety percent of Shahristan's people call themselves Tajik, Qurban-*aka* described nine of the eighteen *baxshis* as Tajiks and nine as Qipchâq Uzbeks—that is, Uzbeks descended from the Qipchâq tribe. Most everyone in Shahristan is bilingual in Uzbek and Tajik, yet Turdijân and Nasri-oi both told us that a *koch* is always performed in Uzbek, even by Tajik *baxshis.* The very name of the ritual, *koch,* is a Turkic word, but the *koch* betrays many Tajik influences.

V. N. Basilov, the influential Russian scholar who has devoted his career to the study of Central Asian and Siberian spiritual culture, published an article in which he distinguished two strains of Central Asian shamanism.[10] The first he called the "'Turkic,' or stock-raising variant," the second the "'Tajik' or agricultural variant." For each strain, he made a list of attributes. The first few items in these lists are reproduced here. (Note Basilov's use of the past tense. For all his erudition, Basilov apparently chose to ignore the living tradition of Central Asian shamanism, or perhaps his use of the past tense was simply a political convenience.)

"Turkic"

1. Shamans were most frequently men.
2. The séance was accompanied by performance on a stringed instrument (*qobyz* or, more rarely, *dombra* among the Kazakhs; *dutar* or, more rarely, violin among the Turkmen; *qobyz* among the Karakalpaks; *qomuz* [three-stringed fretless lute] among the Kyrgyz, particularly in the north).

255

3. The séance was usually held at dusk.
4. The shaman performed divination [e.g., *fâl*] while playing a [stringed] musical instrument.
5. During the ritual, animals were sacrificed to the spirits.

"Tajik"

1. Shamans were most frequently women.
2. The shamanic séance was accompanied by a tambourine (*dâyra*).
3. The shamanic séance usually took place during the day.
4. The basic form of shamanic divination was to the accompaniment of a tambourine. A mirror and glass of water, usually with a piece of cotton in it, were also widely used for divination.
5. The ritual offering to the spirits during the séance was flour and food made from flour.

Basilov concluded that while the contrasting attributes in his lists do have specific cultural references and origins, they have combined in a variety of ways to create numerous local variants of shamanic practice, each composed to a greater or lesser extent of both Turkic and Tajik attributes. Musical instruments play a central role in Basilov's typologies. For him, the tambourine (*dâyra*) belongs historically to Iranian-speaking peoples and is connected through iconographic evidence to drums that existed in ancient Egypt, Greece, and Asia Minor. These drums, without a grip or handle, are distinct from the frame drums found among Siberian peoples, which have handles or crossbars.[11] However, Basilov's Turkic-Tajik complementarity does not work as well with the stringed instruments in his "Turkic" list, which ostensibly form a link between the Siberian instrumentarium and the Turko-Mongol element in Central Asian music. One of these instruments, the *dombra,* is also commonly played in areas of Tajik settlement and is used interchangeably with instruments called *dumbrak* or *dambura* played by Tajiks (as well as Uzbeks).[12]

In the case of Shahristan, with its largely Tajik, if bilingual, population, Basilov's hypothesis would suggest that local shamanism should display a preponderance of attributes on the "Tajik" list, and this is in fact the case: the predominance of female *baxshi*s, the use of the tambourine, the ritual offering of flour rather than meat, the absence of shamanic tricks or stunts, the rubbing of animal blood on the sick person, and so on. (One exception is the time of the shamanic séance: in Shahristan, it seems frequently to be held after dark or toward dusk, as in Basilov's typical "Turkic" séance.) At the same time, the oblïgatory use of Uzbek language to communicate with the spirits (whose names are themselves a mixture of Uzbek and Tajik) shows the deeply syncretic roots of the *baxshi*s' ritual world.

256

The *baxshi*s inhabit not only a doubly syncretic (shamanic–Islamic/Turkic–Iranian) ritual world of their own but are also part of a larger healing community that includes mullahs, *tabib*s (herb doctors), and clinicians trained in Western medical science. And how ironic now, after so many Soviet ethnographers confidently, if not always willingly, predicted the demise of superstition amid the irresistible progress of modern materialism, to find physicians at the local hospital referring patients to *baxshi*s because they lack the medicines to treat those patients. Like Dargh, Shahristan had tried modernity and discovered that it couldn't afford it. Qurban-*aka* told us, "These days, more and more people are going to the *baxshi*s. It used to be the opposite. But there are no drugs. Doctors can't treat their patients. It used to be that if you were a Communist and went to a *baxshi* and someone found out, you'd be kicked out of the party. Now no one cares. Doctors themselves send their patients to *baxshi*s, and sometimes they also go for some sort of spiritual or psychic illness." He added, "I consider those *baxshi*s a lot better than a professor at the Tashkent Medical Institute. They treat their patients sincerely; and that sincerity always redeems people."

From a *bakhshi*'s point of view, nothing seemed illogical about taking a referral from a doctor. Turdijân had put it simply: "There are illnesses that a doctor can treat and there are illnesses that we can treat. If we feel that an illness can be treated by a doctor, we send the person to a doctor. For example, a cold, or coughing, or tuberculosis. Or sometimes after doing a *koch,* I recommend to the sick person to go to a mullah for a healing prayer. People tend to go to the *baxshi* for psychological problems. Ninety percent of the illnesses that are treated by the *baxshi*s are psychological. For example, people can't control themselves or can't control their thoughts. Or they hear voices, or are depressed, or they suffer from fear. There's a psychiatrist at the polyclinic [and a psychiatric hospital in Khojend], but if a specialist doesn't give a clear diagnosis, the sick person will go to a *baxshi*."

Nasri-oi matter-of-factly described one case that she'd taken over from a medical doctor after he had declared it hopeless: "A seventy-two-year-old woman had a heart problem, an irregular heart rhythm. She was black and blue. The doctor said, 'She'll die soon; take her home.' They took her home, and she went to a *fâlbin*. The *fâlbin* said that she should have a *koch*. But instead they [her relatives] brought her back to the hospital. I went to the hospital, and she heard my voice, and asked for me to come to her bedside. She asked to eat, so I went to the home of the patient and prepared *pelmeni* [meat dumplings]. I told her daughter to take the *pelmeni* to her, and I took a black chicken and a black sheep with a white spot on the head. I took the chicken to the hospital and cut its crest off. A lot of blood flowed. I rubbed blood all over her naked body and she started to get some color in her. She kept saying, 'thank you, thank you.' When she came home, she asked to have a *koch*. Now she's much better. Her heart has become normal. Her blood pressure is normal. She fed the *xunxâr* [blood-drinking] spirits with the chicken's blood. The spirits *demanded* something."

In Shahristan, the *baxshi* world and the hospital world merge seamlessly. According to Nasri-oi, no one at the hospital minded that she cut a chicken's crest off in a patient's room and smeared blood over a dying woman's body to feed blood-drinking spirits. And this sort of coexistence of different values and beliefs is not an isolated case. At a time when strong currents of Balkanization are running through Central Asian elites—dividing, separating, distinguishing groups on the basis of language, ethnicity, clan, and regional affiliation, other currents exist at a grassroots level. At this level, where political ideologies echo faintly, belief systems and the physical props that support them tend to overlap and converge: shamanism intermingled with Islam intermingled with Marxist-Leninist materialism. It is curious: seen from above, from the perspective of political leaderships and institutions, Central Asia has a long history of suscep-tibility to ideological dogma. But from below, from a place like Shahristan, one can sense a pragmatic agility and openness that defies ideology. Shahristan offers little space for fantasy: whether overcoming illness, finding food, or marrying off a son or daughter, the most important thing is to seek practical solutions. And in doing so, people have been quite ready to become *bricoleurs*. These days the *baxshi*'s place in Shahristan's *bricolage* seems well assured.

Shahristan's Muslim shamans had assured their cultural survival through strategies not unlike those adapted by other carriers of expressive culture in Transoxania: adaptability, a willingness to mix traditions of various prov-enance, and a keen sensitivity to the social and psychological needs of the population they served. For example, entertainers such as Turgun Alimatov and Mar'uf Xâja, no less than the *baxshi*s, were "master psychologists," as OM had once put it, who had managed to remain popular through an entire lifetime of performing—a feat that might be the envy of many Western entertainers who enjoy a meteoric streak of fame only to burn out as quickly as they appeared. But whatever their artistic eccentricities and whatever the challenges they faced as performers in keeping their expressive art or technology (in the case of the *baxshi*) within the cultural mainstream of their respective communities, figures such as Nasri-oi, Turgun, and Ma'ruf Xâja were Sunni Muslims who could blend at one crucial level of identity into Transoxania's overwhelmingly Sunni majority population. By contrast, entertainers from marginalized minority groups—Jews such as Tohfaxân, the *sâzanda,* and Shia Muslims such as Mahdi Ibadov, the *mavrigixân*—faced the challenge not only of adapting their perfor-mances to shifting tastes and community needs but of doing so as outsiders—at least from the perspective of religion and all that religion dictated about an individual's place in society.

In the case of Bukharan Jews, more than a millennium's experience at cultural survival amid Transoxania's Muslim majority had provided the community with a sure sense of social footing. Adopting the language and, to a large extent, the cultural identity of the urban Tajik-Uzbek milieu in which they lived, Bukharan Jews had made themselves in many ways indistinguishable from Muslims while preserving essential features of their separate religious identity. In Bukhara and other cities, Jews capitalized both on the cultural knowledge they shared with Muslims and on the social distinctions that divided them, in order to flourish in their specialized role as musicians, a calling that at least at the secular end of musical life might have been morally problematic for a devout Muslim. But when those same Bukharan Jews—so competent at assimilating to the conditions of Transoxanian Islam—began to emigrate to Israel and the United States, their complexion as a minority group instantly changed. Could the adaptive strategies that had evolved to guide their lives among Muslims adapt yet again to assure their cultural survival as émigrés in the West? To seek an answer to that question, I did not need to travel far. Tohfaxân (after less than a year in Youngstown, Ohio), along with many other musicians I had known in Central Asia, was in New York City. Probably the most outstanding classical musician among them was Ilyas Malayev, and it was Ilyas whom I first sought out in Queens.

QUEENS

"Well, what does thou think then of seeing the world? Do ye wish to go round Cape Horn to see any more of it, eh? Can't ye see the world where you stand?"

—Captain Peleg to Ishmael, *Moby-Dick*

AN APARTMENT IN FOREST HILLS

The view from the kitchen of Ilyas Malayev's fifteenth-floor apartment in the Parker Towers complex looks east, up the twelve lanes of Queens Boulevard and across the grid of numbered streets, roads, drives, and avenues, whose arrangement, despite a hidden logic, makes navigating around the borough of Queens, New York, a test of both perseverance and imagination. Parker Towers dominates the intersection of Queens Boulevard, 69th Avenue, and 68th Drive in the part of the borough known as Forest Hills. It consists of three identically cheerless twenty-story brick buildings set around a circular drive with an empty cement pool in the center. A symbolic penumbra of manicured lawn fills the tiny space between the pool and the circular drive.

Beyond the entrance to Parker Towers, the row of stores that stretches along Queens Boulevard shrieks to even the most casual observers that they are in what New Yorkers like to call an "ethnic neighborhood." There are kosher bakeries and butcher shops, bagel joints, a restaurant featuring Israeli-Romanian cuisine, and, across the street, the Tel Aviv Haktanah restaurant. Nearby is the Glatt Kosher Kitchen and Take-Out, the Hamakom Kosher Pizza Restaurant, and the Knish Nosh. For the residents of Forest Hills, however, their neighborhood is more than "Jewish," *simpliciter.* It is Jewish with many gradations and distinctions, both of origins and patterns of settlement. There are Polish Jews and Russian Jews. There are Jews whose families emigrated from Russia at the end of the last century and Jews who emigrated from Russia last week. There are Persian-speaking Jews from Iran and Persian-speaking Bukharan

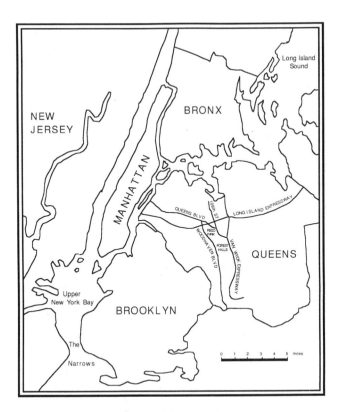

Queens, New York

Jews from Transoxania who distinguish themselves both from Iranian Jews and Russian Jews. There are Bukharan Jews who emigrated to Queens directly from Tashkent, Samarkand, or Bukhara, and there are Bukharan Jews who first emigrated to Israel and then came to Queens. There are Bukharan Jews who speak English and commute daily to the world outside Forest Hills, and there are those whose lack of English limits them to the social milieu of Russian, Turkic, or Persian speakers in Forest Hills and other émigré enclaves. Ilyas Malayev (pronounced "MaLAyev") is one of the latter.

I had met Ilyas a few times in Tashkent and recorded some of his music. During our meetings, there had always been a bustle around him—phones ringing, friends coming and going, musical engagements being planned. Ilyas was perhaps the closest Uzbekistan had to a vaudeville star. OM had told me that Ilyas performed stadium concerts where 25,000 people would squeeze into bleachers to hear him croon, tell jokes, and show his hilarious imitations of drunks and his carefully calculated satires of public figures. Ilyas himself contributed generously to the sense of bustle. He had a frenetic energy that made him seem at times like a man possessed. His speech came in rapid-fire bursts of

261

oratory; he veered between manic displays of physical energy and moments of near physical collapse. In conversations about his music and poetry, about his career, and about those who had helped or hindered him, he heaped magnanimous praise on his idols and lamented with a disgruntled, vengeful wrath the injustices he had suffered at the hands of jealous rivals and incomprehending bureaucrats. With all his local fame and fortune, Ilyas was one of the last people in Uzbekistan I would have expected to emigrate, and it was thus with some shock that I learned of his impending move to Queens.

I saw Ilyas several times during his first year in Queens, but it wasn't until the fall of 1993, a year after his arrival, that we were able to arrange the first of several long visits. I told Ilyas that I wanted to write about his adaptation to musical life in New York, that I'd like to spend several days talking with him and perhaps accompanying him to a performance or two. I said that I'd stay with a friend in Manhattan and drive out to Queens each day for our discussions. "Nonsense! You'll stay with us," Ilyas said emphatically.

"But you've got nine people living in three rooms," I protested.

"No problem," said Ilyas.

Ilyas lived with his second wife and former vaudeville costar, Muhabbat Shamaeva, a vivacious and attractive woman who looked considerably younger than Ilyas, and with his son, Raj, and Raj's wife and two young children, his fourteen-year-old daughter, Violetta, and his elder and recently divorced daughter, Nargis, and her son. Their apartment consisted of an ample living room with a dining alcove at one end, two bedrooms, a tiny kitchen, and a bathroom. A balcony was accessible from the living room, but the noise from Queens Boulevard's twelve lanes of traffic and airplanes on approach to La Guardia airport became deafening whenever the door was opened. The decor of the living-dining room summed up the exuberant collision of imported values and newly acquired tastes that has been such a central rite of passage in the lives of émigrés. A room-size Bukharan rug from Uzbekistan covered the floor, while another large Oriental hung on the wall—Central Asian style—opposite a row of grotesquely large, overstuffed sofa sections set before a large-screen television. Ilyas's collection of Asian stringed instruments covered one wall of the dining alcove, while on the other wall was a picture of the Brooklyn Bridge that lit up with tiny red and green light bulbs when plugged in.

For sleeping, Raj and his family shared one bedroom and Nargis, her son, and Muhabbat shared the other. Violetta slept on the couch, and Ilyas slept Central Asian style on *korpacha*s spread out on the living room floor (I was given a rollaway cot in the living room, next to Ilyas). In this modest space, the family managed to maintain the decorum of a Central Asian household. The living-dining room functioned as an expandable or contractable *mehmânxâna*. The dining table, surrounded by folding metal chairs, was always set with a tea service, fruit, candies, and bread. When Ilyas and his male friends gathered for tea and conversation, the women and children made themselves mysteriously invisible. Dividing up the space in the apartment was especially difficult because no one in the household except Violetta regularly left to go to school or to a job. Nargis, a versatile pop singer, and Raj, an astonishingly accomplished electric guitarist whose playing is reminiscent of John McLaughlin's, had worked with a band at a restaurant in New Jersey, but the band had been displaced by another ensemble that was backed, as Raj explained it, by the Israeli mafia. They had then moved from one poorly paying restaurant job to another, often with long lapses in between. Raj's wife wanted to qualify to become a medical technician but was still struggling to gain a basic command of English. Muhabbat attended language classes a few times a week, and Ilyas had occasional jobs playing music. The days that I was with them, the family spent a good part of each morning gathered around the television watching videos of old Russian and Uzbek movies or of Indian movies overdubbed in Russian or Uzbek, all taped from television in Uzbekistan.

Precarious would not be an alarming enough description of the Malayevs' financial situation. The family received a monthly welfare payment that was barely enough to cover the rent (later Ilyas would move to a smaller and less expensive apartment on nearby 108th Street), plus a food stamp allowance. Any extra income had to come from the various family members' musical engagements. Ilyas worked from time to time with a group of Afghan musicians who entertained at festivities in their own émigré community and had started a Bukharan ensemble called Maqam-i Nawa. The group specialized in performing the classical *Shash maqâm* but also offered lighter musical fare appropriate for weddings.

In Transoxania, the *Shash maqâm* had been brazenly presented as the cultural achievement of the "Uzbek nation" or "Tajik nation" or, in a slightly more enlightened formulation, as the joint achievement of both. But Ilyas had his own ideological spin on the *Shash maqâm*. "Its greatest performers have been Jews," he often reminded me, invoking the name of Leviche Babakhanov, the court singer to Emir Alim Khan, and other departed masters. "The *Shash maqâm* couldn't have existed without Bukharan Jews." Indeed, not only had Jews been leading performers of the *Shash maqâm,* but as listeners they had been among its greatest connoisseurs. At Jewish *toys* no less than Muslim ones, performances of the *Shash maqâm* had once had an enduring role. And in New York, freed from Uzbekistan's and Tajikistan's wearying cultural politics and nationalistic claims of ownership over Transoxania's musical great tradition, Ilyas hoped to restore the *Shash maqâm* to the greatness it had once enjoyed among both Muslim and Jewish audiences, who were often mixed in any case. Although the target local audience for Maqam-i Nawa was overwhelmingly Jewish, Ilyas had been sought out by Uzbekistan's diplomats in Washington and New York and had quickly established a cordial relationship with both diplo-

OM and Ilyas in Queens.

matic enclaves. Invited to perform for embassy functions and at a reception at Kennedy Airport to mark the inaugural flight on Uzbekistan Airways' route between Tashkent and New York, Ilyas had at least partially reassumed the role he had relinquished in Tashkent as a sort of modern-day Jewish court musician to the Muslim establishment.

Ilyas hoped that he could receive a modest but steady income from Maqam-i Nawa's engagements and from publication of his poetry. He had been curious to hear my thoughts about his financial prospects, and it was awkward to explain that while I was glad that he had started an ensemble to perform the *Shash maqâm* and while his Uzbek and Persian poetry certainly deserved more readers, my enthusiasm alone could not support him, and the chances that he'd be able to earn even a modest living in New York from Bukharan music and poetry were pretty slim.

"Perhaps I shouldn't have come," Ilyas sighed, his face creasing. "Sometimes I think about going back, but what would I do there? I've given up my apartment. I have one brother who's supposed to emigrate soon. Everywhere I looked in Tashkent, I was reminded of people who had died or had left: my deceased brother, my mother and father, my ancestors, my friends. I was bored. And besides, they're stingy now with art, stingy with music. I simply stopped writing music. They killed my creativity. Not the people, but the bureaucrats at the radio."

"The bureaucrats who blocked you, was it connected to the 'national question'?"

"I don't want to say that I'm a good poet or a good musician, but anything good that I did irritated them, especially because it was written by a Jew. Once a friend told me, 'If you want people to respect you, write lousy stuff.'"

GROWING UP JEWISH IN KATTAKURGAN

In Uzbekistan, Ilyas had been a musical wunderkind. Born in 1936 in Mari, Turkmenistan, he grew up near Samarkand, in Kattakurgan, where his father worked as a barber in the military commissary. Ilyas recalls his parents telling him that no sooner had he learned to walk than he would regularly disappear to the house of a neighbor who owned a gramophone in order to listen to recordings of local classical musicians. His parents grew tired of these disappearances and, with every kopeck they could scrounge, bought Ilyas his own gramophone. By the time he was eight, Ilyas was playing both a *tanbur,* which he glued together from broken pieces, and a tin-can violin that he fashioned using the can as a resonator and a stick of wood as the instrument's neck.

"There were a lot of teahouses in Kattakurgan where people sang," Ilyas recounted. "My father took me, my *tanbur,* and the gramophone to the teahouses. I'd play along with the recordings, and the listeners would give a little money. Then I started to play the violin and began to get invitations to weddings. I played pure classical Bukharan music. People were amazed, because usually musicians take up the *maqâm* only after they've matured, but I began to play *maqâm* immediately.

"There were many Bukharan Jews in Kattakurgan—maybe a thousand or fifteen hundred—and Bukharan Jewish musicians frequently sang in the teahouses. If singers wanted to become popular, it was important for them to develop a good reputation among the inhabitants of Kattakurgan. It was like an examination center for Central Asian musicians. Few people had radios, and consequently there was a great demand for live music. The teahouses had interesting musical evenings. They'd begin around seven o'clock. There would be one *tanbur* player and one *dâyra* player. They'd sing *maqâm* and they'd sing folk music. There could be five hundred or a thousand or two or three thousand people sitting and listening. They didn't have tables and chairs. People would just sit on the square.

"For a while, I had a teacher in Kattakurgan who taught me to play the violin, Central Asian style. Then one day he said, 'I'm going to write a letter to your father; please give it to him.' He wrote to my father that he needed money. So I stopped going to him. We didn't have any money. And then I saw him one day, and he said, 'Come to me even without money. I'm a sick man'—he had tuberculosis—'I'm going to die soon, and I want to leave my teaching to someone.' I went to him, he taught me, and soon after, he died. His death was difficult for me. After he died, the musical theater invited me to play. I was nine years old, and I played in the pit. There was an ensemble there—violin, *nay, tanbur, dutar, tar.* We played without notation. It was wonderful music.

265

"Later, I was asked to run a big musical amateur's society. They united five collective farms together under one chairman, and I became the music director. I was fourteen, and my students were twenty or twenty-five years old. It wasn't long before some of these students decided to kill me. They cornered me in the park, beat me, and tried to stab me. I managed to escape and ran barefoot through the snow for a kilometer."

"Why did they want to kill you?"

"Because I could play and they couldn't. It was simple jealousy. After that, my father decided that I had to leave Kattakurgan. I came to Tashkent in 1951, when I was fifteen. The next year, I was taken into the Uzbek Ensemble of Song and Dance in the Philharmonia Society, under the leadership of Grigorii Kogan. He was a Jew. He took me on a trial basis and said, 'If you play well for two or three weeks, we'll take you in.' I couldn't read music, but I started playing, and I played the best I could, because I was hungry. I tried to learn to read notes quickly. I took the music home and practiced it and learned to play it. They were astonished. They'd never seen anyone learn to read music so fast.

"From the Philharmonia, I entered the Conservatory. The Conservatory musicians played very academically, without any kind of melodic ornamentation, without any melisma. I stayed there a year, then left. It had been very difficult to get in, but everyone said that I did the right thing to leave. I returned to the Philharmonia, and one day Tamara Xanum, the dancer, came to see our ensemble. She liked my playing and said to the leader of the ensemble, 'Give me that boy to work with me.' And I started to work for her. There were four musicians, all of them older than I. We were very successful. I was the nightingale of the *tar*. The *tar* is a Caucasian instrument, but it had become very popular in Uzbekistan. I figured out how to play Uzbek *maqâm* on it, and brought the *tanbur* sound to the *tar*.

"After Tamara Khanum, I worked as an accompanist with one of the radio choruses, but I wanted to be a soloist. One of the *maqâm* players invited me to a wedding at the home of Dani Zakirov, who was an important figure at the radio station. There were fifteen *tar* players there, and the people asked us to play together. All fifteen of them took their instruments, and I took mine, and what I did, they were supposed to repeat. Then, at the end, I played this riff that no one else could play, and for half an hour, I played a solo. There was great applause. The wedding ended, and I was in a hurry to get home, but I didn't have money for a taxi. Some of the musicians gave me a lift. There was a big hole in the road and they intentionally got their truck stuck in the hole. Then they said, 'Let's all push it out.' They said to me, 'We'll lift the truck up and you put a brick under the wheel so that we can roll it out of the hole.' They lifted the truck up, and I'd no sooner shoved the brick under the wheel than they dropped the truck and the wheel fell right on my finger, which was on top of the brick. It was a three-ton truck. I managed to jerk my hand out of the way, but it caught my index finger."

"Do you think they did it on purpose?"

"Yes, they were jealous. If it hadn't have been done on purpose, five or six musicians from that evening wouldn't have gone with me. Their houses were in a completely different part of town. They took me to a hospital and at three o'clock in the morning, they amputated my right index finger. For three months I was crazy, but I got used to playing without that finger, and I tried to forget the horror of the accident. I became the same Ilyas Malayev, and it wasn't noticeable. Of course, I notice the difference, but an audience can't tell.

"Two years went by. I was working in the Folk Orchestra of Uzbek Radio when the idea came to form an *estrada* orchestra within the radio station [*estrada:* from French *estrade:* "platform," "stage": the peculiarly Russian form of hybrid folk-popular music—one might call it "ethnographic vaudeville"—that persists in myriad "national" varieties, e.g., Uzbek, Ukrainian, Chukchi, and so on all over the former Soviet Union]. I went to the Chairman, and he said that it would be a good idea to create that kind of orchestra.

"The orchestra consisted of violins, violas, trombones, trumpets, saxophones, clarinets, cellos, basses, and an electric guitar. Various composers arranged or composed songs for us. I'll tell you the truth—compositions that I wrote, that had my name attached to them, were always rejected. I had to hide my arrangements under other peoples' names in order to submit them. It was the same with my poetry. I wrote a poem called 'Who's an Uzbek?' A lot of singers sang the text. They brought it to the Artistic Council [at the radio] and the Artistic Council kept rejecting it. Once, an Uzbek girl in a veil recited my poem on television. But when she got to the line where my name was supposed to be [the *taxallus*], she didn't read it. The editor had forbidden her. I went to the Chairman and complained. That editor was fired. He had forbidden the girl to mention my name because it was Malayev, and Malayev is a Jew, even though the poem was about Uzbeks.

"I wrote a lot of *estrada* pieces so that they'd have a little bit of the feeling of folk music. Strictly speaking, there shouldn't be *estrada* music in Asia, because Asian music is richer. *Estrada,* in fact, is European music. It just has Uzbek words. Or you could say it's Europeanized music with an Uzbek accent. They don't go together—*estrada* and Central Asia. But when we went on concert tours to Europe, we were forced to play it."

I asked, "What attracted you to *estrada?*"

"Nothing. It was just the times. I had to go in that direction. I had to help the *estrada* orchestra so there would be some national flavor in it, so that it wouldn't lose its national spirit. It was hard, because audiences wanted to hear folk music. People would throw rocks at the trombone and trumpet players when we'd go around from city to city. They'd swear at us in the theaters. They didn't accept it. We built a kind of bridge between folk music and *estrada* music, and little by little, people crossed that bridge without a mishap. We introduced it little by little, like an injection into the blood. Now there are clarinets and organs at every single wedding. Twenty or thirty years ago, if you'd gone to a wedding with a clarinet or an electric organ, you could have gotten a bullet for it."

"So what you did was ideological?"

"Yes, it was an ideological task. The people themselves didn't ask for it. But I did my best to make it interesting. I wrote *estrada* music in the rhythms of the *maqâm*. I wrote a concerto for the *tar*. It was quite successful. It was played by the radio orchestra of Tajikistan. I was fascinated by the idea that the clarinet or the trumpet could play *maqâm*.

"Under Rashidov [Sharaf Rashidov, First Secretary of the Communist Party of Uzbekistan, 1959–1983, whose regime was disgraced after his death by the "Cotton Affair"], relations with the Bukharan Jews were much better. He wasn't a nationalist. He was a very decent person. He knew who was who. He always called me and my wife 'my son' and 'my daughter.' We were always invited to government ceremonies and to his own family ceremonies. The chairman of the radio, Ibragimov, was a very good person. He was an internationalist. He had good relations with all nations, in particular with Bukharan Jews. At age thirty-three, my wife was already a People's Artist.

"Frequently the Ministry of Culture would write a letter to the radio requesting that we be given to them for a performance. We were in the highest pay category. The Ministry established a tariff rate for us—how much we'd get paid for a performance. We received fourteen rubles and fifty kopecks. We were soloists. At the end, they gave us double pay: twenty-nine rubles. In those days, you could buy six or seven kilograms of meat or good shoes with that money. When we performed in stadiums, so many people came that there were casualties. People even sat on the field. There might have been twenty-five thousand people at a show and the tickets cost two rubles. A few musicians played with us. All of the artists' expenses—salaries, hotel, etc.—couldn't have come to more than a thousand rubles. The government kept the rest. What was important to the audience was not that I played *maqâm* on the *tar*. The people liked my jokes, my imitations. I'd do jokes and songs together. I did these concerts in six languages: Azerbaijani, Russian, Tajik, Uzbek, Armenian, and Afghani [i.e., Dari, which is essentially the same as Tajik].

"We earned our real money in the theater and at weddings. We were often invited to tour with the Bukharan theater, or with the theaters in Dushanbe, Osh, or Ferghana. The theaters all did tours in their own regions. We'd give one concert a day for a month, and we'd get a hundred rubles each for our concerts. At weddings it used to be that if *maqâm* wasn't played it was because musicians hadn't been invited. I'm talking about evening weddings. There would be one *tanbur* and maybe a *ghijak* and a *dutar,* without microphones. Five or six years ago I went to a wedding in Urgut, near Samarkand, and there were still people there who loved *maqâm*. There was a *tanbur* hanging on the wall in very good condition, and the host asked me to play something on it. I began to sing *maqâm* at seven o'clock in the evening and finished at ten. Three hours without stopping. There were three thousand people there, and they sat and listened without moving. I said to the host, 'Even if you don't give me money, my thanks still go out to you, because now I've seen thirty years later the sort of audience that I used to see.'"

I asked, "How is it possible that there would be silence at a wedding where you could play *maqâm?*"

"It wasn't complete silence. There would be *maqâm,* and there would be a dance-like piece, then another *maqâm*. But there would never have been a wedding where they just played dance music or modern-type music. They never had a wedding without *maqâm*. That was in the old days. Ten years ago I played at 108 weddings, and I played contemporary music, because that's what people wanted. I had a clarinet, an accordion, a sound system. For Uzbek music, I used a *tar* and a *dâyra*. I'd do the whole wedding in Uzbek. I liked Uzbek weddings not because the people listen well but because they respect artists. They like a lot of laughter and jokes. And they pay well. Once we earned four thousand rubles even before the wedding began, because the director of a collective farm where we played found out that it was my wife's birthday and everybody gave her money. Another time we earned eleven thousand rubles in one evening. They'd stand in line to put money under your *doppi*. But the only time I received real pleasure from the music was that time at Urgut. I didn't play at Bukharan [Jewish] weddings. The people were condescending. They didn't know how to be hospitable to artists. They'd say, 'Why are you sitting? Come on, get up and play some more.'"

"When Rashidov died and the leadership changed, everything began to change. At the radio, they came to my wife and said, 'You have to be transferred to the chorus.' She said, 'I'm a People's Artist. People know me.' And they said, 'So what?' They said, 'We've gotten rid of district and regional party secretaries and no one said anything.' The people who came to power weren't very smart. So my wife was transferred to the chorus and then they sent home a paper that said that as a consequence of a downsizing of the chorus, she was being laid off and had to go and pick up her documents. We went to the Chairman, and he told us that they were announcing the layoffs simply to get rid of some of the riff-raff and that afterward they'd take her back. Finally, one of her supporters managed to put her in with the folk orchestra, which spent most of its time touring *kolkhozes*. They wanted to make sure that she wouldn't have any fame. It was simply open nationalism at the radio. That went on until 1992, when we'd had enough and decided to emigrate."

I said to Ilyas, "Surely you didn't think you could just move your careers here, start publishing your poetry, and be music stars as you were in Uzbekistan. You'd visited Queens; you knew what you were in for. What did you expect?"

"In the capitalist world you can do everything. No one asks, 'What's your nationality?' or 'What sort of book are you writing?' I've seen books published here that are so vulgar that in the Soviet Union not only would the author have been shot but his whole family would have been shot, like the Romanovs. There's freedom of the press here. I understand that everything depends on how deep your pockets are, but I don't need any great profits. The main thing is that I want my poetry to be published while I'm alive. To tell the truth, I thought I would come to an understanding with a big businessman here for whom money means nothing—someone who could publish my book with the earnings from one day of work. I expected to find someone who would help me do this."

"What language would the publication be in?"

"The original languages: Uzbek and Persian for the poetry and Russian for the text portion. There could be some copies translated into English. That's what I expected. But unfortunately, I haven't found such a person, and now I don't know whether I will. Some people have promised to help me. I don't know what awaits me here. But I understand that as a chicken becomes fatter, its backside becomes smaller and it stops laying eggs. So it seems that the richer people become, the stingier they become. I don't have a lot of hope, and probably I'll find people who aren't rich, but are spiritually rich. I'm looking for that kind of person." Ilyas finally published the book himself. *Shiru Shakar* (Milk and Sugar) appeared in 1994 in an edition of a thousand copies.

A FOOL OF GOD IN QUEENS

Was Ilyas a "fool of God" or simply a fool to have thrown in everything he had in Tashkent for a life on welfare in Queens, all for the sake of trying to publish his poetry? He repeated frequently, "I'm close to the last one who's working with the *âruz* [classical quantitative verse meters]. I'm the only one left who understands *ghazalrâni* [improvisational *rubato* in the performance of classical songs]." In fact, Ilyas admitted that there were several Uzbek poets who wrote in *âruz* meters, but he complained that "besides the poetic form, you have to have philosophy, and these poets have very little of it."

Ilyas was indeed a master of the classical poetic style so central to Transoxania's literary heritage, and his claim to be "close to the last" poet from Uzbekistan writing quantitative verse in the *ghazal* and *muxammas* forms was only a slight exaggeration. Ilyas considered it not at all odd that a late twentieth-century Jewish poet would devote himself to perpetuating an Islamic poetic style that arguably reached its zenith in Transoxania in the fifteenth century. "The *ghazal* and *muxammas* are poetic forms for all times," Ilyas said. He had continued to write poetry after coming to Queens, and he wanted me to read a poem written shortly after his arrival that expressed the disorientation and confusion he had felt in his new surroundings. The poem was in Tajik, and together we translated it into English.

270

Where Is the Body and Where Is the Soul?

People with wisdom can't experience pleasure
And people with a heart of stone can't experience burning heat.

The nightingale and the crow sing in the bosom of the same garden
So go and compare the singing of the nightingale and the cry of the crow.

This world has two kinds of hearts, one pitiless and one compassionate
So go and compare the pitiless one and the compassionate one.

When you cry, tears flow from your eyes, but when you laugh, tears also flow
So go and compare the tears of laughter and the tears of lament.

From the same rain of nature there grew in the garden a thorn and a rose
So go and compare the pile of thorns and the bunch of flowers and basil.

The company of smart people and of stupid are both company
So go and compare the company of smart people and the company
    of stupid people.

You cannot plant and harvest if you spread water with your hands
So go and compare the hand-spilled water and the natural rain.

Two people went traveling, each had his own path
So go and compare the trip to the garden and the trip to the cemetery.

Every pair of lips has its own gesture from the command of the heart
So go and compare the laughing lips and the crying lips.

The rays of the moon are pleasure, the rays of the sun are healing
Both are lighthouses of life, so go and clarify which one is which.

A hundred thousand regrets that Ilyas didn't know what was in his body
So go and find his hands, his feet, his body, his soul.

Tan kujâ-u, jân kujâ

Aqilân hargiz nadânand majlisi rindân
Sangdilan hargiz nadânand ki dili biryân kujâ

Bulbulu zâgh nâlaye dârand ba sahni yak chaman
Nâlai bulbul kujâ-u qarqari zâghân kujâ.

In jahân dârad du manzil hardu âbâd u xarâb
Manzili âbâd kujâ-u, manzili bayrân kujâ.

Ham zi xanda, ham zi girya chakrâye âyad zi chashmi.
Chakrai xandân kujâ-u chakrai giryân kujâ.

Gashta az bârân paidâ xâru gul dar yak chaman
Todai xârân kujâ-u, sunbulu raihân kujâ.

Sohbati dânâ-u nâdân, harduye sohbat buvad,
Sohbati dânâ kujâ-u sohbati nâdân kujâ

Kishtu kâr hâsil naxâhad dâd zi âbi dasti xud.
Abi dasti xud kujâ-u sharshari bârân kujâ.

Har duye raftan ba sairu har yake dâsht râhi xud
Sairi bâghistân kujâ-u, sairi qabristân kujâ.

Har du lab du shevaye dârad chu az fatvâi dil
Du labi xandân kujâ-u du labi larzân kujâ

Sho'lai mâhtab safâu, sho'lai âftâb davâ
Har duye mash'al, valekin in kujâ-u ân kujâ.

Sad daregh, Ilyas nadânist ku chi dârad dar vujud
Sar kujâu pâ kujâ-u, tan kujâu jân kujâ.

Ilyas loved the literary refinement and intellectual rigor of classical poetry—the myriad puns, esoteric metaphors, and double entendres, all worked out within the strict metrical formulas of the *âruz* system. But the intricacies of poetry were multiplied when poetic texts were set to music, and Ilyas was an unusually versatile master of these intricacies. Like the great musician-poets of earlier times, he both set his own texts to preexisting melodies from the classical repertory and set preexisting poetic texts to his own melodies. At the same time, he was a composer in the European sense of fixing his compositions in musical notation, as well as what Uzbeks call a *bastakâr*—a singer-songwriter in the oral tradition.

The ability to match poems featuring a particular quantitative *âruz* pattern to a melodic meter for which they are appropriate was an essential skill for the classical musician-poets of Transoxania. But Ilyas continually repeated, always dolefully, that there were practically no poets left in Uzbekistan who understood the *âruz* and no *bastakârs* who understood how to set quantitative verse to music. "Writing *âruz* isn't easy," he said. "You have to have a feeling for music—the accents in music. If a person can't feel music, he'll never be able to understand *âruz*."

For Ilyas, performing music with texts based on the *âruz* system wasn't simply a matter of matching poetic meters and musical meters. It also involved a more subtle level of rhythmic interplay between music and text.

"What's the point of *maqâm*?" Ilyas asked. "The point is that you have to fight with the rhythm. The rhythm says, 'I'm stronger,' and the words say, 'I'm stronger.' And in the end they find a common language between themselves, and they end together. That's the essence of the *maqâm*—the secret of the *maqâm*. It's a crime to play the *maqâm* with a square rhythmic template. Why is it that when there's a concert of Azerbaijani *mugâm* in Baku, the police can barely hold back the crowds? But when there's a concert of *maqâm* in Tashkent, no one comes. Why is that? Because when music is performed correctly, it will get through to anyone—even to a complete stranger to that music. Why was it that before the war, when there were concerts of the *Shash maqâm* in the Jewish Theater in Samarkand and Bukhara, people didn't sleep at night in order to get a ticket? Because the music was performed correctly and stayed in people's souls. When you have this square, rigid manner of performance, little by little people become turned off by the music and they'll try to love a different music. And history suffers for that."

The "fight" that Ilyas described between rhythm and melody is embodied in the performance technique called *ghazalrâni* (Persian: *ghazal + râni,* from *rondan,* "to cut," "to polish"). *Ghazalrâni* involves a slight syncopation of the vocal line—something between syncopation and *rubato*. One might think of it as the Bukharan equivalent of swing—a rhythmic treatment that is hard to define precisely but that listeners sense immediately. I had never heard of *ghazalrâni* before meeting Ilyas, and Ilyas passed off my ignorance to a simple fact: the art of *ghazalrâni* had become lost. Bukharan Jewish *maqâm* singers like Leviche Babakhanov and Mikhail Tolmasov had been masters of *ghazalrâni,* Ilyas told me, but in the last thirty or so years, *ghazalrâni* had declined, and he was the only one who used it any longer. It had become a hermetic tradition, one that was alive only in exile from its native land.

Ilyas demonstrated the effect of *ghazalrâni* by singing a five-line stanza of poetry set to a classical melody from the *Shash maqâm* ("*Mogulcha-i Segâh*"). His demonstration appears on the accompanying compact disc (track 6). First, to the accompaniment of a *dâyra,* he sang "square," without *ghazalrâni*. Afterward, accompanied by *dâyra, tanbur,* and violin, he repeated the same section of melody with *ghazalrâni,* beginning with a different stanza of poetic text and expanding his rendition of the piece. A listener can follow the transcription given here for both examples, noting digressions from the "square" rhythm in the second example. Like a good jazz singer, Ilyas adds to the rhythmic tension of the vocal line by holding back for a moment at the beginning of melodic phrases and coming in a little after the beat. Throughout each phrase, syllables are rhythmically modulated to create a fluid and shifting flow of text that alternately moves away from the metric pulse of the drum and then rejoins it.

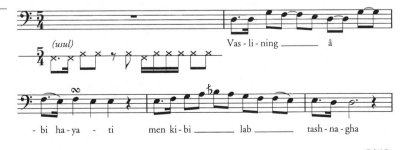

Kop ke-rak ___ er - di ___ ja - fâ - kâ(r) -
- lar yi-ghil - ghan ___ dav - ra - gha "Suv" de - bân ma - y(i) ber -
- di - lar, nam - im chi - qib ___ shar - man - da - gha ___
Dair a - râ ___ ja - mi la - bâ - lab kim i - chir - di ___
may man - gha _ Xâ - nâ - gah ___ aq - li _ (i)chi - qib ___ bir -
- bir ta - mâ - shâ ___ qil - di - lâ (yâr - di jâm - ni - mai) __

1. Vaslining âbi hayati men kibi lab tashnagha
2. Kop kerak erdi jafâkâlar yighilghan davragha
3. "Suv" debân may berdilar, namim chiqib sharmandagha.
4. Dair arâ jami labâlab kim ichirdi may mangha
5. Xânâgah aqli chiqib bir-bir tamâshâ qildilâ

1. I, a thirsty one, needed the water of life from her face
2. I needed it very much, finding myself amidst a gathering of enemies
3. I said "water," but they gave wine, shaming my name.
4. Who poured me a full glass of wine in the wine house?
5. The wise ones leaving the prayer house laughed at me.

In the poem Ilyas had performed a standard maneuver of the classical poets: he had taken a preexisting *ghazal* composed in rhymed couplets and turned it into a five-line *muxammas* by adding his own three verses to the original two. The challenge, of course, was to create a seamless transition from the newly composed lines to those of the original author—in this case, Nawâ'i. The authorship of the poem breaks down as follows: lines 1–3: *muxammas* by Ilyas Malayev, lines 4–5: *ghazal* by Mir Ali Shir Nawâ'i. In composing his own lines,

Ilyas preserved the *âruz* meter of Nawâ'i's *ghazal,* as illustrated here for line 4 (the *âruz* is in boldface, spelled out in the conventional Arabic *afaʿil,* or rhythmic formulas, which serve as paradigms for recognized verse meters; the meter shown here is *ramal mutamman mahdûf*):

Dair a- râ ja- mi la- bâ-lab kim i-chir-di may man-gha
fa: ʿi la:tun fa:ʿi la:tun fa: ʿi la: tun fa: ʿi: lun

‿ ⏑ ‿ ‿ ‿ ⏑ ‿ ‿ ‿ ⏑ ‿ ‿ ‿ ⏑ ‿

Finishing his demonstration of *ghazalrâni,* Ilyas turned to me and asked anxiously, "What will happen to this art if I don't continue to write and perform?"

"It will die," I said. "But it will die anyway. You can't save a moribund tradition by yourself. Dying traditions, however, may sometimes be reincarnated in new forms that one can't guess in advance."

Ilyas was uncharacteristically silent. Sitting close to me, puffing impetuously on a cigarette and jabbing me lightly in the arm—a reflexive movement that Bukharan Jews frequently use as a kind of intensifier or exclamation point in conversation—he asked wearily, "Did I come here for nothing?"

I couldn't bring myself to say anything, but it wasn't a rhetorical question. Ilyas repeated, "Tell me, did I come here for nothing?"

"I can't answer that," I replied. "It's simply that you have to face the reality of the cultural marketplace."

The forces that acted on the marketplace in which Ilyas's music and poetry had currency did not stem from the machinations of corporate media empires and entertainment conglomerates; rather, as Ilyas rightly saw it, his marketplace was most directly affected by two local factors: first, the increasing power of Orthodox religious authorities in the Queens Bukharan Jewish community who were hostile to what they viewed as secular music and secular art; second, an inexorable shift in musical taste among members of the community away from what Ilyas termed "ethnographic" music and toward what he viewed as kitsch. When I asked Ilyas to elaborate on the subject of religion and music, he launched into a long and caustic monologue.

"I knew that if I came here it would be very difficult for me, because I'd be banging my head against the [Jewish] religious authorities," he said. "In Central Asia, religious and secular life are separate. The synagogue takes care of praying, and everything else is handled in the community. In America, religion and social life are both under the aegis of the synagogue. A lot of Bukharan Jews have come back to religion. I don't know whether they believe it in their souls. I believe in religion, but not in religious authorities.

"In Central Asia, despite the fact that Bukharan Jews weren't considered an indigenous people and felt constrained compared to other groups, there were still opportunities. Any artist could find work. Any scholar could graduate from an institute and find work. In Uzbekistan, against the background of twenty million people in the republic, Bukharan Jews were a drop in the bucket. But despite that, about forty Bukharan Jews have their own solo records. I don't know a single Bukharan Jewish performer in Israel or America who has a solo record.

"It's true that not all of our works were published, that there were obstructions and impediments to our creative work. But we shouldn't judge these things, because we weren't Uzbeks or Tajiks. Here there's a hundred-percent possibility to regenerate and revive Bukharan Jewish culture, to revive our dying traditions [Ilyas was referring in particular to the performance tradition of the *Shash maqâm*]. And here the Bukharan Jews themselves are putting sticks in the wheel. That's terrible. I'm a Bukharan Jew. I came to America so that my people would have their culture, would stand on their own feet. We have our language, our music, our traditions. But there are religious figures who impede their expression. They say, 'Only religion. Only Hebrew.' Other peoples have a language and tradition that's separate from their religion. For instance, Uzbeks pray in Arabic, but they have their own language and culture. Azerbaijanis also pray in Arabic, but they speak, sing, and write poetry in Azerbaijani. It ought to be the same with Bukharan Jews." Ilyas's analogy pointed to the "problem" of Bukharan Jewish culture from the perspective of the Orthodox Jewish authorities. Uzbeks and Azerbaijanis who spoke, sang, and wrote poetry in their own vernacular languages were nonetheless drawing their means of expression from a cultural milieu that was, broadly speaking, Islamic. But Jews who spoke, sang, and wrote poetry in their own vernacular languages (Uzbek and Tajik) were *also* drawing their means of expression from a cultural milieu that was, broadly speaking, Islamic, and this was indeed troubling for the Orthodox.

"Here they're trying to change all our traditions," Ilyas continued. "Take funerals, for example. The latest you can have a funeral here is ten o'clock in the morning, and it's usually at eight o'clock in the morning. They bring the body into the synagogue in a closed coffin. Everyone comes into the hall. Five or six people speak, and then they take the body out, and that's it. There it was different. There was a tradition called *shayd-e avaz,* which means 'farewell' or 'epitaph.' It was like when dervishes begin to chant rhythmically the name of Allah in crazy intonations. It's a Bukharan Jewish tradition. One person begins with a solo, and another person answers. Men and women did it together in the home of the deceased person. If the dead person hadn't lived to see his children married, they buried him to the accompaniment of the wedding drum. Here instruments are forbidden in the synagogue, and so is lamenting. And God help you if a woman should show herself during prayers in the same hall as the men [in the Bukharan Jewish synagogue].

"And then there's *kiddush*. The way Bukharan Jews chant *kiddush* is different from the way Russian Jews chant it. The same Bukharan Jews who have been chanting it for a thousand years one way, they come here and all of a sudden they start to chant differently. It would be the same thing as giving up our language and our music to some foreign representatives out of our own stupidity, as if we weren't patriots of our own nation.

"Here, where there's complete freedom to revive our culture, suppose there's a concert of Bukharan music. There might be fifty or a hundred people in the audience. They consider that a ten-dollar ticket is very, very expensive. But one man gave five thousand dollars just to sit in the synagogue to see Simhat Torah. People regularly pay hundreds of dollars at 'auctions' in the synagogue where they auction off worthless religious *mitzvahs*—like opening up the ark, or holding the Torah. They don't know that there will come a time when they can throw a hundred billion dollars to try to revive their nation and their traditions, but they won't be able to revive them. It will be too late.

"Why is this? We have a weak intellect. It looks as if Bukharan Jews were created in this world to work for other nations, to develop other cultures and other traditions. That doesn't happen simply because we're Bukharan Jews and others are Uzbeks or Tajiks. If Bukharan Jews would stand up for themselves, it wouldn't have happened. They should support their own culture, so that someone could say, 'This is mine, and that is yours.' But now it's set up so that 'that is yours' and 'mine is also yours.' And then people look at us and say, 'You don't have any culture. You're just a bunch of cobblers and barbers.'"

I was moved by the intensity of Ilyas's dedication to preserving distinctive Bukharan Jewish traditions amid the forces of assimilation that had arisen from the Uzbek-Tajik cultural milieu of Transoxania and subsequently from the émigré cultural milieu of New York, where Jews of Eastern European origin far outnumber the Bukharans. The pressures on Bukharan émigrés to adopt a more canonical form of religious practice and social life were, in fact, part of a long history of efforts on the part of other Jewish groups to assimilate Bukharan Jews into their own practice. For example, during the nineteenth century, rabbis from Morocco and Yemen conducted rival "missionary" work in Bukhara in which they urged adoption of the Sephardic and Yemenite liturgy, respectively.[1]

Of all the traditions threatened by assimilation, it was the Jewish performance tradition of the classical *maqâm* that most concerned Ilyas. His dedication to "preserving the classics," as he put it, wasn't a dedication born from cultural snobbism or elitism. After all, he had earned his livelihood playing popular music. Classical music and poetry had been more an avocation than a vocation, and he had used the Bukharan classical repertory unrepentantly as a source for his own popular music compositions. But however successful his own creations, Ilyas acknowledged the superiority and sanctity of the classical tradition. "It's not that I don't have respect for contemporary music. I do. But I know that contemporary music is like a brochure or a magazine that people pick up, read, and throw away. Classical music, on the other hand, is religion in music. It doesn't die.

"Contemporary music—it's as if you started to dig with your hands to make a canal. Like it or not, it's not going to be a natural river. A natural river is formed when there's a snowfall in the mountains, and in the springtime, it begins to melt, and it makes its own pathway. No one forces it to go that way. The water goes where it has to go. And in that way, different streams flow together and become a great river. Can you dig the Volga River or the Atlantic Ocean by hand? No, it's impossible, even if you have a thousand pieces of heavy equipment. It's all nature. Classical music is also like that, because every note of classical music is the highest expression of the depths of the soul of a person who has undergone intense spiritual suffering. That's why it becomes a classic. A person can laugh a thousand times and not remember it, but if you cry once, you'll never forget it. And do you know how many tears there are in this music?"

I interrupted Ilyas's monologue and asked, "Why is it, then, that classical music is so quickly being forgotten in the Bukharan Jewish community?"

Ilyas offered a parable that summed up his own view of the rise of kitsch—a topic that has animated some of our century's most distinguished cultural critics. "There's a sickness that overcame music in Uzbekistan and Tajikistan," Ilyas said, "and it's been carried here as well. Imagine that one person becomes sick with the flu. Ten people are healthy. They're performers—ten performers are healthy and the one with the flu is a banal musician. If in two hours those ten people try to cure the one who's sick, they won't succeed, but the sick one, on the contrary, can infect all of the healthy people. Music is like that. That's what happens when music goes along a false path. And if a people doesn't listen to music the right way and starts liking banal music, that people isn't guilty. The guilty ones are the performers who began to infect them with that sickness. So you always have to try not to get sick. What does it mean, not to get sick in music? It means not to allow entry to just any kind of music simply for commercial or political purposes." Later Ilyas would reverse himself and blame not performers but listeners, for straying into the clutches of "false music."

For Ilyas, the locus of "banal music" was the new style of *toy* that had begun to emerge in Central Asia, particularly in Tashkent, and had achieved its fullest expression among Bukharan Jews in New York. Ilyas spoke about these New York *toy*s with a certain luridness whose effect could only have been to make me want to see one for myself, and so Ilyas had arranged to have me invited to the wedding of a friend's daughter.

I had known Nisim casually since the early 1980s.[2] He was a musical dilettante in the best sense of the word: a performer, though by his own admission not a gifted one, and, more important, a connoisseur of *Shash maqâm*. Nisim had been trained as an engineer, but after coming to the United States had worked as a watchmaker and later started his own small import-export business. His elder daughter, Bella, had been fourteen when her family emigrated, and at the time of her marriage was studying to be a hospital administrator. David, her fiancé, also from an émigré family, was a medical student.

The venue of choice for Bukharan Jewish *toy*s is Leonard's, a banquet and catering emporium in Great Neck, just off Exit 33 on the Long Island Expressway, about a twenty-minute drive from Forest Hills when there are no traffic snarls. As I drove Ilyas and his wife through the white brick gate and around the circular driveway with its colored fountain centerpiece to Leonard's grandiose columned entrance, Ilyas told me that he was a regular at Leonard's. He figured that he came there not less than twice a month to attend the *toy* of one or another friend and that he could easily come once a week if he wished.

The theme of Leonard's is glitz and glass. Inside the building's all-glass facade, the main lobby features floor-to-ceiling mirrors and three-foot crystal chandeliers recessed into a faux-marbled ceiling. A two-story-tall upside-down wedding cake chandelier dangles inside a glass tower with a circular staircase that links the lobby with a banquet hall on the lower floor and an auditorium on the upper floor. In the center of the lobby is a platform holding a grand piano made entirely of glass (or plexiglass). A sign informs that it is one of five produced in the world. "Many famous musicians have played at it's bench," says the sign. "Please do not touch. Replacement of any parts are unattainable. Better yet non Existent."

Leonard's is a capacious place, and the seven hundred or so wedding guests flowed easily through the main lobby and down the circular staircase to the ground floor, where they picked up dinnertable place cards, greeted friends, and eyed—but did not touch—an almost unimaginably massive display of desserts. Soon it was time for the ceremony. Everyone trooped back up the circular staircase to the second-floor auditorium, where men, all except the renegade Ilyas, wearing yarmulkas, seated themselves on one side of the center aisle and women on the other. At the front of the auditorium was a *huppah*—in Orthodox Jewish tradition, the portable canopy resting on poles, formerly carried by four young men, under which the marriage ceremony takes place. Leonard's version of the *huppah* was consistent with the overall decor: in place of poles, Doric columns wound with strings of white Christmas-tree lights in front of a floor-to-ceiling mirrored section of wall bounded by stone masonry, or what appeared to be stone masonry.

The ceremony was under the overall direction of a master of ceremonies, called in Russian a *vedushchii* (literally, "one who leads"), a figure imported directly from the former Soviet Union, where the *vedushchii* became a fixture at any sort of event construed as ceremonial—weddings, concerts, poetry readings, political rallies, practically everything except funerals. At a wedding, the job of the *vedushchii* is to narrate the plot of the ceremony, introducing the protagonists, interrogating them at appropriate moments ("What is it like to be nervous?" the *vedushchii* asked the bride. "It couldn't be better," she answered),

279

while at the same time revving up the crowd, adding humorous commentary, and keeping the event moving along. Dressed in a black dinner jacket with mottled gray patterning and holding a microphone, the *vedushchii* held forth in Russian from stage left. To dramatic snare drum rolls provided by an electronic drum machine accompanied by oompah chords from a synthesizer, the *vedushchii* introduced members of the wedding party as they marched down the aisle to take their places in the front: uncles and aunts, grandparents and siblings, a junior bride and groom—he around ten, she around eight—dressed, respectively, in miniature wedding dress and tuxedo (a symbolic presence that Nisim later assured me had been drawn from the stock of American wedding customs and was not a Bukharan tradition), and finally Rabbi Yeshua, followed by the groom and his parents and the bride and her parents.

Rabbi Yeshua came from a Bukharan Jewish family but, after emigrating to the United States, had joined the Lubavitcher Hasidim, the Brooklyn-based ultra-Orthodox sect that had sent representatives to Central Asia as the Soviet Union began to break apart with the aim of recruiting Bukharan Jews to their practices and beliefs. The Lubavitchers had donated money to help restore synagogues, offered Hebrew instruction, and along the way, tried to instill in the Bukharan Jewish community their own ideas about piety. Rabbi Yeshua had studied in Israel and then returned to the United States to work in the Bukharan synagogue in Queens as what Nisim had described as the "chief ideologist."

Rabbi Yeshua conducted his part of the ceremony in a mixture of Hebrew, Russian, and English. After a long section of chanting in Hebrew, he looked up at the bride and groom and asked in Russian, "Did you understand?" The auditorium erupted in laughter. Neither had understood anything.

At the conclusion of the ceremony, the guests descended quickly to the banquet hall (there was no receiving line), and as they found their assigned tables and dug into platters of appetizers, the entertainment began almost immediately. Before the ceremony, Nisim had proudly introduced me to the evening's chief entertainer, a musician descended from one of the most distinguished family lineages of classical musicians in Transoxania, Abram Tolmasov. Tolmasov had grown up in Samarkand in a household steeped in the tradition of the *Shash maqâm*. Mikhail and Israel Tolmasov, Abram's uncles, had been students of Leviche Babakhanov, the court singer to Emir Alim Khan; his father, Gavril Tolmasov, had also been a renowned *maqâm* singer. Abram Tolmasov had emigrated to Israel in 1989 and, realizing quickly that there was little demand for *Shash maqâm* singing, had branched out into more commercially lucrative musical genres. Tolmasov was just shy of forty but looked older that evening. His greased-back black hair and large mustache were set off by an aqua blue suit and matching shirt, worn tieless with a silver chain holding a pendant that dangled at his midriff. High-heeled boots completed the costume. Tolmasov was a childhood friend of Nisim, the father of the bride, and Nisim had paid for his old friend to fly from Tel Aviv to perform that evening. "He's very expensive," Nisim whispered to me in an aside, "but for a friend, he doesn't even mention money."

Accompanied by two young tuxedoed Bukharan Jewish musicians from New York who played clarinet and synthesizer *cum* drum machine, Abram Tolmasov performed a potpourri of popular dance music that included Russian, Israeli, and Neapolitan songs (such as "O Sole Mio," during which Tolmasov strummed his electric guitar like a mandolin). He also performed American songs such as Stevie Wonder's "I Just Called to Say I Love You" and "You Are the Sunshine of My Life" arranged in a Russian pop style (whose effect was to make them either faster or schmaltzier than they already were). A few minutes into Tolmasov's set, the lights dimmed, a smoke machine spewed a bluish haze, and the *vedushchii* announced in a dramatic, quivering voice that the bride and groom were about to take to the dance floor to have their first dance as a married couple.

After about an hour, Tolmasov and his accompanists took a break, and the *vedushchii* informed us that there would be a "show" (Russian: *sho*) featuring Ilyas Malayev and his ensemble performing Bukharan "ethnographic music." Ilyas and his ensemble, dressed in Bukharan silk *chapan*s, mounted the stage and broke into the traditional wedding song *yâr-yâr.* Ilyas sang and played the *tar* while members of his ensemble played accordion, *dâyra,* and the synthesizer and drum machine left on stage by Tolmasov's accompanists. Ilyas's twenty-minute set included traditional Bukharan wedding songs and light classical pieces with his own texts. There was warm applause at the end, and Ilyas went off, turning the stage back over to Tolmasov. Later in the evening, after the slicing of the wedding cake (a three-tiered model with a miniature illuminated water fountain in the middle), there was another variety act—"for the young people," the *vedushchii* explained, as he introduced Angelina and Arsen, adding that they "sang the most contemporary songs in the most contemporary restaurants in the world." Angelina and Arsen indeed looked contemporary, in a distinctly Russian way. Angelina wore black leather hot pants over black tights, a black bustier, and a gold chained belt. Arsen, tall and ponytailed, was dressed more conservatively in a black turtleneck, white slacks, and black blazer. Their act consisted of singing Russian pop songs to an instrumental sound track taped on a cassette and blasted through the speaker system.

Ilyas took a seat next to me during Angelina and Arsen's set, and using the loud music as a cover, I asked him indiscreetly, "How much do you think this wedding cost?" In Central Asia, Muslim and Bukharan Jewish families commonly put away money during the whole of their working lives to be able to stage a respectable wedding. But the economics of weddings in New York were different, and I had wondered how émigré families with little savings, many of them living on food stamps, were routinely able to engage Leonard's for prodigal evenings like the one I had witnessed.

Ilyas calculated for a few moments and replied, "Seven hundred guests means that it cost around thirty thousand dollars. Maybe a little more. But the families of the bride and groom don't pay that amount. Each guest contributes fifty dollars. Relatives of the families come around the tables and collect the money. Whatever is left over goes to buying presents for the newlyweds." Only slowly did it dawn on me that Ilyas, ever the gracious host, had paid my fifty-dollar contribution without mentioning anything to me.

"But a lot of the guests attending this wedding are not well off," I said. "How can they afford to pay a hundred dollars a couple to come here all the time?"

"It's a two-way street," said Ilyas. "Everyone wants a lot of guests to come to their *toy* when their own children get married, so it's important to attend other people's *toy*s. It all works out in the end."

The next morning, over breakfast, I engaged Ilyas in an assessment of the previous evening's event. Ilyas was in high dudgeon. As I switched on my tape recorder to record our conversation, he began speaking formally, as if offering an official critique for broadcast or publication. "Bukharan Jews, notwithstanding their very interesting musical history and their enormous contribution to the art of Central Asia, nonetheless quickly forget about their own culture. I consider that a great stupidity. Present at yesterday's wedding was one of the most famous singers of Central Asia, Abram Tolmasov. Having been raised in the Eastern quarter of Samarkand, Abram Tolmasov inherited the great *Shash maqâm* tradition of his ancestors. I was very surprised when Abram Tolmasov, finding himself at Nisim Davidov's wedding, didn't sing even one song from the *Shash maqâm,* notwithstanding the fact that he's a wonderful performer of that repertory. I don't blame him. I blame our immigrants, who so quickly have forgotten their beautiful and interesting musical history and have gone over to a musical culture that's completely foreign to them. The people yesterday noticed when, in a short length of time between the first and last appearance of Abram Tolmasov, there was a performance of the ensemble Maqam-i Nawa, directed by Ilyas Malayev. It had a great success, and all the people stood and surrounded those musicians. From that it was evident that the people, all the same, in their soul, have their ethnographic music. It would be not a bad idea for our Bukharan Jews who emigrated to think carefully about the danger of the disappearance of their old and interesting culture."

With that peroration, Ilyas retreated into a glum silence, and I was left to ruminate on his words. My first thought: wasn't Ilyas being more than a little patronizing in his notion that Bukharan Jews ought to perform and listen first and foremost to "Bukharan Jewish music," however one defined it? That notion reeked of Soviet cultural politics: Uzbek art by and for Uzbeks, Tajik art by and for Tajiks, and so on. And perhaps jealousy played some role in his condescension toward Tolmasov's performance. Ilyas had also had his moment in the spotlight—the stadium concerts with tens of thousands of admirers, the intimate relationship with the old Uzbek party bosses. The moment had passed, however, and Ilyas had been relegated to the status of a sideshow among the rising generation of Bukharan Jewish entertainers.

Ilyas's most committed audiences were arguably not in Queens but in the small halls in large cities around the United States and Western Europe where aficionados of "world music" came to hear the ensemble he called Maqam-i Nawa perform Bukharan Jewish "traditional music." The energy that Ilyas put into preparing for and performing at these events was astonishing, as if the fate of Bukharan Jewish culture rested entirely on his shoulders. Yet, for all their value as exhibitions of a great talent presenting the treasures of a little-known musical practice, such concerts of "traditional music" completely deterritorialized Ilyas's art. Not only had his music become detached from its social origins in Central Asia; it also had become increasingly removed from the Bukharan Jewish milieu of Queens. Whether the venue was Los Angeles or Leiden, Ilyas's audiences leaned heavily toward seekers, some alienated by the commodification of much mainstream music and searching for alternatives that they could find spiritually meaningful, others interested specifically in Jewish or Central Asian musical traditions. The sponsors were usually arts-presenting organizations carrying out mandates from philanthropic foundations or various levels of government to program multicultural arts events; sometimes they were Jewish groups seeking creative ways to make the full breadth of the Diaspora come alive for their overwhelmingly Eastern European-oriented constituencies: multiculturalism redux, if in a more limited sense. In these contexts, Ilyas's music existed not as an offering to a cohesive cultural community. Rather, it served an ideology—the ideology of multiculturalism, or, more precisely, the idea that artistic manifestations of cultural pluralism elevate the moral character of a liberal society. Thinking about the *Shash maqâm* in these conditions, one might have had a *déjà vu* of Central Asia: music in the service of ideology. Once again the *Shash maqâm* was being asked to be more than itself.

In that light—the light of "traditional" music as ideology, even if enlightened ideology—what about the wedding in Queens and the performance of Abram Tolmasov that Ilyas had dismissed as a great artist's pandering to the hoi polloi? Perhaps, if one could see and hear beyond Tolmasov's aqua suit and high-heeled boots, beyond the synthesizer and drum machine, perhaps that performance had embodied what was active and alive in Bukharan Jewish culture, what was truly traditional. What was Bukharan Jewish music, anyway? Leviche Babakhanov and others in the pantheon of Bukharan Jewish musicians had built their reputations by performing the music of the local Muslim population. Was it odd that musicians of talent who emigrated from Central Asia to Israel and New York should have invested themselves in the musical vernacular that surrounded them? These émigré musicians performed music that people wanted to hear and dance to, in other words, music endorsed by a kind of unspoken community consensus. They didn't present a prearranged "show" but, like Tohfaxân, Ma'ruf Xâja, and other musicians I'd met in Central Asia, actively interacted with their audiences, extemporizing, improvising, extending, or shortening pieces to play to the reaction of the crowd and the flow of the evening.

As Ilyas had made clear in his comments about "banal music," "traditional" musicians' adoption of the contemporary pop vernacular was not only a result of emigration. Tolmasov's performance in Queens had not been so very different from what I'd heard in Tashkent at the evening *bazm* in the basement of the city library—the *bazm* with the grossly amplified *tar,* synthesizer, and pop vocalists. In fact, the entire Queens event had seemed close in spirit to that Tashkent *bazm*. The banquet hall in the basement of the Tashkent Library had been a kind of Leonard's *manqué*. Leonard's brought fully to life a world of the imagination that had been but partially expressed in Tashkent only because the material means to express it more fully did not exist there. Perhaps these *bazm*s were indeed the vehicles for a new kind of musical traditionalism. Yet, if this was the case, there were also distinctions to be made between newer and older practices.

Glitz and pop music were merely the most obvious signs of deeper differences between the contemporary *toy,* whether in New York or Tashkent, and the older style of *toy*. And if one wanted to take the *toy* as a measure of Central Asian expressive and spiritual culture, then these differences between new and old might well run broad as well as deep. At their root was a social mutation clearly represented in music. The repertory that Turgun Alimatov had described as being "for God and the Prophet" in his aphorism about the purpose of music ("Once for God and the Prophet, once for merriment and dance") had receded from the *toy*. It had receded entirely from the Jewish *toy* and remained only residually in the early morning men's gatherings—the *âsh*—of some Muslim *toy*s. In a formal sense, the wedding at Leonard's had been a religious wedding, but music with any hint of spiritual depth had been unambiguously banished. The electronic snare drum rolls and synthesizer-produced oompah chords that accompanied the procession of family members down the aisle in front of the *huppah* had also trumpeted the departure of the sacred in music. Indeed, the Lubavitchers, like strictly orthodox Muslims, had no place for "religion in music," as Ilyas had characterized the *Shash maqâm*. In their ceremonies, it was not for music to serve as an expression of prayer and a link between the sacred and secular worlds, the role it had served for so long among both Muslims and Jews in Central Asia (here, "music" must be distinguished from the more narrowly defined liturgical chant, or cantillation). The musicians I have called fools of God were essential to that expression: men and women who devoted their lives to music as a service to community and to God—the God of Muslims and the God of Jews. Even though both Judaism and Islam existed in all their orthodoxy in Central Asia, stronger and most certainly older histories of local ceremony and celebration had mollified the more rigid attitudes of the religious

Tohfaxân and Ilyas in Queens.

toward music and entertainment. Now, with the "God and the Prophet" side of ceremonial music obliterated by canonical religion in New York and under pressure from Western-style youth culture in Transoxania, the *toy* had nowhere to go except toward the secular, toward "merriment and dance." As of this writing, it seems unlikely that *toy*s in Transoxania will come under pressure from Muslim activists, whose influence in Uzbekistan and Tajikistan is on the wane.

What was left for the fools of God whose musical world seemed to be in the process of disappearing? Ilyas Malayev, Tohfaxân Pinkhasova, Turgun Alimatov, Mutavakkil Burxanov—all of them had told me plaintively, "When I die, there will be no one to continue my tradition." Even more than the lack of a successor, I think, my friends were bemoaning the possibility that in the future society might no longer need their tradition. Musicians achieve artistic immortality through the continual recreation and rehearing of their art, and the idea that one's art could become superfluous, that listeners might approach it with indifference, is like a form of spiritual death.

But I am more optimistic about traditions. I do not accept the dire auguries of "the death of tradition" and "the disappearance of traditional worlds." Even the Soviet "struggle with the old," the centerpiece of the ideological campaign to uproot the "cursed past" of traditionalism—possibly the most massive such campaign the world has known—was not able to achieve its aim. In Central Asia, this campaign produced not a vibrant modern art but mass cultural disorientation—and lots of kitsch. Meanwhile, tradition turned out to be at once

285

more deeply rooted in local tastes and practices and more flexible and open to change than Soviet culture strategists could have imagined. Uzbeks, for example, largely turned their backs on officially sponsored "Uzbek national music." In its place they wanted the lyricism of a Khorezmian *suvâra,* the growl of a *baxshi* reciting a *dâstân,* the pungent rhythms of Bukharan *sâzanda*s thumping their *dâyra*s. These musics, with their strong and intrinsic sense of place, survived not through rigid adherence to local custom and convention— that is, to "tradition" in the narrow sense—but by serving an abiding need in people's inner lives: a need for identity and a sense of community.[3] Even the pop songs of Yulduz Usmanova—perhaps the closest that Uzbekistan presently has to a national music—are an epiphenomenon of the traditional, rooted in Yulduz's attachment to the concerns of everyday life.

Identities and communities, of course, change with time, and so do the traditional musics that serve them. Genres, styles, and techniques constantly evolve, and while traditions can and do really die when they no longer serve a social need, more commonly the energy of moribund traditions is redirected and reactivated in living cultural practices, as I had suggested to Ilyas in his moment of despair about the disappearance of *ghazalrâni.* Talented musicians transform expertise in one kind of music into expertise in another as they search for musical vitality and material sustenance. Abram Tolmasov, the *maqâm* singer turned pop musician, exemplified that kind of transformation. Ilyas, too, had used *maqâm* as a resource for popular music and had passed on his embrace of musical versatility to his children, Raj, the guitarist, and Nargis, the vocalist. As for Ilyas's much-beloved "classics," they hold the potential always to blossom into new life under the care of a master who, like Turgun Alimatov or Munâjât Yulchieva, can reinvent them with grace.

Still, even if the energy of traditions that have run their course can come alive in new forms, what about the aesthetic quality and authority of these forms? Ought one to include "O Sole Mio," the *pièce de résistance* of Abram Tolmasov's wedding performance, in the same category of Bukharan Jewish tradition as the *Shash maqâm* simply because Bukharan listeners like it and endorse it? If a society replaces its musical "high road" by a "low road"—especially one borrowed from elsewhere—does this substitution not reveal a certain lessening of cultural aspirations? In a century in which commerce and ideology have had such a profound influence on the fabrication of artistic taste, has the notion of serving "the higher" become irrelevant in music?

In Central Asia at least, Turgun Alimatov had suggested that "the higher" would take care of itself. "People always search for the best," he had said cryptically in explaining why students sought him out. But perhaps he should have said, "Eventually . . . some people . . . sometimes. . . ." Turgun had made it sound too easy. "The best" musicians might have survived and flourished, but the conditions in which they did so had exacted a formidable price: the long artistic hibernations brought on by the chill of ideological vilification—like Turgun's own years of exile from the radio station; the pathetically misdirected musical talents, set wrong by ideological visions that paid little heed to musical sensibilities. Abduhashim, the energetic but hopelessly constrained director of the Tashkent radio station *maqâm* ensemble, had been one of those.

And yet, in the end, perhaps it was precisely the simplicity of Turgun's formula that pointed toward the future of the fools of God. For Turgun, the essential condition of good music and good musicianship was *sâz,* harmony; not only harmony in music itself, but harmony between performers and listeners who delight in music of high moral purpose offered in an altruistic spirit of service unfettered by commerce or political ideology. As long as those kinds of listeners exist, the fools of God and their musical traditions will in some form live on. At the same time, the communities that embrace them will no longer be communities bound by a common language and territory. Rather, they will be scattered and disconnected, recruited through recordings, radio, concert tours, and music festivals. In these new conditions of performers and audiences separated by language and cultural background and often by the physical distance that is the consequence of recordings distributed worldwide, the fools of God may not always know the effects of their good works on those whom they touch. Perhaps, like the forty *abdâl*s of Sufi tradition, veiled from public view as they carry out their mission to guide humankind toward the just and good, the musical fools of God will have to serve without even the *raxmat*—the "thank you"—that, as Turgun had explained, was remuneration enough when he performed at a *toy.* Or perhaps the fools of God can hear our *raxmat,* even from far away.

GLOSSARY

abdâl	a friend of God or fool of God; a dervish or ascetic
aivân	covered porch or freestanding covered platform
aka	older brother; suffix attached to personal name to show respect
alap	improvised introductory section of an Indian *raga*
âruz	system of quantitative prosody that is the basis of classical poetry in Arabic, Persian, and Turkic languages
âsh	food; an early-morning quasi-religious gathering of men given separately by the fathers of both bride and groom before a marriage
attarchi	literally, "herder"; slang for a low-caste musician who lives outside the moral code that governs musicians' comportment
awj	the melodic apogee of a song
aya mulla	female mullah
bacha	dancing boy
barmâq	a common genre of Turkic folk poetry which in its canonical form is organized into quatrains, all of whose lines contain an identical number of syllables—most commonly 7, 11, or 15
basmachi	counterrevolutionary Muslim guerrilla fighters who resisted the Bolshevik conquest of Central Asia
baxshi	in Transoxania, a reciter of oral epic; also, a shamanic healer
bazm	feast; the culminating feast of a wedding
bukharche	the genre of dance-songs performed by the Bukharan *sâzanda*
chala	a Jew who converted to Islam under coercion but privately preserves elements of Jewish belief or practice

GLOSSARY

chang	struck zither, similar to a hammer dulcimer
chang-qobuz	metal jew's harp
chiltan	in the practice of the *baxshi* healer, an evil spirit
dâmla (*dâmulla*)	reverential name for a teacher
dâstân	heroic or lyrical epic poem
dasturxân	tablecloth; hospitality offered at the table
dâyra	tambourine; also, frame drum, usually with metal jangles attached to the wooden rim
dâyradast	in Bukhara, a male instrumental player who performs at weddings
dombra	short long-necked lute used by a *baxshi* to accompany the performance of oral poetry
doppi	square prayer cap worn by Uzbek and Tajik men
dutar	two-stringed, long-necked lute
duwâ	a prayer
fâl	diagnostic ritual performed by a *fâlbin*
fâlbin	fortune-teller
gap	intimate evening gathering of friends for conversation, food, and music
ghazal	form of lyrical poetry composed in distichs with a single rhyme
ghazalrâni	improvisational *rubato* in the performance of Bukharan classical songs
ghijak	spike fiddle
hafiz	male classical singer
hâwuz	small pool for drinking water placed at strategic locations in cities
ilm-i musiqi	Islamic musical science
ishân	Persian, "they"; a rural religious teacher whose authority comes not from a formal religious post but from a reputation for spiritual mastery among a circle of disciples

290

jinn	a spirit or fury
kaif	intense pleasure or delight
karnai	long ceremonial trumpet played at weddings
Kashgar rebab	plucked lute, adopted in Uzbekistan from the Uighur *rebab*
koch	ritual healing ceremony performed by a *baxshi*
kolkhoz	Russian acronym that means "collective farm"
korpacha	pad or mat filled with cotton used as a mattress or for sitting on the floor
kultprosvet	Russian acronym for "cultural enlightenment"
maddâh	a reciter-performer of lyrical poems, panegyrics, devotional odes
madrasah	theological college
mahalla	neighborhood, residential quarter
maqâm	the modal principle in Turco-Arabic and Persian art music; in Central Asia, used to designate any of the constituent suites of the *Shash maqâm* which are organized with attention to the succession of melodic types and metro-rhythmic genres (e.g., "Maqâm-i Nawâ")
mavrigi	"from Merv"; a vocal suite performed at men's *bazm*s by a *mavrigixân*
mehmânxâna	guest room
mehtar	in Bukhara, a performer of the *surnai;* also, a military orchestra consisting of *surnai*s, *karnai*s, and various sorts of drums played from a portico attached to the exterior wall of the *ark*; *mehtarlik* refers more generally to the prerevolutionary entertainer's guild that included musicians, artists, acrobats, and others
mullah	Muslim religious teacher
munâjât	a chanted or sung appeal to God
murid	disciple of an *ishân* or Sufi sheikh
muxammas	poetic blandishment traditionally bestowed upon women by a *sâzanda*; also, a form of lyrical poetry consisting of stanzas of five lines

GLOSSARY

nâla	melodic ornamentation
nân	round, puffy bread
naqsh	in the Zaravshan Valley, a wedding song; also, a song genre in the Khorezm *maqâm*
na't	a poem praising and expressing devotion to the Prophet Muhammad, sometimes set to music
nâwruz	Persian New Year's, coinciding with the vernal equinox
nay	wooden transverse flute (in Transoxania)
palav	pilaf
qalandar	wandering dervish connected to a loosely organized ascetic movement who performs didactic spiritual songs for alms; the genre of devotional poetry and songs associated with such singers
qâri	reciter of the Qur'an
qâshnay	musical instrument with single reed, double pipe
qobyz	two-stringed fiddle used by the *zhirau* to accompany oral poetry; also, the traditional instrument of the Karakalpak and Kazakh shaman (*baqsy*)
samâ	mystical concert and dance
samodeiatel'nost'	artistic "do-it-yourselfism"; in Soviet cultural praxis, amateur arts activities
satâ	bowed *tanbur*
sâzanda	female wedding performer
shahd	molasses; the first part of a *mavrigi* suite
sharia	exoteric Muslim religious law
shashlik	shishkebab (literally, "a sixsome")
Shash maqâm	six *maqâm*s; a compendium of instrumental and vocal pieces that embody classical Central Asian aesthetic ideals in music and poetry
sheikh	spiritual authority; spiritual master
Sufi	Muslim mystic

surnai	loud oboe, traditionally played at weddings
suvâra	in Khorezm, a song genre devoted to the expression of spiritual and lyric poetry
sybyzyk	short, single-reed pipe made from cane
taksim	improvised introductory section of a suite in Ottoman classical music
tanbur	plucked, long-necked lute with raised frets
tar	plucked stringed instrument from the Caucasus imported to Transoxania and used especially in Khorezm
tariqa	the spiritual path or method of the Sufi
terma	a short, orally composed poem, often improvised in the course of performance
toy	wedding; more broadly, a family ceremony marking life-cycle occasions including marriage, circumcision, first haircut of a boy, first placing of baby in cradle, first day of school, etc.
ustâ	master
usul	the rhythmic principle in Central Asian music; a particular rhythmic cycle
xalfa	in Khorezm, a female entertainer at weddings and other women's ceremonial occasions
xöömei	vocal style particular to Tuva and western Outer Mongolia in which a single vocalist simultaneously articulates an amplified harmonic and a drone fundamental tone
zhirau	in Karakalpakstan, a reciter of oral poetry who accompanies himself on the *qobyz*
zikr	remembrance; the repetition of divine names or religious formulas
ziyâfat	offering; a *gap,* or evening gathering for conversation, food, and music
ziyârat	pilgrimage to the tomb of a saint

NOTES

PREFACE

1. The historical evolution of the concepts of nationality and ethnicity in Central Asia has been widely discussed in scholarly literature. For important recent contributions, see Jo-Ann Gross, ed., *Muslims in Central Asia: Expressions of Identity and Change* (Durham: Duke University Press, 1992); Olivier Roy, "Ethnies et politique en Asie Centrale," *Revue de Monde Musulmane* 59–60, nos. 1–2 (1991): 17–36; and Ingeborg Baldauf, "Some Thoughts on the Making of the Uzbek Nation," *Cahiers du Monde Russe et Soviétique* 32, no. 1 (January–March 1991): 79–96.

2. Broader surveys of music in Central Asia were undertaken by Russian scholars: vol. 1 of Viktor Beliaev, *Ocherki po istorii muzykii narodov SSSR* (Moscow, 1962), available in English as *Central Asian Music,* trans. and ed. Mark Slobin and Greta Slobin (Middletown, Conn.: Wesleyan University Press, 1975); V. S. Vinogradov, *Muzyka Sovetskogo Vostoka: Ot unisona k polifonii* (Moscow: Sovetskii Kompozitor, 1968); T. S. Vyzgo, *Muzykal' nie instrumenty srednei azii: Istoricheskie ocherki* (Moscow: Muzyka, 1980); and I. Vyzgo-Ivanova, *Simfonichesko tvorchestvo kompozitorov srednei azii i kazakhstana (1917–1967)* (Moscow and Leningrad: Sovetskii Kompozitor, 1974).

3. For example, Soviet scholars who conducted ethnographic studies of contemporary cultural traditions with connections to religions (a topic that was implicitly off-limits to non-Soviet researchers) had to frame their work as demonstrating the atavistic existence of cultic practices that would eventually disappear in the face of proper atheistic education.

4. The compact discs are *Bukhara: Musical Crossroads of Asia,* Smithsonian/ Folkways 40050 (1990), and *Uzbekistan: Music of Khorezm,* UNESCO/Auvidis (1996).

5. OM's two completed manuscripts are musical biographies of Turgun Alimatov (who is discussed in chap. 1 of the present work) and Ilyas Malayev (discussed in chap. 7). The Alimatov biography is written in Uzbek, the Malayev biography in Russian. OM's third manuscript, in Uzbek, is devoted to the music of Khorezm.

1. TASHKENT

1. Eugene Schuyler, *Turkistan,* vol. 1 (New York: Scribner, Armstrong, 1877), 77.

2. Mit'hat Bulatov, the Chief Architect of Tashkent from 1940 until 1962, whose solidly classical structures would be as much at home in Central Europe as in Central Asia, complained to me in a conversation in 1993 that "everything you do as an architect [in Tashkent] is obligatory, determined by the need to build rapidly, and with limited materials. Architectural thinking doesn't operate, can't operate, in those conditions."

3. Mark Slobin visited Tashkent in 1968, 1969, and 1976. His meetings with Professor Karomatov and officials of the Tashkent Conservatory in 1976 under the auspices of an International Research and Exchanges Board "ad hoc grant to promote cultural exchanges" directly prepared the way for my acceptance to the IREX exchange program in 1977–1978.

4. Galina Kozlovskaya, "Dni i gody odnoi prekrasnoi zhizni: Vospominaniia o kompozitore Aleksee Kozlovskom," unpublished manuscript, 1990. In 1994, two excerpts from the manuscript were published in the Russian journal *Muzykal'naya Akademiya* (1994, nos. 1 and 3).

5. See Gordon D. McQuere, "The Theories of Boleslav Yavorsky," in McQuere, ed., *Russian Theoretical Thought in Music* (Ann Arbor: UMI Research Press, 1983).

6. In the years following the Second World War, Kozlovsky, despite his history of administrative exile, became a highly decorated cultural figure in Uzbekistan (People's Artist of the Uzbek SSR, Order of Lenin, Honorary Diploma of the Supreme Soviet of Uzbekistan, etc.). As one musicologist in Tashkent put it, "It was a paradox: they exiled him here and then rewarded him. That happened a lot."

7. The tulip festival of Isfara is described by the ethnographer O. A. Sukhareva in "Prazdnestva tsvetov u ravninnykh tadjikov (konets XIX–nachalo XXv.)," in V. N. Basilov, ed., *Drevnie obriady verovaniia i kulty narodov Srednei Azii* (Moscow: Nauka, 1986), 31–46. The broad outlines of Galina Longonovna's description correspond to Sukhareva's. Sukhareva, however, notes that on the second day of the festival, groups of men and women (separately) make pilgrimages to the mausoleums of local saints, giving it an Islamic as well as pagan caste.

8. Emir Alim Khan was not deposed by the Bolsheviks until August 1920. For a detailed chronicle of the complex political situation in Bukhara during the interregnum years, see Seymour Becker, *Russia's Protectorates in Central Asia: Bukhara and Khiva, 1865–1924* (Cambridge, Mass.: Harvard University Press, 1968).

9. Burxanov's account of Fitrat's defense of religion is somewhat questionable. His falling out with Lenin had more to do with his reformist political agenda than with issues about religious freedom.

10. Annemarie Schimmel notes in her wide-ranging study of Sufism, *Mystical Dimensions of Islam* (Chapel Hill: University of North Carolina Press, 1975), that "among the groups in the hierarchy the Forty have gained special prominence in Islam. Numerous stories are told about them, and there are local names in the Near East connected with their presence, such as *kìrklareli,* 'the county of the Forty,' in the European province of Turkey" (p. 202). The tradition of the *abdâl* has an analogy in that of the forty *chiltan*s, supernatural spirits who assume the form of men and, preserving their anonymity, influence the course of events in such a way as to protect people from misfortune. The *chiltan*s seem in turn to have been taken over from a pre-Islamic tradition in which they were considered not beneficent beings but evil spirits. OM and I found traces of this belief in our work with *baxshi*s in the north of Tajikistan (see chap. 6).

11. Alexander Djumaev (oral communication, November 1994) points out that the written treatises that comprised the tradition of *ilm-i musiqi* were probably always relatively limited in their distribution, even when they were being actively produced, and that the level of theoretical knowledge they represented most likely never engaged the musical ideas of most working musicians. Djumaev reports that in the 1930s, attempts had also been made in Soviet Central Asia to trace knowledge of the old theoretical tradition among classical musicians and that the results had been similar to our experience with Ma'ruf Xâja: no trace could be found. John Baily, who studied professional music and musicians in the city of Herat, Afghanistan, in the 1970s, found that in this important Khurasani center, "the science of music . . . was a version of Hindustani music theory" that took root in Herat after Indian court musicians were

brought to Kabul in the late nineteenth century, and Kabuli art music was adopted in Herat in the 1930s. Baily suggests that the imported Indian theoretical tradition did not so much replace an already extant comprehensive science of music as create one *ex nihilo* to provide a representational model for what the musician already knew informally. See Baily, *Music of Afghanistan: Professional Musicians in the City of Herat* (Cambridge: Cambridge University Press, 1988), chap. 4.

12. I am indebted to Jean During for this insight, which he elaborated in a series of lectures presented at Dartmouth College in 1993.

13. For details on Turkish-Iranian language contacts, see Gerhard Doerfer's entry, "Turkish-Iranian Language Contacts," in *Encyclopaedia Iranica,* vol. 5, fascicle 3 (Costa Mesa, Calif.: Mazda): 226–235.

14. The central source of my information about Rajabi is a semiofficial biography written in Uzbek and published in 1980: B. V. Axmedov, *Yunus Rajabi* (Tashkent, 1980).

15. Rajabi's primary informant was Barukh Zirkiev. Rajabi also transcribed parts of the *Shash maqâm* from Mikhail Tolmasov, Mikhail Mullakandov, Yakub Davidov, Gavril Mullakandov, Marafjân Tashpulatov, Sharaxam Shâumarov, Xâja Abdulazziz, and Dâmla Halim.

16. Rajabi's *Shash maqâm* was published in two separate series of musical transcriptions, the first in 1959 (*Özbek Xalq Muzikasi,* vol. 5, ed. I. A. Akhbarov) and the second, between 1966 and 1975 (*Shashmaqâm,* 6 vols., ed. F. M. Karomatov). I have called the second series the Karomatov edition, after its editor.

17. It is instructive to compare Turgun's *segâh* with the beginning of *Saraxbâr-i Segâh* recorded by the *maqâm* ensemble at the radio station (accompanying compact disc, track 3). The two pieces clearly display a strong degree of melodic resemblance in the low-register opening section (*darâmad*) and the middle-register section that follows (*miyânxâna*), yet Turgun's melodies seem much more refined and sharply etched than Rajabi's.

18. Scholars of oral traditions have lately begun to catch up to the traditions themselves with works such as Ruth Finnegan, "The Relation between Composition and Performance: Three Alternative Modes," in Tokumaru Yosihiko and Yamaguti Osamu, eds., *The Oral and the Literate in Music* (Tokyo: Academia Music, 1986), 73–87, which creates a theoretical context for distinguishing between the model of oral extemporization developed by Parry and Lord on the basis of their research on oral epic (elaborated in Albert Lord's now classic *Singer of Tales*) and the kind of memorized oral composition typical of much Central Asian music.

19. Yunus Rajabi had himself been a prolific song composer at the same time that he canonized the *Shash maqâm*.

20. Jean During, "Tradition and Modernity: A Matter of Taste," unpublished lectures delivered at Dartmouth College, 1993.

21. Babaev's decree was paraphrased in an article published in the Soviet Union's most prestigious music journal: S. Babaev, "Dekada uzbekskogo iskusstva; o rabote soyuza kompozitorov uzbekistana," *Sovetskaya Muzyka,* February 1952, 41–45.

22. For a detailed and objective account of the history and practice of Islam, in particular Sufism, in Transoxania, see O[l'ga] A[leksandrovna] Suxareva, *Islam v Uzbekistane* (Tashkent: Izdatel'stvo Akademii Nauk Uzbekskoi SSR, 1960).

23. These questions in fact are more like those commonly discussed in a mosque or *madrasah* than at Sufi gatherings.

24. In other discussions, Turgun-*aka* formulated the aphorism as "Gâh Allâh rasul, gâh ghamza usul."

25. This characterization comes from S. M. Demidov, *Sufism v Turkmenii (evoliutsiia i perezhitki)* (Ashxabad: Ylym, 1978), 112.

26. *Ishâns* frequently belonged to certain "holy" lineages that traced their origins to

the family of the Prophet, e.g., the *xâja*s or *sayyid*s. As a result, all members of these lineages were sometimes considered to be *ishân*s. This is what Xatamov had in mind when he said that he was from the "lineage of the *ishân*s."

27. The Jizzak Rebellion was one of a series of popular revolts that spread through Russian Turkestan in 1916, and in particular through the entire Jizzak District (*uezd*) of Samarkand Region (*oblast'*). The central cause of all of these rebellions was a decree of Tsar Nikolas II on the conscription of the male foreign population of the empire for various work projects connected to the military campaigns of the tsar's army in the First World War. The Jizzak Rebellion was conducted under the banner of a holy war (*gazavat*) against Russia. One person who helped inspire the rebellion was *ishân* Nazir-Xâja Abdusaliamov. Scholarly studies on the 1916 rebellions may be found in the following sources: A. V. Piaskovskii et al., eds., *Vosstanie 1916 goda v Srednei Azii i Kazakhstane. Sbornik dokumentov* (Moscow: Academy of Sciences of the USSR, 1960); Z. D. Kastel'skaia, *Osnovnye predposylki vosstaniia 1916 goda v Uzbekistane* (Moscow: Nauka, 1972); Kh. T. Tursunov, *Vosstanie 1916 goda v Srednei Azii i Kazakhstane* (Tashkent: Gosizdat UzSSR, 1962).

28. This text does not appear in any published edition of Yasawi's *Hikmat*. Xatamov found it in a chrestomathy published in 1941 (*Adabiyet darsligi,* or "Lessons in Literature") in which the poem is attributed to Yasawi.

29. An edition of Yasawi's *Hikmat* recently appeared in Kazakhstan. It is based on a printed edition first published in Kazan (*Dîwân-i Hikmat Yassawî,* Kazan: Kazan University Press, 1311/1893).

30. Xatamov ascribed the origin of the present-day vocal genre known as *katta ashula* to the *zikr maqâm.*

31. Xatamov noted that the *zikr maqâm* employed particular *usul*s (*qashqarcha, talqin', chârzarb, ufar*), as well as the melodies of particular *maqâm*s (*dugâh* and *bayât*).

2. BUKHARA

1. W. Barthold, *Turkestan down to the Mongol Invasion,* 4th ed. (London: E. J. W. Gibb Memorial Trust, 1977), 100.

2. Demetrius Charles de Kavanagh Boulger, *England and Russia in Central Asia* (London: W. H. Allen, 1879), 187–190.

3. Schuyler, *Turkistan,* vol. 2, 65, 70, and 82.

4. Djumaev's explanation of the events surrounding Uspensky's publication are detailed in Aleksandr Djumaev, "Power Structures, Culture Policy, and Traditional Music in Soviet Central Asia," *Yearbook for Traditional Music* 25 (1993): 43–50.

5. The semantic relationship of "Tajik" to "Persian" in discussions of Iranian language and literature in Bukhara is complex. Gerhard Doerfer, in his *Encyclopaedia Iranica* article "Turkish-Iranian Language Contacts" ("Central Asia XIV," vol. 5, fascicle 3, 226–235), describes "literary Tajiki" as "originally a language developed by the Soviets on the basis of dialects that differed most strongly from standard Persian . . ." (231). These dialects contain a large number of loanwords from Uzbek and are characteristic of northern regions of Tajikistan as well as areas of present-day Uzbekistan, e.g., Bukhara, where Uzbeks and Tajiks have a long history of intermingling. However, at the same time that literary Tajik and the spoken Tajik of northern regions is strongly influenced by Uzbek, standard literary Persian is still current in Bukhara. For example, intellectuals can switch quite easily from the spoken dialect to literary Persian when talking to Iranians or to foreigners. In Soviet Tajikistan, the adoption of Turkic-influenced Tajik as the republic's official language has contributed to the alienation of inhabitants of southern regions, where Uzbek linguistic influence is minimal.

6. O[l'ga] A. Suxareva, *K istorii gorodov bukharskogo khanstva* (Tashkent: Izdatel'stvo akademii nauk Uzbekskoi SSR, 1958), 88. For a survey of early sources on Jewish settlement in Bukhara, see Walter J. Fischel, "The Leaders of the Jews of Bokhara," in Leo Jung, ed., *Jewish Leaders (1750–1940)* (New York, 1953).

7. For a list of the "Twenty-One Prohibitions" against Jews that were commonly a part of traditional Muslim societies, see M. M. Abramov, *Bukharskie Evrei v Samarkande* (Samarkand: Cultural Center of the Bukharan Jews of Samarkand, 1993), 6–7.

8. Both Russian and Soviet census figures for "Central Asian" Jews are widely considered to have underreported their numbers. For example, the 1959 census reported approximately 28,000 Central Asian Jews, and the 1926 census, about 19,000. Independent estimates in the mid-1920s, however, were that 30,000–35,000 Bukharan Jews lived in Transoxania.

9. Beliaev's "History of the Musics of the Peoples of the USSR" is the survey whose first volume was translated into English by Mark and Greta Slobin and published in a somewhat abridged edition as *Central Asian Music*.

10. For detailed information about Bukhara's system of guilds, see the excellent account of Bukharan life at the beginning of the twentieth century by L[azar] I. Rempel', *Dalëkoe i blizkoe: stranitsi zhizni, byta, stroitel'nogo dela, remesla i iskusstva Staroï Bukhary* (Far and near: Pages from the everyday life, architecture, handicraft, and art of old Bukhara) (Tashkent, 1982).

11. The first musician to hold the position of *râtifaxâr* is said to have been Ata Jalâl, who worked in the stables of Emir Muzaffar.

12. Much later the recordings were remastered and released by Melodiya on an LP (M30–42091/92).

13. According to Rempel', up to twenty *bacha*s—most of them orphans—and around forty musicians (*dâyradast*) were housed in the *ghalibxâna*. These *bacha*s not only performed for the emir and his circle but, with permission from the *mirshab*, the chief of the night patrol in the emir's police force, also were loaned out to perform at the *toy*s of well-to-do Bukharans. In order to employ musicians or *bacha*s to perform at a *toy*, a host had to have written permission from the head of the *ghalibxâna* (*ghalib*), who acted as their booking agent. Permission was arranged by a middleman who specialized in that particular service. The *ghalibxâna* had carts to take musicians and their instruments to *toy*s around the city. Income from the *toy*s (which came from money which guests gave to performers) was distributed by the middleman who arranged the performance. In addition to paying musicians and dancers, the middleman paid cooks, tea-servers, and the men and women who went from house to house in advance of the *toy* announcing the festivities. This information was supplied orally by Mahmud Axmedov to Otanazar Matyakubov in 1994.

14. The term *mehtar* was used in two other senses in Bukhara: it denoted the military orchestra consisting of *surnai*s, *karnai*s (long trombones), and various sorts of drums that played from a portico attached to the exterior wall of the *ark*. *Mehtarlik* referred more generally to the prerevolutionary entertainers' guild that included musicians, artists, acrobats, and others (Djumaev, "Power Structures," 43). By contrast, in Khiva, *mehtar* (or *mehter*) referred to the "highest official appointed from among the Sarts," according to Yuri Bregel in "The Sarts in the Khanate of Khiva," *Journal of Asian History* 12, no. 2 (1978): 129.

15. Karl Reichl, in *Turkic Oral Epic Poetry: Traditions, Forms, Poetic Structure* (New York: Garland, 1992), describes the *maddah*—or *meddah*—as a "narrator . . . who is often a reader of texts rather than a 'singer of tales.'. . . The activity of . . . *meddah*s . . . was one of the main channels for the transmission of written poetry to a popular audience and hence also to oral singers" (88–89). For a classic survey of the *qalandar* and *maddâh,* see also A. L Troitskaya, "Iz proshlogo kalandarov i maddakhov v

uzbekistane," in G. P. Snesarev and V. N. Vasilov, eds., *Domusul' manskie verovaniia i obriadi v srednei azii* (Moscow: Nauka, 1975), 191–223.

16. For an analysis of current ideas about the correlation of musical taste and class, see Mark Slobin, *Subcultural Sounds: Micromusics of the West* (Hanover, N.H.: University Press of New England, 1993), 48–50.

17. For an example of Bukharan Torah cantillation, see Smithsonian/Folkways recording 400050, *Bukhara: Musical Crossroads of Asia,* track 10. The cantillation of Genesis 41: 11–21 (Joseph's interpretation of Pharaoh's dream) is performed by a *hazzan* in Tashkent (Yakub Meer Ochildiev, b. 1903) in a melodic mode that is not specifically Central Asian but clearly derives from a more universal style of cantillation.

18. *Ghairi Xudâ Yar Nadâram* appears on the recording *Music of the Bukharan Jewish Ensemble Shashmaqam: Central Asia in Forest Hills, New York,* Smithsonian/Folkways 40054.

19. The full song text is printed in Jean During, *Musique et mystique dans les traditions de l'Iran* (Paris and Teheran: Institut Français de Recherche en Iran, 1989), 219–220.

20. Iu. G. Petrash, *Ten' Srednevekov' ia* (The shadow of the Middle Ages) (Alma-Ata: Kazakhstan, 1981), 7.

21. A good example of such writing is Rempel', *Dalëkoe i blizkoe;* see esp. p. 69.

22. Jean During, in *La Musique traditionnelle de l'Azerbayjan et la science des muqams* (Baden-Baden, 1988), makes the same point in discussing changes in the nature of musical repertories and their relationship to patronage in Iran and Azerbaijan. He points out that nineteenth-century Qajar rulers and patrons supported lighter forms of music that were closer to local traditions and were much more integrated into public life than the aristocratic music of earlier times. In the reformation of Iranian and Azeri music in the nineteenth century, says During, the modes and rhythms that tended to survive and flourish were those that existed also in "la musique populaire." He characterizes the present-day great tradition music of Iran and Azerbaijan as having "conserved, or rediscovered a fundamental simplicity which makes for their originality and indicates links with primitive forms of popular traditions, despite their sophistication" (161).

23. While the Soviet vilification of the emirs has been subject to revisionism in post-Soviet Uzbekistan, few historians would go as far as Ari Babakhanov in toasting the enlightenment of the late Bukharan emirs.

24. Alexandre Bennigsen and S. Enders Wimbush, *Mystics and Commissars: Sufism in the Soviet Union* (Berkeley: University of California Press, 1985), 2.

25. Barthold, in "Geographical Survey of Transoxania" (published as a chapter of *Turkestan down to the Mongol Invasion*), provides a different name for this village: Rîwartün. He writes that it was mentioned in the fourteenth century as the residence of Bahâ'uddin Naqshband (129).

26. In 1985, Benningsen and Wimbush could write about the Naqshbandiya, "There is little evidence as to its activity in Uzbekistan and Tajikistan" (*Mystics and Commissars,* 9).

27. Ghafurjân, the Naqshbandi mullah whom OM and I befriended in Bukhara, said that Bahâ'uddin had been known sometimes to do the "loud" *zikr* after finishing the silent *zikr.* While the silent *zikr* became a norm of Naqshbandi practice, contemporary Naqshbandi groups practice both silent and loud *zikr.* An example of a loud *zikr* from a Naqshbandi *xânagâh* in Bosnia was recorded by the author in 1985 and may be heard on the Smithsonian/Folkways recording *Bosnia: Echoes from an Endangered World.*

28. For a thoughtful discussion of *hadith*s concerning music and, more broadly, of the status of music in Islam, see Jean During, *Musique et extase* (Paris: Editions Albin Michel, 1988), annexe II.

29. A Bukharan *qalandar* song may be heard on the Smithsonian/Folkways recording *Bukhara: Musical Crossroads of Asia.*

30. Definition adopted from Schimmel, *Mystical Dimensions of Islam,* 499. Rumî's *mathnawi* is the most famous in Bukhara, but Ghafurjân said that the *mathnawixân*s also recited *mathnawi*s by Jami and Nawâ'i.

31. In the musical culture of Herat, Afghanistan, which shares many features with that of Bukhara, *sâzanda* (or *sâzandeh*) refers to either male or female urban hereditary professional musicians. For a detailed study of male *sâzandeh*s in Herat, see Baily, *Music of Afghanistan.* For a valuable study of the lives of female *sâzandeh*s in Herat, see Veronica Doubleday, *Three Women of Herat* (Austin: University of Texas Press, 1990).

32. Barthold, *Turkestan,* 112.

33. Despite its name, the prosodic form of the *muxammas* is not the five-line *muxammas* proper but the four-line *rubaî,* with the rhyme scheme aaba.

34. *Mavrigi* also occurs as a musical term in regions other than Bukhara but with somewhat different meanings. For example, in Khorezm, *mavrigi* is also the name of a class of songs; in Baysun, it is understood to mean only the dance part of a *mavrigi.*

35. Z[oya] M. Tadjikova noted that "an especially large influx of [Iranian] immigrants occurred in the second half of the eighteenth century, when Emir Shah Murad, the ruler of Bukhara, undertook a series of raids on Khorasan and destroyed the Murghab dam, which for many centuries had nourished the Merv oasis, thus bringing about the ruin of the city of Merv (1784)" ("K voprosu o muzykal'nykh traditsiiakh bukharskikh mavrigikhânov," in *Kniga Barbada: Epokha i traditsii kul'tury* [Dushanbe, 1989], 166). Olga Suxareva notes that other Bukharan Irani were the descendants of slaves from Khurasan and northern Afghanistan freed by an agreement with the Russian government, while still others had moved individually and at various times from Iran to Bukhara (Suxareva, *K istorii gorodov bukharskogo khanstva,* 84).

36. Suxareva (*K istorii gorodov bukharskogo khanstva,* 82) notes that the Bukharan Irâni began calling themselves Fars after the so-called Shi'ite slaughter of 1910, when "strained relations between Bukhara's Sunnites and Shi'ites led to overtones of hostility and abusiveness in the use of the former names 'Irânî' and 'Marvî.'"

37. Tadjikova ("Voprosu," 167), whose fieldwork on the *mavrigixân* was conducted in 1983, points out that the sequence of the *mavrigi* was by no means fixed. The invariant principle of suite-building concerned the juxtaposition of the unmetered *shahd* with the metered pieces that followed in faster and faster tempos. The *shahd* could be followed by *shahd-i gardân,* or by *sarxâna* or *chârzarb.* Later came *makailik* and finally *gharaili.*

38. According to the article "Djamshîd" in the *Encyclopedia of Islam* (New Edition), the celebration of *nâwruz* is one of the two elements in the Djamshid legend that has come down to popular tradition and Persian poetry from older Avestan and Pahlavi sources.

39. Mahdi Ibadov did not provide names to distinguish the style of the unmetered *shahd* from that of the metered songs that follow; however, Tadjikova (169) mentions that *mavrigixân*s themselves distinguish a "Persian" style from a "Tajik" style.

40. Mark Slobin, in *Music in the Culture of Northern Afghanistan* (Tucson: University of Arizona Press, 1976), 172, notes that macaronic texts are also typical of music in the urban centers of northern Afghanistan, where Uzbeks and Tajiks have a long history of intermingling.

41. Jean During wrote about a similar phenomenon in postrevolutionary Iran in his important and eclectic work, *Quelque chose se passe. Le sens de la tradition dans l'Orient musical* (Paris: Verdier, 1995). See esp. 101–118.

3. THE SOUTH

1. OM's account of Gaipov's death is only one of several versions that circulate in Uzbekistan. Another version is that he was killed by "the organs" because he knew too

much about the Cotton Affair through his close connections to the Uzbek Central Committee. A third version is that he was given the opportunity to kill himself. A person who committed suicide (as opposed to being executed or imprisoned) did not have his personal property confiscated, and according to Alexander Djumaev, suicide was a not uncommon choice of arrested officials who wanted to leave an inheritance to their families. As Djumaev put it, "The Cotton Affair remains a dark chapter in Uzbekistan's recent history about which much is still unknown, and much is likely never to be known" (oral communication).

2. The ethnohistory of the Baysun region is exhaustively treated in B. Kh. Karmysheva, *Ocherki etnicheskoi istorii iuzhnykh raionov tadjikistana i uzbekistana* (Moscow: Nauka, 1976). Karmysheva confirms the presence in the Baysun region of the groups mentioned by local people.

3. Enver Pasha, a Turk who served as Minister of War in the Young Turk government during the First World War, came to Central Asia to assist the Bolsheviks in wiping out local opposition to Soviet rule. Later he switched sides and joined the *basmachi* with the aim of promoting pan-Turkism in Central Asia. He was killed in eastern Bukhara in 1922.

4. Abduxaliq's understanding of music as soul has ample precedent in Islamic mythology. The Sufi master Hazrat Inayat Khan, in his 1921 series of lectures entitled "Music" (*The Sufi Message of Hazrat Inayat Khan,* vol. 2 [Geneva: International Headquarters of the Sufi Movement, 1976], 79), quotes the Persian poet Hafiz on music as soul: "Hafiz, the great and wonderful Sufi poet of Persia, says, 'Many say that life entered the human body by the help of music, but the truth is that life itself is music.' What made him say this? He referred to a legend which exists in the East and which tells how God made a statue of clay in His own image, and asked the soul to enter into it; but the soul refused to be imprisoned, for its nature is to fly about freely and not to be limited and bound to any sort of capacity. The soul did not wish in the least to enter this prison. Then God asked the angels to play their music, and as the angels played the soul was moved to ecstasy, and through that ecstasy, in order to make the music more clear to itself, it entered this body. And it is told that Hafiz said, 'People say that the soul, on hearing that song, entered the body; but in reality the soul itself was song!'"

5. In *Turkic Oral Epic Poetry: Traditions, Forms, Poetic Structure,* Karl Reichl, citing the Russian scholar V. M. Zhirmunskii, wrote that "although no known Uzbek *baxshi* of this century combined the art of singing with the art of healing, older singers did in the 1940s still remember such a union of singer and shaman in former times" (65). The etymology of the word *baxshi* is complex. According to Reichl, the term denoted "a scholar and teacher, in particular a Buddhist teacher," in Old Uighur. Reichl adds that "the most likely etymology for this word is Ancient Chinese *pâk-śi* (Modern Chinese *bo-shi*)" (64–65). In the Timurid period, a *baxshi* was a non-Muslim bureaucrat who worked for the Mongols and preserved the use of Old Uighur script. Later the meaning "bureaucrat" began to drop out (although in Urdu it still means "bureaucrat"). According to Walter Feldman (oral communication), the use of *baxshi* as "performer" seems not to have occurred before the seventeenth century.

6. According to several sources, in parts of Surxandarya, the *baxshi* is still called *yuz bâshi,* literally "commander of 100," a rank in the army of the Bukharan emirs given to *baxshi*s because under the Emir, some *baxshi*s received the state salary of a *yuz bâshi.*

7. The Qongrad population of Transoxania is divided into two primary groups; one resides in Surxandarya and Qashqadarya, the other in northern Khorezm and Karakalpakstan. The historical relationship between the two groups is not completely clear. The Qongrad epic tradition of Karakalpakstan is discussed in chap. 4.

8. The refrain line, also called motif-line or key line, is a prominent feature not only of the *terma* but also of the longer and more complex *dâstân*s. See Walter Feldman, "The

Motif-Line in the Uzbek Oral Epic," *Ural-Altaische Jahrbücher* 55 (1983): 1–15, and the section "Thematic Patterning" in chap. 7 of Karl Reichl, *Turkic Oral Epic Poetry.*

9. Tuvan *xöömei* may be heard on a number of widely available recordings. The widest stylistic variety of solo *xöömei* is on the Smithsonian/Folkways recording *Tuva: Voices from the Center of Asia.*

10. For a detailed study of text generation in the oral *dâstân* of Qahhâr *baxshi*, see Walter Feldman, "Two Performances of the Return of Alpamish: Current Performance-Practice in the Uzbek Oral Epic of the Sherabad School," *Oral Tradition* 20 (1996).

11. Qahhâr takes considerable liberties with the natural speech accents and rhythm of his text in order to fit each poetic line into the steady 6/8 meter of the *dombra* accompaniment. Throughout the *terma*, Qahhâr plays with the relationship of text rhythm and musical rhythm, creating subtle desynchronizations of vocal rhythm and *dombra* rhythm when accented text syllables are shifted to unaccented rhythmic beats. A clear example is in lines 16–18.

12. Qahhâr noted that *baxshi*s, like performers of *maqâm*, use the term *awj* to designate a section of a musical item set in a high tessitura. In the *dâstân*, Qahhâr explained, it is usually in the third part that the voice starts to climb higher, while in the fourth part, it descends. The *baxshi*'s *awj*, however, is only moderately higher than the pitch level from which it ascends. *Baxshi*s and their audiences most typically use the term *awj* to convey a somewhat different and more local meaning. For example, a *baxshi* who performs "with *awj*" is one who performs with force or self-assurance.

13. Examples of narrative instrumental music available on recordings include *"Sygyt: Lament of the Igil"* (*Huun-Huur-Tu: 60 Horses in My Herd*, Shanachie 64050) and "Qâradali" (*Uzbekistan: Music of Khorezm*, Auvidis/UNESCO).

4. KHOREZM

1. *Suvâra* literally means "horseback rider." The link between the musical genre and horseback riding is not clear, but the image of a galloping rider may represent a state of spiritual freedom and ecstasy; or perhaps the horseback rider is riding a heavenly horse.

2. The molding of the Khorezmian character must have been influenced by more than the effects of climate, for other, more stereotypically introverted Central Asian peoples live in similar climatic conditions.

3. In post-Soviet Uzbekistan, the title *hakim* has been used generically to replace that of First Secretary, both at the district (*tuman*) and regional (*vilâyat*) level.

4. In this respect, the *suvâra* is very much like the *katta ashula*, popular in the Ferghana Valley, which Arif Xatamov told us corresponds in vocal style and content to the chanting of a *hafiz* during *zikr* but exists as an independent musical genre. A mullah in Khorezm (Sa'id Mahmud, b. 1906), told us that *suvâra* had also been sung during the ceremony of *zikr.* But Sa'id Mahmud's description of a Khorezmian *zikr* differed in important ways from the most common ceremonial forms of the *zikr* among Sufis. Sa'id Mahmud said that in prerevolutionary Khiva, *zikr* had meant a gathering, held, for example, in the *xânâqah* of a *madrasah*, that featured *tafsir* (hermeneutics), readings from the Qur'an, the singing of spiritual poetry by poets such as Bedil and Hafiz (i.e., *suvâra*), and performance on the *dutar* and *tanbur.* "Music wasn't *haram* [illicit]," said Said Mahmud. "It's not written in the Qur'an that music is forbidden. Music gives pleasure for man. It's *mumiyo* [a kind of balm] for the brain. But there were no rhythmic body movements, no chanting at the *zikr.* Everything was peaceful." Sa'id Mahmud contrasted the urban *zikr* conducted by a mullah to the rural *jahr* conducted by an *ishân.* As a mullah, he had a low opinion of *ishân*s. "They weren't educated," he said. "They

didn't read books. And there's nothing in the Qur'an that supports the loud chanting and crying that went on during the *jahr.*" For Sa'id Mahmud, neither the practice of *zikr* nor that of *jahr* in prerevolutionary Khorezm was linked to a particular brotherhood or spiritual lineage. For example, he regarded Kubrawi, the twelfth-century Khorezmian religious figure who gave his name to the Kubrawiya *suluk,* not as a Sufi sheikh but as a *tafsirxân* (interpreter of texts) and a great mullah.

5. A 1910 Russian translation of the so-called *Diwana-i Mashrab,* a kind of folk biography of Mashrab that includes poems and stories attributed to him as well as stories about him, has been published in Tashkent (*Divana-i-Mashrab,* trans. and ed. N. S. Lykoshin [Tashkent: Gafur Gulyam, 1992]). The translation and its republication are an indication of Mashrab's prestige and abiding popularity in Central Asia—and not only among Uzbek-speakers.

6. Like the *maqâm,* the *suvâra* repertory was systematized at some time in the past into a closed set of repertory items. The *suvâra* system, however, is considerably smaller than that of the *maqâm.* Khorezm has its own *maqâm* repertory, which differs in certain respects from the *Shash maqâm.* For a detailed comparative analysis of the Khorezm *maqâm* and the Bukharan *Shash maqâm,* see Angelika Jung, *Quellen der traditionellen Kunstmusik der Usbeken und Tadshiken Mittelasiens* (Hamburg: Karl Dieter Wagner, 1989). The *suvâra* system contains five principal melodic items and about twenty shorter items, called *sawt,* all of them designated by Persian-language titles: (1) Tan-i ["body"] Suvâra + *sawt* [also called Ona ("mother") Suvâra, Tajik Suvâra (because Tajik texts were used), or Katta ("big") Suvâra]; (2) Chapandaz Suvâra + *sawt;* (3) Kajhang Suvâra + *sawt;* (4) Yak Parda Suvâra + *sawt;* (5) Xush Parda Suvâra + *sawt.* A performance of *suvâra* normally includes a principal melodic item plus one or more *sawt*s set to the same *usul* (metro-rhythmic genre) but played at a faster tempo (the five principal *suvâra*s are not in themselves metro-rhythmic genres like the constituent *shu'be*s of a *maqâm* suite; rather, each *suvâra* is set to one and the same *usul*). Including the twenty *sawt*s, there are in all only twenty-five separate *suvâra* melodies, but these may be performed to hundreds of different texts.

7. Bâla *baxshi* had distinguished two *dukkan*s—literally, two "shops," or styles—of performing Khorezm *dâstân:* Shirvani and Irani. In the Irani style, the *baxshi* accompanies himself on a *dutar,* much the way the *baxshi*s of Qashqadarya and Surxandarya accompany themselves on the *dombra* (the Irani style shows many affinities to the Khurasani and Turkmen style of *dâstân* performance documented on the compact disc *Turkmen Epic Singing/Köroglu,* recorded by Slawomira Zheranska-Kominek and released by Auvidis/UNESCO). In the Shirvani style, the *baxshi* plays the *tar* and is accompanied by a violin and *dâyra.* The Shirvani instrumental trio is analogous to the classic *mugam* trio of Azerbaijan (which contains a *kemanche* instead of a violin and a *daf* instead of a *dâyra*).

8. The purported existence of seventy-two *name*s is most certainly not based on an empirical cataloguing of melodic forms or tune families. Rather, as John Baily notes in describing the seventy-two *maqâm*s performed by *sornâ* players in nineteenth-century Herat, Afghanistan, "Seventy-two is an auspicious number in Persian culture" (*Music of Afghanistan,* 18). Another example of a closed musical system of seventy-two items is the seventy-two *melakarta*s of south Indian music theory. The systematic properties of the *dâstân name*s are only now beginning to be analyzed by Uzbek scholars, and their work has not yet resulted in any publications.

9. Julian Baldick, *Imaginary Muslims: The Uwaysi Sufis of Central Asia* (New York: New York University Press, 1993), 1.

10. In *Imaginary Muslims* (18), Baldick writes of other purported tombs of Sultan Uways: 'The eastern Iranian traveller 'Ali Harawi (d. 1215), in his *Guide to Places of Pilgrimage,* which is based on journeys which he made in the 1170s, notes tombs of

Uways at Damascus (seen by other authors, but today no longer there), Raqqa (also in Syria), in Egypt, at Alexandria, and in Diyarbakr in south-eastern Turkey."

11. Karl Reichl, in *Turkic Oral Epic Poetry,* provides a brief artistic biography of Jumabay (p. 66) and notes that he "went to school for seven years."

12. Abdurauf Fitrat, *Ozbek Klasik Musikasi va uning Tarixi* (Samarkand/Tashkent, 1927).

13. Abdulxamit Raiymbergenov and Saira Amanova, *Kui Qainary/Golosa Narodnykh Muz* (Almaty: Öner, 1990), 15.

14. For an overview of Maxtum Quli's life and work, see Walter Feldman, "Interpreting the Poetry of Mäkhtumquli," in Gross, ed., *Muslims in Central Asia,* 167–189.

15. The most thorough recent study of the *Yedigei* (*Idige*) epic is in Devin DeWeese, *Islamization and Native Religion in the Golden Horde* (University Park, Penn.: Pennsylvania State University Press, 1994), 411 ff., which includes a range of references to earlier *Idige* studies.

16. The Bâbâ Tughul of Jumabay's account is presumably a variant of the figure of Baba Tükles, discussed by DeWeese in *Islamization and Native Religion.* "Baba Tükles," writes DeWeese, "was the object of a truly remarkable range of narrative elaboration, popular devotion, geneaological appropriation, and saintly and shamanic invocation, among the peoples of the western half of the Inner Asian world" (5).

5. THE UPPER ZARAVSHAN AND YAGNÂB

1. These visitors have left a considerable bibliography on Yagnâb, most of it in Russian. Among the most notable works whose focus is ethnography are M. S. Andreev, *Materiali po etnografii Yagnoba* (Dushanbe, 1970); A. N. Kondaurov, "Otchet ob ekspeditsii Instituta antropologii, arkheologii i etnografii Akademiia nauk SSSR po izucheniiu zhilishch Yagnobtsev i gornykh Tadjikov," *Sovetskaia Etnografiia* 6 (1937): 11–116; N. G. Mallitskii, "Yagnobtsi," *Isvestiia Turkestanskogo otdelenii Russkogo Geograficheskogo obshchestva* 17 (1924): 165–178; and E. M. Peshchereva, *Yagnobskie etnograficheskie materialy* (Dushanbe: Donish, 1976). The only published work on music in Yagnâb is a brief report: Zoya Tadjikova, "Muzyka tadjikov Yagnoba," in *Tezisy dokladov na sessii, posviashchennoi itogam polevykh etnograficheskikh i antropologicheskikh issledovanii v 1974–75gg.* (Dushanbe, 1976), 274–275.

2. If Tughral and Aini in fact had a bad relationship, as the local Zasun version of Tughral's life proposes, these bad feelings were not widely publicized. For example, Aini included Tughral's verse in his chrestomathy of Tajik poetry published in 1926.

3. *Komsomoletz Tajikistana,* October 10, 12, 14, 1990.

4. Panfilov points out that before the resettlement, a gradual out-migration of Yagnâbis to other parts of Tajikistan had been going on for decades as a natural consequence of population growth: as the valley's population reached a point beyond which the geographically limited grazing and farming land could not adequately support more herders and farmers, younger Yagnâbis left. Panfilov estimates that as many as 20,000 Yagnâbis may be scattered throughout Tajikistan, while the population of Yagnâb itself was around 3,200 before the resettlement.

5. Yagnâbis use the Tajik word *dilshekast* for "melody."

6. The same song, with a substantially different text, is transcribed in During, *Musique et mystique dans les traditions de l'Iran* (200–201). During, who recorded his version in Pakistan from a Baluchi member of the Cheshti Sufi order, notes that he also recorded a version in Khurasan. The song's 7/8 meter, he adds, is rare for Iran and Baluchistan but common for Central Asia.

7. Sattâr was using "Tajik" to describe spoken language and "Persian" to describe literary language.

8. The term *âxun* (Persian *axond:* "learned man," "teacher") is also used in the Ferghana Valley of Uzbekistan to mean "bard." It is cognate with Kazakh and Kyrgyz *aqin*, also "bard."

9. Yu. N. Nuraliev, "Abu Ali Ibn Sînâ o teorii Mizadja (natury)," *Isvestiia akademii nauk Tadjikskoi SSR, otdelenie biologicheskikh nauk* 80, no. 3 (1980): 25–34.

10. The existence of an analogous practice in the traditional Russian wedding leads to intriguing speculation about early contacts between Slavs and Iranians. In the Russian wedding, the bridegroom is called *kniaz'* (prince) and his male attendants are called by other noble titles.

11. Angelika Jung, in *Quellen der traditionellen Kunstmusik der Usbeken und Tadshiken Mittelasiens,* mentions various descriptions of *naqsh* in fifteenth–eighteenth-century manuscript sources and provides a transcription of a contemporary *naqsh* from the 1958 edition of the Khorezm *maqâm* (210–213). The transcription suggests that the Khorezm art song *naqsh* is far more elaborate than the wedding *naqsh* of the Upper Zaravshan. J. Rabiev and Z. M. Tadjikova, in *Uratiubinskii variant naksha* 20, no. 4 (1990): 27–37, also discuss manuscript sources that mention *naqsh,* admitting that from the descriptions it is difficult to establish what the early *naqsh* might have sounded like.

12. The men's *naqsh* are a mirror image of the *yâr-yâr* wedding songs sung by women, which are also grouped into cycles organized according to the principle of progression from sacred to worldly.

13. Rabiev and Tadjikova (see n. 11) offer the following sequence for the *naqsh* cycles of Ura-Tyube: *naqsh-e kalân, naqsh-e mulla, naqsh-e xurd.* In Dargh, however, the terms *naqsh-e kalân* and *naqsh-e xurd* were not used, and in two separate recording sessions *naqsh-e mulla* was performed as the first song in the cycle. This first song was also referred to as *peshrav,* which is used synonymously with *naqsh-i mulla* to mean a *naqsh* sung to a classical text. Our first recordings of *naqsh* in Dargh were in 1991, in the performance of three singers: Mirzâsaid Xâlmirzâ, Niyazi Bâbâ (b. 1959), and Jumâi Bâbâ (b. 1944). Returning to Dargh in 1994, we recorded *naqsh* in the performance of a group of eight men ranging in age from thirty to seventy-five that did not include the singers recorded in 1991. The 1991 singers performed three *naqsh,* while in 1994 the group of eight men performed five *naqsh,* including the three performed in 1991. For these three, text and tune were essentially identical in the two recordings.

14. Rabiev and Tadjikova discuss the same *naqsh-e mulla* and mention that they heard it referred to as *Naqsh-e Mulla Jâmi,* i.e., the *naqsh-e mulla* of the fifteenth-century Herati poet Jâmi. However, they explain the attribution as the result of the popular custom of crediting classical poets with the authorship of anonymous texts, even when these texts are most certainly the work of poetasters or epigones.

15. Rabiev and Tajikova (33–34) note that the text is composed according to the (rarely found) quantitative *âruz* verse meter *hazaj-e musamman-e akhrab* ($\_\_$ v/v$\_\_\_$/ v$\_\_$/v$\_$) and that the pattern of long and short syllables in the text matches perfectly the long and short rhythmic values in the melody. For example, the first line of text can be scanned as follows:

$$\_\_ \ \text{v} \ / \ \text{v} \_ \_ \_ \ / \ \text{v} \_ \_ \_ \ / \ \text{v} \_$$

av- val zi xu- dâ go- ya-   mu, du-yum zi   ra-sul

16. As performed, the *naqsh* text continued on for over thirty lines.

17. The best estimates in Central Asia are that about 20,000 civilians died in the civil war.

18. Central Asian instrumental polyphony is typically characterized by the parallel, or near parallel, movement of two melodic lines, by the movement of one melodic line against a drone, or by some combination of the two.

19. The *naqsh* is transcribed in Rabiev and Tajikova (29–33) from the singing of a group of elderly men in 1963. Vinogradov's *yâr-yâr* is in *Muzyka Sovetskogo Vostoka*, 87.

20. In *The Sufi Orders in Islam* (Oxford: Oxford University Press, 1971), J. Spencer Trimingham writes at some length about the Qâdiriya and provides an appendix listing Qâdiri groups in a number of countries, but neither text nor appendix offers clues about the *silsila* (transmission) of the Qâdiriya in Transoxania, nor about the practice of *zarb*. Khaliq Ahmad Nizami, in "The Qâdiriyyah Order," in Seyyed Hossein Nasr, ed., *Islamic Spirituality: Manifestations* (New York: Crossroad, 1991), 23, mentions that among the Qâdiriya, *zikr* "may be performed . . . sitting in circles after morning and afternoon prayers" (as opposed to the more typical practice in which *zikr* is performed on Thursday evening or after the Friday midday prayer).

6. SHAHRISTAN

1. V. N. Basilov, "Dva varianta sredneaziatskogo shamanstva," in *Sovetskaia Etnografiia* 4 (1990): 71, and Suxareva, *Islam v Uzbekistane*, 62, both note that the healing ritual may be called by a variety of local names, all of which derive from the Turkic verb *kochmak* (move, travel, migrate): *koch, koch-koch, kochurma, kochuruk*. Basilov suggests a relationship between these words and the term *kovuch-kovuch*, which appears in a description of a shamanic séance in the eleventh-century *Divanü lughat-it-türk* of Mahmud Kashgari.

2. Suxareva, *Islam v Uzbekistane*, 40.

3. For a detailed study of a less stable and more antagonistic relationship between shamanic healers and Islamic authority in Central Asia, see Viviane Lièvre and Jean-Yves Loude, *Le Chamanisme des Kalash du Pakistan* (Paris: Editions du CNRS, 1990), a superb study of a small group in the Chitral district of northern Pakistan who have preserved an ancient tradition of polytheism surrounded by Muslims.

4. In "A Muslim Shaman of Afghan Turkestan," *Ethnology* 10, no. 2 (1971): 70, Micheline and Pierre Centlivres and Mark Slobin describe a similar *zikr*-like phase in a *baxshi* séance in northern Afghanistan. According to the authors, this phase was called *sobkhat kardan*, or "conversation (with the spirits)."

5. Working in the 1920s in Ura-Tyube, about fifteen miles from Shakhristan, O. A. Suxareva ("Perezhitki demonologii i shamanstva u ravninnykh tadzhikov," in G. P. Snesarev and V. N. Basilov, eds., *Domusul' manskie verovaniia i obriady v srednei azii* [Moscow: Nauka, 1975], 12–13) also found a tripartite division of spirits. Suxareva's three categories, however, were a bit different from those provided by Nasri-oi and Turdijân (who were in agreement on categories of spirits). It is interesting that Suxareva's fieldwork on shamanism and demonology, conducted largely in the 1920s, was not published until 1975. In an introduction to her report that explains the rationale of her work, Suxareva concludes by pointing out that her research "could be useful in the work of providing atheistic education to the workers," as well as in showing "how far the Tajik people have come in their cultural development during Soviet times" (11); in other words, how far they have moved away from primitive religious beliefs toward enlightened atheism. This sort of ideological spin, typically isolated in the introductory section of Soviet-era ethnographies dealing with religious practices and beliefs, was *de rigueur* for scholarly publications. Scholars were required to present ritual and ceremonial practices as vestiges of ancient cults, superstitions, or magical beliefs that would inevitably succumb to the rationality of atheism, if only atheistic education could be broadly enough deployed and the reactionary forces opposing it could be eliminated.

6. This view is supported by V. N. Basilov, a leading Russian ethnographer of Siberian and Central Asian shamanism ("Dva varianta sredneaziatskogo shamanstva," *Sovetskaia Etnografiia* 4 [1990]: 73). Basilov wrote "that ritual dance was characteristic of shamanic traditions of the Iranian-speaking population of Central Asia and Kazakhstan. Even several centuries ago, dance as an element of shamanic ritual could have been widely extant. Its decline was precipitated first by the influence of the Turkic-speaking population. Here it is appropriate to remember that until the nineteenth or twentieth century, dancing was foreign to the culture of the once-nomadic and seminomadic peoples in the region, but characteristic of the settled population. Second, dancing could have disappeared from the shamanic cult as the result of the gradual Islamization of shamanism. Uighurs told [the Russian Orientalist and Buddhist scholar] S. F. Oldenburg [1863–1934] that dancing and other shamanic activities are opposed to the *shariat.* Evidently that was the point of view of the local clergy. However, as shamanic ritual absorbed new Islamic elements, it also absorbed the Sufi *zikr.* The *zikr,* with its cries and specific body movements, apparently became established in shamanic ritual on already well-prepared ground: it became a substitute for shamanic dancing."

7. See, for example, Suxareva, *Islam v Uzbekistane,* 50–51; M. Köprülü, "L'Influence du chamanisme turco-mongole sur les ordres mystiques musulmans," *Mémoire Institut de Turcologie Université Stamboul* (Istanbul, 1929); M. Molé, "La danse extatique en islam," *Les Danses sacrées* (Paris, 1963).

8. See A. L. Troitskii, "Zhenskii zikr v starom Tashkente," in *Sbornik muzeia antropologii i etnografii,* vol. 7 (Leningrad, 1927).

9. When asked whether she had ever participated in *samâ,* Turdijân replied, "No, it's not our road. It's not a good idea to go to a place where someone has died—not for three days. If we go there—to some relative's house—we don't eat there. People bring us food from a neighboring house, or we go somewhere else to eat. We never participate in the *samâ.* Death is an evil event. If we see a dead person, we won't be able to cure people. We have to start again—repurify ourselves, do a sacrifice and a *koch,* and sit again in *chilla* for seven, fifteen, or twenty-one days."

10. Basilov, "Dva varianta sredneaziatskogo shamanstva."

11. Ibid., 70.

12. For a detailed study of the *dombra/dumbrak/dambura,* see Mark Slobin, *Music in the Culture of Northern Afghanistan,* 83–88.

7. QUEENS

1. The work of Jewish "missionaries" in Bukhara, including the Moroccan rabbi Joseph Ma'man, who arrived there at the end of the eighteenth century and stayed for sixty-one years, is described by Walter J. Fischel in "The Leaders of the Jews of Bokhara," in Jung, ed., *Jewish Leaders (1750–1950).*

2. Nisim is a fictitious name. The names of the bride and groom are also fictitious.

3. The protean nature of tradition seems to have remained opaque to many scholars and cultural strategists from the former Soviet Union whose views of tradition have been strongly colored by the ideologically charged Marxist-Leninist opposition of "tradition" and "modernity." An example of such a scholar whose work is available in English is Sergei Poliakov; see his *Everyday Islam: Religion and Tradition in Rural Central Asia,* ed. Martha Brill Olcott (Armonk, N.Y.: M. E. Sharpe, 1992).

BIBLIOGRAPHIC & DISCOGRAPHIC GUIDE

Primary sources are identified in the notes; this guide describes recordings and publications in English, French, and German whose focus is Central Asian music and musical life. It does not include scholarly work on Central Asia that stems from other disciplines—history, political science, literary studies, art history, linguistics—bibliographies of which are available elsewhere.

I. MUSICAL ETHNOGRAPHIES OF CENTRAL ASIA

Fieldwork conducted in Afghanistan in the 1960s and 1970s led to the publication of four valuable musical ethnographies. Mark Slobin, *Music in the Culture of Northern Afghanistan* (Tucson: University of Arizona Press, 1976), surveys the region's music subcultures—including those of Uzbeks and Tajiks—as they existed before the Soviet occupation. John Baily, *Music of Afghanistan: Professional Musicians in the City of Herat* (Cambridge: Cambridge University Press, 1988), focuses on urban male hereditary musicians and, like Slobin, provides a sense of both important similarities and significant differences between the musical cultures of Afghanistan and Transoxania. Veronica Doubleday, *Three Women of Herat* (Austin: University of Texas Press, 1990), is a fascinating memoir of the author's friendship with women she met while living in Herat in the 1970s with her husband, John Baily. Hiromi Lorraine Sakata, *Music in the Mind: The Concepts of Music and Musician in Afghanistan* (Kent, Ohio: Kent State University Press, 1983), analyzes local interpretations of the concepts "music" and "musician" in three locations: Herat, Faizabad, and Khadir.

Jean During, *Musique et mystique dans les traditions de l'Iran* (Paris-Teheran: Institut français de recherche en Iran, 1989), is an important study of the musical traditions of Iranian Sufi orders, some of which have strongly influenced spiritual and expressive culture in Transoxania.

Mark and Greta Slobin, *Central Asian Music*, a partial translation of volume 1 of Viktor Beliaev, *Ocherki po istorii muzyki narodov SSSR* (Sketches of the music history of the peoples of the USSR) (Middletown, Conn.: Wesleyan University Press, 1975), is the only book-length work by a Russian specialist on Central Asian music that is available in English. *Central Asian Music* surveys musical genres and repertories associated with the major ethnic group within each of the former Soviet Central Asian republics (Kazakh, Kyrgyz, Turkmen, Tajik, Uzbek), while avoiding discussion of the music of minority ethnic groups—for example, Bukharan Jews, Uighurs, Koreans—and glossing over issues raised by musical genres and repertories that cannot be neatly correlated with particular ethnic groups.

II. THE HISTORIOGRAPHY OF CENTRAL ASIAN MUSIC

Amnon Shiloah, *Music in the World of Islam: A Socio-cultural Study* (Detroit: Wayne State University Press, 1995), contains a brief entry on Central Asia but perhaps is more useful, at least from the Central Asian point of view, for its extensive "thematic bibliography." *The New Grove Encyclopedia of Music and Musicians* (London: Macmillan, 1980) discusses Central Asia in two articles: "Mode," section V, 2(i): "Modal Entities in Western Asia and South Asia"; and "Union of Soviet Socialist Republics, XI, 1: "Central Asian peoples." Angelika Jung, *Quellen der traditionellen Kunstmusik der Usbeken und Tadshiken Mittelasiens* (Hamburg: Karl Dieter Wagner, 1989), deftly summarizes and analyzes extant historical sources pertaining to the development of the Transoxanian *maqâm* repertories. Alexander Djumaev, "Power Structures, Culture Policy, and Traditional Music in Soviet Central Asia," *Yearbook for Traditional Music* 25 (1993): 43–51, illuminates the politics that surrounded musical culture in Uzbekistan and Tajikistan during the 1920s and 1930s.

III. THE CONCEPT OF "TRADITION"

Jean During, *Quelque chose se passe: Le sens de la tradition dans l'Orient musical* (Lagrasse: Verdier, 1994), probes the concept of "tradition" in the Iranian cultural sphere from perspectives both ethnographic and hermeneutic, and links the understanding of "tradition" to aspects of Islamic practice and belief. A work that critically addresses the concept of "tradition" in Central Asia from the very different perspective of a social scientist (who has nothing to say about music per se) is Sergei P. Poliakov, *Everyday Islam: Religion and Tradition in Rural Central Asia* (ed. with an introduction by Martha Brill Olcott, Armonk, N.Y.: M. E. Sharpe, 1992).

IV. CENTRAL ASIAN EPIC POETRY

The classic work on Central Asian oral poetry is that of Wilhelm Radloff (1837–1918). Radloff's collecting, however, focused on Kazakhs, Kyrgyz, Uighurs, and the Turkic peoples of southern Siberia—not the Uzbeks, Karakalpaks, and Tajiks of Transoxania. A more geographically comprehensive survey that analyzes not only texts but also performance practice is Karl Reichl, *Turkic Oral Epic Poetry: Traditions, Forms, Poetic Structure* (New York: Garland, 1992). See also Nora K. Chadwick and Victor Zhirmunsky, *Oral Epics of Central Asia* (Cambridge: Cambridge University Press, 1969). Devin DeWeese, *Islamization and Native Religion in the Golden Horde: Baba Tükles and Conversion to Islam in Historical and Epic Tradition* (University Park: Pennsylvania State University Press, 1994), contains a detailed discussion of the epic tale *Idige* (*Yedigei*), which figures in chapter 4 of the present work. The Turkmen epic tradition, closely related to that of Khorezm, figures in Slawomira Zeranska-Kominek, "The Classification of Repertoire in Turkmen Traditional Music," *Asian Music* 21, no. 2 (1990): 91–109.

V. RECORDINGS OF MUSIC FROM TRANSOXANIA AND CONTIGUOUS GEOCULTURAL REGIONS OF AFGHANISTAN, XINJIANG, AND TURKMENISTAN

1. *Afghanistan: The Rubâb of Herat.* Performed by Mohammad Rahim Khushnawaz. Recordings (1974) and accompanying notes by John Baily. Archives Internationales de Musique Populaire & VDE-GALLO, 1993. An outstanding virtuoso performs traditional Herati tunes as well as several items that represent the Indian-influenced instrumental art music of Kabul.
2. *Bukhara: Musical Crossroads of Asia.* Recordings (1990) and accompanying notes by Ted Levin and Otanazar Matyakubov. Smithsonian/Folkways Recordings, 1991. Wedding music, liturgical and paraliturgical chant, and art song performed by both Jewish and Muslim musicians, including Tohfaxân Pinkhasova, Mahdi Ibadov.
3. *Central Asia: The Masters of the Dotâr.* Recordings (1978–1992) and accompanying notes by Jean During. Archives Internationales de Musiques Populaires & VDE GALLO 1993. A compilation of performances by *dutar* players in Uzbekistan, the Pamir region of Tajikistan, Iranian Khurasan, and Turkmenistan.
4. *Asie Centrale: Traditions classiques.* Recordings (1990–1993) and accompanying notes by Jean During and Ted Levin. Ocora Radio France, 1993. Double CD of classical singers and instrumentalists from Uzbekistan and Tajikistan, including Turgun Alimatov, Monâjât Yulchieva, Ma'ruf Xâja Bahâdor, Arif Xâtamov, Ilyas Malayev, and Ari Babakhanov.
5. *Davlatmand: Musiques savantes et populaires du Tadjikistan.* Selections, notes, and translations by Sorour Kasmaï. Maison des Cultures du Monde, 1992. Vocal and instrumental performances on *ghijak, setâr,* and *dutar* by Davlatmand Kholov and Abdussattar Abdullaev featuring *falak,* a style of popular music, as well as art song.
6. *Music of the Bukharan Jewish Ensemble Shashmaqam: Central Asia in Forest Hills, New York.* Produced in collaboration with the Ethnic Folk Arts Center. Project directed by Ethel Raim and Martin Koenig. Annotated by Ted Levin. Smithsonian/ Folkways Recordings, 1991. Popular and classical songs performed by a Bukharan Jewish ensemble whose members emigrated from Central Asia to New York.
7. *Tadjikistan: Musiques populaires du Sud.* Field recordings by Sorour Kasmaï (1989–1990). Accompanying notes by Sorour Kasmaï and Henri Lecomte. Fonti

310

Musicali, 1991. Five performers (with accompanists) of popular songs, tunes, and epic from the south of Tadjikistan.

8. *Tadjikistan: Falak. Goltchereh Sadikova.* Recorded in Tadjikistan in 1991 by Sorour Kasmaï. Fonti Musicali, 1992.

9. *Turkestan Chinois/Xinjiang: Musique Ouïgoures.* Recordings (1988–89) and accompanying notes by Sabine Trebinjac and Jean During. Ocora Radio France and Archives Internationales de Musique Populaire, 1990. Double CD survey of Uighur *muqam,* Dolan *muqam,* and popular Uighur songs.

10. *Turkmen Epic Singing/Köroglu.* Recordings and accompanying notes by Slawomira Zeranska-Kominek. Auvidis/UNESCO, 1994. Excerpts from the Köroglu tale performed by various Turkmen *baxshi*s.

11. *Ouzbekistan: Monâjât Yultchieva (Maqam d'Asie Centrale 1: Ferghana).* Recordings (1994) and accompanying notes by Jean During. Ocora Radio France, 1994. Art songs of the Tashkent-Ferghana region performed by the leading female classical vocalist of her generation.

12. *Ouzbekistan: Turgun Alimatov.* Recorded in Paris (1995). Accompanying text by Theodore Levin. Ocora Radio France, 1995. Instrumental performances on *dutar, tanbur,* and *satâ* by a virtuoso instrumentalist.

13. The Ilyas Malayev Maqâm Ensemble: Buzruk. Recorded in New York (1995). Accompanying text by Theodore Levin. Shanachie Entertainment, 1996. Instrumental and vocal sections in their proper cyclic sequence of a single *maqâm* suite from the Bukharan *Shash maqâm: Buzruk.*

14. *Uzbekistan: Music of Khorezm.* Recordings (1990–1994) and accompanying notes by Otanazar Matyakubov and Theodore Levin. Auvidis/UNESCO, 1996. A survey of Khorezmian musical traditions, including epic, art song, women's music, and instrumental genres.

15. Yulduz Usmanova, "Alma Alma." Produced by Yulduz Usmanova, Marcus Kröger, and Lenny MacDowell. Blue Flame Records, 1993 (released in the USA by Miramar). Also "Jannona" (Blue Flame/Miramar) and "Binafscha" (Blue Flame). Uzbek "traditional" pop performed by Uzbekistan's premiere female pop singer.

INDEX

INDEX

THEODORE LEVIN

grew up in New England and was educated at Amherst College and Princeton University. Trained from childhood as a pianist, he became interested as a teenager in the musical life of other cultures. He has focused at various times on music of the Celtic lands, the Balkans, the Caucasus, South Siberia, and Central Asia. His recordings of music from Bosnia, Georgia, Tuva, and Uzbekistan/ Tajikistan have been released on the Nonesuch, Smithsonian/Folkways, Ocora, and Auvidis/UNESCO labels. He teaches in the Music Department at Dartmouth College.

SELECTIONS ON COMPANION COMPACT DISC

All recordings are by Theodore Levin except tracks 1 and 2. Track 1 was recorded by Blue Flame Recordings and released on *Alma Alma*, Blue Flame 398 40572. Track 2 is performed by the Moscow Radio-Television Symphony Orchestra under the direction of Alexander Mikhailov; a new recording of this excerpt was made possible by Boris Dubrinin and Alexander Krol. Acknowledgment is also made to Smithsonian/Folkways Recordings for permission to include tracks 9 and 10 recorded by Levin and previously released on *Bukhara: Musical Crossroads of Asia*, Smithsonian/Folkways 40050, and to OCORA/Radio France for permission to include tracks 3 and 4, recorded by Levin and released on *Asie Centrale: Traditions classiques*, OCORA/Radio France C560035-36.

Playing time: 73:56

1	Yulduz Usmanova, "Schoch va Gado" (Tashkent)
2	Alexei Fedorovich Kozlovsky, "Night in a Ferghana Garden," from *Lola* (Tashkent)
3	Munâjât Yulchieva, "Bayât-i Shirâz Talqinchasi"(Tashkent)
4	Turgun Alimatov, "Segâh" (Tashkent)
5	Maqâm Ensemble of Uzbekistan Radio, excerpt from "Saraxbâr-i Segâh" (Tashkent)
6	Ilyas Malayev, excerpt from "Mogulcha-i Segâh" without and with *ghazalrâni* (Queens)
7	Mutavaqqil Burxanov, "Yarlarim" (Tashkent)
8	Baysun Ensemble, "Sus Xâtin" (Baysun)
9	Mahdi Ibadov, "Shahd" (Bukhara)
10	Tohfaxân Pinkhasova, "Taralilalalai" (Bukhara)
11	Shirin Jumaniyazov (*xalfa*), "Yâr-Yâr" (Khiva)
12	Arif Xatamov, setting of poem attributed to Ahmad Yasawi (Tashkent)
13	Qalandar *baxshi,* excerpt from *dâstân,* "Ashiq Gharib va Shâhsanam" (Khiva)
14	Azad Imbragimov, "Suvâra" (Khiva)
15	Qahhâr *baxshi,* "Terma" (Xâja Mahmud)
16	Jumabay *zhirau* Bazarov, "Ode to Maxtum Quli"
17	Xushvakt, Jew's harp (Xâja Mahmud)
18	Sattâr Adinaev, "Afarid" (Yagnâb)
19	Sattâr Adinaev, "Yak Dâna Gul" (Yagnâb)
20	Xalmirzâ Mirzâsayi, Niyazi Bâbâ, Jumâi Bâbâ,"Naqsh" (Dargh)
21	Girls in Dargh, Field Hollers
22	*Zarb* in Dargh Mosque
23	Nasri-oi, excerpt from *koch* (Shahristan)